CLAIRE TOMALIN

Jane Austen

A Life

PENGUIN BOOKS

PENGUIN BOOKS

Published by the Penguin Group
Penguin Books Ltd, 80 Strand, London WC2R ORL, England
Penguin Group (USA) Inc., 375 Hudson Street, New York, New York 10014, USA
Penguin Group (Canada), 90 Eglinton Avenue East, Suite 700, Toronto, Ontario, Canada M4P 2Y3
(a division of Pearson Penguin Canada Inc.)
Penguin Ireland, 25 St Stephen's Green, Dublin 2, Ireland (a division of Penguin Books Ltd)
Penguin Group (Australia), 250 Camberwell Road, Camberwell, Victoria 3124, Australia
(a division of Pearson Australia Group Pty Ltd)
Penguin Books India Pvt Ltd, 11 Community Centre, Panchsheel Park, New Delhi – 110 017, India
Penguin Group (NZ), 67 Apollo Drive, Rosedale, Auckland 0632, New Zealand
(a division of Pearson New Zealand Ltd)
Penguin Books (South Africa) (Pty) Ltd, Block D, Rosebank Office Park,
181 Jan Smuts Avenue, Parktown North, Gauteng 2193, South Africa

Penguin Books Ltd, Registered Offices: 80 Strand, London WC2R ORL, England

www.penguin.com

First published by Viking 1997
Published in Penguin Books 1998
The revised and updated edition pubilshed 2000
Reissued in this edition 2012

002

The acknowledgements on pp. xiii-xiv constitute an extension of this copyright page

Printed in England by Clays Ltd, St Ives plc

ISBN: 978-0-241-96327-2

www.greenpenguin.co.uk

MIX
Paper from
responsible sources
FSC™ C018179
www.fsc.org

Penguin Books is committed to a sustainable
future for our business, our readers and our planet.
This book is made from Forest Stewardship
Council™ certified paper.

ALWAYS LEARNING   **PEARSON**

For my good neighbours,
Sue and David Gentleman

Contents

List of Illustrations   ix
Acknowledgements   xiii
Map Showing Steventon and the Austens'
    Hampshire Neighbours   xvi

  1 1775   1
  2 Meritocrats   11
  3 Boys   24
  4 School   34
  5 The French Connection   45
  6 Bad Behaviour   61
  7 Weddings and Funerals   75
  8 Neighbours   87
  9 Dancing   103
10 The Doll and the Poker   110
11 A Letter   114
12 Defence Systems   120
13 Friends in East Kent   133
14 Travels with My Mother   143
15 Three Books   156
16 Twenty-five   169
17 Manydown   178
18 Brotherly Love   193
19 A Death in the Family   206
20 At Chawton   212
21 Inside Mansfield Park   225
22 Dedication   242

CONTENTS

23 The Sorceress   257
24 College Street   270
25 Postscript   277

Appendix I: A Note on Jane Austen's Last Illness   289
Appendix II: 'An African Story' from Fanny Austen's Pocket-book,
    1809, with a Note on Attitudes to Slavery   291
Notes   295
Short Bibliography   342
Family Tree   346
Index   349

List of Illustrations

between pp. 78–7

Revd George Austen, miniature (Jane Austen Memorial Trust)

Mrs George Austen, née Cassandra Leigh, silhouette (Jane Austen Memorial Trust)

Cottages at Steventon, drawing by Anna Lefroy (collection of the great-grandsons of Admiral Sir Francis Austen)

James Austen, miniature (Jane Austen Memorial Trust)

Edward Austen, later Knight, detail from a portrait painted during his Grand Tour, 1789 (Jane Austen Memorial Trust)

Henry Austen, miniature, *c.* 1820 (Jane Austen Memorial Trust)

Cassandra Austen, silhouette (Jane Austen Memorial Trust)

Francis Austen, miniature (Jane Austen Memorial Trust)

Jane Austen, pencil and watercolour on paper, by Cassandra Austen, *c.* 1801 (The National Portrait Gallery, London)

Charles Austen, portrait by R. Field, 1807 (Jane Austen Memorial Trust)

Steventon rectory (front view), drawing by Anna Lefroy (collection of the great-grandsons of Admiral Sir Francis Austen)

Revd George Austen presenting his son Edward to Mr and Mrs Thomas Knight, silhouette, *c.* 1778 (D. Rose Esq./Jane Austen Memorial Trust)

Mrs Tysoe Saul Hancock, née Philadelphia Austen, after a miniature by J. Smart (Jane Austen Memorial Trust)

Warren Hastings, portrait by Sir Joshua Reynolds, 1768 (The National Portrait Gallery, London)

Eliza Hancock, miniature (Jane Austen Memorial Trust)

Château de Jourdan, photograph (collection of the author)

ix

William John Chute, pastel and pencil portrait, 1790 (The National Trust, Southern Region)

Mrs William Chute, née Elizabeth Smith, drawing (The National Trust, Southern Region)

Thomas Vere Chute, drawing (The National Trust, Southern Region)

John Portal of Laverstoke and Freefolk, painting by Henry Calvert (private collection. Photo: Nathan Kelly)

Hon. Newton Wallop, 'Leavers' portrait from Eton (The Trustees of the Portsmouth Estates. Photo: Nathan Kelly)

Hon. Coulson Wallop, 'Leavers' portrait from Eton (The Trustees of the Portsmouth Estates. Photo: Nathan Kelly)

Sir William Heathcote, the Revd William Heathcote and Major Gilbert out Hunting, painting by Daniel Gardner (National Trust Photographic Library/John Hammond)

St Nicholas Church, Steventon, photograph (Hampshire Record Office 65M89/Z217/1)

Page from the Marriage Register of St Nicholas Church, Steventon (Hampshire Record Office 71M82/PR3)

West doorway of St Nicholas Church, Steventon, photograph (Hampshire Record Office 65M89/Z217/12)

between pp. 271–2

Thomas Langlois Lefroy, miniature by G. Engleheart, 1799 (Photo: Hampshire Record Office 23M93/83/1/1)

Manydown, from *Select Illustrations of Hampshire* by G. F. Proser, 1833

James Leigh-Perrot, miniature by J. Smart (Hampshire Record Office 23M93/51/2/1)

Mrs James Leigh-Perrot, née Jane Cholmeley, silhouette (Jane Austen Memorial Trust)

Revd (Isaac Peter) George Lefroy, miniature (Helen Lefroy)

Mrs George Lefroy, née Anne Brydges, miniature (Helen Lefroy)

Godmersham Park, Kent, from *The History and Topographical Survey of the County of Kent* by E. Hasted, 1799

Mrs Thomas Knight, née Catherine Knatchbull, portrait by George Romney (private collection)

Mrs Edward Austen, née Elizabeth Bridges, miniature (Jane Austen Memorial Trust)

Revd George Austen, silhouette (Jane Austen Memorial Trust)

'A General View of Bath from the Claverton Road', from *Bath* by John Claude Nattes, 1806

View of Lyme Regis, watercolour (Fotomas Index)

Chawton Cottage, early photograph (private family collection/Jane Austen Memorial Trust)

The Prince Regent Driving a Curricle, engraving by Thomas Rowlandson (Courtauld Institute of Art)

Engraving from *Raison et Sensibilité*, Arthus Bertrand, Paris, 1828 (Bibliothèque Nationale de France, Paris)

Title-page engraving from *Sense and Sensibility*, Richard Bentley, London, 1833

Title-page engraving from *Pride and Prejudice*, Richard Bentley, London, 1833

Engraving from *La Famille Elliot, ou L'Ancienne Inclination*, Arthus Bertrand, Paris, 1821 (Bibliothèque Nationale de France, Paris)

Title-page engraving from *Mansfield Park*, Richard Bentley, London, 1833

Engraving from *Emma*, Richard Bentley, London, 1833

Lady Austen, née Martha Lloyd, daguerreotype (Jane Austen Memorial Trust)

Cassandra Austen, silhouette (collection of the great-grandsons of Admiral Sir Francis Austen)

Admiral Sir Francis Austen, daguerreotype (Jane Austen Memorial Trust)

Text Illustrations

(pp. 16–17) The apprentice register in the Public Record Office, showing Philadelphia Austen's apprenticeship to Hester Cole, milliner, Covent Garden, 9 May 1745 (Public Record Office IR 1/18f 146).

(p. 41) Endpaper of Jane Austen's copy of *Fables choisies* (collection of the great-grandsons of Admiral Sir Francis Austen)

(p. 72) 'Sir Thomas Grandison and his daughters Caroline and Charlotte', an 1886 engraving from the original copper-plate of 1778 by Isaac Taylor, from *Sir Charles Grandison* by Samuel Richardson (1754)

(p. 100) Page from Eliza Chute's diary, 1799 (Hampshire Record Office 23M93/70/1/7)

(p. 200) 'Nutting', from the 1794 edition of *The Seasons* (1726–30) by James Thomson

(p. 216) Poem by Jane Austen to her brother Frank on the birth of his son (British Library Add. MSS 42180, f. 7)

(p. 250) Dedication page addressed to the Prince Regent, from the first edition of *Emma*, 1816

(p. 273) Page from Mary Austen's diary, 1817 (Hampshire Record Office 23M93/62/1/8)

Acknowledgements

I should like to extend warm thanks to the many institutions and individuals from whom I have received advice and help. They include the Jane Austen Society; the Kent County Archives; the Hampshire County Archives and especially Claire Skinner; Winchester Cathedral and its archivist John Hardacre; Winchester College and its headmaster J. P. Sabben-Clare and bursar Bill Organ; the National Trust and in particular Charles O'Brien; the London Library; the British Library; Hoare's Bank and its archivist Mrs Hutchings; and the College of Arms.

This edition incorporates some corrections and important new material relating to Philadelphia Austen, given me by Robin Vick and drawn from his meticulous and wide-ranging studies, which he has most generously shared with me.

I must record that it was Jane Tapley who, after hearing me speak on Mrs Jordan at the Theatre Royal in Bath, put the idea into my head that I might approach the subject of Jane Austen. I doubt if I should have been bold enough to do so without her encouraging suggestion, and I remain very grateful to her for making it.

Others to whom I am indebted are Tom Carpenter, Jean Bowden and all at Chawton Cottage; Mrs Matilda Taylor; Lord and Lady Fitzwalter; Mr and Mrs Nigel Havers; Eric Beck; Anthony Storr; Irvine Loudon; Wendy Cope; Brian Southam; Anthony Neville; Paul McQuail; Nicholas Monck; Leslie Mitchell; Olwen Hufton; Eric Korn; Gráinne Kelly; Donna Poppy; Julian Litten; Sir Jonathan and Lady Portal; The Earl of Portsmouth; Christine Jackson; the Revd Professor Owen Chadwick; Valerie Fildes; Charles Elliott; and Tony Lacey.

With my daughter Jo Tomalin I have shared a love of Jane Austen for many years; discussions with her have been helpful and enjoyable.

In France, thanks are due to my father Emile Delavenay and my sister Marguerite Smith for much assistance; also to the Archives du Ministère des Affaires Etrangères; to Mme Odette Bigeon; to M. Jean Ducourneau, the Abbé Michel Devert, M. Yves de Coincy of the Château de Jourdan, M. Michel A. Rateau and M. Gaël Henaff.

I owe a particular debt to Deirdre Le Faye, for her kindness in answering my queries and for her invaluable book, *Jane Austen: A Family Record*, as well as for her discovery of the date of Leonora Austen's death.

Clive Caplan shared his admirable research into Henry Austen's military career with me, gave me a copy of Susan Ferrier's novel *Marriage*, and encouraged me with his enthusiasm. Alwyn Austen, great-grandson of Jane Austen's brother Francis, has been another cheering and generous friend; I recall my visits to him in Kent and our trips together with especial pleasure and gratitude.

My husband Michael Frayn walked many miles with me about Hampshire in the footsteps of the Austens, as well as around Bath and Lyme Regis, and in the Gers in France on the track of Cousin Eliza. He was patient and forbearing with my working habits, and made valuable suggestions for improving the book.

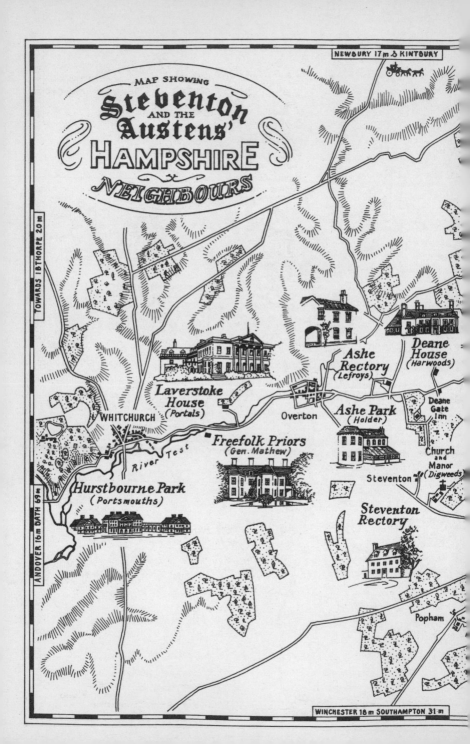

MAP SHOWING
Steventon
AND THE
Austens'
HAMPSHIRE
NEIGHBOURS

NEWBURY 17 m & KINTBURY

TOWARDS IBTHORPE 20 m

ANDOVER 16 m BATH 69 m

Deane
House
(Harwoods)

Ashe
Rectory
(Lefroys)

Laverstoke
House
(Portals)

WHITCHURCH

Overton

Ashe Park
(Holder)

Deane
Gate
Inn

Church
and
Manor
(Digweeds)

River Test

Freefolk Priors
(Gen. Mathew)

Steventon

Hurstbourne Park
(Portsmouths)

Steventon
Rectory

Popham

WINCHESTER 18 m SOUTHAMPTON 31 m

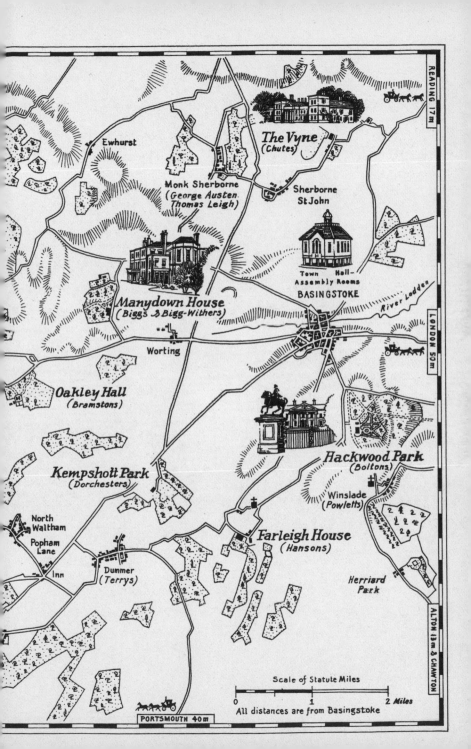

Ewhurst

The Vyne
(Chutes)

Monk Sherborne
(George Austen.
Thomas Leigh)

Sherborne
St John

Town Hall—
Assembly Rooms
BASINGSTOKE

River Loddon

Manydown House
(Biggs & Bigg-Withers)

Worting

Oakley Hall
(Bramstons)

Hackwood Park
(Boltons)

Kempshott Park
(Dorchesters)

Winslade
(Powletts)

North
Waltham

Popham
Lane

Farleigh House
(Hansons)

Inn

Dummer
(Terrys)

Herriard
Park

Scale of Statute Miles

0   1   2 Miles

All distances are from Basingstoke

PORTSMOUTH 40 m

I

1775

The winter of 1775 was a hard one. On 11 November the naturalist Gilbert White saw that the trees around his Hampshire village of Selborne had lost almost all their leaves. 'Trees begin to be naked,' he wrote in his diary. Fifteen miles away, higher up in the Downs, in the village of Steventon, the rector's wife was expecting the birth of her seventh child from day to day as the last leaves fell. She was thirty-six and had been married for eleven years. Four sturdy little boys ran about the parsonage and the big garden at the back, with its yard and outhouses, rising to the fields and woodland beyond. The eldest, James, at ten already showed promise as a scholar, sharing his father's taste in books, and the only daughter, Cassy, kept her mother entertained with her constant chatter as she followed her round the house and out to visit the dairy and the chickens and ducks. Cassy would be three in January. Outside Mr Austen's study the house was seldom entirely quiet.

The November days went by and the rains set in, keeping the boys indoors; by the end of the month it was dark in the house at three in the afternoon, and dinner had to be eaten very promptly if they were to do without candles. Still no baby appeared. December came, bringing an epidemic of colds and feverish complaints. There was a sharp frost, putting ice on the ponds, enough for the boys to go sliding; then, on the 16th, White noted, 'Fog, sun, sweet day.'

The 16th of December was the day of Jane Austen's birth. The month's delay in her arrival inspired her father to a small joke about how he and his wife had 'in old age grown such bad reckoners'; he was forty-four.[1] The child came in the evening, he said, without much warning. There was no need for a doctor; it was rare to call one for something as routine as childbirth, and the nearest, in

Basingstoke, was seven miles away over bad roads. In any case, 'everything was soon happily over'. They were pleased to have a second daughter, 'a present plaything for her sister Cassy and a future companion. She is to be Jenny.' George Austen's letter went on to talk of the prospects of a ploughing match in which he was interested, Kent against Hants for a rump of beef, weather permitting. A village rector in a remote country parish was as much a real farmer as a shepherd of souls.

The baby was immediately christened at home by her father, like all the Austen children. There would be a church ceremony later. And now winter set in in earnest. Mr Austen's ploughing match could not take place, as snow fell steadily, thickly and persistently, drifting right up to the tops of the gates. Soon the lanes were filled and almost impassable. The poultry would not stir out of the hen house, and wild birds appeared at the kitchen door for crumbs. 'Rugged, Siberian weather,' wrote White, remarking that the snow formed romantic and grotesque shapes as it continued to fall and then freeze. Newborn lambs were frozen to the ground, and hares came into the gardens looking for food.

Inside the parsonage, Mrs Austen lay upstairs in the four-poster, warmly bundled under her feather-beds, the baby in her cradle beside her, while someone else – very likely her sister-in-law Philadelphia Hancock – supervised the household, all the cleaning and cooking necessary where there were many small children, together with the extra washing for the newly delivered mother.[2] The maids stoked the fires and boiled coppers, and when she could the washerwoman made her way from the village and toiled for a day, although laundry froze before it dried and the house was full of airing sheets and baby things. Mr Austen might read to the children after their three o'clock dinner, but boys like to run and slide up and down stairs, and there were no carpets to dull the noise. Mrs Austen would not be expected to set foot on the floor for two weeks at least.

Neighbours could not easily call, except for a few robust gentlemen on horseback, bringing congratulatory messages and gifts from their wives. On Christmas Eve the children laid out the traditional holly branches on the window ledges, and on Christmas morning Mr Austen, well booted and coated, set off up the hill to his tiny, unheated stone church, St Nicholas, hoping the light would suffice to read the lesson and serve the sacrament to those farmers and villagers who turned out to hear him. The Digweed family could be relied on, long-term tenants of the old brick manor house next to the church; Hugh Digweed farmed most of the land around Steventon and acted as squire. Then back down the hill, through the snow and silence. There were not more than thirty families living in Steventon, the single row of cottages at some distance from the parsonage; and there was neither shop nor inn.

If Aunt Philadelphia was indeed in charge, it meant their cousin Betsy was also there: grave, dark, delicately pretty Betsy, who had been born in India, where her father was even now, and where Aunt Philadelphia sometimes talked of taking her back. Betsy was fourteen, almost grown up; older than any of the Steventon children, and infinitely more sophisticated in their eyes. She lived mostly in town, meaning London. There she had her own horse, something none of the Austen boys could yet boast, and when she was not riding she was more likely to travel about in her mother's carriage than on foot. She was learning French; she had performed in a play with some other children when she was only ten; she owned a harpsichord, and four strings of pearls, a present just arrived from her father.[3] James, Edward and even precocious four-year-old Henry watched and listened to their cousin admiringly.

When the children were allowed into their mother's room, they saw that the new baby had a round face, fat cheeks and bright dark eyes. It was agreed that she looked most like Henry, who had been the longest and finest of all the babies so far, so it is safe to assume that Jane was also long and large. Mrs Austen fed her daughter at the breast, as she had all her children. She would not dream of going outside the house for at least a month after the birth, whatever the weather.[4] The continuing Siberian winter did not encourage her, and when the thaw began, in February, there were floods, which still kept her in. So the baby enjoyed undivided attention, and three cosy months in the first-floor bedroom.

Then winter ended, Aunt Philadelphia and Betsy departed, and Mrs Austen again took up her duties in the house, the dairy and the poultry yard. On 5 April, after a harsh, dark morning, the sun came out. Little Jane was well wrapped in shawls, her mother put on her pelisse and an extra shawl or two for herself, and the family processed up the lane to the church, with its great yew tree in the graveyard in which the key was kept, its ancient bells, and its two stone heads, one of a man, one of a woman, carved on each side of the pointed arch through which you entered. This was her formal, public christening. Two of her godmothers, or 'sponsors', were Janes, one a Kentish aunt of her father's, the other an Oxfordshire cousin of her mother's. It is unlikely they made the difficult journeys needed to be present for the occasion, or that her godfather, another clergyman married to another of Mrs Austen's cousins and living in Surrey, was there; it was normal for their promises to be made for them at the ceremony.[5] As it turned out, they none of them did anything for their goddaughter; but as evidence of the great connecting web of cousins, mostly clerical, spread over the southern counties, they are a significant part of Jane Austen's story.

It is not an easy story to investigate. She herself wrote no autobiographical notes, and if she kept any diaries they did not survive her. Her sister destroyed the bulk of the letters in her possession, a niece did the same for those preserved by one of her brothers, and only a handful more have turned up from other sources. There are 160 in all, and none from her childhood; the earliest known letter was written when she was twenty. The first biographical note, written in the aftermath of her death, consisted of a few pages only, and her brother Henry, who wrote it, explained that hers was 'not by any means a life of event'. Nothing more was published for another fifty years, when a memoir by her nephew James-Edward Austen-Leigh appeared. It confirmed Henry's view of her. 'Of events her life was singularly barren: few changes and no great crisis ever broke the smooth current of its course.' The uneventful life of Jane Austen has been the generally accepted view. Compared with writers like Dickens or her contemporary Mary Wollstonecraft, the course of her life does seem to run exceedingly quietly and smoothly. Jane Austen did not see her father beat her mother, and she was not sent to work in a blacking factory at the age of twelve; yet, if you stop to look closely at her childhood, it was not all quiet days at the parsonage. It was, in fact, full of events, of distress and even trauma, which left marks upon her as permanent as those of any blacking factory. That she was marked by them will become clear in the course of her story; and that she also overcame them and made them serve her purposes.

Mr and Mrs Austen must have hoped that this would be their last child. Her sister Jane Cooper had only two, and 'has not been breeding since, so perhaps she has done' observed Mrs Austen with interest in a letter to a sister-in-law;[6] to have finished breeding safely was enviable. And then the Austens' financial situation was not good. George was heavily in debt, owing money on all sides, to Jane Cooper's husband among others. He had also borrowed from Mrs Austen's brother, James Leigh-Perrot, and from his own sister Philadelphia Hancock, and, separately, from her husband. His annual income was small, around £210 from the combined tithes of Steventon and the neighbouring village of Deane. The sales of his farm produce were an important supplement to this, but not enough to keep him solvent. Three years before Jane's birth he began to take in pupils; the parsonage, with its seven bedrooms and three attics, was big enough to be turned into a small school. At the same time he sold off the last of his small capital. Just before her christening he had to borrow another £300, through the good offices of Philadelphia, from a London lawyer.[7] His accounts show a perpetual juggling of debt repayments and new borrowings which must have made his wife extremely uneasy if she knew their full extent. The plain fact was that children cost money to launch into the world, and the Austens had enough with James, George, Edward, Henry, Cassandra, Francis and Jane. Separate bedrooms was the usual form of birth control; but the Austens did not adopt it, and there was one more Austen baby to come.

Mrs Austen's system of child-rearing was an unusual one. She was a well-organized woman, and her practice was to give each baby a few months at the breast as a good start – we know from her own account that it was three months in the case of Cassandra – and then hand the child over to a woman in the village to be looked after for another year or eighteen months, until it was old enough to be easily managed at home.[8] For Jane, this handing over is most likely to have followed her christening. A baby of fourteen weeks will be firmly attached to her mother, and to be transferred to a strange person and environment can only be a painful experience. The idea that this was an exile or an abandonment would not have occurred to Mrs Austen; bonding between mother and child is a largely modern concept, and babies were handed about freely. It does not mean they did not suffer, both in going and in coming back. Cobbett deplored the practice, asking, 'Who has not seen these banished children, when brought and put into the arms of their mother, screaming to get from them and stretching out their little hands to get back to the arms of the nurse?'[9] Poor village mothers were naturally glad of the extra income brought by nursing children of the gentry; a country wet nurse could earn about two shillings and sixpence a week, and even a dry nurse would be helping her own family by taking on such work. Whether Mrs Austen found a wet nurse ready for each of her children in the village, or whether she felt they could be spoon-fed after their first few months of breast-feeding, we do not know; but she did use the word 'weaning' in the case of three-month-old Cassandra, which suggests the latter. Whatever the system, there was something impersonal about it; the name of the nurse is never mentioned.[10]

So the Austen babies were cared for in the village, fed, washed, encouraged to crawl in a cottage, taking their first steps there and learning their first words from their foster family. When they approached the age of reason and became socially acceptable, they were moved again, back to their original home. From the physical point of view the system worked very well. In an age when few families were spared the deaths of several children, the Austens did not lose a single one; in London at this time over half the children born died before they could reach the age of five, and although things were better in the country, the mortality rate was still alarmingly high.[11] The Austen children grew up, and grew up healthy.

All the same, you have to wonder what effect Mrs Austen's treatment had on them. In Jane's case, the emotional distance between child and mother is obvious throughout her life; and not only between child and mother. The most striking aspect of Jane's adult letters is their defensiveness. They lack tenderness towards herself as much as towards others. You are aware of the inner creature, deeply responsive and alive, but mostly you are faced with the hard shell; and sometimes a claw is put out, and a sharp nip is given to whatever offends. They are the letters of someone who does not open her heart; and in the adult who avoids intimacy you sense the child who was uncertain where to expect love or to look for security, and armoured herself against rejection.

Mrs Austen's system made for a tidier and more easily run parsonage, and she did not see herself as doing anything cruel or unusual. She believed, along with most other people, that infants required no more than to be kept reasonably clean, reasonably warm and well fed, until their intelligence showed itself in obvious form. One of her contemporaries, also mother of a large family, wrote that she would just as soon be a stepmother as a mother: 'think of being quit of their plague while they are mere vegetables, and then become mere animals'.[12] The Austen parents are said – by a grandson – to have visited the absent babies daily, at least whenever possible, and had them brought to the parsonage regularly, which may have encouraged their children to feel that they had two families and homes where they were loved. The system was certainly a good deal better than that of parents who placed their children too far away to visit, and became total strangers to them. 'She sent him forth to be nursed by the robust wife of a neighbouring farmer, where, for the space of upwards of four years, he was honoured with no token from father or mother, save some casual messages, to know from time to time if the child was in health,' was Henry Brooke's summary of his hero's infancy in *The Fool of Quality*, published in the late 1760s and recognized as a perfectly credible account.[13]

One Austen child did not come home from his village nurse. This was the second, George, nearly ten years older than Jane; he suffered from fits and failed to develop normally. For Mrs Austen, this was a sad repetition of her early experience with her brother Thomas. He was born when she was eight, just of an age to enjoy a baby brother; but when his backwardness was obvious, he was sent away to be cared for. George was destined for the same fate, although he was occasionally at the parsonage as a small boy.[14] Since he was probably still in Steventon village in 1776, he may have been the first of Jane's siblings of whom she became aware. He could walk, and he was not a Down's Syndrome child, or he would not have lived so long, lacking modern medication. Because Jane knew deaf and dumb sign language as an adult – she mentioned talking 'with my fingers' in a letter of 1808 – it is thought he may have lacked language; it would not have stopped him joining in the village children's games.

'We have this comfort, he cannot be a bad or a wicked child,' wrote his father of George, with touching Christian resignation.[15] The Austens cared about goodness, but they also cared deeply about success; and their child-rearing system worked remarkably well, for all, with the partial exception of George, grew up tough, not given to self-pity and notable for their mutual affection and support. And even George lived to a ripe old age, cared for alongside his Uncle Thomas in another Hampshire village, Monk Sherborne; he is rarely mentioned, but survived his elder brother and his sister Jane, and was not forgotten by the others, who contributed to his upkeep. On his death certificate in 1838 he is described as a 'Gentleman'.[16]

In June 1776, before Jane was six months old, her parents did absent themselves from Steventon in order to make a visit to London. Neither two-year-old Frank nor three-year-old Cass had long been promoted from the village themselves, so they may have been sent to keep their baby sister company, happy enough to return to what had been their home, and the games of the long summer days with the small Bets, Bobs and Nans from the cottages. And if Cass now saw herself as a little mother to the baby, and the baby held out her arms to Cass, it was the first stage of a deep and lifelong bond between the sisters.

Mr and Mrs Austen were in London partly at least to visit his sister Philadelphia and niece Betsy. While they were with them word came from India of the death of Phila's husband, Tysoe Saul Hancock. He had in fact died months earlier, in November 1775, even before the birth of Jane, but news travelled slowly, letters from India taking six months or more. Mrs Hancock was naturally afflicted to hear of her husband's end. Worse, it appeared that he died penniless: 'all his effects will not more than clear his debts here', wrote Mr Woodman, the lawyer who advised her, and the same man who had lent George Austen money.[17] Sadly, Hancock was little George's godfather, and now there was no hope that he would be able to contribute to the cost of his care; he had worried about the growing number of Austen children, and how the family would manage. The situation of his own wife and daughter was not, however, as bad as it appeared at first.

Three years earlier, Mr Hancock's patron in India, the great Warren Hastings of the East India Company, on becoming Governor of Bengal, had made a gift to his god-daughter, Betsy Hancock, of £5,000; and in 1775 he doubled the sum, making Betsy an heiress – not a great one, but with enough to ensure she would find a husband. The Hancocks were sworn to secrecy about the whole matter, but the two trustees for Betsy's fortune were the lawyer, Mr Woodman – Warren Hastings's brother-in-law – and Mrs Hancock's brother, George Austen, who was doubtless in London partly to carry out whatever duties his trusteeship demanded.

It turned out there was not much cause for concern about Philadelphia. Quite apart from her daughter's wealth, we can see from the bank account she opened a few months later that she received £3,500 paid in by Woodman, and another sum of nearly £5,000 in the form of a 'bill on Ind. Co.'.[18] The opening of the account is a sign of her independence as a well-to-do widow. Her late husband had advised her to do as much earlier, but she had not complied; now she chose a different bank from the one he recommended, and deposited her money with Messrs Hoare & Co., her brother's bankers.

The Hancocks, mother and daughter, closely bonded as single parent and single child, were free to embark on living as they pleased; and although Philadelphia was fond of her brother, and Betsy of her uncle, they had no thought of burying themselves in the English countryside. Betsy, having lost a father she hardly remembered and come into a considerable fortune, announced she was no longer to be known as Betsy. From now on she would be called Eliza. No one thought of contradicting her wishes.

Eliza Hancock is a central figure in Jane Austen's life for many reasons. She was her first cousin, and they became warmly attached to one another. Although Eliza was the senior by fourteen years, both died relatively young, and Jane outlived her by only four years, bringing the span of their lives close together. The difference was that Eliza was always an exotic, a bird of bright plumage with a story that might have come from one of the romances Jane liked to mock. Eliza was a true Austen in her fluent pen and her enjoyment of acting, music and dancing, and she had a quick ear; in other ways she was markedly different from her Austen cousins. She was incautious in marrying, and could write frivolously of her feelings or lack of them; and yet she was always a most loving daughter, and became a tenderly attentive mother.

There are some unsolved questions in the lives of both Philadelphia Hancock and her daughter, the central one being Eliza's parentage, which will be considered later. For now, in the summer of 1776, George Austen was reassured about the situation in which they found themselves, and continued to repay the money he had borrowed from his sister at the same rate. He and his wife returned to Hampshire and life went on in its usual way. For him this meant supervising the work of the farm and sales of wheat, barley and hops; teaching his older boys; performing his pastoral duties of baptism, burial, Sunday services, and keeping a kindly eye on any parishioners in need or trouble. The one exceptional event of the winter happened three days before his little daughter's first birthday, on Friday, 13 December, when, in common with every clergyman in the land, he held an extra service in Steventon church, reading out prayers against the American rebels.[19] After which he walked down the hill to his cheerful home, whose atmosphere reminded one observer of 'the liberal society, the simplicity, hospitality, & taste, which commonly prevail in different families among the delightful valleys of Switzerland'.[20]

2

Meritocrats

Jane Austen's novels do not ramble. They are tightly constructed stories that cover a short span of time. In the novels, only Lady Catherine de Bourgh and Sir Walter Elliot take much notice of ancestry and pride themselves on it, and neither is an advertisement for the preoccupation. Jane Austen also chose to write about small familics; the Bennets with their five daughters was the largest to be put under close scrutiny. Her experience in life was different. Not only was she one of eight, she lived with a perpetual awareness of a *cousinage* extending over many counties and even beyond England. Family history and connections on both sides were seen as important. The large numbers of brothers, cousins, uncles and aunts, the repeated names, the convolutions of the family trees, are dismaying to outsiders; but they have to be sorted out, summarily at least, by anyone who aims to inhabit the world in which she was at home.

To begin with her mother: Mrs Austen was a Leigh and, down-to-earth and practical as she was, she was proud of her family history and links with the aristocracy. The Leighs knew themselves to be descended from the Lord Mayor of London who proclaimed Elizabeth Queen. Since then, some had been ennobled and become owners of Stoneleigh Abbey in Warwickshire; others had married aristocrats. Her curious name of Cassandra, shared with several cousins, owed itself to the fact that a Cassandra Willoughby had been the wife of a great-uncle who became the first Duke of Chandos; and a ducal connection was something to be proudly remembered and signalled.[1] There were brains in the family too: her uncle Theophilus Leigh was Master of Balliol for fifty years. Her father, Thomas Leigh, was a more modest parish priest at Harpsden, near Henley-on-Thames, where she was reared. She was a clever child who wrote poetry and impressed her Uncle Theophilus; but it was her brother James who came into a fortune through another great-uncle, adding a Perrot to his Leigh in the process. There was no fortune for her, only a small inheritance worth less than £2,000.

When her father retired from his parish, she and her sister Jane, by then in their mid-twenties, were taken to Bath, considered the most agreeable of places for elderly couples and husbandless young women, combining as it did urban pleasures and health care. Unfortunately the delights of the place finished off the Revd Leigh smartly. Shortly after his death, Cassandra chose to marry George Austen. She took to the tough life of the country parson's wife brisk and confident powers of organization, intellectual vitality and pride in her family history.

The Austens had no aristocratic connections. They were however a family for whom putting things down on paper was important. In 1708 George's grandmother had written out a long document headed 'Memorandums for mine and my Children's reading, being my own tho'ts on our affairs 1706, 1707'. She explained that she was making this 'rough draft in a retired hour' as a help to her memory and 'for my own satisfaction'. It was also for her children, to encourage them in the belief that intelligence and articulateness could count for more than an inherited fortune.[2]

Elizabeth Austen was born Elizabeth Weller some time in the reign of Charles II; she was the daughter of a Tonbridge gentleman, and in 1693 she married John Austen, only son of a rich cloth manufacturer. With money on both sides, they were able to settle in a comfortable manor house in Horsmonden, and in the next ten years she gave birth to seven children, a daughter followed by six sons. The drawback to this idyll was that his health was declining from year to year, and at the same time the debts he had acquired before his marriage were piling up. He did not have to face the results himself because he died when his youngest son was still a baby. The dying man made a will entrusting the education of the children to his wife, but appointing his two sisters' husbands executors; and on his deathbed he asked his father to look after his children. Old Mr Austen promised to do so, and also that the household goods should not be sold to pay off his son's debts; but even before the funeral could take place, relations between father, daughter-in-law and executors soured. Wills, and the avarice and bad behaviour induced by wills in otherwise normal people, are a running theme of comedy, and some blackly comic scenes were now played out.

Old Mr Austen 'forgot' his promise that her household goods should not be sold. She had to remind him, and under pressure, he said he would give £200 to save them. Just as the money was about to be handed over, he too died suddenly. When *his* will was read, it showed open hostility to his daughter-in-law. Her eldest son was magnificently provided for as heir to the estate, while the other six were left almost penniless. Mrs Austen begged her brothers-in-law to remember the verbal promise he had made, but they easily talked themselves into overriding it. 'These things I did not well take of them, for I tho't they did not perform ye promise made me at my ffather and husband's death to be kind to me and my children.'

Indeed: but there was nothing she could do. She was too poor to appeal: 'I had no pockett to know ye opinion of my Lord Chancellor.' So over the next few years she sold off her silver, her bed with its hangings and much of her household linen. She had to borrow money to keep the household going, but she did manage to pay off her husband's debts. Then, as the children grew, she began to worry about their education, because there was no school at Horsmonden.

Now Elizabeth showed her exceptional spirit. She made inquiries, and was told of a schoolhouse to be let at 'Sen'nock' (Sevenoaks). The applicant must be prepared to lodge and look after the Master of the school and take some pupils as boarders: in effect, the head-master was looking for a housekeeper and matron. She applied and was successful; she also made an agreement with the Master that all her boys should receive free education in return for her work. It was a social step down, but the good far outweighed considerations of that kind: 'it seem'd to me, as if I cou'd not do a better thing for my Children's good, their education being my great care . . . for I always tho't if they had Learning, they might ye better shift in ye world.' It is the voice of a meritocrat, and a very sensible one she was.

In June 1708 she took up her work at Sevenoaks. She kept her accounts carefully for eleven years, and saw her daughter married and her sons launched on careers. The eldest son was brought up quite separately by his aunts and uncles, sent to Cambridge, and came into his grandfather's estates; he showed no disposition to befriend his less fortunate brothers. Elizabeth Austen died in Seven-oaks in 1721, and was buried where she was born, at Tonbridge.[3] She cannot have been much more than fifty. Her life had been hard, but also heroic; father, husband, father-in-law and brothers-in-law had all failed her and her children, and she had saved them single-handed, by a combination of grit and ingenuity. She was Jane Austen's great grandmother.

Her son Francis became a lawyer, settled in Sevenoaks, worked steadily, invested shrewdly in property and became very rich; two astute marriages made him still richer. When her fourth son, William, finished his apprenticeship to a surgeon, he set up practice in Tonbridge and married, in 1727, the widow of another medical man, with one son, William Walter.[4] Four more children were born, a girl who died, a second girl, Philadelphia, in 1730, a son George – Jane Austen's father – in 1731 and another girl, Leonora, a year later; her birth killed the mother. William married a second, much older wife in 1736, only to die himself within a year. His widow felt neither affection nor obligation towards his children, who found themselves turned out into the care of a reluctant Uncle Stephen in London, while their stepmother remained in their father's house. Orphaned and ejected from the nest, they had a hard time.

Stephen Austen was a bookseller in St Paul's Churchyard, with a wife Elizabeth and one son. They had no wish to acquire a large family, and, although they agreed to keep little Leonora, Philadelphia was passed on to a maternal aunt, and George to his father's sister, Aunt Hooper, in Tonbridge. There he did well, attending the school from 1741 for six years, studying some mathematics but mostly the classics, since Greek and Latin texts provided the standard educational fare. He was a hard-working boy, and at sixteen he was awarded a Fellowship reserved for scholars of Tonbridge School to enable him to go to St John's College, Oxford. Happy and successful at Oxford, he had no difficulty in taking his degree and decided to remain to study divinity, winning a further Exhibition to do so in 1751.

Meanwhile his sister Philadelphia had a more difficult time. As soon as she reached her fifteenth birthday in May 1745, she was apprenticed to a Covent Garden milliner, Hester Cole. The apprenticeship records at the Public Records Office show that a sum of £45 was paid for her to spend five years learning how to make and sell hats from Mrs Cole, widow of Christopher Cole, milliner. So while George was at Oxford on the way to becoming a gentleman, she was in central London serving her apprenticeship to a trade that was only on the border of respectability.[5] To be described as a little milliner carried a suggestion of something altogether more dubious. John Cleland's famous pornographic novel *Fanny Hill* made good use of this equivocal status when he delivered his heroine Fanny into the care of a Mrs Cole of Covent Garden, 'a middle-aged discreet sort of woman', ostensibly a milliner, actually a bawd: 'In the outer parlour, or rather shop, sat three young women, very demurely employed on millinery work, which was the cover of a traffic in more precious commodities; but three beautifuller creatures could hardly be seen . . . as it happened, I could not have put myself into worse, or into better hands in all London.' The coincidence of names and professions is all the more startling in that *Fanny Hill* was published in 1748–9, which was exactly the period of Philadelphia's employment by Hester Cole. Two things may be said about this. First, that it seems unlikely Cleland was unaware of the existence of the real Mrs Cole – Covent Garden was not a vast area – and that if he intended his allusion to her business purely as a joke, it must have caused some embarrassing moments for Philadelphia and her fellow apprentices, Sarah and Rose. But secondly, even if it was not a joke, and Hester Cole was indeed engaged in more than one type of activity, we are not entitled to conclude anything about Philadelphia from Cleland's fiction. The two Mrs Coles of Covent Garden remain no more than a striking coincidence.

As soon as she had served her time with Hester Cole, Philadelphia, showing some of the same enterprise as her grandmother, gave up all thought of millinery and announced that she was taking off for India. Men went to India to make their fortunes through trade, honest or dishonest, and women went with a somewhat similar object, as everyone knew even if no one said so. Their business was to find a husband, the richer the better, among the Englishmen working there; and they had a fair chance, because Englishwomen were in very short supply. Phila, as she was known in the family, was bright and pretty, but none of this had brought her proposals of marriage

The apprentice register showing Philadelphia Austen's
apprenticeship to Hester Cole, milliner, Covent Garden, 9 May 1745

in England, where men looked for brides with money as well as
charm, and little milliners were not well placed to catch husbands.
In India, there was a better hope. It sounds a bleak way of going
about things, but for many decades it was quite a standard procedure
for young women to be shipped out to British colonial territories in
this way.[6] It may even be that in her case the whole process was set
in motion by her lawyer uncle Francis, acting for a client in the
employ of the East India Company who wanted a wife. Still, Phila
must have shown some enthusiasm, a great hatred of millinery and
a lot of spirit to embark on so risky and uncertain a venture. She had
to apply for permission from the Directors of the Company, and give
the names of friends in India and sponsors, or 'sureties', in England.

The permission was given, and Philadelphia's story began in
earnest. Her years as an apprentice milliner were blotted out, and
seem never to have been mentioned in the family. The trip round
Africa and through the Indian Ocean took six months, and she was
entirely responsible for herself from the moment she stepped aboard
the *Bombay Castle*. Two years before her, the same journey had been
made by a clever Westminster boy of eighteen; his headmaster grieved
that he was not allowed to go on to the university, but his guardians

were convinced he had a better chance in life as a clerk in the East India Company. His name was Warren Hastings, and he and Philadelphia, both poor orphans, both intent on improving their status, already had much in common although they did not meet for some years yet. He went north to Calcutta, while she remained where she landed in August 1752, in Madras. India was in a state of turmoil, violence flaring, the Company uneasily poised between attempts to assume the role of government and concentration on its trading enterprises; and in these it was often fleeced by its own employees, many of whom preferred amassing fortunes privately to performing their official duties.

One of these employees became the husband of Philadelphia. Six months after her arrival in Madras, in February 1753, she was married to a man named Tysoe Saul Hancock. He was thirty, had been in India for five years, nominally as a surgeon to the East India Company, really with his eye on making a fortune for himself by trading. So far he had done only moderately well, and he was scarcely the husband a young woman dreams of. He was not particularly able, or amusing, or charming; on the other hand, Francis Austen was his lawyer in England, so perhaps the deal had been made in advance. Hancock was very pleased to have a delightful young wife, and eager to treat her well. News of the marriage must have reached George in Oxford by the summer of 1753.

There was no marriage in prospect for Leonora. She remained with Uncle Stephen and Aunt Elizabeth Austen; he was doing well enough to acquire a house in Islington, where she provided a useful pair of hands. No one put up money to apprentice her to any trade, although it is conceivable she helped out with the bookshop. She and her sister presumably saw one another during Phila's years in Covent Garden, but just at the time Phila left for India Stephen Austen died, and since no one else wanted Leonora or had anything to offer her, she stayed on with his widow. Elizabeth Austen soon married another bookseller, a Mr Hinton, who accepted Leonora as an unremarkable fixture of the household.[7]

Brother Austen and sister Hancock wrote regularly to one another. The years went by; both approached thirty, but there came no word of any little Hancocks from India, and there seemed no prospect of marriage for George. Then Philadelphia's life in India changed spectacularly in 1759 when the Hancocks moved north to Bengal and there formed a close friendship with Warren Hastings. By now Hastings, the biggest meritocrat of them all, was advancing on the brilliant path that would make him governor first of Bengal, and then of India. He was dedicated to work, and he loved and understood Indian life and literature as no one else in the Company did. He was also an arrogant man, behaving more like an Indian despot, it was said, than a British civil servant; a good master but a bad colleague. Against this, he was lonely and unhappy following the death of his wife in 1759; their infant daughter had lived for a few weeks only, and their small son George was about to be sent back to England for the good of his health and his education. Hastings owned a town house in Calcutta and another with a garden at Belvedere, Alipur; airy, splendid palaces, they must have felt painfully empty.[8] It is possible that Philadelphia had known his wife aboard the *Bombay Castle*; if so, she must have been doubly welcome as a friend.[9]

The two men, Hastings still in his twenties and on a rising wave of success, and Hancock, an undistinguished man in his forties, now appear to have embarked on a private business partnership involving a whole series of trading ventures, 'in salt and timber and carpets,

Bihar opium, and rice for the Madras market'.[10] Money was made, and Hancock felt he had a valuable friend and patron. We do not know how he reacted when, after eight years without children, Phila told him she was expecting one; but he welcomed the baby girl born in December 1761 and conducted himself thereafter as a devoted father. She was christened Elizabeth and known as Betsy or Bessy for the first years of her life; later she became Eliza. Hastings agreed to be her godfather; her name was of course the same as that of his dead daughter.

Was she Hancock's child or Hastings's? Lord Clive asserted that Mrs Hancock 'abandoned herself to Mr Hastings', warning his own wife not to keep company with her; and the question is not an unreasonable one to ask even if there is no certain answer.[11] On one side of the argument is the fact of Phila's childlessness for the first eight years of her marriage. Then there is the likelihood that a widower, young, lonely, rich and handsome, might well become the lover of a pretty and entertaining married woman of his own age whose husband is not very agreeable to her. The other side of the argument is that Hancock was always a fond husband and father. Would he have behaved as he did if he suspected that there was anything wrong? I believe he might. He may simply have decided not to think too closely on the subject; although he was a grumbler, he was an affectionate man, and glad to have a daughter he could claim as his own. Pride too may have decided him to brazen out the situation.

Whatever the facts, everyone concerned behaved with outward decorum, and it is unlikely that any gossip reached Philadelphia's brother George in Oxford, although he may have wondered privately. In 1764 Hastings and Hancock were winding up their opium transactions together; Hastings had by now built up a spectacular private fortune, and Hancock had put by what seemed a comfortable sum.[12] The whole party was preparing to sail for England together, Hastings, the Hancocks with four-year-old Betsy, and their Indian servants; the trip cost Hancock £1500.

Meanwhile George Austen's progress had continued smoothly. At twenty-four he was ordained in Rochester Cathedral. He was now at the age considered by Sir Thomas Bertram as the most suitable for marriage in a young man; but there was no question of marriage for him yet. He had as little fortune as his sisters, and no home; their stepmother was still living in their father's house in Tonbridge. Yet Kent drew him back. Uncle Francis was there, growing more prosperous from year to year, as were his other uncles and aunt; and George found a position as Second Master at his old school. It gave him a house, and he was able to supplement his earnings by lodging some of the boys, as his grandmother had done; but it was not enough to launch him on a properly independent life. During the school holidays he sensibly returned to Oxford to keep up his contacts, and when after three years his college invited him to be assistant chaplain, he went back gladly. He took another degree in divinity. He was well liked, and was soon appointed Proctor, in charge of discipline among the undergraduates, and known as 'the handsome Proctor' for his bright eyes and good looks. By now he had certainly met the niece of the Master of Balliol, Miss Cassandra Leigh, and may have begun to think the life of a bachelor Fellow, however comfortable, had its drawbacks.

But it was some time yet before he was able to marry, even though he was presented with the living of Steventon in 1761, through the good offices of a second cousin married to a land-owner with estates in Kent and Hampshire. Cassandra Leigh's father may not have thought such a modest and out-of-the-way parish a good enough prospect for his daughter; at all events, another three years went by, and the death of her father, before George persuaded her that this, together with the small inheritances each expected, did offer a sound enough basis for a life together, and she accepted his proposal.[13] A marriage contract was drawn up and signed, and the ceremony took place on 26 April 1764 at the old church of St Swithin, Walcot, Bath. He was thirty-two, she twenty-four. No other Austens were present; her mother was there, and her brother James Leigh-Perrot and sister Jane were the witnesses. She wore a red riding habit for the occasion, suitable for the journey across Somerset, Wiltshire and Hampshire. They set off at once, stopped overnight at Devizes, and arrived the following day at the parsonage at Deane, which was to be their first home before the ramshackle rectory at Steventon was put into better order.

That autumn Philadelphia had news of her brother's marriage, and in January 1765 left India for England, arriving six months later on 16 June.[14] The Hancocks took a house in Norfolk Street and Hastings settled near by in Essex Street, off the Strand. On Hastings's arrival in England he was given the news that his son George, whom he had not seen since he was four, had died of diphtheria the previous autumn, before they set sail. The death was both upsetting and even embarrassing for Mrs Hancock, because it happened while the boy was in the care of her brother George and his newly married wife; he can have been with them at most for six months. It looks as though Phila recommended her brother to Hastings as an experienced schoolmaster with a wife and a suitable country residence, with the thought that he would make a kindly foster father, and that the income would be useful to him. There was nothing wrong with the plan; only the child, having already lost his mother, been separated from his father and sent half way across the world to be cared for by strangers, might have fared better without further disturbance. He could even have been more resistant to sickness; as Betsy Hancock said later, 'mental & bodily sufferings are ever closely connected'.[15] Family tradition says Mrs Austen loved the boy, and both she and her husband must have been appalled at his death in their care, while she was pregnant with their own first child.[16]

George and Philadelphia continued to be devoted to one another. In the summer of 1766 she and her husband visited the Austens in Hampshire; she was there to help with the arrival of their second son, another George, to whom Mr Hancock stood as godfather. In London he seems to have been introduced to Leonora also, still living in Islington with the Hintons, and took a kindly interest in her. Over the next two years Mr Austen occasionally borrowed money from Hancock, on one occasion a substantial sum of £228. Then Hancock, realizing he could not hope to maintain his wife and child in the style he had dreamt of without increasing his fortune considerably, decided he must return to India. Leaving them in London, he set off once more in 1768.

In his absence, Hastings gave some financial help to Philadelphia, for which her husband expressed gratitude; he also kept up a correspondence with her, again with the knowledge of Hancock, who sometimes forwarded their letters. The only one that survives from Hastings to Philadelphia is perfectly correct, not a love letter, but warm and full of feeling. He addresses her as 'my dear and ever-valued friend', and asks her to 'Kiss my dear Bessy for me, and assure her of my tenderest affection. May the God of goodness bless you both!'[17] A few months after this letter was written, Hancock wrote to his wife telling her that Hastings had a new 'favourite among the Ladies', a Mrs Imhoff, very lively and pretty, with a German husband. This was indeed the woman Hastings married as his second wife, after she obtained a divorce from her husband. Philadelphia's response to hearing about Mrs Imhoff was an immediate proposal that she herself should return to India with Betsy, who was now ten. A long answer from her husband forbade her to think of doing any such thing, listing the possible disasters that might befall Betsy, from the deaths of either of her parents, which could leave her stranded, to being debauched by the gallant young men of Calcutta, or simply too early a marriage: 'You know very well that no girl, tho' but fourteen years old, can arrive in India without attracting the notice of every Coxcomb in the Place, of whom there is very great plenty at Calcutta with very good persons & no other recommendation.' He expressed another fear, that she might fall into 'false notions of happiness, most probably very Romantick'.[18] A few weeks later he wrote again to tell Phila that Mr Hastings had informed him that he was settling £5,000 on his god-daughter.

The subtext of these letters seems clear: Philadelphia did not want to lose her place, or her daughter's, in Hastings's affections, and was prepared to travel to India to try to keep them. Hancock saw the futility of such a move, and pointed out the risks involved in doing so. Phila herself may have written to Hastings asking him to do something tangible for Betsy, to ensure that she was not forgotten now he had a new interest. Dignity was preserved all round, not least that of Hancock.

He was always the prudent and sensible one, as he reminded Philadelphia when he commented on her brother's situation: 'That my brother & sister Austen are well, I heartily rejoice, but I cannot say that the News of the violently rapid increase of their family gives me so much pleasure; especially when I consider the case of my godson who must be provided for without the least hope of his being able to assist himself.'[19] It was true that the Austens were breeding fast. Their first three sons were born in three successive years, and the next batch of four children, after they had moved the short distance from Deane to Steventon, in four more years. Mr Hancock had a point, but he need not have worried overmuch. Despite the death of George Hastings in their care, despite the affliction of their own second son, and despite their singular system of baby rearing, George Austen and Cassandra Leigh were raising a family of clever and ambitious children.

Did the Austen children know they had an Aunt Leonora living in London as well as a dazzling Aunt Philadelphia? In 1769 the woman who had effectively mothered Leonora, Elizabeth Hinton, died, leaving her on the hands of Mr Hinton. Soon after this, a letter from Hancock mentions 'poor Leonora', the noble behaviour of Hinton, and the lack of any legacy from his late wife; Hancock offers to take his share of financial responsibility for his sister-in-law.[20] Clearly, there was no question of her going to her brother's. Why she was not considered suitable remains guesswork: 'poor Leonora' could cover anything from very low intelligence to some moral lapse, easy enough for a motherless girl in London to have fallen into. After Hancock's reference no more is heard of her. Even her death goes unremarked in any surviving letters. In fact she lived until 1784, when she was fifty, and was buried in Islington on 4 February. Her sister Philadelphia was absent in France, and her brother George busy with his family. By then he had eight children. Leonora's eldest nephew James was already at Oxford, and her niece Jane just eight.[21] But in a family in which you had to fight your battles hard to get and keep a good place, it was easy for the unsuccessful to drop out of sight, and one way or another Leonora – plain, dim and poor – had ceased to count.

3

Boys

The Austen parents were also running a boys' school. When the small Jane Austen was brought back to the parsonage, toughened by the life of the mud-floored cottage and unpaved village street, she found herself in a still busier place, full of the clatter of boys, a mixture of brothers and pupils, the eldest of them fourteen and fifteen. Boys' talk and boys' interests dominated the breakfast and dinner table, and even from the nursery you could hear the sound of boys' voices and boyish activities inside and outside the house. There were her four brothers, reasonably familiar, who remained at home all the year round; and the other, stranger boys who came and went as pupils. Twice a year these big creatures arrived, in February and again at the end of August, and twice a year they departed, for the Christmas season, and in June; the school year was divided into two halves at Mr Austen's, just as at the great public schools.[1]

Some were sons of local squires. Other boys, travelling from a distance, might be brought to the parsonage by their parents when they first arrived, and then, once they knew the way, were simply put off the coach that stopped at the Deane Gate Inn on the main road, and walked the last half mile down the hill. Their heavy boxes, full of clothes and perhaps a favourite book and a cake from home, arrived separately, brought to the door on the carrier's cart, then lugged up two flights of stairs to the top of the house. All these were events to be watched by Jenny and explained by Cass.

A houseful of young men meant noise, the clumping of boots in and out of the doors and up and down the stairs; it meant shouts and laughter from the garret rooms where they slept, and sometimes groans and giggles from the parlour where they sat preparing their lessons. In Mr Austen's study they might be allowed to look through the microscope and learn from the large globe, but mostly they were kept busy at their Latin grammar, and reading and translating, with some Greek for the clever ones like Jemmy. Ned and Henry did lessons, but Frank was still too young, and he and Cass learnt their letters in the approved way from counters and cards with their mother; Jenny could easily have picked up hers as younger ones do, without anyone paying much attention except Cass, in her role of little mother.

For Mrs Austen always had her hands full. As well as the work of the vegetable garden, poultry yard and dairy, she had to supervise the preparation of meals for so many hungry growing boys, and make sure they and their linen remained reasonably clean. Nine shirts, seven pairs of stockings, two of breeches, seven handkerchiefs, two nightcaps and just one towel was the packing list of one young contemporary bound for Oxford; he listed neither underwear nor night wear, and the boys may well have done without either, sleeping naked or in their shirts.[2] There must have been a good deal of rough and tumble to be controlled at the top of the house.

The number of pupils was small enough for the Austens to run the school as a large family rather than as an institution. When the boys were not at their lessons, they were much like extra elder brothers to the girls, and no doubt they petted and played with them. A favourite country-house game of the time was one in which the girls were sat on a good thick tablecloth at the top of the stairs, the boys then taking hold of the corners of the cloth and pulling it down to the bottom; you can imagine what fun it was, and the shrieks of laughter as everyone ended in a heap.[3] Apple-pie beds were as popular as blind-man's buff, and there was dancing at Steventon sometimes, when even the youngest could attempt to join in.[4] In summer there was cricket on half holidays, in winter the boys might go out to see the hunt meet, and to run a mile or two with it; James sometimes climbed a tree for the huntsmen, to chase down a marten cat that was distracting the hounds from the scent of fox.[5]

Some of the boys became lifelong friends of the Austen children, among them the four Fowle brothers from Kintbury in Berkshire, sons of an Oxford contemporary of Mr Austen, all of an age with the older Austen boys: Fulwar-Craven, Tom, William and Charles. You can tell the school was a cheerful place from a poem written by

Mrs Austen and sent to one of the pupils, a Berkshire baronet's son called Gilbert East, who stayed away from school longer than he should have done after Christmas, enjoying the season of dances at home. She urged him to return to 'the Mansion of Learning' where, she wrote, 'we study all day, Except when we play':

> Of Dan Virgil, we say
> Two lessons each day,
> And the story is quite entertaining;
> You have lost the best part,
> But come, take good heart,
> Tho' we've read six, there's six books remaining . . .
>
> That you dance very well
> All beholders can tell
> For lightly and nimbly you tread;
> But pray, is it meet,
> To indulge thus your feet,
> And neglect all the while your poor head?
>
> So we send you this letter
> In hopes you'll think better,
> And reflect upon what is here said:
> And to make us amends
> Pray return to your friends,
> Fowle, Stewart, Deane, Henry, & Ned.[6]

A mother who could make magic with words must have caught all her children's attention. Mrs Austen's pen brought Gilbert back; he went on to Oxford, and preserved her poem carefully. It tells us not only what a clever writer she was, but how deeply she involved herself in all the activities of the school.

When Jenny was not quite three, and her mother was thirty-nine, Mrs Austen found herself pregnant again; and if she and her husband were not delighted, they were both of a temper to resign themselves to the will of God and make the best of the situation. At the end of June 1779 a sixth and last son, Charles, made his appearance; at least he had the grace to arrive during the summer holidays, when the only children around were his brothers and sisters. Two weeks after his birth, James set off with his father to be enrolled as an undergraduate at his old Oxford college, St John's. At fourteen he was two years younger than Mr Austen had been on starting at the university, but he did not have to win his scholarship by any demonstration of intelligence or learning, as his father had done. He was able to claim it through his mother's family connections.

St John's awarded scholarships to those who could prove they were 'Founder's Kin', that is, related, however distantly, to the Sir Thomas White to whom the college owed its existence. Because the Leighs were such enthusiastic keepers of their family history, James was able to supply the necessary pedigree without difficulty.[7] They dined with Mrs Austen's formidable uncle, still Master of Balliol at eighty-six and as sharp as ever: when James politely began to remove his newly acquired gown on sitting down at table, he was told, 'Young man, you need not strip, we are not going to fight.'[8] After enrolling, James came home, but from October he would travel to and fro between Steventon and Oxford as the short university terms dictated. He was beginning to write poetry, like his mother.

Edward was also away in the summer of 1779. In May, the Austens were called on by the absentee landlord of Steventon, their distant cousin Thomas Knight, with his newly married wife Catherine; they were on their bridal tour, and they took such a fancy to twelve-year-old Edward that they asked if they might take him with them for the rest of the trip. They may have thought too that Mrs Austen had a good deal on her hands, and she may have agreed. The idea of inviting a boy of twelve as a honeymoon companion is an unusual one, but Edward was always a sunny and uncomplicated boy, and the plan worked so well that the Knights became deeply attached to him. They maintained their particular interest in him after returning him to his parents, and asked if he might visit them in Kent; and, as they showed no sign of having any children, they began to think of Edward as almost their own.

About this time arrangements must also have been made for George to be settled further from home. Mr and Mrs Austen would have consulted with her brother and her sister Jane, now married to another clergyman, Edward Cooper, in Bath, about the care of their handicapped brother Thomas; and a family called Culham was found at Monk Sherborne, a quiet village on the other side of Basingstoke, to look after both Thomas Leigh and George Austen. In Crabbe's poems you read of idiots endangering themselves by wandering into the paths of fast-travelling coaches, and other accounts of village life mention them falling into wells, so it was important to find reliable people; evidently the Austens and the Leighs did. There is no record of any visits to their afflicted brother and son, but it is reasonable to suppose they took place, if only to pay the Culhams.

A single glimpse of nursery life comes from Jane Austen herself. It is the only direct reminiscence she gave of her early childhood, apart from saying she had been shy, but it is vivid enough to make you feel you are in the room with her and her brother Francis, and hear the Hampshire dialect the children spoke with their nurses. It comes in a poem written for Francis thirty years later, when his eldest son was born, in 1809. She expressed the formal hope that the new baby would resemble him, then turned to the past, when Frank, who had been small for his age, and agile, was the leader of their infant group, given to 'saucy words and fiery ways'; in particular, she recalled an occasion when he peeped disobediently round a door, presumably after they had all been put to bed, and explained himself to their nurse with words that imitated her soft speech: 'Bet, my be not come to bide.'

> My dearest Frank, I wish you joy
> Of Mary's safety with a Boy . . .
> In him, in all his ways, may we
> Another Francis William see! –
> Thy infant days may he inherit,
> Thy warmth, nay insolence of spirit . . .
> May he revive thy Nursery sin,
> Peeping as daringly within,
> His curley Locks but just descried,
> With 'Bet, my be not come to bide.' –

You can see the little sister behind him, half shocked, half admiring; to a four-year-old there is nothing like a hero of five, and Frank was known in the family for his unruliness: 'Fearless of danger, braving pain/And threaten'd very oft in vain'.

A girl growing up in a boys' school is likely to take up boys' games. This is the best reason for believing Jane made Catherine Morland in *Northanger Abbey* partly in her own image, 'fond of all boys' plays', and preferring cricket and base ball* to playing with dolls or keeping a pet dormouse or canary. There was certainly a green slope to roll down at the back of Steventon rectory, as there was behind the Morlands'; and a few years of being 'noisy and wild', hating 'confinement and cleanliness' and even running about the country and riding on horseback fit in very well with the fact that Frank managed to buy himself a pony called Squirrel when he was seven, and took himself hunting as soon as he could. His mother made him a red coat, cut down from her wedding clothes, and he would help himself to early breakfast in the kitchen; it is not hard to see six-year-old Jane getting astride Squirrel when he gave her the chance.

Running about the country with her brothers meant sometimes going in the direction of the village, where each cottage was entirely familiar and each face known; any stranger caused a stir, the odd pedlar, or a sailor making his way home across country. Up the lane in the other direction the children could walk to their father's church and the Digweeds' house among the trees. It was much bigger than the parsonage, with an ancient porch three storeys high, and very dilapidated; and here again there were boys, four of them, keen riders and followers of the hunt, and all of an age with the Austen brothers.

In rainy weather they could play in their own big barn, a great resource for children. They could walk up the hill to Cheesedown Farm beyond the village, where everyone worked for their father; and beyond that was the main road along which the coaches travelled unimaginable distances to and from places whose names gradually became familiar: Winchester, Southampton, Portsmouth, Andover, Reading, Newbury, Bath and London. The coaches carried not only people but letters, which the children might bring home from the Deane Gate Inn where they were left. These were greatly valued by their parents, read, reread and talked over in the parlour, with their news of aunts, uncles and cousins: Aunt Hancock and Cousin Eliza in town; Aunt and Uncle Cooper and their children Jane and Edward in Bath; Aunt and Uncle Leigh-Perrot at Scarlets, in Berkshire; old Uncle Francis Austen in Tonbridge; and many more.

* This is one of the few early English references to baseball before its official invention in America in the 1860s.[9]

In the study their father kept his rows and rows of books; one of his bookcases covered sixty-four square feet of wall, and he was always collecting more, not just the classics but new ones, from which he read aloud.[10] He also knew enough science to show them the worlds in miniature revealed by his microscope, the 'animalcules' living in a drop of rainwater infused with hay, or the exquisite workmanship of a butterfly's tongue, an insect's egg or a fish scale. These were thrilling sights, and proof of the way in which the divine organizer patterned and planned everything in the universe.[11] But Mr Austen's world was as much the farm as the study. The children often saw him riding about on his horse, and conferring with his bailiff John Bond. He had to worry about the price of wheat, barley, sheep and pigs, take on labourers and lay them off, decide what crops to sow and when to harvest. Then there was his parish business to attend to, and his Sunday services. He wrote some of his own sermons at least, although he was frugal with them; the manuscript of one shows that he preached it seven times at Deane and eight at Steventon.[12] He was a busy man but good-tempered, no doubt prizing domestic life the more for having been an orphan himself. He took to neither drink nor gluttony, the traditional supports of the country clergyman, and managed to be his sons' schoolmaster without losing their friendship. He accepted that his children's different temperaments set them off on different paths: James and Henry scholars; Edward not cut out for classical studies but with a more practical turn of mind; and Francis born to be a man of action. All received his kindness and interest. He could be down-to-earth. When he gave advice to Francis as a young man setting off for his first sea voyage, he reminded him to be vigorous not only in saying his prayers but also in brushing his teeth and washing regularly.[13] There is something fresh and pleasant about Mr Austen's concern for well-brushed teeth.

Every week rose to a sort of climax on Sunday when Mr Austen, transformed by his black gown, presided in church. Their mother's province was the dining parlour, the kitchen, the poultry yard, the dairy and the vegetable garden, with their succession of regular events. Bread was baked, and beer was brewed at home and stored down in the cellars; the parsonage had its own cows to be milked, and the cream churned by the dairy maid for their butter. The washerwoman came once a month to tackle the piles of dirty linen, disrupting everything with steam and suds. In June there was haymaking, when the children were supplied with small hayrakes; in July there was boiling of jams and jellies; in August the harvest; in September you heard shooting. The freedom conferred by good summer weather and long hours of daylight was precious; as the year moved round and candles were lit earlier and earlier, and fires in the parlour and the dining room, the children longed for bright, frosty days that allowed them to get out of the house freely. James Austen wrote of the 'female foot' not getting through the lanes in mud, snow and flood, while men and boys could almost always manage on horseback; it was one of the sexual distinctions everyone accepted, and made bad weather a sort of imprisonment for women and girls. Itching chilblains on fingers and toes afflicted almost everyone; and Mrs Austen caught colds that were worse than anyone else's. Energetic as she was, she sometimes took to her bed. But there were no epidemics, and no repetition of the tragedy of George Hastings.

Growing up in a school meant that Jane knew exactly what to expect of boys, and was always at ease with them; boys were her natural environment, and boys' jokes and boys' interests were the first she learnt about. This is obvious in what has survived of her earliest writing; although there is none from before the age of twelve, the influence is clear. It is full of boys' humour, starting with the talk of horses and vehicles, journeys and accidents, all topics young men were as much obsessed with then as modern boys are with motor bikes and cars. There is a lot about drunkenness too, always good for a laugh among boys. There are drunken quarrels, and characters are found 'dead drunk', or actually die of drink.

Food is another source of jokes, 'stinking' fish and game, underdone veal and curry with no seasoning, and other dishes likely to have been unpopular with schoolboys, fried cow-heel and onion, tripe, red herrings, liver and 'crow' (i.e., giblets). A man at an inn orders 'a whole egg' to be boiled for his and his servants' dinner. Food is funny in itself, and by association. A girl's face turns 'as White as a Whipt syllabub' when her future husband is killed; another – called Cassandra – devours six ices at a pastry-cook's shop, refuses to pay for them and knocks down the pastry-cook; a third remains, under provocation, 'as cool as a cream cheese'. Of two sisters, one loves drawing pictures, the other drawing pullets: schoolchildren's word play. And there is a fine boys' joke about a man jilting his bride because the marriage date coincides with the first day of shooting.

Ugly and deformed girls provide another source of humour: one is 'short, fat and disagreeable', another has a 'forbidding Squint', 'greazy tresses' and a 'swelling Back'. Female efforts to improve appearances with red and white cosmetic paint are good for a laugh too. There is a great deal of cheerful violence, including several incidents which might be called fun murders. There is a hanging. There is a steel mantrap that catches a girl by the leg. There are characters driven by hunger to bite off their own fingers.

Jane Austen was a tough and unsentimental child, drawn to rude, anarchic imaginings and black jokes. She found a good source for this ferocious style of humour in the talk she heard, and doubtless sometimes joined in, among her parents' pupils, bursting out of childhood into young manhood. If she was sometimes shocked as she listened, she herself was learning how to shock by writing things down.

At Christmas 1782, when Jane was seven, there was something new for her to listen to. Her brothers put on a play. It was a tragedy called *Matilda*, and perhaps responsible for Jane's smart dismissal of another play a few years later, 'it is a tragedy and therefore not worth reading'.[14] *Matilda* may have been chosen because it was the work of a respectable Surrey clergyman, had been premièred by Garrick only seven years before, and needed only five principal actors; but Jane's judgement was better than Garrick's. The action is set in the time of William the Conqueror, when Morcar, Earl of Mercia, and his brother Edwin are both in love with Matilda, daughter of a Norman lord. She loves Edwin, but they are held prisoner by Morcar, who decides to have his brother murdered. A trick prevents the foul deed, Morcar repents, and the lovers marry. The writing is an all too familiar sub-Shakespearean:

> Confusion! horror! misery! O heaven!
> Canst thou behold such complicated guilt,
> Such unexampled perfidy, and yet
> Withhold thy vengeance? Let thy lightnings blast
> The base betrayer! O Matilda! false,
> Deceitful, cruel woman! . . . [15]

Two sets of brothers, Austens and Fowles, seem to have taken part in this fratricidal play, for which James wrote the epilogue, spoken by Tom Fowle. As to Matilda and her waiting woman, Cassandra and Jane were ten and seven, surely too young, which leaves you to wonder whether Henry, aged eleven, put on one of his mother's gowns for the occasion. I rather hope so, but it is also possible their cousin Jane Cooper, another eleven-year-old, was allowed to come from Bath to take the part.

James took his theatricals very seriously, and contributed a prologue as well as an epilogue, contrasting the ancient stage with the modern, and showing off his knowledge of the special weather effects required in *Matilda*:

> When Thespis first professed the mimic art
> Rude were his Actors, and his stage a cart;
> No scene gay painted, to the eye displayed
> The waving honours of the sylvan glade.
> No canvas Palace pleased the wondering sight,
> Nor rosined lightning flashed its forked light:
> No iron bowl the rolling thunder forms,
> No rattling pease proclaim the driving storms . . .

And so it goes on for many more couplets: he has done his research, but he cannot quite match his mother's light touch with verse. One hopes the evening was relieved by unintentional humour at least; *Matilda* must have made considerable demands on the attention of those friendly neighbours – Digweeds, Portals, Terrys, Lyfords – who were invited to the performance in the Austen barn, even if their sons figured as spear-bearers and attendants. That James had some doubts about the enterprise appears in the opening of the epilogue: 'Halloo, good gentlefolks! What, none asleep?' You can be sure that the seven-year-old girl in the audience was wider awake than anyone.[16]

4

School

'One's heart aches for a dejected Mind of eight years old,' wrote Jane Austen when she was thirty-two, hearing of two small nieces being sent unwillingly away to boarding school. She knew what she was talking about, because she herself was sent away at the age of · seven. While the Austen boys were kept at home until they were twelve at least, the two girls were subjected to much tougher treatment. There may have been a financial motive for this brisk decision, their parents reasoning that they could more than cover the cost of the girls' school fees by using their room for further boy pupils. Mrs Austen was also surely influenced by loyalty to her sister Cooper, who had decided to send her daughter Jane to school and wanted companions for her there. And there was another point that weighed with the Coopers: the school was set up by Mr Cooper's widowed sister, a Mrs Cawley, and sending her pupils was a piece of family support. No one seems to have worried that Jane Cooper was eleven to Jane Austen's seven.

Even before the school plan was laid, the Coopers, wanting companionship for their daughter, were in the habit of inviting Cassandra to stay in Bath. Jane felt the loss of her sister, signalling it on one occasion, when their father had gone to collect her at Andover on her return from Bath, by setting off with Charles to meet them on the road, to the considerable surprise of Mr Austen when he saw the two children trudging along so far from home. This powerful dislike of being left behind by Cassandra was enough, perhaps, to make her think she would rather go to school with her than stay at home without her.

Mrs Cawley, as well as being Jane Cooper's aunt, was eminently respectable, as the widow of a Master of Brasenose, and her school was in Oxford, familiar territory to both Austen parents. James was now at St John's, and Mrs Austen's uncle was still master of Balliol; not perhaps much comfort to two small girls, but in principle able to keep an eye on things. Essentially, Mrs Austen must have decided she could trust her sister's choice, and brushed aside any anxiety about sending such a young child as Jane away from home. There is, however, a note of defensiveness about her explanation, decades later, that it was Jane herself who insisted on going: she was 'too young to make her going to school at all necessary, but it was her own doing; she *would* go with Cassandra; "if Cassandra's head had been going to be cut off, Jane would have her's cut off too"'.[1] According to Mrs Austen's granddaughter Anna, who is the source of the story, this actually applied to her later departure for another school, when she was nine; if so, it makes the earlier decision even harder to understand.

It does suggest that Jane, following Cassandra's absences in Bath, felt that the prospect of losing her again was more than she could bear; and that her sister, sharer of her bedroom and her secrets, represented something she did not find in her ever active mother. But she was too young to grasp what it would really mean to be far from home and consigned to the care of strangers. Other children endured as much, of course, and Mrs Austen may have feared that Jane would become wild and out of control at home among so many boys. She may have recalled too that her sister-in-law Jane Leigh-Perrot had been packed off from the West Indies at six to be sent to boarding school in England, and survived the experience well enough. In any case she had a house full of boys to look after; and she convinced herself it would be best for all concerned. It was Jane's second banishment from home.

Whether Mrs Austen even met Mrs Cawley is not on record; one of the Austen parents presumably took their daughters to Oxford in the spring of 1783, but as soon as they were delivered, both parents set off on a holiday trip. It meant they were out of touch for some time. Mrs Cawley would have taken her pupils into her own house, just as the Austens did; a child used to the countryside must have found the contrast between life at Steventon and life in a town house difficult to cope with. Then, to a seven-year-old who has never thought about time before, a term stretches like a limitless desert ahead; and the sense of loss and powerlessness on finding yourself cut off from home, parents, brothers, familiar faces and familiar places can turn the world into a very bleak place indeed.

Boarding schools for girls were not hard to find in the 1780s, not least because keeping a school was one of the very few ways in which a woman could hope to earn a respectable living; but accounts of what went on in them make depressing, and sometimes horrifying, reading. At the time the Austen girls were sent to Oxford, a seven-year-old called Elizabeth Ham, daughter of well-to-do parents in the West Country, found herself at 'Ma'am Tucker's Seminary' in Weymouth, where the pupils were fed on the principle 'eat the bread and smell the cheese', and all made to sleep in the drawing room. By day Elizabeth was kept confined in the same unaired room, sewing on a wooden bench for hours at a time until she and her eyes were worn out, Mrs Tucker occasionally enlivening things by reading aloud from *The Pilgrim's Progress*. The child was removed when she was found to have caught the itch, but once recovered she was sent to a far worse school at Tiverton, run by two genteel sisters. Here she was put to share a bed with a girl five years older than herself, thought a suitable friend because both came from Weymouth; but the big girl took to turning the little one out of bed before daybreak so that she could have it to herself; and Elizabeth sat shivering in the early morning cold.[2]

Sharing a bed was more common than not; Arthur Young's dearly loved daughter Bobbin fell ill at her fashionable boarding school in London, where she shared a 'vile' small bed with a deaf girl who would lie on one side only, forcing Bobbin into excruciating discomfort. Like Jane, she was a country child, used to running about in the fresh air, and this she was no longer allowed at school: running was forbidden, very little time was spent out of doors, and the food was poor and scanty. 'She abhorred school,' wrote her father after her early death. 'Oh! how I regret putting her there.'[3]

Children were often half starved by their schoolmistresses because they were struggling against poverty themselves. This was the case at Elizabeth Ham's Tiverton school, where breakfast was hot water – the girls could supply their own tea – a dash of milk and a halfpenny roll; dinner, boiled mutton or suet pudding. At tea-time an old woman came round selling biscuits, three for a halfpenny, and there was the same provision of hot water. Supper was bread, cheese and cider. As for their studies, they learnt by rote from the Dictionary, the Grammar and a book of Geography; there were never any questions. They read from the Bible in the morning and the history of England or Rome in the afternoon; a master came to teach writing and arithmetic each morning from eleven to twelve, and the Dancing Master came twice a week. Every now and then there was a half-holiday, when the girls were allowed to visit nearby farms, and able to gorge on fresh bread and clotted cream. They could not complain in their letters home, because these were 'corrected' and sealed by their schoolmistresses; and the worst time of all was when Elizabeth was left at school with some other girls over the Christmas holidays, and they had to endure being frozen as well as starved. One night she enterprisingly crept down and stole a leg of roast goose while the teachers were enjoying a party; you feel like cheering the little thief.[4]

Not all girls went through such horrors as this, and one hopes Mrs Cawley at least fed her charges better. Maria Edgeworth, also sent at seven to school in Derby, after the death of her mother and her father's remarriage, and left there for at least a year without going home, nevertheless remembered the school with affection. She was taught French, Italian, dancing, embroidery and copperplate hand-writing, and she entertained herself and the other girls by telling stories when they were in bed at night. When it was decided to send her on to a smart London boarding school she was much less happy, for there she was made to wear backboards and iron collars to improve her posture.[5]

There are many more examples of the wretchedness of girls' schools chosen by rich and seemingly well-informed parents. Dr Johnson's friend Mrs Thrale sent her four- and five-year-old daughters, Harriet and Cecilia, to boarding school in 1783; there was a measles epidemic, Harriet died, and Cecilia was only just saved by her mother's intervention; she was then sent to another boarding school when she was ten. Mary Butt, who became the writer Mrs Sherwood, and was the same age as Jane Austen, also went through a measles epidemic at her boarding school in which a small girl in her room died, uncomforted by her parents; they probably did not even learn of her illness until it was over.

*

Mrs Cawley's school narrowly avoided the same thing. First she decided to move her little group from Oxford to Southampton, which the Austen parents either accepted as a *fait accompli* when they heard of it, or welcomed, since Southampton was closer to home. Unluckily it was also a port where troops returning from abroad were arriving in large numbers, and in the summer of 1783 they brought an infectious fever with them, which spread around the town. Both the Austen girls and their cousin became ill. Mrs Cawley thought it unnecessary to inform their parents, whether from a belief that she could manage and did not want them disturbed, or out of incompetence and callousness. Most fortunately Jane Cooper ignored her instructions not to write home and managed to send a message to her mother in Bath. It was alarming enough to bring both Mrs Cooper and Mrs Austen to Southampton. Jane Austen was by then in danger of her life.

She was nursed back to health by her mother, and taken home. Cassandra and Jane Cooper also recovered; but Mrs Cooper had caught the infection and, back in Bath, she died of it in October. Her husband was left grief-stricken and hardly able to cope. After this, Jane Cooper spent more time at Steventon, becoming a part of the family, and a favourite with all her cousins.

The adult Jane Austen wrote both scathingly and pityingly of schoolmistresses. 'To be rational in anything is great praise, especially in the ignorant class of school mistresses.' ' "I would rather be Teacher at a school (and I can think of nothing worse) than marry a Man I did not like." – "I would rather do any thing than be Teacher at a school – said her sister. *I* have been at school . . . & know what a Life they lead: *you* never have." ' But there are no references to her own time at school beyond one passing phrase in a letter to Cassandra, where she wrote, 'I could die of laughter . . . as they used to say at school.'[6] Better to die of laughter than of infectious fever, at least; beyond this, she did not choose to recall her schooldays.

Their very wretchedness may also have done something for her. She described herself as a shy child, and shy children withdraw into themselves when they are unhappy; one thing a seven-year-old can retreat into is reading any and every book that comes to hand. Other people's worlds offer an escape. Then her own imagination may have offered her another escape route, as Maria Edgeworth's did. So the dreadful Mrs Cawley may claim some indirect credit for Jane Austen's mental and imaginative development.

Charlotte Palmer, in *Sense and Sensibility*, is said to have spent 'seven years at a great school in town to some effect' – the effect being the production of a landscape in coloured silks, and a social manner carrying silliness into surreal realms. In contrast to such places, the motherly Mrs Goddard's establishment in *Emma* 'had an ample house and garden, gave the children plenty of wholesome food, let them run about a great deal in summer, and in winter dressed their chilblains with her own hands'. This has Jane Austen's approval, and Mrs Goddard and her twittering assistants are kindly women, clearly not modelled on Mrs Cawley; the parents of the illegitimate Harriet Smith, who is dumped there, are luckier than many more careful and respectable fathers and mothers. But Mrs Goddard's also becomes a pretext for an attack on schools that 'professed, in long sentences of refined nonsense, to combine liberal acquirements with elegant morality upon new principles and new systems – and where young ladies for enormous pay might be screwed out of health and into vanity'.[7] All her life Jane found it hard to see girls' schools as anything but places of torment for pupils and teachers alike.

For the moment, the girls were at home again. Edward had now left for good, officially adopted by Mr and Mrs Thomas Knight. Henry said their father was less keen on the adoption plan than their mother, but that she urged it for Edward's good. As with the decision to send the girls away to school, hers seems to have been the dominant voice. In this case she was justified by events. The move was made gradually, he was old enough to understand and appreciate what was happening, and to keep up his contacts with Steventon; and he fitted perfectly into the world of the Knights. They were rich, kindly and not particularly clever; and Edward was neither an intellectual nor an imaginative boy, but one with a good heart and a steady nature. Although he would have to change his name to Knight one day, he remained an Austen for the present, and devoted and attentive to his natural family, a devotion unshaken by his years of Grand Touring, his marriage to a baronet's daughter or his inheritance of the Knights' large estates and fortune.

Edward's adoption and the girls' illness coincided with James taking his degree at Oxford. He remained there as a Fellow of his college, but was often at home, and planning more theatricals. Encouragement may have been sought, and would certainly be given, from new neighbours at Ashe, the next village to Deane, where the Revd George Lefroy moved into the rectory with his wife Anne and three small children. She was known as 'Madam Lefroy', in tribute to something exotic about her as much as to her Huguenot husband; and she came from Kent with a reputation as a great reader and writer of poetry, with a knowledge of Milton, Pope, Collins, Gray 'and the poetical passages of Shakespeare'. She was a beauty and a spirited woman, clever, quick, witty and popular, a different being from the lumpish wives of the hunting squires of the district. She enjoyed entertaining, and was 'the life of every party into which she entered'. This is her brother's view of her, and it is borne out by others. She dressed elegantly, her hair was beautifully arranged and powdered, her expression sweet; and she did not let children or domestic cares stop her sitting down to talk over a poem or a piece of writing by a friend. She soon became Jane Austen's best loved and admired mentor, the person she would run to for advice and encouragement, and who always made time for her, the ideal parent to be preferred to the everyday one.

It looks as though 1784, when Jane was eight, was spent at home again. By now she was able to read anything in English on her father's shelves that took her fancy. She could also read some French, probably taught her at Mrs Cawley's, for she owned a volume of *Fables choisies* with her name inscribed in December 1783. On its advertisement page her brother Francis practised writing his name with various flourishes, and a tired student – it could be Jane herself – scrawled 'I wish I had done'; in tiny letters, the words, 'Mothers angry father's gone out' may be a glimpse into a cross afternoon at the parsonage.[8] Mrs Lefroy could also encourage her in her choice of books, supplementing her father's and mother's suggestions. The death of Dr Johnson occurred in 1784, which may have inspired her to start reading his essays from the *Rambler*, with their fine rolling prose and their short, dramatic life studies: the fortune-hunter, the flighty Miss of fifteen impatient of control, the adopted niece who is betrayed and abandoned and becomes a prostitute, and many more stories,

Endpaper of Jane Austen's copy of *Fables choisies*

all told with such point and concision that any intelligent child would seize on them as a window on to the adult world.

Jane later associated Johnson's name with Anne Lefroy's in a memorial poem she addressed to her, touchingly citing his greatness as 'the first of Men' alongside her pre-eminence among her friends. The poem is warm but disappointingly general in its terms. 'Angelic woman!', 'solid worth', 'captivating grace', 'energy of soul sincere' are none of them phrases that give any impression of a living personality, or allow us to see what form this friendship took in day-to-day life. While Jane's adult letters mention Mrs Lefroy as hostess or fellow guest, and we hear of her calling on the Austens for informal conversation, no solid picture of her character or of the exchanges between the young woman and the clever child appears; we have to take on trust the way in which she demonstrated her early friendship.

In July, there was another production in the Steventon barn, this time a comedy, Sheridan's *The Rivals*, first produced at Drury Lane in the year of Jane's birth and now 'Acted by some young Ladies & Gentlemen at Steventon', as James wrote at the head of his prologue, to be spoken by thirteen-year-old Henry at the performance. This was altogether more ambitious than *Matilda*. Uncut, its playing time is five hours, and it has a cast of twelve principals, with three important parts for women; James must either have called on Oxford friends or cast children. There is some evidence that he did the latter from the final words of his prologue, where he addresses the girls in the audience:

> Ye blooming Fair, from whose propitious smile,
> We hope a sweet reward for all our toil,*
> Though yet too young your stronger powers to own,
> We fondly wait your smile, and dread your frown
> Smile but this evening, and in riper years,
> When manhood's strength has damp'd our boyish fears,
> Our hearts, with genuine grace and beauty caught,
> In fervent sighs shall thank you as they ought.
> You'll see us suppliant at your feet again,
> And they who liked as Boys, shall love as Men.

This is a real advance on his earlier prologue, and rather surprising for a boy of fifteen, not an age when it is usual to look forward in this graceful fashion to the prospect of adult love. If it does suggest there were children in the cast as well as in the audience, we may speculate boldly that Jane Cooper and Cassandra played Lydia and Julia, and even that Jane Austen may have been given Lucy the maid. There was plenty to laugh at for children who were growing up in a house full of books, starting with the scene in which the maid Lucy hides the library books for her mistress Lydia, nervous of being caught out reading unsuitable ones:

Lydia Here, my dear Lucy, hide these books. Quick, quick! Fling *Peregrine Pickle* under the toilet – throw *Roderick Random* into the closet – put *The Innocent Adultery* into *The Whole Duty of Man* . . . put *The Man of Feeling* into your pocket – so, so – now lay *Mrs Chapone* in sight, and leave *Fordyce's Sermons* open on the table.

---

* Note that the Austens pronounced 'toil' to rhyme with 'smile'; a much later poem of James's similarly rhymes 'join' with 'thine'. This suggests the same usage as that of Pepys, whose shorthand renders 'point' as 'pint', 'boil' as 'bil' (*bile*) and 'join' as 'jin' (*jine*). Readers aloud of Jane Austen might like to take note: 'Mr Elton, in very good spirits, was one of the first to walk in. Mrs Weston and Emma were sitting together on a sopha. He jined them immediately . . .'

Lucy   O burn it, ma'am! the hair-dresser has torn away as far as *Proper Pride.*

Lydia   Never mind – open at *Sobriety.* – Fling me *Lord Chesterfield's Letters.* Now for 'em.

And in comes Mrs Malaprop (Mrs Austen, perhaps?), ready to declare she would send a girl 'at nine years old, to a boarding school, in order to learn a little ingenuity'.

The truth was, after a year at home, and with Jane Cooper motherless, the girls were to be sent off to school again. This time it was to Mrs La Tournelle's in Reading. This was a well-established place, with the use of a good house built beside all that was left standing of Reading Abbey, and a garden overlooking the ruins of the rest, where the children could run about and play as they liked; but even here the headmistress left something to be desired. Although she was known by the impressive name of Mrs, or Madame, La Tournelle, her real name was Sarah Hackitt. The false name was merely a tribute to the expectations of prospective parents, and she spoke no French. The school did, however, have a French connection, its proprietress being a Madame St Quintin; and a few years later, when the French Revolution began, *émigrés* came to teach there.

Mrs La Tournelle was an odd creature. She was in her forties, had a cork leg of mysterious origin, and a passion for the theatre. What she most enjoyed was telling stories of actors and actresses; it seems unlikely the Austens expected this when they chose the Abbey School. She did not attempt any teaching herself, content with acting as matron, or housekeeper, always dressed with a good deal of white muslin, apron, cuffs, ruffles, scarf and two large flat bows on her cap and her bosom; and she sat in a wood-panelled parlour with chenille pieces representing tombs and weeping willows on the wall behind her, and a row of miniatures set over the high mantelpiece. She served an early breakfast to the children, sitting by the fire, with a large plate of bread and butter supported on an ebony tripod known as a 'cat'; it was all quite cosy, and the young women teachers were allowed to come in with their hair in curl papers. After this, morning prayers were read by Mrs La Tournelle's niece Miss Brown, their effect sometimes diminished by urgent whispers of 'Make haste!' from her aunt, because the washerwoman was waiting in the next room.

This school sounds a harmless, slatternly place. The girls slept six to a room, and were taught some spelling, needlework and French. They would certainly have had dancing lessons, essential basic training for every girl; and perhaps piano was taught too. A pupil who was there a little later took part in performances of plays, so plays may also have been a feature of Jane's and Cassandra's education.[9] They were given plenty of free time, for after morning lessons they were left entirely to their own devices; and they did not fall ill again. On one occasion they were taken out to dinner at a nearby inn in Reading by their brothers, Edward Austen and Edward Cooper, eighteen-year-olds who must have thought it rather a lark to visit a girls' school; easy-going Mrs La Tournelle made no objection. The only other recorded visit is from a Gloucestershire cousin of their mother, the Revd Thomas Leigh of Adlestrop, who gave them half a guinea each on his way through Reading. He may have reported that the girls were being taught very little, causing Mr Austen to wonder whether it was worth paying £35 a year to have his daughters kept idle away from home. Whatever the reason, they were removed from Mrs La Tournelle's towards the end of 1786; and that was the end of Jane's formal education.

5

The French Connection

Whatever 'Madame La Tournelle' had done for Cassandra's and Jane's French, they were going home to something better. Their French-speaking cousin Eliza was due to spend Christmas at Steventon with her mother, Aunt Hancock, and her six-month-old baby, Hastings François Louis Eugène Capot de Feuillide. The arrival of a French countess with her tremendously named son and heir was something to stir the imagination. Eliza had been living abroad since Jane was a baby, so she knew her only through hearing her parents talk of her and the letters that came from France; although they also had her portrait, sent as a gift to Mr Austen, in which she appeared slight, intense, unsmiling, with widely spaced dark eyes and teased out, powdered hair. Mysterious Eliza: everything about her history spoke to the ten-year-old, from her birth in India to her recent dash all the way from remote southern France to London in an advanced state of pregnancy, determined that her child should be born on English soil. She had the magic conferred by marriage and mother-hood, and she was still young and beautiful; she also shared Jane's birthday month of December, and would be twenty-five just as Jane was eleven.

There were only two brothers at home when Cassandra and Jane arrived, little Charles and delightful Henry, full of jokes and at fifteen grown to a man's height. No George, of course; and the three others were embarked on adventures. James was making his first trip abroad, on his way to France to visit cousin Eliza's unknown French husband, Count Jean François Capot de Feuillide, on his estates near Nérac in the south-west; although the latest news was that James's ship was still becalmed at Jersey. Edward the fortunate was in Switzerland, and would be travelling on to Dresden and later Italy; and Francis was at the naval school in Portsmouth. The regime there was tough, not to say brutal; discipline was maintained with a horsewhip, and there were complaints about bullying, idleness and debauchery.[1] Francis himself did not complain; he had chosen to enter for the school and been there since April, was doing very well, and due home for a short holiday at Christmas.

Before Christmas the busy parsonage emptied itself of homebound schoolboys and filled up again immediately with visitors. 'We are now happy in the company of our Sister Hancock Madame de Feuillide & the little Boy; they came to us last Thursday Sennet & will stay with us till the end of next Month,' Mrs Austen wrote to her Kentish niece Phila Walter. She was also expecting her Cooper niece and nephew; and 'Five of my children are now at home, Henry, Frank, Charles & my two Girls, who have now quite left school.'[2] Mrs Austen did not give her niece her title, but the French countess cast her glamour over the whole family party. It was as though a bird of paradise had alighted on the parsonage. She talked gaily of life in London, where she and her mother had taken a house near Portman Square and acquired a carriage and four in which she went out to attend court Drawing Rooms, wearing a dress so heavily hooped it was quite fatiguing to stand in. She told them how she called on duchesses and went to Almack's, which everyone knew as the most select assembly rooms in town; and stayed out until five in the morning.[3]

Cousin Eliza wore French fashions, had a French maid, and talked French as though it were her native tongue; and although Monsieur le Comte was not able to be with her, she could tell stories of his regiment, his estates and *châteaux*, of journeys with him into the Pyrenees and through remote parts of France, of theatrical parties among their aristocratic friends and of their brilliant life in Paris. Like Mrs Lefroy, she had crossed the great divide of a woman's life without giving up her own tastes and pleasures. Nothing about Madame la Comtesse was dull or domestic; and although she was devoted to her baby, she talked of his having 'two Mammas' – herself and her mother – and remained girlishly dependent on Mrs Hancock.[4] She was lively, light-hearted and kind, interested in all her cousins and ready to join wholeheartedly in the family's amusements as if she had no responsibilities or cares in the world.

Every day she sat down at the pianoforte especially borrowed by the Austens, and played to them; Jane's love of playing and transcribing music was surely inspired by Eliza on this visit. And there was dancing: 'on Tuesday we are to have a very snug little dance in our parlour, just our own children, nephew & nieces . . . quite a family party'. All the guests were expected to stay until the end of January.[5] Henry, as the eldest son at home, was quite ready to take up his position as Eliza's host and dancing partner. He had a turn for wit and flattery, and knew how to tease; and she enjoyed the teasing, especially since it was so evidently admiring. Henry was his father's favourite, and adored by Jane too; and Eliza quickly saw his charm, and had no objection to acquiring an English Cherubino among her admirers. Before she left Steventon it was agreed that he should visit her in London in the spring. 'Madame is grown quite lively,' wrote her aunt.

Eliza and her mother are the most likely people to have brought with them a birthday present of books for Jane by the French children's writer Arnaud Berquin, whose *L'Ami des enfants*, a series of moral stories and plays, was newly published and hugely popular. There were already English translations, but Jane received the original French, printed in small volumes to suit small hands.[6] The virtues Berquin sought to encourage were generosity, kindness to servants and also to animals, charity to the poor, hard work and, for girls, 'prudence de conduite': when in doubt about anything they were told they should seek their mother's advice. His playlets were meant to be performed by parents and children together as 'domestic festivals' within the family, designed to drive home the moral lessons and give children 'courage, grace, and ease in their address, deportment and conversation'. Eliza, who had a taste for private theatricals, may have been particularly keen on this aspect of Berquin, and expected the Austens to warm to it. If so, she underestimated them, because one look at Berquin was enough to show that, in his eagerness to inculcate moral values in a family context, he wrote bland, sentimental, wishy-washy stuff. Jane would have thanked Eliza politely for her present, but her own earliest attempts at writing plays and stories provide her comment upon the improving Berquin. Where he sought to teach and elevate, she plunged into farce, burlesque and self-mockery, and created a world of moral anarchy, bursting with the life and energy Berquin's good intentions managed to squeeze out. Berquin's plays are dead on the page; some of Austen's juvenile stories could go straight into a Disney cartoon.

Whatever she thought of Eliza's present, Eliza herself was quite a different matter. Jane attached herself then and there, and the friendship was maintained until the end of her cousin's life. Four years later, when she was fourteen, she dedicated to Eliza one of her most ambitious early stories, *Love and Freindship*, the one everyone remembers for the scene in which the two heroines 'fainted alternately on a sofa'. This particular joke was cribbed from Sheridan, but many of the other jokes are crisp enough to be worthy of him, and the humour does not flag in all its thirty-three pages.[7] Laura, who tells her own story in a series of letters, has a background to match Eliza's: she was 'born in Spain and received my Education at a Convent in France', her father an Irishman and her mother 'the natural Daughter of a Scotch Peer by an italian Opera-girl'. She writes to the daughter of a middle-aged friend, as Eliza might tell her story to Aunt Austen's daughter, and with a touch of Eliza's insouciance. Most of it consists of travels, often with her friend Sophia, and both meet with sentimental and violent adventures, including carriage crashes fatal to their loved ones. In one episode a venerable old gentleman makes a sudden discovery of four separate and hitherto unknown grandchildren, to each of whom he gives a £50 banknote, only to abandon them again immediately afterwards: a hint of Eliza's expectations from her godfather, Warren Hastings, for little Hastings?

Laura and Sophia fly in the face of every lesson Berquin spells out. They not only fail to take parental advice, they manage not even to notice the deaths of parents. They encourage friends and lovers to 'disentangle themselves from the shackles of Parental Authority'. A fifteen-year-old girl is persuaded to elope with a fortune-hunting officer, and two other young men, the illegitimate sons of well-born ladies, rob their mothers, leave them to starve, and take to the stage, first as strolling actors and then as stars at Covent Garden. All the young people steal, run up debts and refuse to settle them. It is black comedy, absurd and riotous, rejecting domestic virtue and decorum with *élan* and authority. For Jane to dedicate it to her cousin, she must have felt confident that Eliza would see and enjoy the jokes with her.

Eliza was well aware of Jane's 'kind partiality to me', and enjoyed her company more than Cassandra's: 'still My Heart gives the preference to Jane'.[8] Clearly, they were friends and talked together; Jane must have questioned her, Eliza must have told her about her experiences at home and abroad. James too would have described Capot de Feuillide's character and estates; and Henry came to know every aspect of Eliza's life and character. The cousins' stories were woven together; but Eliza's history was more like something out of a novel than anything you expect of a cousin.

Eliza's childhood memories went back to the years in London with her young mother and old father, and the great personage of her godfather in the background. When she was six Mr Hancock disappeared back to India. Affectionate, grumbling letters came from him which she rarely answered. As for her young godfather, he also soon went away, also back to India. Eliza was not sent away to school. She lived with her mother in a fashionable London street, and had good teachers. She learnt to ride, to sing, to play the harp and the pianoforte, to dance, to write a good hand and to do simple arithmetic. She performed in little plays with other children; she studied French, read poetry and was taken to the theatre. She wore beautiful, well-made clothes. She went to church and gave to the poor. She was attached to her Austen uncle and aunt, and visited them with her mother, as we have seen; and also to her Kentish cousins the Walters. Cousin Philadelphia Walter – who was also Jane Austen's cousin, and was named for Eliza's mother – carefully kept the affectionate, teasing letters Eliza wrote her; they are our main source of information about her.[9]

The expensive life in London continued, but there was something unsatisfying to Mrs Hancock about it, perhaps because she did not know quite where she belonged in society. People were snobbish about Indian money unless it was amassed in such outrageous amounts that its lowly origins could be overlooked, which was not quite the case with the Hancocks. When Eliza was ten, the distant figure of her godfather came into clearer focus, as her mother told her he had provided her with a small fortune. Mr Hancock warned his wife not to talk of it to anyone: 'Let me caution you not to acquaint even the dearest friend you have with this circumstance. Tell Betsy only that her godfather has made her a great present, but not the particulars: let her write a proper letter on the occasion.'[10] Perhaps she wondered about her parentage then; she was a bright child in an odd situation.

Her presumed father, Mr Hancock, died when she was thirteen, and at the same time her godfather doubled the amount of money he was giving her. She was now possessed of £10,000, placed in trust under the care of Mr Hastings's brother-in-law Mr Woodman, and her Uncle Austen. So Eliza grew up with an awareness that she was different, mysterious in her Indian origins, set apart by them and by the money.

It may have been the uncertainty of their social position that led her mother to take her abroad when she was fifteen; also the encouragement of another friend, Sir John Lambert, an Anglo-French baronet with whom Mrs Hancock had many dealings.[11] She and Eliza visited Germany, were in Brussels in June 1778, and went on to Paris, where they began to move in glittering society, their connection with 'Lord Hastings', as the French liked to call him, a subject for comment. Eliza was made a fuss of, and felt she had entered a world as splendid as the Arabian Nights. Her letters to her Cousin Phila became very conscious accounts of the grand and glamorous company in which she found herself. Marie Antoinette is described in Turkish dress at a ball, covered in diamonds, feathers, flowers, silver gauze and jewels of all kinds. She gave the fashion gossip, hats, hairstyles, earrings, and the Queen's favourite new colour, 'a kind of Pompadour shot with black', wittily known as *la mort de Marlborough*. She evoked Longchamps, 'a monastery situated in the Bois de Boulogne', with its parade of *élégants* and *équipages*, and a new opera house at 'the Thuilleries', big enough to hold 'a troop of five hundred horse', although she had not actually attended an opera yet. She saw the balloonist Monsieur Blanchard ascend, with wings and rudder. She mocked the French for 'murdering' Shakespeare with their translations of *Romeo and Juliet, Lear, Macbeth* and *Coriolanus*; and reported the tremendous success of Beaumarchais' *Le Mariage de Figaro*. She declared her heart 'entirely insensible' to any sentiments 'but those of friendship', and enjoyed a particular friendship with a Paris convent girl, with whom she exchanged pictures; and when she and Mrs Hancock left Paris for Combs-la-Ville, near Fontainebleau, in the heat of the summer of 1780, she said she would write weekly to her convent friend, like any romantic heroine.

Her letters are energetic, and conscientious in describing what she thought would amuse; but it is not always easy to learn her real feelings from them. The first great event of her adult life, her marriage to a French officer at nineteen, seems to have taken her by surprise. It was not a love match. She claimed she did not choose him for herself but acted 'much less from my own judgment than that of those whose councils & opinions I am the most bound to follow', people she referred to as 'advisers of rank & title'.[12] Who were these advisers? Certainly not the two trustees of her fortune, well out of the way in England. The most likely person is her mother's friend Sir John Lambert. Eliza had asked Cousin Phila to address her letters care of 'le chevalier Lambert' in Paris.[13] He had the rank and title Eliza spoke of, and the influence with her mother. He was also more than half French by blood; his father had taken French citizenship, and they had connections with south west France.[14]

Whether Sir John had reasons of his own for wanting to make the match we don't know, but someone presented Eliza to the thirty-year-old Jean François Capot de Feuillide as a wealthy heiress, related to 'Lord Hastings', and presumed to have more expectations from him; and he was presented to her as an aristocrat with large estates in the south. Both descriptions had an element of truth in them, but neither was entirely true. Eliza's fortune, though good, was not great. Capot de Feuillide was the son of a lawyer who had risen from modest beginnings to become mayor of Nérac and been placed in charge of the 'Eaux et Forêts' in his region, the remote and unprosperous Landes where they touch on the Bas-Armagnac. He had no title, and Eliza's claim that she was becoming a countess by marrying him was based either on fantasy or, more likely, on some misrepresentation. Capot de Feuillide presumably hoped to be ennobled, helped by his bride's fortune, and did a bit of Gascon boasting on the subject. Perhaps Sir John expected to benefit from the matchmaking. There is no doubt that he was involved in the affairs of Capot de Feuillide, for years after Eliza's death Henry Austen was doing business with Lambert's heirs.[15]

Eliza was introduced to de Feuillide when he was serving in one of the French Queen's regiments. He was known as the handsomest officer in the army; he attended court balls and, in the festive atmosphere of the French court in the early 1780s, seems to have been a captivating figure. Mrs Hancock liked him well enough to give her assent to the match, and soon to lend him her own money. This was exactly what Eliza's trustees feared. 'They [the de Feuillide family] seem already desirous of draining [her] of every shilling she has,' wrote Mr Woodman to Warren Hastings, after complaining that Eliza's marriage was not very advantageous, although Mrs Hancock 'says it is entirely to her satisfaction, the gentleman having great connections & expectations.'[16]

Mr Austen was also concerned that Eliza might convert to Catholicism – and indeed she does mention a nun who tried to convert her, perhaps at her friend's convent – but he need not have worried on that score. Nérac had a strong Protestant tradition, and some Capots were Protestants, however they conformed outwardly.[17] Capot de Feuillide was also an Anglophile; 'the Comte has the greatest desire to see England', wrote Eliza. Later he expressed a wish that his child should be 'a native of England'.[18] This is so unusual for a Frenchman that you seek a reason. It could be a religious one, though more likely the hope that the birth of the child would interest 'Lord Hastings', who had no legitimate children and might look kindly on Eliza's offspring – a conjecture supported by the naming of the baby.

Eliza made jokes about her husband: 'he is young & reckoned handsome, in the Military & a Frenchman besides – how many reasons to doubt his constancy'; although at the same time 'he literally adores me'.[19] In truth, Jean Capot de Feuillide was a man with an obsession that had nothing to do with Eliza. He wanted money, not for *équipages* or high living in Paris, but to carry out a project in his native Landes. This was the draining of a large area – 5,000 acres – of mostly useless and insanitary swamp near Nérac, known as 'le Marais', in order to turn it into profitable agricultural country. The idea is likely to have come from his father, from his time in charge of the Eaux et Forêts; the French government was eager to encourage land improvement, and granted exemption from taxes to those carrying out such work. De Feuillide applied to the King for permission to take the land and drain it, and for exemption from taxes. It was a good plan, likely to make him rich if it succeeded; but it needed a very large amount of capital.

His father had left him some land and money at his death in 1779, but not enough. In 1780 he went on half-pay, and in 1781 he married Eliza Hancock. At the beginning of 1782 he got his licence from the King to embark on his project, and went south to supervise the work, leaving his bride and her mother in Paris. The work did not proceed entirely smoothly, partly because local land-owners disputed his right to some of the land, still more because the peasantry began to object to their common land, where they had pastured beasts and collected reeds from time immemorial, being enclosed. Everything cost far more than he had expected. The whole of his inheritance went into it, plus some of his wife's income; he borrowed more from Mrs Hancock.

Eliza's story becomes an economic romance at this point, providing a fine example of how money was moved about the world in the late eighteenth century. The English bride was the conduit for money made in India – or plundered from its people – reaching the French Landes; and there it served to drain the ancient swamps, a good purpose but also enraging to the ordinary local people, since the financial benefits were all for Capot de Feuillide. This was by no means the end of the story of the money or the land improvement. In May 1784 Eliza and her mother travelled south to observe the work in progress. To receive them suitably, Capot de Feuillide was obliged to find a house, because he had none of his own good enough for Eliza. He contrived to rent one fit for a countess, and installed his mother, who prepared a warm welcome for her rich daughter-in-law. The Château de Jourdan, which became their residence for the next two years, was (and is) a preposterously romantic place, more like a setting for the Sleeping Beauty than a base for a land reclamation project. It stands between Nérac and the area of the Marais, and is a *château* strictly in the French sense, not a fortified building but a large, stone-built three-storey gentleman's house with a mansard roof, shuttered windows and pepper-pot turrets at the corners of the façade. Set on the top of a steep hill, it looks out over woodland to miles of empty countryside and sky. In the 1780s the area was wild and the nearest town twenty miles away.

Mrs Hancock and Eliza made the 450-mile journey south in June. Eliza spent so much time out and about that she began to acquire the 'tan with which I have contrived to heighten the native brown of my complexion'.[20] There were a few aristocratic families within driving distance to be called on, otherwise only a sparse population of peasants speaking an unintelligible patois and living in conditions so primitive they seemed almost another species: this was provincial life in the Landes. Winter drove her indoors, and struck most of the household down with fever; and as winter ended her mother-in-law died suddenly. Her husband, grieving and feverish himself, remained deeply absorbed in his *travaux*. You can appreciate the scale of what he undertook by walking across the area; the canals can be seen today, there are fields of corn, vines and miles of woodland, in which you stumble on stone marker blocks engraved with the date '1785'.

He was also building a *château* of his own, a square, unromantic house on a road; and, undeterred by mounting debts, many other buildings, stables, farms, cottages and a house for a brother currently in the West Indies. Eliza began to take so much interest in the works that she wrote to Phila, and no doubt to the Austens too, enthusiastically explaining that the land was a gift from the King to 'Mons. de Feuillide & his heirs for ever'.[21] What's more, an heir now seemed in prospect. Then she had a miscarriage, which upset her badly. She was now committed to the place. Encouraged by her account, James Austen began to plan a visit.

Before he could set off, Eliza and her husband took themselves and Mrs Hancock to the Pyrenees for their health. Bagnères-de-Bigorre was a spa much favoured by English families, and Eliza boasted of meeting young Lord Chesterfield, remembered now chiefly for being so lackadaisical that, appointed Ambassador to Spain, he never managed to reach Madrid.[22] Bagnères had the desired effect. Capot de Feuillide recovered from his illness, and she became pregnant again. This did not deter her from planning another trip in the new year, this time to visit friends for a house party to be devoted to amateur theatricals: 'I have promised to spend the carnival . . . in a very agreeable society who have erected an elegant theatre for the purpose of acting plays amongst ourselves'.[23] After this her husband seems to have reminded her of the importance of their child being born in England, especially now that Warren Hastings was in London. Unfortunately the work on the Marais made it out of the question for him to accompany her; so Eliza and Mrs Hancock packed up the coach once more and set off at the end of May, trundling over the hundreds of miles of bad roads, making the ever unpredictable crossing from Calais to Dover, for which you had to be carried from small boat to shipboard; all particularly difficult and exhausting for a woman far advanced in pregnancy. They reached London just in time for the birth of the baby in June.

This was Eliza's story so far; and at Christmas 1786, as she told it, or part of it, everything seemed to be going as well as possible for her. Her cousin James Austen was on his way to Nérac, bringing the two families closer together. She had given her husband a son and heir, and her mother, still the dearest person in her life, was with her to help and advise. Meanwhile the Count proceeded with works that would enrich him and his heirs for generations to come. At this stage no one seems to have noticed that the six-month-old Hastings, who was fat, fair and pretty according to his Aunt Austen, had anything wrong with him. Yet in the new year it became gradually apparent that, once again, the family was to go through the bitter experience of finding a child, apparently healthy at birth, failing to develop as expected.

At two Hastings could neither stand up nor speak, though he made a great noise. He had frequent convulsive fits. His eyes looked odd; anyone could see this was not a normal little boy. Eliza reacted differently from her aunt. Whether she wrote the bad news to her husband we don't know, but she kept her son with her and did everything she could to encourage him to develop. Touchingly, she insisted that he was always acquiring new accomplishments, even if it was only 'doubling his *prodigious* fists' and boxing 'quite in the English style'. Cousin Phila wrote to her brother expressing fears of 'his being like poor George Austen', but Eliza continued to boast of 'the wonderful endowments of my *wonderful brat*', and never considered putting little Hastings into care away from home. For all her cultivated reputation as frivolous and pleasure-loving, Eliza had a streak of stubborn goodness.

On the surface she did not change. She was lucky to have her mother's support, and a great deal of domestic help, which allowed her to continue her social round much as usual. Henry spent his month in town with her in April, and came home happy and pleased with himself. He kept up his studies for Oxford – like James, he would claim a 'Founder's Kin' scholarship – and prepared brilliant futures in his imagination. He and Eliza were concocting a plan that he should accompany her to France the following year, an arrangement 'particularly harped upon on both sides' according to family gossip.[24]

Eliza next descended on Tunbridge Wells and struck even that sophisticated place into admiration. Her dress was 'the richest in the room' and her capacity for extravagant shopping notable. 'On Friday morning the countess & I hunted all the Milliners' shops for hats . . . She presented me with a very pretty fancy hat to wear behind the hair, on one side, and as a mixture of Colours is quite the thing I chose green & pink, with a wreath of pink roses & feathers; but the taste is all the most frightful colours,' reported Cousin Phila, divided between admiration and disapproval. They went to the races, heard some celebrated Italian singers, danced with a party of gentlemen until midnight and attended the local theatre. Eliza bespoke a special performance of *Which is the Man?* and *Bon Ton*, the first an up-to-date play by a woman writer, Hannah Cowley, about a fascinating widow who cannot make up her mind among several admirers, the second a decidedly risqué farce by Garrick about a couple, both on the brink of adultery and only saved from it by a hair's breadth. Bad French behaviour is contrasted with good old English morality, and Miss Tittup, thoroughly infected with French ways, declares, 'We must marry, you know, because other people of fashion marry; but I should think very meanly of myself, if, after I was married, I should feel the least concern at all about my husband.' Eliza liked both these plays so much that she proposed them for performance at Steventon. No doubt Henry and Jane read them over together; Jane knew Hannah Cowley's plays well enough to quote lines from them in her letters.

While Cousin Phila was with her in Tunbridge Wells, Eliza confided to her that, although the Count her husband loved her 'violently', she did not love him at all, but felt only respect and esteem. After this they had another evening in the ballroom, staying until two in the morning and ending with an energetic French country dance, 'La Boulangère', six couples keeping going without a break for half an hour, with constantly changing figures. Dancing like this, continuous and unrestrained, was a liberating pleasure, a permitted high in women's lives. Even staid Phila felt this, as Eliza appreciated when she wrote to her subsequently, hoping that 'your favourite amusement *dancing* has exhilerated [*sic*] your spirit'. It was something women understood among themselves; for Eliza, tormented by anxiety over her baby son, it must have been a heavenly release to dance.

The next family event was the return of James from his continental trip in the autumn. He was half in love with France, somewhat shocked by the easy French manners, and eager to set up more theatricals at Steventon.[25] Encouraged by Eliza's enthusiasm, he and Henry started to plan for a Christmas even better than last year's. Mr Austen agreed that they might fit up the barn with proper painted scenery, everyone set to work, and two plays were settled on, both old favourites on the London stage. Neither was Mrs Cowley's *Which is the Man?*, but the first at least was by a woman, Susannah Centlivre, and called *The Wonder! a Woman Keeps a Secret*. The 'Wonder' is that Donna Violante, the daughter of a Portuguese nobleman, risks losing her lover by sheltering his sister, escaping from an arranged marriage; even when her own reputation and marriage are at risk, Violante keeps the secret. Eliza played the heroine and spoke the epilogue written by James in praise, if not quite of the emancipation of women, at least of their increased power over men since the days when Portuguese noblemen oppressed their ladies:

> But thank our happier Stars, those times are o'er
> And Woman holds a second place no more.
> Now forced to quit their long held usurpation,
> These Men all wise, these 'Lords of the Creation',
> To our superior sway themselves submit,
> Slaves to our charms and vassals to our wit;
> We can with ease their ev'ry sense beguile,
> And melt their Resolutions with a smile . . .

For James, the writing of the prologues and epilogues seems to have been half the fun of the enterprise. His prologue was in praise of Christmas, its cheerful customs 'imported from the mirthful shores of France' – a compliment to Eliza and the Count no doubt – and wickedly interrupted when 'Cromwell and his Gang' found 'rank Popery in a Christmas pye'. There were two performances of *The Wonder!* after Christmas, and then, such was the enthusiasm, they followed it up in January with another old comedy, *The Chances*.[26]

On top of this they did finally put on *Bon Ton*, so that Eliza got her chance to play Miss Tittup.[27]

Theatrical fever reigned. All this was offered as entertainment to local friends, but everyone knows it is the participants who have the most fun, and that the most exciting and emotional exchanges take place backstage. Henry felt he had an already established claim to Eliza, but James was five years older; since she was married, any dispute over her was out of the question; but Eliza was a flirt by her own account – 'highly accomplished, after the French rather than the English mode' wrote James's son carefully, eighty years later – and both brothers were fascinated by her.[28] Their younger sister watched and listened to the arguments over casting, costume arrangements, readings and rehearsals. When Jane dedicated a play of her own to James some time after this, she began with the words 'The following Drama, which I humbly recommend to your Protection & Patronage, tho' inferior to those celebrated Comedies called "The School for Jealousy" & "The travelled Man" . . .' What can she have been thinking of?

Before Christmas, Eliza had predicted 'a most brilliant party & a great deal of amusement, the House full of Company & frequent Balls', and she at least was not disappointed. Plays and dancing provided a distraction from her anxieties over her son, who had yet to be seen by his father; indeed, she herself had not set eyes on him for more than two years. She appeared to be in no great hurry to leave for France.

The return of Mr Austen's pupils in February meant that Eliza had to leave Steventon at least. She went back to Orchard Street, leaving the Austens to get up yet another entertainment, this time Fielding's *Tom Thumb*, a burlesque on the grand tragic style. It may have been about now that Jane produced three scenes of a play of her own, called *The Mystery*. It was dedicated to her father, and strikes a distinctly twentieth-century note:

ACT THE FIRST
Scene the 1st
A Garden
Enter CORYDON.

CORY:) But Hush! I am interrupted.

[*Exit* CORYDON

Enter OLD HUMBUG *& his* SON, *talking.*

OLD HUM:) It is for that reason I wish you to follow my advice. Are you convinced of its propriety?

YOUNG HUM:) I am Sir, and will certainly act in the manner you have pointed out to me.

OLD HUM:) Then let us return to the House.

[*Exeunt*

In London, Eliza now had her godfather to worry about as well as her son. Warren Hastings had returned from India to be put on trial, accused of a whole catalogue of crimes against the people over whom he had ruled, and facing an array of parliamentary prosecutors renowned for their oratorical skills: Burke, Sheridan and Fox. The trial, terrible and humiliating for him, was treated by the public as the fashionable entertainment of the season, and crowds gathered at dawn to queue for the next day's show in Westminster Hall, where Sheridan's eloquence reduced men to tears and women to fainting fits, and Hastings, pale-faced, slight and disdainful, evoked sympathy from many, but was completely outshone by his famous accusers.[29]

At the same time, he remained a very rich man. During the trial he lived with his wife in St James's Square, keeping a second mansion at Windsor. They entertained Eliza and, one assumes, Mrs Hancock, offering them the use of their box at the opera and receiving them in splendid style in spite of the ordeal he was undergoing. Eliza also went to Westminster Hall, where she sat one day from ten until four to hear him attacked. The Austens were naturally fervent supporters of Hastings; and the case against him did eventually collapse, although not until 1795, too late to restore him to anything like his former wealth or position. Here was another crack in the fabric of Eliza's world.

Her plan to take Henry to France fell through because he was obliged to go – reluctantly – up to Oxford, to join James at St John's. In July, Eliza and her mother entertained Mr and Mrs Austen, accompanied by Cassandra and Jane, in Orchard Street, on their homeward journey from a visit to Kent. Then Eliza decided to visit James and Henry in Oxford. Her account of the entertainment provided by her cousins is delicious:

We visited several of the colleges, the museum etc & were very elegantly entertained by our gallant relations at St John's, where I was mightily taken with the garden & longed to be a *Fellow* that I might walk in it every day, besides I was delighted with the black gown & thought the square cap mighty becoming. I do not think you would know Henry with his hair powdered and dressed in a very *tonish* style, besides he is at present taller than his father. We spent a day in seeing Blenheim. I was delighted with the park & think it a most charming place, I liked the outside of the mansion too, but when I entered it I was disappointed at finding the furniture very old-fashioned & very shabby . . . [30]

So much for Blenheim; and there is no doubt which of her cousins pleased her best. As for her husband, he did not see his son Hastings until the boy was two and a half, in the winter of 1788, when at last his wife and mother-in-law appeared in Paris again. What he made of the heir to the Marais was never told. He is unlikely to have shared his wife's determined optimism; fathers look with a colder eye at disappointing children. He was in any case distracted by financial difficulties, and the political unrest all over France increased his anxieties. It must have taken an effort to laugh with Eliza when Hastings tried to chatter in a mixture of English and French, and generously offered his 'half-munched apples or cakes to the whole company'.[31]

'We have not been fortunate here. The Ct de Feuillide has had an intermitting Fever which he brought from the Country,' wrote Mrs Hancock. Eliza was also 'thinner than ever' this winter, and troubled with headaches; only 'our dear little Boy' was really well.[32] Mrs Hancock and Eliza were back in London in June 1789, on financial business; they brought their own maid and stayed in Mr Woodman's house, mother and daughter sharing a bed to save trouble. After this there is a gap in the letters. The date explains why. On 14 July the people of Paris attacked and destroyed the Bastille, symbol of the despotic power of the French crown. The Revolution transformed France and Europe; and on the smaller scale of this narrative it changed everything for Capot de Feuillide and his schemes, for his wife, and for her English family.

6

Bad Behaviour

In the summer of 1788 the Austens took a holiday in Kent. They dined in Sevenoaks with Uncle Francis, at ninety still keeping a patriarchal eye on the fortunes of his clan. Phila Walter was at the dinner, and conveyed the liveliness of the family in a letter to Eliza; they were all, she said, 'in high spirits & disposed to be pleased with each other'.[1] In the same letter, Phila also gave a bad report on Jane. Its importance is that it is the first direct description of Jane, in which she is singled out within the Austen family, and we are at once made aware of the power of her personality. Jane, wrote Phila, was 'whimsical and affected', 'not at all pretty', or feminine, it seems, since she was 'very like her brother Henry'; also 'very prim', and generally not what Phila expected a girl of twelve to be. Cassandra, on the other hand, was pretty, sensible and pleasing. Phila was not always an amiable witness, and she said herself that it was a hasty judgement, but it does suggest that Jane did not conform to the conventional pattern of girlhood. An exceptional child is not always lovable; perhaps she made jokes Phila found disconcerting, or laughed in the wrong places when Phila and Cass were enjoying their 'very sensible and pleasing' conversation; or simply fixed her bright attentive eyes on Phila in a way that made her uneasy.[2]

On their way home from this trip the Austens dined with Eliza and her mother in Orchard Street, and found them starting to pack up the house in preparation for their to return to France. Eliza mentioned the visit in her answer to Phila's letter, did not argue with her unkind remarks about Jane beyond a tactful, 'I believe it was your first acquaintance with Cassandra & Jane'. She did, however, sing her uncle's praises: 'he appeared more amiable than ever to me. What an excellent and pleasing man he is; I love him most sincerely as indeed I do all the family.'³ His hair was now white, and Mrs Austen had lost several front teeth, but they continued as vigorous as ever, steadily meeting the triple demands of parish, school and farm. They were no longer in financial difficulties, although they knew they would have to go on working into their sixties. The girls could not be expected to marry for some years yet; meanwhile they helped their mother with her household and garden routines, and with making clothes for themselves and shirts for their father and brothers. They had their conventional young ladies' accomplishments too. Cassandra had taken up drawing, and a visiting piano teacher, George Chard, assistant organist at Winchester Cathedral, was arranged for Jane. Jane's other skill, the ability to turn out stories and plays, already noticed in the family, was not quite classed as an accomplishment; but it did keep them entertained.

The futures of the boys promised well. At Christmas, Francis left naval school with a high recommendation and, after coming home to say goodbye, sailed for the East Indies aboard the frigate *Perseverance*. He was not fifteen, and did not reach the rank of Midshipman for another year. He took with him his father's beautifully composed letter of advice on how to conduct himself. He was urged to remember the importance of religion and prayer; to write letters to those who might be in a position to do him good; and to keep careful accounts. Mr Austen assured him that he could count on regular letters from the family, and told him,

> Your behaviour as a member of society, to the individuals around you may be also of great importance to your future well-doing, and certainly will to your present happiness and comfort. You may either by a contemptuous, unkind and selfish manner create disgust and dislike; or by affability, good humour and compliance, become the object of esteem and affection; which of these very opposite paths 'tis your interest to pursue I need not say.⁴

This is a fine statement of Mr Austen's ethos, which saw practical as well as moral advantages in good humour and compliance, and encouraged his son to cultivate the virtues of corporate man in the closed world of his ship. His younger daughter would later suggest that there were times when affability, good humour and compliance must be set aside for the greater virtues of honesty and a clear conscience. For the moment her writing was more concerned with violence and vice.

Francis did not see his family again for five years. In the navy so long a separation from family, even for a boy as young, was accepted as part of the job; and in his case the bonds with his family held very firm. Jane wrote and inscribed stories proudly to 'Francis William Austen Esqr Midshipman on board his Majesty's Ship the Persever-ance'. All her early works were given these dedications to friends and members of the family, whether present or absent, and she inscribed *Jack and Alice* to Francis more than a year after his departure. It must have made him laugh, this story of a quiet country village with a cast of bad girls, ambitious, affected, 'Envious, Spitefull & Malicious' as well as 'short, fat and disagreeable'. One girl is found with her leg broken in a steel mantrap; subsequently she is poisoned by a rival, and the rival is hanged. The ambitious girl captures an old Duke, the affected one leaves the country and becomes the favourite of a Mogul prince. Another village family is so 'addicted to the Bottle & the Dice' that a son dies of drink and a daughter starts a fight with the local widow, the pious Lady Williams, who is herself carried home 'dead drunk' after a masquerade. Particular interest is shown in the effect of drink on women; Jane sagely notes that their heads are said to be 'not strong enough to support intoxication'. This sounds so like an older brother's piece of worldly wisdom that it is not surprising Jane crossed it out; perhaps she and Francis had started on the story together before he went to sea. Two children intensely curious about the adult world, laughing at drunkenness, cruelty and death, seem plausible originators of *Jack and Alice*. Jane had already faced death when she was away at school, Francis might now face it even further from home; better to die laughing than be pitiable, was tough Jane's word for tough Francis.[5]

Frank was gone, and Edward settled in Kent after returning from his Grand Tour, but Charles remained at home, and James and Henry were often with them, the Oxford term being short and the attractions of hunting and shooting around Steventon considerable: both had game licences, and their contribution to feeding the house-hold would have been appreciated.[6] And there was more theatrical business at Christmas 1788, when they put on two well-known farces,

The Sultan and *High Life Below Stairs*. In the first an English girl puts down the harem system single-handed by sheer cheek and courage, in the second a group of servants on the fiddle are caught out aping their masters' ways.[7] Eliza was in Paris, but she was sent a report of the performances, in which Jane Cooper – now seventeen and a beauty – played opposite Henry. Eliza passed on the news to Cousin Phila with, 'I hear that Henry is taller than ever.'[8]

This was the last burst of theatrical activity, because James was turning his attention to something more ambitious. It was clear at this point that he was the writer of the family, with serious poetry to his credit as well as his prologues; and now he turned to prose, and to editing.[9] In January 1789 he produced the first issue of his own weekly magazine. There was nothing amateur about it; it was printed, published and sold to the public for threepence. He called it *The Loiterer*, and it was modelled on Dr Johnson's great periodicals, the *Rambler* and the *Idler*, each number consisting of a single anonymous essay or story. Contributions were solicited, and two contributors are known, one being his brother Henry, the other Benjamin Portal, who was at Oxford with them; but the largest number of essays was his. *The Loiterer* was distributed in London, Birmingham, Bath and Reading as well as Oxford; it lasted for fourteen months and was admired enough to receive an accolade which must have delighted James, when one of his own essays was reprinted in the *Annual Register* for 1791.

The essay chosen for reprinting was an urbane sketch narrated by a young Fellow of an Oxford college on the subject of his friends' marriages. One, a land-owner, has married the daughter of a tenant 'with no charm excepting a little health and freshness, and no acquirements beyond those of a country boarding-school', to find his *cara sposa*, as he calls her, transformed into a vulgar and expensive termagant. His brother has married a Scottish noblewoman who prides herself so much on her relations that she has brought half a dozen to live permanently with them. A third claimed to have done better; but when the narrator goes to stay with him, he overhears, through a thin partition wall, the wife scolding the husband for bringing a friend when there is not much for dinner, and the servants are all busy ironing; the guest cannot be given the chintz room because of his dirty boots, and will have to make do with the curtainless green garret. This is enough for the Oxford man, who makes an excuse and returns to his bachelor fireside in college, thinking with 'peculiar complacency' of his escape from the green garret.

Writer's privilege allowed James to laugh at land-owner and nobility in his magazine, although he was in truth a penniless and landless young fellow who was beginning to feel he needed a wife himself. The questions of how to marry money, and how to get a good Church living, were raised in several humorous pieces; there was also a steady tone of mild misogyny which was probably standard at Oxford, even among men with sisters. The claim has been made that Jane Austen was the 'Sophia Sentiment' who wrote to *The Loiterer* for 28 March 1789 – two months after its first issue – complaining that it did not cater for women readers, and recommending that they should run 'some nice, affecting stories' about lovers with 'very pretty names' who are separated, or lost at sea, or involved in duels, or run mad. The trouble with attributing this to her is that the letter is not an encouragement to *The Loiterer* to address women readers so much as a mockery of women's poor taste in literature. 'Sophia Sentiment' is more likely to have been a transvestite, Henry or James.[10]

The best of James's stories describes the attempt by a curate to collect money for a village Sunday school. Sir Charles Courtley suggests he should apply to the Bishop, and offers to drop him off in his carriage at the Palace. A rich maiden lady lectures him on the bad consequences of encouraging learning among the common people. Another feels she has already paid so much to the poor rate that she cannot be expected to give any more. Finally Mr Humphrey Discount, to whom the curate urges that a little money spent on the school would save him from mischievous youths breaking into his garden, gives his answer by pointing out of the window to two steel traps already installed there: 'I warrant the young rascals will keep clear of my premises by the time I have broken two or three of their legs.' Mantraps figure in both James's and his sister's stories, and both were obviously appalled by them; though she makes hers into a joke, while his becomes part of a political argument. If the rest of *The Loiterer* were as good as this, it would be a fine periodical; but few of the other numbers come near it. There are some knockabout essays on the difference between the French and the English ('the

English might grow gay, and the French grave; the English might learn to talk, the French to hold their tongues'). There is a story of a household driven to distraction when the children see some strolling players and are inspired to put on plays themselves, which could be an allusion to the theatricals at Steventon. There is a sage piece on how curates can better themselves by learning to ride and shoot well. There is one on Oxford types, the man with plastered hair and large buckles, the scholar with beard and dirty shirt, the 'Knowing Man' and those who try 'to appear more idle, uninformed and ignorant than we really are'. From Henry there is a breezy account of a ballroom in a country town hall, where a particularly energetic dancer turns round to reveal herself, shockingly, as old enough to be someone's mother; a couple who appear mutually devoted have just agreed to a divorce; and a reluctant male dancer looks at his partner 'as if he wished it had been his hunter'. All taken from life, no doubt, at the Basingstoke Assembly Room balls.

Henry's pieces are surprisingly brash, and he seems more anxious than assured when he writes about women. The most awkward of his attempts at comedy is narrated by a man with a cousin who is trying to trap him into marriage; she lets him see too much ankle and bosom, paints her face and wears false hair, drags him off for a walk and talks about *The Sorrows of Young Werther*. Worst of all, she is older than him. Henry's conversation must have been more entertaining than this routine stuff, or his own older cousin would hardly have found him as charming as she did.

Jane's comic writing was already in another class; and although she did not dedicate anything to Henry for another two years, when she did it was something exceptional. *Lesley Castle* is told in letters, and each character has an individual voice. Charlotte Lutterell, busy cooking for her sister's wedding at the start, can hardly take in the news that the bridegroom has been thrown from his horse and is expected to die. She can think only of all the food she has prepared, and her address to her grief-stricken sister is a monologue of Dickensian brilliance. We laugh because this is a situation we all recognize; none of us wants to be distracted from our own pressing concerns, even by the tragedies of friends.

Dear Eloisa (said I) there's no occasion for your crying so much about such a trifle. (for I was willing to make light of it in order to comfort her) I beg you would not mind it – You see it does not vex me in the least; though perhaps *I* may suffer most from it after all; for I shall not only be obliged to eat up all the Victuals I have dressed already, but must if Henry should recover (which is however not very likely) dress as much for you again; or should he die (as I suppose he will) I shall still have to prepare a Dinner for you whenever you marry any one else. So you see that tho' perhaps for the present it may afflict you to think of Henry's sufferings, Yet I dare say he'll die soon, and then his pain will be over and you will be easy, whereas my Trouble will last much longer for work as hard as I may, I am certain that the pantry cannot be cleared in less than a fortnight.

Charlotte is the precursor of a line of obsessed and eloquent women to come from Jane's pen, among them Mrs Bennet, Mrs Norris and Miss Bates; and she is quite as good as they are. When the thought of a visit to London comes to her, she writes, 'I always longed particularly to go to Vaux-hall, to see whether the cold Beef there is cut so thin as it is reported, for I have a sly suspicion that few people understand the art of cutting a slice of cold Beef so well as I do.' Any writer would be pleased with lines like these; for a sixteen-year-old they are prodigious.

These early pieces, composed over several years, were transcribed, in somewhat random order, into three notebooks. *Lesley Castle*, which seems to have been written between January and April 1792, was copied, unfinished, into the second. At the front of this notebook Jane wrote 'Ex dono mei Patris' ('A gift from my Father'). His appreciation and encouragement of his daughter's skill was admirable. He must have bought her paper for her writing, an expensive item. He also supplied Cassandra with drawing paper; and to Cassandra, Jane inscribed her *History of England* ('by a partial, prejudiced, & ignorant Historian'), and gave the task of illustrating it. It was the only one of her works to have contemporary illustrations.

The *History* is full of family matters. There is a tease for her father, when the author claims to be partial to the 'roman catholic religion'. There is an allusion to the absent Francis in the prediction that Sir

Francis Drake will be surpassed by 'one who tho' now but young, already promises to answer all the ardent and sanguine expectations of his Relations and Freinds'. There is a knowing 'sharade' on the word 'car-pet' which refers to James I's favourites, Car and Villiers: 'My first is what my second was to King James the 1st, and you tread on my whole.' The Austens went in for verbal games, and the *History* sounds like Christmas entertainment to be read aloud around the table or the fireside. Jane could rely on her parents to pick up her reference to a novel by Charlotte Smith, a former neighbour, when she likened Queen Elizabeth's favourite, Essex, to one of Smith's characters, the romantic Delamere, who throws away his life in a duel. Her interest in history was, as she acknowledged, more to do with romance than with fact and date; and perhaps more still to do with making her family laugh.

She dated her *History* at the end, 'Saturday Nov: 26th 1791', just before her sixteenth birthday. By then *The Loiterer* had ceased publication; and although James continued to write poetry for his private satisfaction, and Mrs Austen to produce her occasional verse, Jane's claim to be considered an aspiring writer now was accepted by the most important member of the family. At the front of her next notebook, Mr Austen wrote his own graceful tribute: 'Effusions of Fancy by a very Young Lady Consisting of Tales in a Style entirely new'.[11] He appreciated her work enough to put up with some strong stuff. *Lesley Castle* has, for instance, an adulterous elopement by a young mother who abandons her baby; later in the story her husband converts to Catholicism, enabling him to get an annulment, and both parties remarry cheerfully. These are quite daring jokes for the daughter of a clergyman of the Church of England.

It is clear too that he gave her uncensored access to his books; for if she was allowed to read Richardson's *Sir Charles Grandison* as a child, which gives detailed accounts of maternal drunkenness and paternal adultery, and lays out the correct attitude to adopt towards a father's mistress and illegitimate half-brothers, Mr Austen cannot have kept much from her. In this as in his unruffled response to her bold stories, he was an exceptional father to his exceptional daughter. According to Henry, her reading started very early, and it was difficult to say 'at what age she was not intimately acquainted with the merits and defects of the best essays and novels in the English language'. This pious memorializing does not mean she was reading Dr Johnson and Samuel Richardson at the age of five, but it does set Henry's remembrance of a very young and precocious child curled over her books squarely before us. She was, he added, blessed with an enviably 'tenacious memory'.[12] So their father's bookshelves were of primary importance in fostering her talent, given that the first impulse to write stories comes from being entertained and excited by other people's.

But it is hard to make any very systematic account of her early reading. For one thing, the 500 volumes in Mr Austen's library were sold off; and for another, Henry in 1817 was more concerned to stress her piety and respectability than the eclecticism of her taste. He stated in his biographical note that Johnson and Cowper were her favourite 'moral writers', and that she admired Richardson more than Fielding. 'She recoiled from every thing gross,' he explained; recoiled, possibly, but read and enjoyed first. She was never prim. She did enjoy Fielding, and not only his farce *Tom Thumb*, brought to her by her brothers, but *Tom Jones* too.[13] She was also familiar with Sterne's *Tristram Shandy* and his *Sentimental Journey*: again, not mentioned by Henry. He did not name any of the women novelists and playwrights who were important to her, among them Charlotte Lennox, Fanny Burney, Charlotte Smith, Maria Edgeworth, Hannah Cowley. Plays were after all read in the family, discussed, performed and enjoyed; but Henry may have felt it inappropriate to say so in 1817. Nor did he mention Shakespeare, although Shakespeare was 'part of an Englishman's constitution', according to Henry Crawford (in *Mansfield Park*), and Edmund Bertram agrees with him: 'one is familiar with Shakespeare in a degree . . . from one's earliest years . . . We all talk Shakespeare, use his similes, and describe with his descriptions.' We can take it that Edmund is speaking for the Austen family as well as for the Bertrams here; Catherine Morland is reared on Shakespeare, and the Dashwoods read *Hamlet* with Willoughby. Yet it is true that there are only three scant references to his work in her letters.

With Johnson it is easier to point to direct influence. We know she read *Rasselas*, and his essays in the *Rambler* and the *Idler*. Later in life she called him 'my dear Dr Johnson' in a letter, and read Boswell;

and his turn of phrase and thought both appear in her writing. There is a Johnsonian ring, grave and witty at once, about a sentence like 'She had nothing against her, but her husband, and her conscience.' This is from an early story, *Lady Susan*; the same note is heard in the famous opening sentence of *Pride and Prejudice* ('It is a truth universally acknowledged . . .'), which could easily be the opening of a *Rambler* essay.

Yet looking over her shoulder at what we know her to have read in those early years tells us chiefly how original she was; how she appreciated, took what was useful to her, and kept her own voice and imaginative ground clear. There is no early Austen novel written in the manner of Richardson, or Fanny Burney, or Charlotte Smith, with a heroine of undeviating saintliness and a hero who carries indecisiveness through five volumes. In her teens she enthused about Charlotte Smith, the Daphne du Maurier of the 1780s and 1790s, and still entertaining today, with her thrilling heroes and gorgeously picturesque scenery – Grasmere, the Welsh mountains, Switzerland, America, the south of France – and her rambling narratives: *Emmeline*, *Ethelinde* and *The Old Manor House* are each four or five volumes long. Austen alludes to Smith several times in her juvenile writings; one of Smith's characters, the passionate and uncontrollable Frederic Delamere mentioned in her *History*, caught her fancy particularly. Delamere is driven by feeling, impulsive in all his actions and liable to fits of near-madness when he is thwarted. He is darkly handsome, proud, well-born, tormented, abominably behaved but never dishonourable: having abducted Emmeline with the intention of carrying her off to Scotland, he repents before they reach Barnet. Emmeline did not love him, but he fascinated her, as he did the young Jane Austen.[14] Smith's heroines, tearful innocents prone to fainting and falling off horses, slighted and ill-used by their social superiors, are like nothing in Austen (unless you count Fanny Price, their very distant cousin). But Smith's romance is vigorous, well written and genuinely imaginative, and you can see why Austen took pleasure in it, and defended it with 'if a book is well written, I always find it too short'.[15]

Too short could never apply to Samuel Richardson. 'An amazing horrid book,' Austen made Isabella Thorpe call his *Sir Charles Grandison* in *Northanger Abbey*, giving herself away in those four words, since it was Austen's favourite. 'Her knowledge of Richardson's works was such as no one is likely again to acquire,' wrote her nephew in his *Memoir*, going on to say that every incident in it was familiar to her, and every character like a friend.[16] A book so important to her, and now so little known, is worth some attention. It is built around a pair of paragons, Sir Charles and the beautiful Harriet Byron. She falls in love with him after he saves her from abduction and likely rape in Volume I, and remains in love throughout seven volumes and 800,000 words; whereas he is divided between her and an Italian lady to whom he has given his word and half his heart, and from whom he extricates himself honourably, but at a snail's pace. This allows the reader to be entertained by their families and friends; and they are so diverting that you see how the young Jane Austen chose to inhabit the book, like a great house with many rooms, corridors and stairs to explore and re-explore.

Richardson is at his best in describing Grandison's sisters, who become Harriet's friends, in particular the younger, Charlotte, sharp-witted and fierce, the most interestingly developed character in the book. Charlotte is unwilling to bear fools gladly and averse to getting married; she talks of the 'matrimonial noose', and when she does reluctantly agree to enter the state, she behaves badly at her own wedding, muttering during the service and forbidding her bridegroom to sit beside her in the carriage afterwards. She quarrels with him for intruding on her privacy, and her teasing drives him to such rage that he breaks up her harpsichord with his fists; but he loves her passionately, and when his rage passes tells her never to give up her high spirits, or her teasing.

The chief cause of Charlotte's wildness is the behaviour of her father, Sir Thomas Grandison, and a great theme of the book is the bad behaviour of parents and the ways in which the younger generation are affected by it, or try to put it right. After the death of Lady Grandison, when the girls were in their mid-teens, their father invited a Mrs Oldham, the widow of a friend, to become their governess; when she became his mistress, they refused to have any more dealings with her, and he moved her to a house in another county (Grandison's main estates are in Hampshire, which must have amused the Austens). During this period Charlotte, neglected by her father, engaged herself to a fortune-hunting army officer. Mrs

Isaac Taylor del. et sculp.

Published as the Act directs 1.st June 1778. by T. Cadell in the Strand.

Sir Thomas Grandison and his Daughters

'Sir Thomas Grandison and his daughters Caroline and Charlotte'
from Samuel Richardson's *Sir Charles Grandison* (first published 1754)

Oldham meanwhile bore two sons, but Sir Thomas neither married her nor made any provision for her or them; and when he died, it was left to his legitimate son and heir to treat the lady with kindness, allow her some dignity, give her a pension and see that his half-brothers were given a start in life. There are similar stories involving his uncle, and the mother of an heiress to whom he stands as guardian, each of whom he helps to redeem by acts of good sense and generosity.

Grandison is full of discussions about the place and condition of women, and of love, marriage and eroticism. There is even a mannish Miss Barnevelt, who makes a distinct pass at Harriet Byron, telling her that she 'wished twenty times, as I sat by her, that I had been man for her sake . . . if I had, I should have caught her up, popt her under one of my arms, and run away with her'. Sir Charles objects to love at first sight because it is too sexual: 'a tindery fit', 'an indelicate paroxysm', dangerous to women especially. The question of lifelong constancy to a lost love is debated, and 'constant nymphs' are ruled against: 'Must a woman sit down, cry herself blind, and become useless to the principal end of her being, as to this life, and to all family connections, when, probably, she has not lived one third of her time?' Another discussion concerns itself with 'girls of slender fortunes', comparing their 'peculiarly unprovided & helpless' state as single women with that of men, who 'can rise in a profession, and if he acquires wealth in a trade, can get above it and be respected'. These were all subjects likely to interest Austen; and some were later raised in her own work. In *Grandison*, a respected old lady suggests that 'women of large and independent fortunes, who have the hearts and understanding to use them as they ought' may do better not to marry, but poor women do not have the same freedom of choice. On the whole, the older women take the view that young girls should not be too romantic in expecting love as well as a decent husband. Harriet Byron, who does achieve both, asks, 'Is not marriage the highest state of friendship that mortals can know?', a view all Austen's principal heroines would support.

Important as all these points were to her, the characterization of Charlotte was, I believe, most useful to Austen's purposes. Here was an outspoken young woman, very often wrong in her judgements and behaviour, yet always captivating, brilliantly lively and wholly human, whether speaking for herself or presented through the eyes of others. With her sisterly love and loyalty, her teasing, her articulacy, her repartee, her 'archness rising to the eye that makes one both love and fear her', Charlotte Grandison was surely an early inspiration for Elizabeth Bennet.[17]

There is another witty young woman in Fanny Burney's *Cecilia*, Lady Honoria Pemberton, who teases Cecilia and her humourless lover so mercilessly that you wish she were allotted more than the few pages she gets in that extraordinary book. Nearly a thousand pages long, it too must have filled many winter evenings by the fire at Steventon and taken its toll on Jane's eyes, which at times became tired and troublesome. She admired Burney's comic monsters and her dialogue, but most of what she learnt from her was negative: to be short, to sharpen, to vary, to exclude. Also, to prefer the imperfect and human heroine to the nearly flawless one. What Burney had demonstrated with her first book – concise as none of the later ones were – was that there was a public for social comedy finely observed through female eyes. After *Evelina*, a man such as Mr Austen could feel it not unreasonable or disreputable for his daughter to try her hand at fiction.

7

Weddings and Funerals

At the end of the 1780s, when Jane was in her mid-teens, the Austen clan was changing its shape, scattering, spreading here, diminishing there, some of its members prospering serenely, others beginning to be overshadowed by political events. As yet Mrs Hancock and Eliza did not appear much troubled by the slow spreading effects of the French Revolution. They came to England in 1790 on one of their regular trips; at this stage nobody was prevented from travelling, and few thought themselves in any personal danger in Paris. They spent some time in the summer of 1790 at Steventon, and this is when Jane dedicated *Love and Freindship* to Eliza. It was the longest story she had written so far, and the strongest proof of her attachment to her cousin. But although she and Eliza were the best of friends, relations between Henry and Eliza were ruffled; a coolness arose between them, which Eliza at any rate blamed on him.[1] Since they had been flirting for several years, and since Henry was now no Cherubino but a fully grown nineteen-year-old, it looks like a power struggle. How far did such flirtations go? A grass widow with a husband for whom she feels no love, but with an appetite for life and an active young admirer, may put on a performance of switching between hot and cold and then express surprise at the effects of such behaviour; a young man may rage, protest or sulk. Evidently there was a quarrel. Henry went back to Oxford.

Eliza also returned to Paris with Mrs Hancock and Hastings, but was soon in England again; her husband went south to his swamp-draining projects. He was a fervent royalist, as was to be expected of one who held his land from the King; so she stated in 1791, adding that he had already 'joined, in his heart, the royalist clan in Piedmont and Turin', where some of the French princes were gathered in exile.[2] The revolution rolled on, becoming fiercer, more doctrinaire and bloodier; and the English, together with other unreformed European powers, began to feel threatened. Life in Paris became difficult for someone who loved to call herself Madame la Comtesse, and early in 1791 she brought her son and mother to England again, this time with no immediate plans to return to France. After a stay at Margate, where the sea bathing was recommended for Hastings, they settled in their old house in Orchard Street, near Portman Square; and Mrs Hancock succeeded in teaching her grandson his letters.

At this point the Austens were full of the engagement of Edward: he was to marry a baronet's daughter, Elizabeth Bridges of Goodnestone Park in Kent.[3] The bride was eighteen, younger than Cassandra, and only two years older than Jane; the marriage was approved by Bridges, Knights and – rather distantly – Austens, and would take place at the end of the year. All the Bridges girls were elegant and pretty. They had been educated at the smartest of girls' boarding schools in Queen Square in London; and two of Elizabeth's sisters became engaged at the same time. The world was set on marriage, it seemed. Even Jane dreamt of future husbands. She took a page of her father's parish register and tried out names for these fictitious beings: 'Henry Frederick Howard Fitzwilliam, of London', 'Edmund Arthur William Mortimer, of Liverpool'. There is nothing surprising about the fantasy until the bottom of the page, when a populist note is struck with 'Jack Smith', to be married to 'Jane Smith late Austen'. For a moment the Tory parson's daughter seems to be letting her imagination travel in an unusual direction: one would like to know more about that particular dream.

However much she lived in her imagination, in books and stories, she had to make the transition from child who observes adult life to woman who experiences it. Mrs Austen was in her fifties before Jane reached fourteen, a wide gap between mother and daughter; once again Cassandra is likely to have taken over most of the maternal role in giving help and advice to Jane as she grew up. Menstruation started late for most girls in the eighteenth century, at fifteen or sixteen; they had to learn to deal with an awkward and unpleasant process just when they were being told to prepare for the crucial years in which they were expected to attract admirers and most wanted to appear elegant and imperturbable.[4] Imagine coping without running water or indoor plumbing, and being obliged to conceal, wash and dry your napkins, while a lot of teenage boys thundered about the house. This is another piece of lost, unrecorded history; but even in the most brisk and practical families, girls must have felt themselves vulnerable, and at a disadvantage, in the cumbersome arrangements they were obliged to make.

Friendships with other girls became more important. Jane Cooper was in and out of Steventon, and then two new families with daughters arrived in the district. Martha and Mary Lloyd came in the spring of 1789; Mrs Lloyd was the widow of a clergyman, with aristocratic connections of the kind Mrs Austen herself boasted, and she made them welcome as a congenial addition to local society. They were cousins of the Fowles, who had been pupils at Steventon, and a third Lloyd daughter had married the eldest Fowle. James Austen went to his friend's wedding and got to know them all, and soon after this Mrs Lloyd rented Deane parsonage from Mr Austen. Mary was Mrs Austen's favourite; but, although she was close to her in age, Jane never liked her. She preferred Martha, nearly ten years older but with a sense of humour. Stories and poems were dedicated to Martha, and she and Jane were happy to share a bed when necessary; they would lie talking and laughing until two in the morning.[5] From now on the Lloyds were a constant part of the Austens' lives.

In the same year a family with three unmarried daughters, Catherine, Elizabeth and Alethea Bigg, inherited Manydown, a large manor house four miles beyond Deane. Mr Bigg, or Bigg-Wither, was a well-to-do land-owner and they were heiresses in a small way, but this did not prevent a real friendship developing with the penniless Austen sisters; the Biggs were clever too, and they found they had similar tastes. There was now a community of young women with whom Jane could talk about shared experiences, exchange and discuss books, compare clothes, practise dance steps and music, take walks, drive into Basingstoke for shopping, and gossip about their own families and their neighbours.

James had left Oxford to take up a curacy and was installed in the vicarage at Overton, not far from home. He cultivated good company and even hunted alongside visiting royalty; and he met a young woman who fulfilled all the dreams of an aspiring curate.[6] Anne Mathew was the daughter of a general and the granddaughter of a duke; she had good financial prospects; she was slim and dark, with beautiful eyes; and, at thirty-two, she was on the shelf. James saw his chance, took it, and was accepted by Anne, and welcomed by her family, despite being a mere curate. Her father promised her an allowance of £100 a year; it meant that, together with James's income, they could furnish a house and keep a carriage and a pack of hounds.

While these cheerful matters were arranging themselves, Eliza and her mother were suffering. Mrs Hancock was ill, with a hard and painful swelling in one breast, and Eliza was desperate to find a remedy for what they both knew must be a serious condition. There are always charlatans ready to prey on the desperate by offering miracle cures; they heard of, and called in, a 'Doctress' who offered 'most flattering hopes of a perfect cure'. And whatever her method, which she warned would take time, it may not have been any worse than most other available treatments.[7] Mrs Hancock said the pain was reduced, and Eliza allowed herself to hope for 'the unspeakable happiness of seeing my beloved parent restored to Health'. Each tried to reassure the other. As the summer went by, Eliza gave up all other activities and remained shut up in Orchard Street, trying to divert her mother's thoughts from the illness, and suffering her own 'racking anxiety'. She was too busy and unhappy even to inform the Austens until June; after this Edward called on her. He was bound for the Lake District, and Eliza was able to summon enough of her old spirit to tease him about his indifference to making such a pleasure trip without his beloved. 'I asked him how he would be able to exist; which enquiry he answered with that calm smile of resignation which his sex generally wear under circumstances of this nature.'[8] There was no word of Henry.

Mrs Hancock could not travel to Steventon. In August she was experiencing acute pain. Eliza wrote, 'the progress of her amendment is so very slow, that in spite of all my endeavours my spirits sometimes sink, and I shudder at the possibility that all our efforts may be ineffectual . . . how dreadful it is to experience even the shadow of uncertainty where those we love are concerned!'[9] The Doctress

Jane Austen's father as a young man, dark eyed, precise of feature, neatly wigged: the hard-working orphan who achieved an Oxford Fellowship. He left Oxford on marrying Cassandra Leigh, niece of the Master of Balliol, and became a country clergyman.

The only known image of Jane's mother, showing the aristocratic nose of which she was proud. Mrs Austen ran her large family and household on tough, practical lines; she was also a reader, and in her few leisure moments wrote accomplished light verse.

A view of Steventon village, a straggle of labourers' cottages set along a lane in a remote part of north Hampshire. There was no shop, no public house, no school, no doctor, and church and rectory stood at some distance. In one of these cottages Mrs Austen put out her babies to be cared for by a village woman until they reached the age of reason.

James, the eldest Austen son and his mother's favourite, inherited her aptitude for verse and saw himself as the writer of the family. A good scholar, he went up to Oxford at fourteen, when Jane was only four; he wrote serious poetry and dramatic prologues for the plays he put on with his brothers at home, and founded a magazine, *The Loiterer*, for which he wrote most of the contributions. His other passion was hunting.

There is no picture of the second Austen son, George, handicapped from birth. The third, Edward, was the lucky one: a pleasant, easy-going boy, he took the fancy of some distant cousins of his father, and when they proved childless they asked to adopt him. Mr Austen resisted the idea at first, but Mrs Austen urged letting him go; and he became heir to a fortune and large estates.

This staid portrait, done after Jane's death, conveys none of the panache of her fourth brother, Henry. 'Oh, what a Henry!' she once wrote; he was the charmer of the family, witty, dashing and not always reliable, but his father's favourite and hers. He took his Oxford degree while serving as an officer in the militia, made a romantic and advantageous marriage, and on leaving the army set up as a banker, living in high style in London. Later the bank crashed and he fell back on the Church for his final profession. He took the keenest interest in Jane's writing, and dealt with publishers on her behalf both during her lifetime and afterwards.

Cassandra, Jane's elder sister and closest companion, was a beauty; but after the death of her fiancé she retreated into voluntary spinsterhood and sadly premature middle age. She described Jane memorably as 'the sun of my life, the gilder of every pleasure, the soother of every sorrow'.

Francis, known as Frank, or Fly, closest in age to Jane, an energetic and enterprising boy who saved up to buy himself a hunting pony at seven, left home at twelve for the Royal Naval Academy in Portsmouth, and went to sea for a five-year stint in the Far East at fourteen. He ended his career as Admiral of the Fleet.

The only member of the Austen family to have no formal portrait, apart from her handicapped brother, George, was Jane. This sketch by Cassandra was regarded as inadequate and unflattering by those who remembered her, but it is the single image of her face drawn from life.

Charles, the sweet-natured baby of the Austen family, followed Frank into the navy. He was devoted to Jane, and read all her books as they came out, *Emma* three times in quick succession. 'I am delighted with her, more so I think than even with my favourite Pride and Prejudice.'

Steventon rectory was pulled down in 1824, and this is one of several drawings done from somewhat hazy memory by James Austen's elder daughter, Anna. It shows the front, with the windows of the garret rooms where Mr Austen's pupils slept. His study was at the back, looking on to the flower garden and strawberry bed; there was also a vegetable garden, yard and out-houses, where Mrs Austen kept poultry and a cow.

A silhouette showing young Edward Austen being formally presented by his father for adoption into the wealthy Kentish family of Thomas Knight of Godmersham. After this Edward spent his holidays in Kent but continued to be educated at Steventon by his father before being sent on the Grand Tour. Although his circumstances were transformed, he always maintained close contacts with his natural family.

(*left*) Philadelphia Austen, sister of Jane's father, orphaned as a child and poor like him, travelled alone to India at the age of twenty-one to find a husband, and made a loveless match to Tysoe Saul Hancock, who was twice her age.

(*below*) Warren Hastings, painted by Reynolds as a successful young officer of the East India Company, well on his way to becoming Governor-General and fabulously rich. He was Hancock's patron, and a young widower when Philadelphia met him.

(*left*) The wistful face of little Betsy – later Eliza – Hancock, Phila's only child, god-daughter and probably also natural daughter of Warren Hastings, who settled £10,000 on her. Clever and affectionate, she became warmly attached to her cousin Jane; she also enjoyed flirting with her male cousins.

(*right*) The Château de Jourdan, near Nérac, to which Eliza Hancock's French husband, Jean François Capot de Feuillide, took her with her mother in 1784, and where he spent a good part of their money on land-drainage schemes, by which he hoped to make his own fortune.

Among the Austens' neighbours were (*above left*) Norfolk-born William Chute, MP, who inherited The Vyne, one of the great houses of Hampshire. His younger brother Thomas (*below left*) was a good friend of James and Henry Austen and dancing partner of Cassandra and Jane. Possession of The Vyne made William Chute a most eligible bachelor, but he was more interested in hunting than in any other form of social life, and he chose his bride Eliza (*above right*, a late portrait sketch) in London, the daughter of a fellow fox-hunting MP. Eliza Chute had no children; she read, gardened, did charitable work among the rural poor and kept a diary, in which the Austens often appear; and her niece married James Austen's son. John Portal (*below right*), another hunting neighbour, was from a French immigrant family that became rich printing notes for the Bank of England at their papermills on the River Test. They built a mansion at Laverstoke in the 1790s, visited by Jane Austen in 1815; and Mrs Portal was one of her last visitors. Two of Edward Austen's sons married Portal daughters.

The Hon. Newton and Coulson Wallop (*above*), the handsome younger sons of the second Earl of Portsmouth, were well known to Jane; she quoted with amusement Coulson's 'delicate language' for a pregnancy – '*in for it!*' Their elder brother Lord Lymington, who became the third Earl, was one of the Revd George Austen's earliest pupils. His pathetic and sometimes terrifying eccentricity as an adult, and the efforts of the family and others to control him, led to dark and horrible scandals in the neighbourhood.

Left is a portrait of the Revd William Heathcote (with his father and the Master of the Hounds), who figures in Jane's letters and married her close friend Elizabeth Bigg of Manydown. After Heathcote's early death Elizabeth moved to Winchester, and it was she who found lodgings there for Jane in the last weeks of her life.

The tiny, isolated and peaceful thirteenth-century church of St Nicholas at Steventon, where the Revd George Austen officiated for over thirty years, and where Jane was christened. In the churchyard is a 900-year-old yew tree with a hollow trunk in which the key of the church door was kept. One of the three bells dates from 1470, and they have always been rung in the entrance porch, reached through a simple arch with a man's head carved on one side, a woman's on the other. Below left is a page of the parish register in which Jane Austen was allowed to scribble by her father, and where she tried out the names of imaginary husbands: Henry Frederick Howard Fitzwilliam of London, Edmund Arthur William Mortimer of Liverpool and – in another mood – Jack Smith.

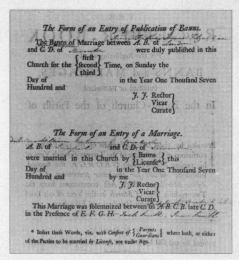

continued to promise a cure, but Eliza now called in a surgeon, Mr Roops; and by October Mrs Hancock was confined to bed and seeing no one but her daughter and Roops. At the end of the month she suffered a 'very dreadful attack' and Eliza summoned a physician. He prescribed laudanum. Eliza was in a state of distress 'bordering on distraction', unable to make out Roops's real opinion of the case.

The sequence of hope, despair and revived hope continued. 'Never will the year 1791 be effaced from my memory for from the first Month of its commencement . . . my feelings have constantly been exposed to some fresh trial,' wrote Eliza.[10] At Christmas Mrs Hancock had a violent cough, no appetite, disordered bowels, as much pain as ever, and the tumour remained as before; gallantly, she told Eliza she thought 'the complaint itself' was getting better. 'To my unutterable Sorrow – I cannot flatter myself with a similar Belief.' A flash of the old Eliza appears when she tells Phila she has been invited to two elegant balls; but she has no intention of attending either. Phila wrote sanctimoniously to her brother about poor Eliza's 'gay and dissipated life' now bringing its just deserts, and predicted that she would be left 'friendless and alone'.[11]

The care of five-year-old Hastings became more difficult now that his 'second Mamma' was unable to take part in it, but she refused to give up her hopes for him. Eliza promoted him from petticoats to trousers and jacket, in the hope that they would help him to walk better, although he had difficulty in keeping upright at all.

There was nothing but bad news from France. In September the Count was attacked by a mob of angry peasants at the Marais; he escaped with his life, but his new house was pillaged, and all work on the drainage scheme stopped. He made his way to Paris; he had no money and owed his mother-in-law £6,500.[12]

Mrs Hancock died at the end of February 1792, in Hampstead, where Eliza took her in the hope of better air for the last weeks of her life. She had adventured and endured much in her sixty years; the inscription on the tombstone spoke of 'Philadelphia wife of Tysoe Saul Hancock' as one 'whose moral excellence united the practice of every Christian virtue', and of the pious resignation with which she bore 'the severest trials of a tedious and painful malady'.[13] Jean Capot de Feuillide managed to make his way to England to comfort his wife and son, and they took a rather grim trip to Bath; he soon heard that his whole property would be forfeit and he himself declared an *émigré* if he remained abroad, and hurried back to Paris.

Edward's marriage had taken place in December 1791; it was a double wedding, shared with one of Elizabeth's sisters. Jane's dedication to him of a distinctly brutal story about mercenary matchmaking, *The Three Sisters*, made a somewhat two-edged wedding gift; even the most good-humoured bride might have found it tactless. Weddings did not then call for large gatherings of relatives, so Jane is unlikely to have attended Edward's, but she may have been at James's in March 1792, since it took place close to home, at Laverstoke. James and Anne soon moved closer to Steventon, taking over Deane parsonage from the Lloyds. On their departure Jane wrote a poem for Martha and dedicated to Mary her story *Evelyn*, full of hasty marriages and marriage settlements, house moves, forgetfulness and funerals. The Lloyds moved eighteen miles away, to Ibthorp; it was too far for daily calls, but Cassandra and Jane were soon invited to stay.

In June, Eliza was frightened by a mob fighting with mounted Guards in Mount Street in central London. She was not alone in asking if the spirit of revolution might be about to cross the Channel. The principal county personages of Hampshire gathered to express their approbation of Pitt's government, their lack of sympathy with the national Convention in France, and their disapproval of revolutionary societies in England.[14] Since Hampshire was solid Tory, the mere fact of its land-owners finding it necessary to mention the French and the English revolutionary societies indicates their disquiet.

Later in the summer Eliza and her little boy appeared at Steventon, where Hastings became 'the plaything of the whole family'. She relaxed and allowed herself to be happy looking at Mr Austen, whose 'likeness to my beloved mother is stronger than ever', and sometimes reduced her to tears: 'I always tenderly loved my uncle, but I think he is now dearer to me than ever, as being the nearest and best beloved relative of the never to be sufficiently regretted parent I have lost.' Jane had grown taller than Eliza, was as fond of her as ever, and remained her favourite; she commended both sisters for their greatly improved manners and appearance, and their good sense.

And Henry – Henry was now over six foot, also much improved, in fact 'endowed with uncommon abilities'. The coolness was over, or partly over, and they were on 'very proper relation-like terms; you know that his family design him for the Church'.[15] And Eliza queened it at the Club balls in Basingstoke.

Jane was sixteen, an uncomfortable age in itself, and made no easier when you are the youngest member of the family at home, and a witness to elder brothers and sisters engaging in romances beyond your reach. Another wedding was planned for December. Jane Cooper was also living at Steventon, following the death of her father; she was engaged to a naval officer, Captain Thomas Williams. They had met in July on the Isle of Wight, and before the month was out he had proposed and been accepted, and they were to be married before Christmas. A naval bridegroom with his fortune to make, confident enough to sweep beautiful Jane off her feet and silence any prudent warnings, made this the most romantic of the family weddings. It was solemnized in Steventon church, with Jane as one of the witnesses and Cassandra another. The service was taken by Tom Fowle; he and Cassandra were also on the brink of becoming engaged.

Only there was no whirlwind courtship for them, since Tom Fowle had hardly any resources beyond his almost worthless parish in Wiltshire, and no immediate prospect of anything better; Cassandra had no money at all. Both were dutiful and sensible, and they knew, without either family having to put any pressure on them, that they would have to wait, possibly for years, before they could marry. Without money there could be no marriage. Both James's Anne and Edward's Elizabeth were already 'in the increasing way' as Eliza put it; or, in the less delicate language of Lord Portsmouth's brother Coulson, '*in for it!*'[16] The gleeful menace contained in this phrase struck Jane forcibly enough for her to quote it later; even the most treasured wife had no control over this part of her fate.

The question of how much control a woman had over her own life was one to ponder during that year of weddings and engagements. Money, money, money, again. There was no freedom for a woman without it, married or unmarried. Eliza talked to Jane about her mother's experience, how Aunt Philadelphia had been obliged to travel out to India alone as a girl and marry a man she did not care for, making the basic bargain, her body and companionship for his money; and Jane was so struck by this part of her aunt's story that she incorporated it into her writing that summer. In *Catharine, or the Bower*, Catharine's friend, the orphaned Miss Wynne, is given the experience of young Philadelphia Austen:

> The eldest daughter had been obliged to accept the offer of one of her cousins to equip her for the East Indies, and tho' infinitely against her inclinations had been necessitated to embrace the only possibility that was offered to her, of a Maintenance; Yet it was *one*, so opposite to all her ideas of Propriety, so contrary to her Wishes, so repugnant to her feelings, that she would almost have preferred Servitude to it, had Choice been allowed her – . Her personal Attractions had gained her a husband as soon as she had arrived at Bengal, and she had now been married nearly a twelvemonth. Splendidly, yet unhappily married. United to a Man of double her own age, whose disposition was not amiable, and whose Manners were unpleasing, though his Character was respectable. Kitty had heard twice from her friend since her marriage, but her Letters were always unsatisfactory, and though she did not openly avow her feelings, yet every line proved her to be Unhappy.[17]

This bleak, frank summary of her late aunt's experience was written out a few months after Mrs Hancock's death. What Mr and Mrs Austen thought of it is not known; Jane was sixteen, and it was dedicated to Cassandra. In the story, the brutal selling of the girl stands apart from other experience, which seems to be ruled by sunnier conventions, and is a satirical comedy of English country life, beginning to approach the tone of Austen's later novels; but it is recurred to several times, as though the writer does not want to let it go. Catharine's friend Camilla Stanley, the daughter of an MP, declares Miss Wynne very lucky to have been sent out to India to be married to 'an immensely rich man'. To which Catharine responds, 'Do you call it lucky, for a Girl of Genius and Feeling to be sent in quest of a Husband to Bengal, to be married there to a Man of whose Disposition she has no opportunity of judging till her Judgement is of no use to her, who may be a Tyrant, or a Fool or both for what she knows to the Contrary. Do you call *that* fortunate?' Camilla's speech is that of an empty-headed rich girl who talks of 'good fun'. Catharine, who has an imagination, expresses her shuddering repulsion. Camilla brushes this aside again: 'she is not the first Girl who has gone to the East Indies for a Husband, and I declare I should think it very good fun if I were as poor'. We are hearing a real argument here, provoked by the direct reporting of Aunt Phila's experience: a unique moment in Austen's wriring.

Eliza and Hastings stayed on into the autumn. There was room for them even when the pupils were in residence, because there were no longer any Austen boys left at home; Charles had followed Francis to the Portsmouth naval school at twelve, and Francis, promoted to Lieutenant, was still in the East Indies. Mr Austen's finances were stable, thanks to his pupils and helped by a legacy from Uncle Francis, who died at last at the great age of ninety-two; he might not have approved of his nephew spending some of it on a government lottery ticket, a flutter that failed.

Edward's and Elizabeth's daughter Fanny was born in Kent in January, soon after Jane's seventeenth birthday; James's and Anne's daughter Anna in April when, according to family legend, Mrs Austen was summoned to Deane in the middle of the night, and rose from her bed to walk stoutly through the muddy lanes with a lantern to be with her daughter-in-law for the birth of the grandchild who became her favourite.[18] Jane took due notice of becoming an aunt by writing nonsense offerings for her new nieces: 'Opinions and Admonitions on the conduct of Young Women' for Fanny, 'Miscellaneous Morsels' for Anna.

The distant thunder in France had grown steadily more menacing for three years, and now war broke out between England and France in February 1793. An immediate effect on the Austens was that Henry gave up his plan to become a clergyman, took leave of his college studies, was signed up with the Oxford Militia as a 'Gentleman to be Lieutenant' and joined his regiment in Southampton. For the next seven years he served as an officer, taking time off to complete his degree but rising in rank, popular with his fellow officers, and stationed in places as various as Brighton, Ipswich and Dublin. A new world opened to him, and proved much to his taste. Eliza was more deeply affected by the combined effects of revolution and war. In February 1794 her husband was arrested. He was in Paris, and had gone to the assistance of an elderly marquise imprisoned for allegedly conspiring against the Republic. With more gallantry than understanding of what he was up against, he set out to bribe one of the secretaries of the Committee for Public Safety. The man tricked him and testified against him. Other witnesses were his housekeeper and a woman described as his former mistress; his maidservant Rose Clarisse, a coloured girl, could neither read nor write, and was not called. On 22 February, Jean Capot de Feuillide was condemned to death and guillotined within hours of his trial. Eliza's marriage had lasted for twelve years.

At some time during the next two years Jane Austen wrote a short novel called *Lady Susan*.[19] Like most of her juvenile stories, it is about bad behaviour; but it is finished and polished, sophisticated in its analysis of behaviour, and quite unlike anything she had yet written or was ever to write again; an altogether extraordinary piece of work to come from the pen of a country clergyman's daughter. Told in letters, it is as neatly plotted and characterized as a play, and as cynical in tone as any of the most outrageous of the Restoration dramatists who may have provided some of her inspiration.[20] But Austen's tone is her own. She creates a female predator who holds centre-stage throughout, and wittily tells her own story; her wickedness is real, but she is also attractive, and so entertaining that we find ourselves sympathizing with her in her battle with the dullards who are her victims.

Lady Susan is sometimes associated with Eliza de Feuillide, and not only because she was a clever and beautiful young widow. Clearly it is not a portrait; but it has been suggested that Austen was influenced by Laclos' novel of 1782, *Les Liaisons Dangereuses*: and who could have shown her a copy of that scandalous book but Eliza? On the other hand, although Eliza may well have owned a copy of *Les Liaisons*, it is hard to believe she would have shown it to her unmarried cousin. Its cynicism was one thing; its outspoken sexual element quite another. But she could have talked about the book; and in fact there are considerable points of resemblance. Both stories, while maintaining a strictly moral framework, subvert it by giving the evil characters all the enterprise and charm. Lady Susan is a bad mother who is also a dazzling female Don Juan; she uses her charm very much as Madame de Merteuil does, to manipulate, betray and abuse her victims, whether lovers, friends or family. For both women, power is pleasure.

Lady Susan adjusts to new situations faster than anyone she meets, and never allows herself to be taken by surprise, or to appear upset or angry. Even when things turn against her she remains sweet-tempered, polite and obliging; and even those who distrust her allow that 'her Countenance is absolutely sweet, & her voice and manner winningly mild'. One of the points Austen is making is that Lady Susan is just what the conduct books advised ladies to be. You could even add that she displays exactly the 'affability, good humour and compliance' recommended by Mr Austen to his son Francis. She has perfectly mastered the art of using the conventions of society to get what she wants.

She will try to force her daughter into marrying the man she has chosen for her, but will not be seen to bully her. She sends her to boarding school at sixteen both to humiliate her and to 'make good connections': how well she understands English society. She exerts her power over those who are prejudiced against her by charming them: 'There is exquisite pleasure in subduing an insolent spirit, in making a person predetermined to dislike, acknowledge one's superiority.' Where she cannot overcome distrust, she can at least disarm by her sweet irreproachable manners. The worst mistake she could make, as she knows, would be to betray her real feelings (except to the obligatory confidante). Austen hands out the message in the coolest manner: it is not doing but seeming that counts, not character but reputation. Lady Susan commits adultery and breaks up a marriage, but she will not allow her married lover to visit her in the country *incognito*: 'I forbid anything of the kind. Those women are inexcusable who forget what is due to themselves & the opinion of the World.' As long as she reveals nothing, she has nothing to fear; she remains the perfect lady.

The story has been found sinister, and that is surely part of its point; so is Lady Susan's 'unfeminine' predatory nature.[21] It is much less developed as well as much shorter than *Les Liaisons*, as you would expect, given the relative ages and experience of the two writers. *Lady Susan* would be a better book if its heroine were provided with an opponent worthy of her skills; as it is, she does her worst, is partly foiled, grows bored, and ends her story with a shrug. But the energy and assurance shown in trying out such an idea and such a character are truly remarkable. It stands alone in Austen's work as a study of an adult woman whose intelligence and force of character are greater than those of anyone she encounters, and who knows herself to be wasted on the dull world in which she is obliged to live.

The exercise is brilliant. So brilliant, that Austen may have frightened herself, and felt she had written herself into a dangerous corner, and been too clever, too bold, too black. She set the story aside and, although she copied it out a decade or so later, never tried to have it published, and was clearly not encouraged to return to it by anyone in the family. Had she not felt some interest and pride in it, she would not have kept it. The fact that she did not follow it up with anything remotely resembling it suggests that she decided to censor the part of her imagination that interested itself in women's wickedness, and particularly sexual wickedness. Not until *Mansfield Park* and Mary Crawford did the spark of Lady Susan take a little fire again: only to be quickly re-extinguished. But the fire was there, however banked down.

8

Neighbours

At home, she read, wrote and followed her own imagination; outside, among the neighbours, she entered another world that sprang its own surprises and dramas. The society in which the young Austens found much of their entertainment was made up of the households of clergymen, squires, aristocrats, Members of Parliament, entrepreneurs, doctors and lawyers, mostly living within a range of about fifteen miles. A steady, backbone-of-England, unchanging rural society is what you expect to find; but the strange fact is that they formed a very unstable group, and that many were what has been called in this century pseudo-gentry, families who aspired to live by the values of the gentry without owning land or inherited wealth of any significance. There were remarkably few Dashwoods or Darcys, Bertrams, Rushworths or Elliots; Bingley's uncertainty about where he belonged and where he might settle comes much closer to them.

Far from making up a solidly established network of old families, many were recent arrivals in Hampshire, coming from other counties and countries, often changing their names in the process; few had more roots in the place than the Austens themselves, and some moved on again, either from choice or driven by debt or scandal. The more closely you look at them, the more they appear as a fluid, arbitrary group, families who merely happened to be where they were at that particular time, some floating in on new money, others floating out on their failure to keep hold of old.

Among the aristocratic families at whose balls Jane put in occasional appearances in the 1790s, the resoundingly named Lord Dorchester of Kempshott Park turns out to be an Irishman of very modest origins. He had worked his way up through the army, carving out a brilliant career for himself in Canada; he then married the daughter of an earl, and was made a baron and awarded a pension of £1,000 a year for life in 1783. He was an honourable man who deserved well of his country for saving Quebec, and he chose a title with a fine English ring to it, but inside it he was Guy Carleton of Strabane, a thorough-going meritocrat without local affiliations; and he merely took a lease on Kempshott for a few years, before moving on to another house near Maidenhead.[1]

The Dorchesters' neighbour at Hackwood Park, Lord Bolton, also sported a brand-new title. He came from Northumbria as simple Thomas Orde, achieving his transformation by marrying, in 1778, one of the illegitimate daughters of the fifth Duke of Bolton; and he took the name of Bolton when she had the good fortune to inherit some of the Bolton estates. This was in 1795, when Jane Austen was twenty; he was created Baron two years later. He aroused Mr Austen's interest by building particularly elegant pigsties, which he visited 'every morning as soon as he rises', according to a letter Jane sent her sister. She also told Cassandra she had preferred to sit down 'two Dances in preference to having Lord Bolton's eldest son for my Partner, who danced too ill to be endured'; and in another letter passed comment, not very politely, on Lady Bolton's improved appearance in a new wig.

A few years before these Boltons took over Hackwood Park, it had been the childhood home of the Revd Charles Powlett, a clergyman serving the tiny nearby parish of Winslade when the Austens knew him, and appointed one of the Prince of Wales's chaplains in 1790, despite never managing to take his degree at Cambridge. He was the son of a naval officer who died young, but more significantly the grandson of the third Duke of Bolton and his long-time mistress (and finally wife), the actress Lavinia Fenton, who played the first Polly Peachum in *The Beggar's Opera*. Powlett was something of a character, witty, diminutive in size, and with oddly shaped limbs; and he could be charming, for Jane Austen does not seem to have been too offended by his attempt to kiss her during the Christmas party season in 1796. Two years later she was rather more severe about him when he gave a dance, having by then acquired a wife 'discovered to be everything the Neighbourhood could wish her, silly & cross as well as extravagant'. He became a byword for extravagance himself; and his wife appeared 'at once expensively & nakedly dress'd' on social occasions,

otherwise failing to arouse Jane's interest. After her death, the Powletts' spending habits proved their undoing, and they were forced to
leave for the Continent, from which they were never able to return.
You can easily imagine them as figures in a Thackeray novel, living
on remittances in a Brussels boarding house, and sometimes surprising
new guests with reminiscences of parish life on the one hand, and
the Prince of Wales, dancing at Hackwood and 'the Duke my
grandfather' on the other.[2]

The Portsmouths of Hurstbourne Park were older and more solidly
established aristocrats; but they were struck by tragedy and a long-
running and horrific scandal during the period in which the Austens
knew them. It is impossible to believe that knowledge of it failed to
spread in the district where, to use Jane's own phrase, every man
was 'surrounded by a neighbourhood of voluntary spies'; although
no word of it survives in any Austen letters.[3] The Austens had
particular reason to be aware of it, because the third Earl was known
at Steventon from his childhood when, as Lord Lymington, he was
brought to be Mr Austen's pupil. This was two years before the birth
of Jane, in 1773. The little lord was 'between five and six years old,
very backward of his age, but good tempered and orderly', according
to Mrs Austen, and her Jemmy and Neddy were 'very happy in their
new play-fellow'.[4] But after about six months Lord Lymington's
mother removed him, 'alarmed at the hesitation in his speech, which
certainly grew worse'.[5] He was taken to London to be cured by a
Mr Angier; whatever his methods, the stammer remained, and the
young lord grew disturbed and eccentric. Outwardly he appeared to
live a normal life; in fact the Portsmouth family kept a very strict eye
on him. His two younger brothers, Newton and Coulson Wallop,
also well known to the Austens, were both sent to Eton.

In 1799, when Lord Lymington had succeeded to the title and
reached the age of thirty-two, his brothers obliged him to marry the
Hon. Grace Norton. She was then forty-seven and, whatever her
reason for agreeing to the marriage – to become a countess was
generally thought to be a sufficient one – the family's chief reason
was to make sure he produced no children, or at any rate no legitimate
ones, so as to ensure the succession to the next brother, Newton. The
Earl's knowledge of the process of human generation was so uncertain

that he believed it took fifteen months from conception to birth, and he was said to be impotent; still it was thought better to be on the safe side. The family further appointed trustees to superintend his property, one of whom was John Hanson, a London lawyer who was also the young Lord Byron's man of business.

One of Lord Portsmouth's eccentricities was that he took an obsessive interest in funerals ('black jobs') and slaughterhouses. He would get his servants to stage mock funerals for his amusement, and visit slaughterhouses in order to strike the animals awaiting death with a stick or an axe, saying as he did so, 'Serve you right.' It sounds horribly like a compulsive repetition of some punishment received as a child himself, perhaps from Mr Angier, although that can be no more than a guess. He also enjoyed having his servants and animals beaten, and once, when his coachman was lying in his room recovering from a broken leg which had been set by a surgeon, the Earl visited the injured man and re-broke his leg. Despite these habits, his social façade was kept up, and in November 1800 Jane Austen reports that he spoke kindly to her at a ball and particularly asked to be remembered to Cassandra in her next letter; she gave no indication that she found his manner in any way out of the ordinary. 'Lady Portsmouth had got a different dress on,' she added, indicating that she had seen her recently at another social occasion. The Portsmouths then gave a ball at Hurstbourne, their great mansion in its landscaped park, to which she went with pleasure; no sign of 'black jobs' or beatings as the Hampshire gentry went through their paces in the cotillion, although she did report that her hand shook the next day from drinking too much wine at the ball.[6] The house was one of James Wyatt's, built in the 1770s and enormous, with a central block and two wings each as big as the main building; it stood in a grandly landscaped park, with a lake and carefully placed knolls of trees.

In a later stage the Portsmouth saga became more diabolical. John Hanson, Lord Portsmouth's lawyer trustee, 'rented' a Portsmouth house and estate for himself at Farleigh, close to Basingstoke; in effect he got it for nothing, the rent being supplied by the legal fees due to him from the Earl. Hanson introduced his daughters to Lord Portsmouth, and entertained shooting parties; Byron came down in August 1805 for some 'destruction of the feathered Tribe' in the

'*Rural Shades* and *Fertile Fields* of Hants', just before going up to Cambridge, and met some local sporting families, among them the Terrys of Dummer, well known to the Austens.[7]

Hanson had a very good reason for installing his family in Hampshire; he made careful plans, and, when Lady Portsmouth died at the end of 1813, acted rapidly. He had Lord Portsmouth brought to London, drew up a marriage settlement between him and his daughter Mary-Ann Hanson, and asked Byron to be a trustee to the settlement, telling him that Portsmouth wanted to marry a young woman and was resisting his brother's efforts to force him to marry another old one. Neither Lord Portsmouth's brothers nor any of the other trustees were informed of what was going on.

Hanson's son Charles procured a marriage licence with blanks for names, and the ceremony was hurried through at St George's, Bloomsbury, in the presence of Byron, who noted in his diary that Portsmouth 'responded as if he had got the whole by heart; and, if anything, was rather before the priest'. He also reported him as saying 'he had been partial to Miss Hanson from her childhood' on the way to church, then afterwards telling his coachman that he had not expected to have a new wife, and didn't want the one he had got, but her sister. The younger Hanson sister, Laura, was beautiful; Mary-Ann was not. But Byron 'saw her fairly a countess – congratulated the family and groom (bride) – drank a bumper of wine (wholesome sherris) to their felicity, and all that – and came home. Asked to stay to dinner, but could not'.[8] He seemed unaware that he had been a party to something sinister.

The new Countess dismissed all the servants from Hurstbourne Park and instituted a reign of terror, having her husband regularly whipped and installing a barrister friend of her father who tortured and beat him into total submission. This regime continued until 1822, when Portsmouth's brother Newton began proceedings to have the marriage declared void and Mary-Ann's three children – one of them named Byron – illegitimate. Byron himself was accused of having been one of Mary-Ann's lovers but denied it ('my liaison was with the father, in the unsentimental shape of long lawyer's bills'), and there is no reason to doubt his word. All the Hansons fell into disgrace and poverty, but Lord Portsmouth, rescued from his persecutors, proved remarkably tough and lived on into his eighties.

This last part of the Portsmouth story happened after Jane Austen's death. At the time of the marriage, however, she took note of it: she was in London herself, in Henrietta Street with her brother Henry, in March 1814, and wrote with enigmatic brevity to Cassandra, 'What cruel weather this is! And here is Lord Portsmouth married to Miss Hanson!' As a tale of horror, it is far beyond the fashionable Gothic fiction she knew and satirized in *Northanger Abbey*, the novel she began in 1798, worked on and rewrote intermittently over many years, during which the Portsmouth–Hanson story unfolded.[9] Even supposing she heard no more than faint rumours of the Earl's taste for mock funerals, beating and torture of men and animals, some connection between having such a nightmare neighbour at Hurstbourne Park and the second half of *Northanger Abbey* does come to mind. Catherine Morland was wrong in her fears and suppositions about the goings-on at the Abbey, but she was not wrong in fearing its master, General Tilney, who was indeed both eccentric and cruel. The Portsmouth saga makes Catherine's dark suspicions of an ill-used and murdered wife in *Northanger Abbey* seem mild stuff.

The Terrys, whom Byron met when he stayed in Hampshire in 1805, were an old-established family, with a very handsome small manor house in Dummer, within easy walking distance across the fields from Steventon.[10] Thirteen Terrys were born there to the squire and his wife between the mid-1770s and the 1790s, and a good many of them figure in Jane's letters. As a group, she called them 'noisy'; but she was on friendly terms with the girls and danced with the boys, among them Stephen, the eldest son, who joined the North Hants Militia, Robert, who went into the regular army, and Michael, who became a clergyman and was later engaged to Jane's niece Anna. The second Terry girl in due course read *Emma* and particularly admired Mrs Elton; and two of her sisters married neighbouring squires' sons, one a Digweed at Steventon, the other a Harwood at Deane. But the Harwood family too was in trouble, with an accumulation of debts and mortgages they could not hope to settle. The eldest son felt unable to marry and spent his life paying off his father's debts, and the younger sank with his Terry wife from land-owner to humble yeoman farmer; they became something like Hampshire Durbeyfields. The Digweeds also had problems, and Jane's 'dear Harry

Digweed', his Terry wife and most of their children ended their days in exile in Paris, more victims of economic decline.

Old money failed and new money took its place. The Portals of Laverstoke were an enterprising Huguenot family from Languedoc who arrived in Southampton in the early years of the century, driven out of France by religious intolerance, and wasted no time making their mark. Henry de Portal was naturalized in 1711, bought a lease on Bere Mill on the River Test in 1712, and began to make paper. He was so successful that he acquired Laverstoke Mill, rebuilt it in 1719, and in 1724 got the contract to make the Bank of England notes; it was his idea to watermark them.

Henry Portal's son Joseph became High Sheriff and bought the Laverstoke estate, the next generation prospered further, and by the 1790s the Portals were important Hampshire land-owners. Jane Austen included them in her list of the grandest families at a ball in 1800; they demolished Laverstoke House in 1796 and had it hand-somely rebuilt in neoclassical style.[11] The brothers of this generation also owned the manor at Freefolk Priors, and Ashe Park House, which they rented out to a bachelor with a West Indian fortune, James Holder, the man whose tendency to lunge at ladies made Jane Austen keep hold of the door handle when she found herself alone with him in his drawing room.[12]

Other new money had thoroughly murky origins. Sir Robert Mackreth, who acquired an estate at Ewhurst in 1802, had begun life as a billiard marker at White's Club, become rich as a bookmaker and unscrupulous money-lender, and been given a pocket borough and then a knighthood for his services to the government without ever losing his unsavoury reputation where financial matters were concerned.[13]

The Biggs were also newcomers. They did not appear in Hampshire until 1789, when Lovelace Bigg of Wiltshire inherited Many-down from cousins called Wither, and moved in, a well-to-do widower with five daughters and two sons. To complicate matters, father and sons changed their names to 'Bigg-Wither', while the girls strong-mindedly kept to their simple original 'Bigg'. The two elder daughters soon married and the elder son died young in 1794, leaving the three sisters who became the Austen girls' friends. Their little brother Harris, then thirteen, was a stammerer like Lord

Portsmouth; his father had him educated at home by a private tutor, with no bad effects.

Elizabeth Bigg attracted two serious wooers, one of them John Harwood, her neighbour at Deane House, the other William Heathcote, a baronet's son from Hursley Park near Winchester. The Heathcotes were old friends of the Portals, and a highly respectable and conventional family; one son went into the navy, the daughters made comfortable marriages, and William was a fine, fox-hunting clergyman who became a prebendary of Winchester. The portrait of him in his hunting coat, flanked by his father and the Master of the Foxhounds, shows what a good-looking creature he was, with a face that could have modelled for Darcy or Willoughby.[14] His elder brother became one of the MPs for Hampshire; they were generally returned unopposed in that Tory county.

The simple slogan on which the Tories contested Hampshire was 'Heathcote and Chute for ever'. William Chute, Heathcote's fellow Member, was, however, another who grew up somewhere else – in Norfolk – and under another name: he was called William Lobb until he was nearly twenty, when his father inherited The Vyne through a Chute grandmother. The Vyne was (and remains) a large, handsome Tudor house outside Basingstoke, and the inheritance was magnificent enough to warrant a change of name for the whole family, which included a sister Mary and a much younger brother, Thomas, born in 1772.[15] They kept their property in Norfolk, but moved to Hampshire in 1776. Tom Chute was of an age to make friends with the Austen children, and he grew up to hunt with James and Frank, and to dance and play cards with Cassandra and Jane. He was 'full of wit and fun', and it is very possible that the young Chutes, neighbours of just the right age, either joined in or at least were in the audience for the theatricals at Steventon; Tom was particularly close to James, whose friend he remained for life.[16]

William Chute was educated at Harrow – where he was the statesman Spencer Perceval's fag, which may be what propelled him into Parliament – and then Cambridge. He enjoyed a Grand Tour on the Continent and spoke good French. Thomas missed going abroad because of the war, but went straight from Cambridge into one of the cavalry regiments raised in Hampshire in 1792; like Henry Austen, he became an enthusiastic officer, and did a lot of recruiting around Basingstoke. He was also a reader, and almost certainly the more intelligent of the two brothers.

Still, when William Chute succeeded his father as owner of The Vyne in 1790, he was thirty-three, single, and in possession of a decent fortune and estate, and one of the best houses in the district. It is to be supposed that neighbouring families with daughters of marriageable age thought him in want of a wife, and that the matter was talked over from time to time among the ladies of the district in the usual way. At that point Jane Austen was fourteen, old enough to hear what was said and speculate as to which of the young ladies of the district might be lucky enough to be chosen.

On coming into his estate, William Chute also entered Parliament, in principle establishing himself as one of the most influential as well as the most eligible young men in the county. As it turned out, Parliament failed to engage his interest much; although he voted steadily with the Tories for the next thirty years, he never spoke in the House. His heart was always in Hampshire, where he kept a pack of hounds and a stable of fine horses; politics simply could not compete with hunting. He would sometimes send instructions from the House of Commons for his hounds to be brought out to meet him on his ride home from Westminster – it took him about seven hours – so that he could enjoy a gallop with them over the last stretch. Not surprisingly, he became a noted local character on the hunting field. One day he slipped at a fence while hunting and his horse trod heavily on his thigh. His fellow huntsmen gathered round in alarm, fearing he was badly injured, and when he managed to get up, his friend John Portal said anxiously, 'I thought we were going to lose our member.' 'Did you?' replied Mr Chute, rubbing the injured part. 'Well, I can tell you I thought *I* was going to lose *mine.*'

He was a robust and cheerful man, did his duty at the Winchester assizes, dined the freeholders when an election was due and attended the Basingstoke Club. In 1793 a marriage was arranged between his sister Mary and the neighbouring squire of Oakley Hall, Wither Bramston. The prospect of losing Mary – who no doubt ran his house for him – may have spurred William to look for a bride. He had no difficulty in finding one, but he disappointed the Hampshire mothers. The Member for Devizes in Wiltshire, Joshua Smith, had four daughters, three of them unmarried, and in April, when they were all in London, he introduced Chute to Elizabeth, a shy, serious girl in her early twenties whom he decided to court. Her diary records the wooing, not quite in the terms of an Elizabeth Bennet. 'Mr Chute to dinner' at the end of April is followed by 'Mr Chute in the morn.' on 15 May. On 10 June, 'Mr Chute to dinner. Sopha conversation.'[17] Two days after the sofa conversation she wrote, 'Mr Chute in the morn. Mr Chute to dinner. Answer.' It was not settled yet, because the next day's entry goes, 'Mr Chute to dinner. Miss Cunliffe to supper & slept with me. Final decision.' This signalled the engagement. She then set off for Weymouth, where she rode on the sands and read Thomson's *Seasons* until Mr Chute arrived and replaced Thomson with Robertson's *History of America*, which he read aloud. Later, at her home in Wiltshire, there were musical evenings and they enjoyed *Much Ado about Nothing* together. The diary risks nothing about what she felt for Mr Chute; it merely notes that she spent sixpence on a toothbrush.

All the Smiths returned to London in October, and Mr Chute's visits multiplied, morning, evening, breakfast and dinner, sometimes with his brother Tom. On 6 October the two men went off to Hampshire for their sister's wedding, returning three days later. Then, on Tuesday, the 15th, Eliza wrote, 'I was married at St Margaret's at 1/2 after 9 set off a quarter before 12 stopped 20 mns at Bagshot & arrived at the Vyne quarter after 5. white frost sunny unclouded sky may it be a happy omen.' She had never seen her new home before, with its beautiful brickwork and Palladian porch, its chapel adorned with Tudor stained glass and wood carving, Gothic rooms, long panelled gallery and exquisite classical hall and staircase installed in 1770. Splendid as it was, she must have found it an ordeal to be faced with so much that was strange, as well as the housekeeper, butler, footmen and maids, all on the evening of her wedding day.

The next day they were called on by the Miss Biggs of Manydown House and their father. Two days later there were a great many morning calls, from James Austen and his father and mother with one of his sisters ('Miss Austin'); and other local families, John Harwood from Deane House, the Revd Mr and Mrs Lefroy from Ashe, and Chute's sister, Mrs Bramston from Oakley Hall. The bride returned some of these visits on 13 November, calling at Manydown to see the Miss Biggs, at Ashe on the Lefroys, and at Steventon on the Austens, where again only one daughter put in an appearance. She then dined at Oakley Hall with the Bramstons, staying for supper and playing cards, a version of Snap, which she called 'snip snap', until eleven. The following evening she went to a ball in the Basingstoke Assembly Rooms, where she danced with the Revd Charles Powlett and with one of the Wallop brothers; and a week later she met Lieutenant Francis Austen, just back from the Far East, at a dinner at the Lefroys.

The lives of the Chutes and the Austens touched at many points. The Vyne stood within the parish of Sherborne St John, where James Austen was vicar, and they had him to dinner – without his wife – almost every week; he hunted with the Chute brothers, and he and his wife used Chute's franks for their letters.[18] There are innumerable references to 'Mr Austin' in Eliza Chute's diaries and a fair number to other 'Austins': she never managed to spell their name as they did. For example, '16 Jan. [1794] Basingstoke ball. I danced six dances with Mr H. Austin': Henry's charm working as usual, for Eliza rarely records dancing more than twice with the same partner. 'Tues. 26 March [1799] Dined at Mr Austins comp [i.e., company]: Mrs Miss Austins Mr Digweed & us two.' The 'Mrs Miss Austins' here are Mary, Cassandra and Jane.

Eliza Chute was exactly the sort of young woman you would expect to become a friend of the Austen sisters, and not only because she formed an immediate bond with their great friends the Biggs. She was gentle and sometimes uncertain of herself, very nervous, for example, about appearing at public balls that first Christmas in Hampshire, when her mother wrote to her, 'I am glad for your Sake there are no Minuets at Basingstoke, I know the terror you have in dancing not that you have any occasion for such fears'.[19] She had intellectual stamina; she learnt French and Italian well enough to read in both and to write serviceable French. She was, like the Austens, a devourer of novels, Fanny Burney's, William Godwin's, Charlotte Smith's, *Gil Blas* and Rousseau's *La Nouvelle Héloïse*; she read Mme de Sévigné, Mme de Maintenon, Clarendon, Voltaire, Johnson's *Rambler* and Shakespeare. She enjoyed theatre-going and music, and owned a harpsichord. She painted well: her husband put this talent to use by setting her to make portraits of his foxhounds, on the grounds that they were as deserving as humans. She was a keen gardener, turning the long hall at The Vyne into a conservatory. She responded to the natural world, commenting in her diary on 'a falling star', 'glow worms in the lane', a September evening when she stayed out late because it was 'so heavenly & the moon so beautiful'; and the effect of frost on a bright day, 'trees in sun uncommonly beautiful in appearance, glittering like glass or diamonds'. A trip to Box Hill in September 1802 inspired her to lyrical praise of its magical slopes, woods and views; she praised it as one of the most beautiful spots in England.[20]

But Eliza Chute did not form a friendship with either of the 'Miss Austins', and Jane's few words about the Chutes suggest she did not care for either of them, much as she liked Tom. In 1796 she notes William's call at Steventon with 'I wonder what he means by being so civil.' Four years later she reports a meeting with Mrs Chute and her sister-in-law at Deane House: 'They had meant to come on to Steventon afterwards, but we knew a trick worth two of that.'[21] The note of hostility is so strong that there must have been a reason for it. Perhaps she felt the Chutes condescended from their grand house and superior social position. Perhaps Eliza Chute stole too much of the time and attention of the Lefroys and the Biggs, with whom her diary records regular dinners and joint expeditions. It remains odd, because Eliza Chute needed friends. Coming as she did from a merry and comfortable family, she suffered from loneliness at The Vyne, made worse by her husband's passion for hunting. Many entries in her diary read only 'the gentlemen hunted' or 'Mr Chute hunted' or simply 'a blank day'. And as the months and years went by, and no children appeared, she became sad.

After ten years of marriage, in 1803, she adopted a child. The wife of a cousin of Mr Chute died, leaving a large family, and three-year-old Caroline Wiggett was brought to The Vyne to cheer Mrs Chute. All her life Caroline remembered crying for her nurse and her father; but she became the pet of the house, overcame her fear of the tapestries on the walls, and for five years slept in Mrs Chute's bedroom. Then she was put into her own room, without a fireplace: these are her reminiscences. She was particularly fond of Uncle Thomas (Chute), who came for three months every winter from Norfolk, bringing his horses, Kicker, Slyboots and Thunderbolt; but nobody thought of letting her visit her family, even when her brothers were at school in Winchester. She was twelve before contact was re-established. There is something here of Fanny Price's story in *Mansfield Park*. There are several such parallels between Chute experience and Austen imagination.

The most stable group of the Austens' neighbours is very little documented. This was the Steventon village community, among whom all the children had spent their first years. In spite of this, the gulf between the gentry and the lower orders – what James Austen called the 'nine parts of all mankind' who were 'designed' for labour – remained absolute and unquestioned; both sides believed that God had arranged the system.[22] The death of an old family servant, reported in a letter to Eliza Chute from her mother, allows her the grace of neither a first name nor a 'Mrs': 'Poor Old Stevens died the death of the righteous, worn out with length of days she resign[ed] her Spirit without a Groan into the hands of her maker.' It goes on with the formal phrase about her 'having performed the duties of the Station of life in which he had pleased to place her in this world', and ends by wishing her 'a better lot hereafter'.[23]

The Austens were a little closer. Many of the names of the Steventon families appear in Jane's letters. She called the married women with children Dames: there was Dame Staples (Elizabeth) and her many children, Dame Kew (another Elizabeth) with her husband William and four children. Robert and Nanny Hilliard, the Steevens family, Mary Hutchins, Betty Dawkin, the Batts, Matthew and Susannah Tilbury and their four children, and other Tilburys with their four, are all mentioned. So is Daniel Smallbone and his Jane with their eight; and the two farm bailiffs, Corbett and John Bond, who worked for Mr Austen; and the Littleworths, or Littlewarts. Bet Littleworth emerges as a character because she was remembered by the adult Edward Austen as a childhood playfellow, and is one of the few whose subsequent life can be traced; she became a 'rather small and delicate looking' woman who chose to do the work of a man, once walking from Hampshire into Kent and back on an errand, presumably for the Austens.[24]

Almost all the men were employed in farm work, at between seven and eight shillings a week; around Steventon the women eked out the family income with home spinning until mills took over in the

March—April, 1799. APPOINTMENTS. *The time*	MEMORANDUMS and OBSERVATIONS.
Monday 25	
Tueſday 26 The gentlemen hunted	Dined at Mr Austin's Comp: two Miss Austins Mr Digweed & us two
Wedneſ. 27	Mr & I went to a Justice meeting at Basingstoke
Thurſday 28	
Friday 29 I rode to Basingstoke The gentlemen hunted	Mr J. went to a Justice & Commissioner's meeting at
I & C & I rode to Mr Bramston's	Bedham dined there.
Saturday 30	
The gentlemen hunted	
Sunday 31 Church	

Page from Eliza's Chute's diary

later years of the century, leaving them poorer. The brighter and luckier village children might find work at the manor houses or rectories. Boys could be employed in the stable or the garden, and if they did well go on to become coachman, gardener or even house servant; and the more presentable girls might become dairymaids, nursemaids, kitchenmaids or housemaids. Jane Austen calls a kitchen-maid an 'Under' and a housemaid a 'Scrub'. If this sounds impersonal, the differences between their experience and hers must have been almost unbridgeable.[25] Few village children learnt to read or write; they went to work as soon as they could be put to watching cattle or sheep, or scaring off crows. By far the best jobs in the district were at the Portal papermills, where men were paid twenty-two shillings a week and women seven pence a day, with 'red letter days' allowed as paid holidays; this was quite exceptional.

Villagers were not expected to behave like their betters in all ways. The Austens' bailiff, John Bond, gave his sweetheart a child before they married, and no one seems to have minded.[26] On the other hand, Mrs Austen mentions Mr Digweed discharging his manservant for making a village girl pregnant; the man married the girl, and Digweed was 'sorry to part from him as he liked him much – but it was right to do so'.[27] Discrepancies of this kind must have been puzzling to the servants. The Austens were capable of real goodness to theirs on occasion; when the Bonds' cottage burned down in their old age, James Austen took them into his rectory, where they were presumably given a garret room and a place in a corner of the kitchen in which to live out their days.[28] The alternative would have been the workhouse, where the destitute were maintained on two shillings and sixpence a week from the parish rates. There children were separated from parents and set to work winding silk or preparing hemp and flax; and families were known to endure frightful hardship rather than accept such a separation, to the surprise of their betters.

Ladies knew they had a duty to give charity to village families, in the form of blankets, clothes, and children's and baby things. Such gifts were much relied on, as necessities rather than as luxuries. Mrs Chute handed out blankets in almost wholesale quantities. Jane Austen also gave Christmas gifts: 'I have given a pr of Worsted Stockgs to Mary Hutchins, Dame Kew, Mary Steevens & Dame Staples; a shift to Hannah Staples, & a shawl to Betty Dawkins.' This is from a letter to Cassandra in 1798. Since she had no money beyond the little allowance her parents made her, the six Christmas offerings to women in the village suggest how seriously she took the obligation to help the poorest of her neighbours. One of them, of course, may have been her own nurse.

The Austens' neighbours, shifting, diverse, eccentric and sometimes outrageous in their behaviour, look like a great rich slab of raw material for a novelist to work on. In fact their lives were far too rich and heterogeneous for Jane Austen's adult purposes. She was attentive to them, as her letters show; but military heroes, forced marriages, mad earls and bastard sprigs of the aristocracy make no appearances in her novels; nor do ruined squires, brilliant factory-owners of foreign origin, or village girls, foster sisters of the rector's children, who grow up into enterprising women. What Jane Austen wanted from the life around her, she took and used, finely and tangentially. We can make a few guesses. The noisy, cheerful Terrys may have made their contribution to the Musgroves in *Persuasion*. William Chute's arrival in the neighbourhood may have distantly inspired the opening chapters of *Pride and Prejudice*. Lawyer Hanson's daughter Mary-Ann could even have suggested Mrs Clay, daughter of Sir Walter Elliot's 'civil, cautious lawyer', Mr Shepherd, with her aspirations to the baronet. Eliza Chute's enthusiastically described trip to Box Hill may be echoed in *Emma*, and her adoption of her husband's sad little niece in *Mansfield Park*. Some of these may be true links, others not; what is certain is that Austen took precisely the elements she wanted from her neighbours and no more; and that she transposed them to characters and locations which had very little in common with the people and places she knew so well in her Hampshire neighbourhood.

9

Dancing

'Are any of your younger sisters out, Miss Bennet?' asks Lady Catherine of Elizabeth, who answers 'Yes, Ma'am, all,' and Lady Catherine is duly shocked, because the youngest is only fifteen. Keeping Lydia Bennet in would have been a hard task even for a determined parent, and, like the Bennets, the Austens took a relaxed view of what it meant to be out. This was the country; the Austen daughters had been joining in country dances at home from their earliest years, and knew all the neighbours' sons and daughters; children took part in dancing, brothers danced with sisters, girls with one another. Each year there were newly named dances – you can read lists of them printed in ladies' pocket-books – but they were all made up of the same familiar steps, jumping, setting, forming a ring, linking hands and arms, moving up and down the sets, clapping, bowing and curtsying: variations on themes everyone knew as well as they knew how to run up and down their own stairs in the dark.

From dancing at home to dancing at the Lefroys or the Digweeds was a natural and easy progression; to the Terrys at Dummer and the Biggs at Manydown only a slightly bigger one. By the time she was fifteen Jane might have a white muslin dress kept for evening occasions which required any degree of formality, and a special ribbon for her hair, but more often dancing would be impromptu, a matter of someone suggesting, after a neighbourly dinner or tea at half past six, that they might push back the furniture and make up a set with anyone present who felt like joining in. Dancing was the chief evening amusement among the Hampshire families in winter, the music depending mostly on mothers and aunts at the keyboard, or occasionally a servant with a fiddle. Jane could play the piano, but at her age would not be expected to sacrifice herself when there were older fingers to work in the good cause of the young people's pleasure. Like her cousins Eliza and Phila, 'Jane was fond of dancing, and excelled in it.'[1] She loved it, but she could also mock its social purpose and supposed powers: in *Pride and Prejudice*, she makes the mothers of Meryton, eager to catch sons-in-law, believe that 'to be fond of dancing was a certain step towards falling in love'. Mr Darcy is allowed to voice the reservations of his sex on the subject: 'Every savage can dance.' True, but, as it turns out, the mothers are proved right, and even Mr Darcy grows less rigid and more energetic. And it was to be a dance that brought Jane the one young man we know to have fallen in love with her, and whose love was returned.

By the age of seventeen Jane was attending the balls held at the Basingstoke Assembly Rooms over the town hall, where all the local families gathered, paying a small subscription. Even here there was no great formality: as we have seen, there were no minuets. On 14 November 1793, a month before Jane's eighteenth birthday, there was a ball at the Assembly Rooms at which the new Mrs Chute met many of her neighbours. Cassandra and Jane were likely to have been there with Frank, home from the Far East after five years, nineteen, and a fine sunburnt figure in his lieutenant's uniform. A few days later he was invited to a large dinner party given by the Lefroys for the Chutes, but his sisters were not; of course he was a useful single man. Nor were the Austen girls at the Chutes' dance on 5 December, at which eight or nine couples enjoyed a cold supper, and kept going until after two, among them the Lefroys, the Harwoods and the Biggs.

In fact Cassandra and Jane were preparing for a visit to a Kentish cousin, planned by Mrs Austen, no doubt, in which the girls would make themselves useful and at the same time have the opportunity to meet a wider circle. Elizabeth Austen from Tonbridge had married money and moved to Southampton, where her husband was now Sheriff; and she was about to have a baby. So the girls helped out, and were also taken to the Assembly Ball at the Dolphin Inn for the company and the dancing. Jane stood godmother to the new baby, and stayed for the christening; Cassandra returned to Steventon, and she and Henry attended the next Basingstoke ball together, when Henry danced his six dances with Mrs Chute; Alethea and Harriet Bigg were there, the Lefroys, a Terry brother and sister, Coulson

Wallop (Lord Portsmouth's brother) and Charles Powlett. Mrs Austen
wrote a verse account of the occasion for Jane's entertainment. It
began:

> I send you here a list of all
> The company who graced the ball
> Last Thursday night at Basingstoke;
> There were but six and thirty folk,
> Altho' the Evening was so fine.
> First then, the couple from the Vine;
> Next, Squire Hicks and his fair spouse –
> They came from Mr Bramston's house,
> With Madam and her maiden Sister;
> (Had she been absent, who'd have missed her?)[2]

Mrs Austen had a sharp tongue for neighbours, appreciated by her
daughter and passed on to her.

Dancing, as the new year of 1794 came in, was not the major
preoccupation in Hampshire. The county was busy with plans to
augment the militia and raise more cavalry regiments. They were
wanted to fight the French, now on the offensive and sunk into infamy
of every kind: terror reigned, the Queen as well as the King had
been guillotined, the Christian religion thrown out and an entirely
new calendar, in which a week lasted ten days, invented. The militia
was also needed to suppress seditious gatherings at home in England,
where some sympathy with French ideas could still be found among
radical thinkers and the discontented poor. Basingstoke felt the full
effects. The little town buzzed with officers of the 84th, Colonel Rolle
and Captain Rodd and so many more of them were quartered there
that they made 'a great fracas' later in the year.[3] Henry Austen's
regiment was kept busy guarding French naval prisoners at Portsmouth; he managed to be stationed at Petersfield, which meant he
could get home easily.[4] Eliza was nowhere to be seen; when news of
the death of her husband reached England, she retreated to the
north and spent the rest of the year with friends on the borders of
Northumberland and County Durham. Meanwhile all the furniture
from the Marais was sold up, without the least regard to her or her
son's claims upon it.[5]

Four of the Austen brothers were now concerned in one way or another with the war; remotely in the case of James, whose father-in-law, the General, had him appointed to a military chaplaincy. It was intended simply to bring him a useful income, and asked nothing of him but the appointment of a deputy to do his work for a fraction of his pay; this was the accepted jobbery of the time. Mr Austen also did his utmost for Frank, corresponding assiduously with Warren Hastings about his promotion prospects, and suggesting the names of the contacts who might further them, lords and admirals right up to Chatham, First Lord of the Admiralty.[6] Hastings was still officially on trial, but the momentum had gone out of the prosecution, and Mr Austen was probably right in thinking he had influence in these quarters. For the moment Frank was kept in home waters, helping to evacuate British troops from Holland. Charles, who had finished his schooling at Portsmouth, had his introduction to life at sea taking part in a similar exercise off East Friesland, 'in support of British Army then retreating'; he got badly frostbitten.[7]

Early in 1795 some soldiers in Henry's regiment joined with the half-starved poor around Newhaven in rioting for food. Henry had been allowed leave in Oxford to work for his degree; in the crisis he was urgently summoned back. He sent a message to say he was sick, and got away with it. The rioting was brutally put down and the mutineers condemned to the severest punishments; Henry was back with his regiment in time to see the men executed by firing squad by their fellow soldiers before the whole Brighton garrison, 10,000 strong. Then in September he marched his men to winter quarters in Chelmsford before resuming his studies in Oxford. It was an odd way of life, divided between cloistered scholarship and the camp, where the young officers under their colonel, Charles Spencer, kept up a cheerful social round while maintaining an unrelentingly harsh discipline over the men.[8]

Henry had something else on his mind. In February 1795 Eliza de Feuillide had been widowed for a year; and in April, when her godfather was finally acquitted of all the charges brought against him, Henry wrote from St John's College to congratulate him: 'Dear Sir, An humble, and hitherto a silent spectator of national concerns, permit me at the present interesting moment to transgress the strictness of propriety, and though without permission, I hope without offence to offer you the warm & respectful congratulations of a heart deeply impressed with a sense of all you have done & suffered. Permit me to congratulate my country & myself as an Englishman.' He went on to allude to 'many instances of your kindness shown to me'.[9] We don't know what these kindnesses were: presumably either introductions or money. Henry's tone reads stickily, but he wanted Warren Hastings to approve of him.

It was eight years since he and Hastings's god-daughter had acted together at Steventon, Henry as a boy of sixteen, Eliza a flirtatious matron of twenty-six. Now she was free, and he was fully grown; and at some point this year he asked her formally to become his wife. There was no reason why they should not marry: it was common for first cousins to do so, she was loved by his family and reciprocated their love; he was earning something as a lieutenant, and she had an independent fortune, and possibly further expectations. But she turned him down: ambitious Henry, resplendent in his red officer's coat, was sent away with his tail between his legs. Perhaps she thought they knew each other too well; perhaps she cherished her independence. Perhaps she expected a longer wooing; but if she regretted her refusal, Henry was too proud to be kept dangling. He does not appear to have informed his family of his plans, and that was that.

Eliza's other male admirer among the Austens had been James, now of course married and father of a baby daughter. That May of 1795, when Anna was two and his wife Anne not yet forty, she was taken suddenly unwell after dinner one day, and died, inexplicably, within hours. James, left to deal with his own and his child's shock and grief, naturally turned to his family for comfort and help, and Anna was taken from Deane to Steventon to be cared for by her grandmother and aunts. James, mourning but free, began to think of his widowed cousin again, while Anna became a dearly loved part of the Steventon family, and the nearest thing to a child of their own for Cassandra and Jane. Jane's acute observation of children must have sprung first from this little niece; when the small Gardiners in *Pride and Prejudice* express joy in purely physical fashion, 'over their whole bodies, in a variety of capers and frisks', we are surely seeing Anna at a happy moment.

Anna in turn stored up her impressions of the rectory at Steventon, and years afterwards wrote an account of the two rooms Jane and Cassandra shared upstairs, the inner bedroom, the outer called 'the Dressing room', but actually more like a private sitting room, with its blue wallpaper and striped blue curtains.

> I remember the common-looking carpet with its chocolate ground that covered the floor, and some portions of furniture. A painted press, with shelves above for books, that stood with its back to the wall next the Bedroom, & opposite the fireplace; my Aunt Jane's Pianoforte - & above all, on a table between the windows, above which hung a looking-glass, 2 Tonbridge-ware work boxes of oval shape, fitted up with ivory barrels containing reels for silk, yard measures, etc.[10]

Anna was enamoured of the work boxes with their neat fittings, and mentioned neither Cassandra's paints and pencils, nor a small mahogany writing desk that may have held Jane's pens and paper.[11]

During that autumn of 1795 the war reached further into the sisters' lives when Cassandra's fiancé Tom Fowle agreed to act as chaplain to a regiment bound for the West Indies to fight the French. This was nothing like James's sinecure. Tom had to sail with the soldiers; the chaplaincy was offered by the colonel of the regiment, Baron Craven, his distant cousin, who was also going out. Tom's acceptance was a bold step intended to secure his future with Cassandra, because Lord Craven promised him a good living in Shropshire once the military expedition was over. But Tom, discreet as Cassandra, did not mention his engagement to his patron; only, with admirable prudence, he made his will before setting off. He was due to sail some time at the end of the year.

Another severe winter threatened; the Prime Minister, Pitt, recommended the poor to eat meat instead of bread, the price of which kept rising, with disastrous consequences for those who depended on it. Pitt's advice sounds dangerously like Marie Antoinette's, and in Berkshire the magistrates were so anxious at the prospect of riots they resolved to raise poor relief out of the rates; other counties felt it wise to follow suit. In October a mob of self-styled democrats attacked the King as he went through St James's Park on his way to Parliament, breaking the windows of the state coach, hissing, hooting and shouting, 'Give us peace and bread!', 'No King!' and 'No War!' The crowd was dispersed, and the next day the King, who never lacked courage, went out again, with the Queen and princesses, to Covent Garden Theatre; this time there was no trouble.[12] Pitt decided to raise money from the middle classes by putting an individual tax on hair powder; the result was effectively to end its use. A few held out, like Edward and Elizabeth Austen – and no doubt George Austen continued to wear his old-fashioned powdered wig – but more followed Frank and Charles, who simply had their dark hair cropped short. The result is that they both look entirely modern in their portraits, inhabitants of a different world from their brothers James and Edward, who were both immortalized as men of an *ancien régime*.

So much for the world and the family. Another world and another family occupied Jane's mind all through 1795. Some time after she had finished *Lady Susan* she started work on a new story planned on a larger scale. *Elinor and Marianne* was the name given to the first version of *Sense and Sensibility*, and Cassandra remembered that it was read to the family before 1796, and that at this stage it was written in the form of letters, like *Lady Susan*. Since all the manuscripts are lost, there is no way of knowing how much of *Elinor and Marianne* survived into the published book; we can at least be sure that it centred on two sisters with contrasting characters, an elder sensible and discreet, a younger ready to live less decorously and more dangerously.

IO

The Doll and the Poker

Biographers soon learn that there is no such thing as a reliable description or portrait, so it is not surprising to find Jane Austen remembered as 'fair and handsome' by one observer, and by another as having 'a clear brown complexion' with 'darkish brown' hair and hazel eyes. A third witness writes of her having a 'complexion of that rather rare sort which seems the peculiar property of *light brunettes* – A mottled skin, not fair, but perfectly clear & healthy in hue . . . fine naturally curling hair, neither light nor dark'; while a fourth gives her 'large dark eyes and a brilliant complexion, and long, long black hair down to her knees'.[1]

These are only the beginning. The silhouette that surfaced in 1944 (tucked inside an 1816 edition of *Mansfield Park*), labelled 'l'aimable Jane' and approved by the greatest of all Austen scholars, R. W. Chapman, shows someone with a large nose and a small mouth; yet her nose was described by Anna as small. Long narrow noses and dark-seeming eyes appear in her father, her Aunt Hancock and Cousin Eliza, and in all her brothers, as far as can be made out from miniatures; but we are told that Mr Austen had hazel eyes, and that both Henry and Jane inherited them. She certainly did not have her mother's aquiline nose, a source of pride to Mrs Austen, who considered it a mark of aristocratic blood.[2]

The eldest of the Fowle sons, who knew Jane from her early childhood, insisted that she was pretty: 'certainly pretty – bright & a good deal of colour in her face – like a doll – no that would not give at all the idea for she had so much expression – she was like a child – quite a child very lively & full of humour'. It is the most attractive of all descriptions of her, because you feel he has searched his memory and come up with a real vision, inspired but not distorted by affection.

Another witness, who was her neighbour later in her life, makes her 'a tall thin *spare* person, with very high cheek bones great colour – sparkling Eyes not large but joyous & intelligent', and criticizes the engraving made for the 1870 *Memoir* as making her face too broad and plump. The very high cheekbones fail to appear in Cassandra's sketch, and others thought her real cheeks were 'a little too full', and that her face was round. Her niece Anna, who loved her aunt dearly, ends her description with the words, 'One hardly understands how with all these advantages she could yet fail of being a decidedly handsome woman': a convoluted phrase which I take to mean she was *not* generally considered handsome.[3] Anna pronounced Cassandra's sketch to be 'hideously unlike' her aunt and it was not shown during Cass's lifetime.[4] But one cannot help noticing that the only two Austen children for whom there is neither formal portrait nor silhouette are George and Jane

Cousin Phila Walter's pronouncement that Jane was not pretty as a child has already been given. Eliza called Jane and Cassandra 'two of the prettiest girls in England', but this is Eliza's good nature running over into gush. Henry praised his sister's complexion, and the character that shone through her separately good features, without suggesting they added up to conventional beauty. Adapting John Donne, he said her eloquent blood spoke through her modest cheek, a lovely phrase which suggests a blushing pink or even red; and others noticed her high or brilliant colour.[5] Her nephew James-Edward described her in his *Memoir* as 'very attractive . . . a clear brunette with a rich colour . . . full round cheeks with mouth and nose small and well formed, bright hazel eyes, and brown hair forming natural curls close round her face . . . not so regularly handsome as her sister'. And he adds, 'she and her sister were generally thought to have taken to the garb of middle age earlier than their years or their looks required; and . . . were scarcely sufficiently regardful of the fashionable, or the becoming'.[6] Jane chose to have her curls cut short at the front, leaving only the hair at the back to pin up, tucking it into a cap when she felt like it, and making the whole process quicker and simpler; she had no need of curl papers. 'My hair was at least tidy, which was all my ambition,' she wrote after a ball at Lord Portsmouth's, suggesting she was unwilling to be too much bothered.[7] On another occasion she expected Cassandra and Edward to be amused by the news that her hair has been dressed by Nanny Littlewart, one of the village family who served the Austens in many capacities, and unlikely to be skilled hairdressers; impossible to imagine Jane with the swept-up and powdered creations of Mrs Lefroy or her sister-in-law Elizabeth.

She was never scarred by smallpox, the ruin of so many faces in her generation, and so often used as a threat and a warning against the perils of vanity. Jane Austen was not vain. She struggled to concern herself with fashion and dress design – which seems to have interested Cassandra more, for it is clear from Jane's replies that she raised the subject regularly in her letters – but Jane does not write about them as though they held real interest for her: 'I hate describing such things,' she says of an ultra-fashionable borrowed cap she is to wear at a ball; and 'I have got over the dreadful epocha of Mantuamaking much better than I expected.'[8]

This is not the voice of someone prepared to devote much time and trouble to her appearance. 'I cannot determine what to do about my new Gown; I wish such things were to be bought ready made' (in a letter of 1798) confirms this unwillingness. Many years later, when she was persuaded to have her hair done to the latest fashion in London (in 1813), she 'thought it looked hideous', and regretted her concealing cap. At the same period she wrote to Cassandra to tell her she was trimming a dress with ribbon: 'With this addition it will be a very useful gown, happy to go anywhere.' A useful gown, happy to go anywhere, is not what someone who cares for fashion wants to be seen in.

Nor did she concern herself with clothes in the novels: in *Northanger Abbey*, Mrs Allen's obsessive interest in fashion – 'dress was her passion' – is roundly mocked, both by the author and by the most sensible voice in the book, Henry Tilney's. 'There goes a strange-looking woman! What an odd gown she has got on! – How old-fashioned it is! Look at the back': this is Mrs Allen's tedious level of interest in other people. And in a famous passage in which the young heroine, Catherine Morland, worries about what to wear to a dance, the author interpolates her own comment: 'Woman is fine for her own satisfaction alone. No man will admire her the more, no woman will like her the better for it.'

This was her considered voice, whether the passage was written in the 1790s or added in 1803. In her letters she may comment on the fact that ladies are wearing fruit on their hats, and that it seems more natural to have flowers growing out of the head, and be precise about the colour she requires for dress material; but the impression we get is that, had she lived two hundred years later, she would have rejoiced in the freedom of a pair of old trousers, with a tweed skirt for church, and one decent dress kept for evening.

About her figure there is general agreement: 'slight and elegant', 'tall and slight, but not drooping'; 'a tall thin *spare* person'; even 'a thin upright piece of wood or iron' makes the same point.[9] This casts more doubt on the silhouette, whose bosom is not that of a spare person. Henry called her stature 'that of true elegance. It could not have been increased without exceeding the middle height,' a very elegant, brotherly formulation. Her nephew James-Edward described her figure as 'rather tall and slender, her step light and firm, and her whole appearance expressive of health and animation'.[10] Anna also testified to her quick, decisive step.[11]

From this jumble of accounts, what emerges? She was tall and thin, with curly hair that was closer to dark than fair. One lock of Jane's hair survives; although it is now bronze coloured, hair is known to fade with time, and the curls that can be seen emerging from her cap in Cassandra's portrait sketch are certainly dark.[12] Her eyes were not large and not blue, but possibly hazel and possibly dark; they were bright, although she had a tendency to eye trouble, which must have affected them at times. Nose and mouth on the small side. Round, doll-like cheeks, likely to glow into high colour with exercise or emotion. Not a beauty, but attractive to those who knew her best and responded to the animation, responsiveness and intelligence of her expression. And of course, like most people, she had looks that changed. When she was at ease and happy among those she loved, she sparkled joyously. When she was bored or mistrustful, her features tightened and her face closed up; no doubt she did then become as alarming as an unfriendly witness, Mary Mitford, made her sound when she likened her to a poker, perpendicular, precise and taciturn.[13]

11

A Letter

The earliest of Jane Austen's letters to survive was addressed to Cassandra, wishing her a happy birthday. Jane wrote it sitting at home in her father's parsonage on Saturday, 9 January 1796, and it is a remarkable document. Everyone in the family turned out a good letter, and her pen must have flown along neatly and fluently, as much for the sheer enjoyment of writing as from any sense of duty towards her dear sister. Because the letter was not intended for any eyes but those of the recipient, it takes a little decoding, but then it becomes as enjoyable as the first page of a novel, a familiar type of novel in which two young women will exchange news of their adventures and flirtations and gradually work their way towards the crowning point of their lives: which is marriage. As it happened, just such a novel in letters as Jane Austen herself had been writing – a fact which must have amused her.[1]

Cassandra was away from home for the Christmas of 1795, staying with her future in-laws the Fowles in Berkshire. She was there to cheer them and be cheered in turn, for Tom was now at Falmouth, waiting to sail for the West Indies; there was always danger when young men sailed halfway across the world, but enough Austens had survived such trips to give them confidence, and there was no question of Tom being away for as long as Francis. So there was no display of sympathy, only a teasing reference to the odd name of Tom Fowle's ship – it was called the *Ponsborne* – tucked in at the end of the page. Another Fowle brother, Charles, is also mentioned, who has rather boldly promised to get hold of some silk stockings for Jane; and she says she has spent so much on white gloves (for dancing) and pink silk (for underwear) that she has no money left for the stockings.

The main theme for Jane's letter was to be a description of the ball attended the night before, at Manydown House, with the Biggs; but alongside this topic she was signalling something more important, and more intimate. Her second sentence reads, 'Mr Tom Lefroy's birthday was yesterday, so that you are very near of an age.' Another Tom, and in truth, almost the same age as Jane herself, both of them just twenty. This dazzling stranger was from Ireland: Tom Lefroy was a visitor to Hampshire, not one of the dancing partners she and Cassandra had known most of their lives, but someone quite new. He was fair-haired and good-looking, clever and charming; he had completed a degree in Dublin and was about to study for the Bar in London, and was just taking a few weeks' holiday over Christmas with his Uncle and Aunt Lefroy at Ashe parsonage. After this first mention, Tom Lefroy keeps putting in more appearances in Jane's letter. In fact she can't keep him out, this 'gentlemanlike, good-looking, pleasant young man', as she covers the sheet of paper so cheerfully, dipping her well-sharpened pen into the little ink bottle at her side.

That Jane has just reached the age at which Cassandra became engaged to *her* Tom is something both are well aware of: these are things young women notice. Jane's letter plunges on into talk about the ball of the night before: who was there and what happened, together with what plans are being made for more festivities. There is plenty of gossip to pass on to Cassandra, and the list of guests is so familiar to her that it needs no explaining. There are neighbours and neighbours' friends and relatives, cousins, ex-pupils of their father and *their* sisters, and Oxford friends of James and Henry. Both these brothers are present, although she mentions only James among the dancers. There is no reference to his recent bereavement, only to 'the very great improvement which has lately taken place in his dancing'. This is Jane's tough streak; perhaps his sisters encouraged him to improve his skills on the dance floor as a means towards courting a new wife.

Clergymen outnumbered all other kinds of men at the dance, almost as though Hampshire were a special breeding ground for the Church; but there were also local land-owners, a baronet and the widow of another baronet – he had also been a prebendary of Winchester Cathedral – who brought along three daughters and a son in her carriage, for the fun, the exercise, the small dramas of the dance floor, and the chance to extend the limited social circles of country life.[2] Jane records the presence of a son of the Basingstoke doctor, John Lyford, whom she considered bad news, and her relief at avoiding him as a partner; she was better pleased by John Portal, whose handsome cousin Benjamin had called at Steventon the day before.

The Bigg sisters, encouraged perhaps by their fifteen-year-old brother Harris, had persuaded their father to illuminate the Many-down greenhouse to add to the splendour of their occasion. James Austen danced with Alethea Bigg, Cassandra would be pleased to hear; and she would be even more entertained by her account of the behaviour of Elizabeth Bigg, who was at the interesting stage of rejecting one suitor and encouraging another. She opened the ball with the Revd William Heathcote, a good-looking, lively, well-to-do, fox-hunting sort of clergyman, and by the end of the evening everyone knew Heathcote had cut out John Harwood, a lesser land-owner's son, who would dearly have liked to marry Elizabeth. The Harwoods had given last week's ball, but the attractiveness of Deane House had not softened Elizabeth's heart towards their son.

Jane wrote, 'Mr H [Heathcote] began with Elizabeth, and after-wards danced with her again; but *they* do not know how *to be particular*. I flatter myself, however, that they will profit by the three successive lessons which I have given them.' She means her behaviour with Tom Lefroy. She calls him 'my Irish friend' and teases Cassandra, who has already scolded her about her behaviour in a letter, by telling her to imagine 'everything most profligate and shocking in the way of dancing and sitting down together'. Her delight in announcing this shines out unashamedly, but she goes on to explain that 'I *can* expose myself . . . only *once more*', as Tom Lefroy will be leaving the country soon after the next ball. They have had only three balls in which to get to know one another, and he is being 'laughed at about me' by his uncle and aunt, the Lefroys, so much that he is 'ashamed of coming to Steventon' and 'ran away' when Jane last called at Ashe. The next ball, however, is to be held at Ashe itself, in the Lefroys' rectory, on the following Friday, 15 January.

Here the letter breaks off. She takes it up again later with more about her Irish friend, who has just called. It is a polite custom for gentlemen to call on ladies they have partnered on the day after the dance, so there is nothing special about the visit, and in any case Tom comes chaperoned by his thirteen-year-old cousin, George. 'The latter is really very well-behaved now; and as for the other [i.e., Tom], he has but *one* fault, which time will, I trust, entirely remove – it is that his morning coat is a great deal too light. He is a very great admirer of Tom Jones, and therefore wears the same coloured clothes, I imagine, which *he* did when he was wounded.'

The reference to Fielding's *Tom Jones* is another provocative remark. Jane is making clear that she doesn't mind talking about a novel which deals candidly and comically with sexual attraction, fornication, bastard children and the oily hypocrisy of parsons, and roundly states that the sins of the flesh are of little account, and much to be preferred to the meanness of spirit of sober, prudent people. By telling Cassandra she and Tom Lefroy have talked about the book together, she lets her know just how free and even bold their conversation has been. She also lines herself up with its badly behaved hero – another shocking and profligate creature – against the correct and discreet characters who are his enemies in the book, and might be hers in the world outside it; for some would be displeased to hear of the daughter of a clergyman reading such a bawdy story. With this flourish, she puts down her pen until the next day.[3]

Who else was in the house at Steventon as she sat writing this letter? She does not mention her father, who might be reading, or dozing, or thinking about tomorrow's sermon in his study at the back of the house, overlooking the garden; or talking with his bailiff John Bond in the yard. There were undoubtedly servants in the kitchen and the outhouses, but they do not at this moment in Jane's life seem worth a mention in a letter; later they will. Of her brothers, only Henry was at home. He had brought a friend to stay, John Warren, known to them from his schooldays with their father, and so quite accustomed to sleeping in one of the attic rooms, even though he was now a Fellow of Oriel College. He and Jane were good friends too, and he was one of her dancing partners the night before; but they had left him at the inn on the main road after the ball, to catch an early coach to town. He was back in Hampshire a few days later, when Jane discounted the idea that *he* might be in love with her, on the grounds that he presented her with a portrait of Tom Lefroy, drawn by himself; a gesture that made it quite clear that the flirtation had attracted attention and become common knowledge.

Henry was also due to set off towards Oxford the next day to collect his Master's degree before returning to his regiment in Chelmsford. He was not entirely committed to the militia; sometimes he thought of joining a new regiment which might be sent to the Cape of Good Hope. (Jane: 'I heartily hope that he will, as usual, be disappointed in this scheme'.) Much as she loved Henry, she was clear-sighted about his not always realistic ambitions and his vacillations; although even she may not have known that he was simultaneously pursuing a quite different plan to become a clergyman at nearby Chawton.[4] He was also engaged in complicated financial dealings, and was about to pay off a debt to his father and borrow a very much larger sum from Eliza.[5] At the same time, he was pursuing a young woman who might be expected to bring him a dowry, since her father was Sir Richard Pearson, in charge of the Naval Hospital at Greenwich. 'Oh, what a Henry!' as Jane exclaimed on another occasion.[6]

Mrs Austen is given only a passing reference in her daughter's letter, as the creator of some old paper hats 'we' have trimmed up and given away, probably to some neighbouring children; this sounds like a way of amusing Anna on a midwinter afternoon. Of her other brothers, she refers only to Charles, now sixteen and serving as a midshipman at Portsmouth under the command of Cousin Jane Williams's husband; Jane Williams's brother, with wife and children, is expected at Steventon in a few days. Frank is at sea with the home fleet, keeping discipline among his sailors, a subject he probably does not discuss much with his sisters; his log entry during the week of this letter of Jane's reads: 'Punished sixteen seamen with one dozen lashes each for neglect of duty in being off the deck in their watch.'[7] Frank is a good, steady officer who knows how to do his duty.

The last paragraph of the letter, added on Sunday, is chat about Cassandra's date of return and the bits and pieces of news she has sent from Berkshire. The death of a child and losses and gains at card games are mentioned in the same sentence, a juxtaposition brought about by limited space, but also by a brisk attitude towards mortality. She signs off, '. . . and am ever yours, J. A.'

The fact that the manuscript *Elinor and Marianne* was lying completed somewhere in the house as she wrote gives this first letter an extra resonance. But there is more to it than that: it is also the only surviving letter in which Jane is clearly writing as the heroine of her own youthful story, living for herself the short period of power, excitement and adventure that might come to a young woman when she was thinking of choosing a husband; just for a brief time she is enacting instead of imagining. We can't help knowing that her personal story will not go in the direction she is imagining in the letter; that, as it turned out, it was not Tom Lefroy, or anyone like him, who became her adventure, but the manuscript upstairs. Not marriage but art: and in her art she made this short period in a young woman's life carry such wit and human understanding as few writers have managed to cram into solemn volumes three times the size. But just at that moment, in January 1796, you feel she might quite cheerfully have exchanged her genius for the prospect of being married to Tom Lefroy one day, and living in unknown Ireland, with a large family of children to bring up.

Then, if you turn back to the very beginning of the letter, you find its opening sentence suggests there was some thought of the future in her mind as she wrote: 'In the first place I hope you will live twenty-three years longer.' The birthday greeting takes them through another twenty-three years to 1819, when she will be forty-three and Cassandra forty-six. What they had to expect was that both would be living in other parts of the country, under different names, with husbands and troops of children. They would be following a pattern laid down for them by their mother, childbirth and child-rearing, housekeeping, gardening, supervising the dairy and poultry yard, charitable work for the poor, visits paid and received among a circle of neighbours. In all likelihood they would be planning marriages for their own daughters. They would still be writing to one another, the sort of cheerful informative letters their mother wrote to her friends and relations; but the significant adventure of their lives – the brief, high moment which set a young woman at the centre of the stage and saw her determine her future by her actions – would have been accomplished long since and passed into history. Eighteen-nineteen: the date in another century was almost unimaginable, conjured out of the air by Jane's pen.

12

Defence Systems

'Don't think a young Man of 20 is a harmless being,' wrote Eliza Chute's mother to her that Christmas of 1795, warning her against the dangers of ballroom flirtations in words that could have been meant for Jane. Thomas Langlois Lefroy was not a harmless being, but Jane had her system of defences, and even before his departure she started putting them up. In her second letter to Cassandra she joked about her other admirers and contradicted herself with apparent gaiety: 'I mean to confine myself in future to Mr Tom Lefroy, for whom I do not care sixpence.' Then she adopted the solemnity of one of her own most absurd creations to announce that 'the Day is come on which I am to flirt my last with Tom Lefroy, & when you receive this it will be over – My tears flow as I write, at the melancholy idea.' It's a joke, yes, but made with the intention of misleading her sister; the joke is undermined when you look back at the letter of the week before, with its unequivocal message that she was in love.

Tom Lefroy was also in love with her, even if he was not yet making proposals of marriage. He confessed as much to a nephew when he was an old man: 'he said in so many words that he was in love with her, although he qualifies his confession by saying it was boyish love'.[1] Boyish love is after all the most passionate love there is, and the qualification, far from diminishing the remembered flame, makes it blaze up brighter. There must have been something more than dancing and sitting out together: kisses, at least, a stirring of the blood, a quickening of the breath. But however he admired Tom Jones, he was no Jones himself when it came to the point, any more than Jane was a Sophia Western; both were of the wrong class, and brought up to the wrong habits to sacrifice family approval in the name of love. Since the Lefroys were Huguenots, they had to make their way diligently in their adopted country. Tom's father, who had been an army officer and made an unwise marriage himself, was now retired in Ireland, with many mouths to feed; five daughters preceded Tom, the eldest son, and he was dependent on a great-uncle who had already put him through college in Dublin and was now financing his law studies in London. The expectations of the whole family were clearly laid on him, and he could not be allowed to risk his future by entangling himself in a love affair with a penniless girl.

He knew it as well as they did, and whether he was sent away by the Hampshire Lefroys to protect Jane from his philandering, or to protect him from her hopes of a declaration, is uncertain. Mrs Lefroy was too worldly-wise not to see that any prospect of marriage between them was out of the question. Her sons – one of them the George who called on Jane with Tom – said later that their mother sent Tom packing so 'that no more mischief might be done', and that she blamed him 'because he had behaved so ill to Jane': the implication is clear that Jane took his attentions seriously.[2] No doubt Mrs Lefroy offered her sensible advice of the kind Mrs Gardiner gave Lizzy when she saw she was in love with Wickham.

Tom may have reappeared in Hampshire once or twice, although kept carefully away from the Austens, for a 'young nephew' was taken by the Lefroys to a grand dinner given by the Chutes for the Dorchesters in December 1797, at the point Jane was returning from a visit to Bath. Her bleak remembrance, and persistent interest in him, is sufficiently demonstrated in a letter written in November 1798, nearly three years after their brief romance. She described how Mrs Lefroy called but said nothing of her nephew, 'and I was too proud to make any enquiries; but on my father's afterwards asking where he was, I learnt that he was gone back to London in his way to Ireland, where he is called to the Bar and means to practise'. The 'gone back' suggests he had been in Hampshire once again, sent smartly back to London perhaps before Jane returned from a stay in Kent. Mr Austen is the hero of this little anecdote, a model of sensitivity and paternal tenderness in putting to Mrs Lefroy the inquiry Jane longed to but could not make.

So Jane never saw Tom Lefroy again after his Christmas visit of 1795; and from 1798 he was settled in Ireland. That December, Jane told Cassandra that 'the third Miss Irish Lefroy is going to be married', but after that she remained silent on the subject. A year later Mr Irish Lefroy himself married a Wexford heiress, the sister of a college friend. He continued to work hard at the Bar, fathered seven children and, as the years went by, became extremely successful and deeply pious at the same time. He sat for eleven years in Parliament as a Tory; he opposed Catholic emancipation and founded a society to send missionaries into traditional Roman Catholic areas; and in 1852, in the aftermath of the Famine, was appointed Lord Chief Justice of Ireland. Had she lived to see all this, it might have pleased Jane Austen's sense of irony that the oppressed Catholic Irish should have justice meted out to them by one whose forebears had fled from just such cruel religious oppression in France.

A small experience, perhaps, but a painful one for Jane Austen, this brush with young Tom Lefroy. What she distilled from it was something else again. From now on she carried in her own flesh and blood, and not just gleaned from books and plays, the knowledge of sexual vulnerability; of what it is to be entranced by the dangerous stranger; to hope, and to feel the blood warm; to wince, to withdraw; to long for what you are not going to have and had better not mention. Her writing becomes informed by this knowledge, running like a dark undercurrent beneath the comedy.

Writing is what she increasingly turned to now. During the summer after Tom's departure, life at Steventon was transformed by Mr and Mrs Austen's decision to give up taking pupils. It meant that the household was reduced to four adults and little Anna, bringing not only freedom from teaching for Mr Austen, but the easing of all the work involved in the planning and preparation of meals, laundry, cleaning and bedmaking, the province of his womenfolk. Greater leisure and privacy undoubtedly played their part in allowing Jane to be more ambitious both in planning and writing her work. Her output suggests just how much; it became phenomenal. In October 1796 she began on *First Impressions*; this was completed in about nine months, by the following summer. Then around November 1797 she returned to *Elinor and Marianne*, having decided that the letter form did not suit her purposes well enough. The change to direct narrative required fundamental restructuring and rewriting, which she carried out over the winter and spring of 1798, renaming the work *Sense and*

Sensibility. She went on between 1798 and 1799 to produce a first draft of the book that would become *Northanger Abbey*, at this stage called *Susan*. So in four years three major novels were under way; and she was not yet twenty-four.

The tradition of reading her work aloud to the family was well established. You can imagine her at work in the blue-papered dressing room upstairs before coming down for dinner at three thirty, or after tea at six thirty, testing her dialogue first on her own ear, cutting and amending whatever embarrassed her or struck a false note in the dialogue, as you do if you are going to be reading aloud to others; and marking her text in the neat hand she had developed, paper being always expensive. By whatever process of inner composition or redrafting, her characters rarely fail to speak to one another like real people, not in set speeches but as though they are actually exchanging information, exploring or undermining one another's views or feelings, putting one another down, flirting, deceiving, or simply expressing the life with which she has endowed them; whether it is rich Mrs John Dashwood voicing her envy of her penniless sister-in-laws' breakfast china ('twice as handsome as what belongs to this house. A great deal too handsome, in my opinion, for any place *they* can ever afford to live in. But, however, so it is.'), or good Mrs Jennings offering olives, round games and Constantia wine ineffectually one after another for Marianne's broken heart. There is no knowing whether the listening Austens made suggestions or criticisms; what we do know is that father, mother and sister all had the wit to appreciate what she wrote, and to see that the promise of her early sketches was flowering into something still more exceptional.

Mr Austen indeed thought so well of *First Impressions* that he wrote to the publisher Thomas Cadell in London in November 1797, asking if he would consider it. This Cadell had only recently inherited his business from an eminent father, the publisher of Gibbon and friend of Dr Johnson, and with such a pedigree Mr Austen felt it appropriate to use the sort of flattering words he knew so well how to deploy: 'As I am well aware of what consequence it is that a work of this sort should make it's first Appearance under a respectable name I apply to you.' He did not name an author but simply indicated that he had 'in my possession a Manuscript Novel, comprised in three Vols. about the length of Miss Burney's Evelina', and asked what would be the expense of publishing it 'at the Author's risk; & what you will venture to advance for the Property of it, if on a perusal, it is approved of?' Thus he was generously prepared to put up money for it if necessary. His letter was posted on 1 November and answered with unusual rapidity for a publisher: 'Declined by Return of Post' is written across the top.[3]

You can see why Cadell might not want to bother to look at a novel by an unknown Hampshire clergyman. As publishing blunders go it was still one of the worst ever made through laziness. It meant that *First Impressions* was reworked into *Pride and Prejudice*, but if you believe, as I do, that *First Impressions* was pretty good already – from what we know of her later juvenile writing, and to have pleased her father so much – you may also believe that, with publication and success in 1798, Austen might have written another equally good novel before 1800. But whether Mr Austen told his daughter about his letter to Cadell or not, he did not repeat the attempt.

During the late 1790s the Austen children went through major upheavals. Some can be glimpsed through Jane's letters, most not at all. Only twenty-eight letters exist for the five years 1796 to 1801, and none at all for the very important year of 1797, because Cassandra took particular care to destroy personal family material. The first letter about Tom Lefroy can have survived only by mistake.

Cassandra's culling, made for her own good reasons, leaves the impression that her sister was dedicated to trivia. The letters rattle on, sometimes almost like a comedian's patter. Not much feeling, warmth or sorrow has been allowed through. They never pause or meditate but hurry, as though she is moving her mind as fast as possible from one subject to the next. You have to keep reminding yourself how little they represent of her real life, how much they are an edited and contrived version. What is left is mostly her attempt to entertain Cass with an account of what's been happening, usually to other people. She leaves out the empty spaces, the moments of solitude and imagination, the time spent thinking, dreaming and writing. Even the weather is always connected to social activity; there is none of Eliza Chute's frost like diamonds, or falling stars.

What you do pick up from the letters of the 1790s is the sisters' great reliance on one another for information and understanding that could not be expected from anyone else. When, for instance,

Jane made a summer trip to Kent to stay with Edward and Elizabeth at Rowling in 1796, she felt she could ask Cassandra's advice about tipping servants more easily by letter than by asking her brother or sister-in-law. She could grumble to Cassandra that she was stuck there until one of their brothers chose to move her, because she could not, of course, travel alone. 'I am very happy here,' she explained in September, 'though I should be glad to get home by the end of the month.' Meanwhile, she earned her keep in Kent by helping the other ladies to make her brother's shirts; and 'I am proud to say that I am the neatest worker of the party.' Jane did not resent having to sew, as some clever women did; but she did notice that, while the ladies of the house were at their sewing, the men went shooting. This inspired her to: 'They say that there are a prodigious number of birds hereabouts this year, so that perhaps *I* may kill a few.'

Was she really telling Cassandra she wanted to go out with a gun? Women's rights were a topic of the brilliantly amusing novel *Hermsprong, or Man as He is Not* that appeared that year, and of which Jane owned a copy. Robert Bage, the enlightened author, spoke up for democracy and women's rights, and expressed his admiration for Mary Wollstonecraft, who had already claimed for her sex the right to take up farming, the law and other male pursuits. So why should Jane not shoot birds? Two weeks later she was joking about the possibility of becoming a medical student, a lawyer or an officer, should she find herself stranded in London on her journey home. Either that, or she might fall into the hands of a fat woman who would make her drunk, and set her off on a more conventionally womanly career.

There were plenty of jokes for Cassandra. On arriving in London, 'Here I am once more in this Scene of Dissipation & vice, and I begin already to find my Morals corrupted.' She turned her cutting edge against Edward: 'Farmer Clarinbould died this morning, & I fancy Edward means to get some of his Farm if he can cheat Sir Brook enough in the agrement.' Dear Edward swindle his own brother-in-law? No wonder she relied on her letters being cut up: 'Seize upon the Scissors as soon as you possibly can on the receipt of this,' she wrote after blackening another reputation. As it turned out, Edward did not swindle Sir Brook, if only for lack of a spare £500 or £600; and 'What amiable Young Men!' wrote Jane sweetly when he and brother Frank, on leave, walked in from their shooting with two and a half brace of birds.

The jokes are well built, the sentence structure doing the work that makes the reader smile: 'Mr Richard Harvey is going to be married; but as it is a great secret, & only known to half the Neighbourhood, you must not mention it.' Perfect timing. The letters gossip, and describe simple dances given by Edward's Kentish in-laws and friends, one at Goodnestone, the Bridges' beautiful house, where country dances were accompanied by various ladies on the piano, and Jane opened the ball. No doubt they kept going late into that night with the table pushed aside in the long dining room, its doors open through into the oval hall, and the hall doors open on to the terrace; and after supper the Rowling party walked home in the dark and the rain, a mile across country, under two umbrellas. The rain was welcome that exceptionally hot summer, when people were dropping in the streets of London with the heat, and the walk in the fresh, damp night air must have been delectable. The heat continued, and Jane put down one of her best-known remarks a few days later: 'What dreadful Hot weather we have! – It keeps one in a continual state of Inelegance.' Elegance required the denial of most of the physical facts of life, like sweat, blood and tears; every young lady who aspired to take her place in society was required to defend herself perpetually against them.

In one letter she says a Kentish friend supposes that Cassandra is making her wedding clothes, which was no doubt true. Only now the sequence of letters ends, and in the gap between their ending and resumption came the ending of Cassandra's happiness and hopes. In the spring of 1797 the news of the death of Tom Fowle came from the West Indies. He was expected back from St Domingo in May 1797, 'but alas instead of his arrival news were received of his death'.[4] He had died of fever in February, and this is Eliza de Feuillide writing, informed by Jane. The whole family was afflicted around her, for Tom was James's close friend as well as Cassandra's intended husband. James wrote of his grief years later, imagining the body of Tom lying

> . . . where Ocean ceaseless pours
> His restless waves 'gainst Western India's shores;
> Friend of my Soul, & Brother of my heart! . . .

Our friendship soon had known a dearer tie
Than friendship's self could ever yet supply,
And I had lived with confidence to join
A much loved Sister's trembling hand to thine.[5]

The rhyme of 'join' and 'thine' startles for a moment as it reminds you about the Austen pronunciation; the feeling rings true, and touches the heart. James never forgot his friend, and for Cassandra the loss was an absolute one. But there was no screaming in agony or refusing to eat; religion, reason and constant employment were Cassandra's resource. 'Jane says that her sister behaves with a degree of resolution & propriety which no common mind could evince in so trying a situation,' wrote Eliza to Phila Walter.[6] Tom's legacy of £1,000 became her widow's portion; and she seems never to have thought of another man, although she was only in her twenties, and beautiful. Later Jane sometimes encouraged her to notice the attentions paid to her by other men, but she turned her face against them, and there were no more of the jokes that had made the younger sister praise her as 'the finest comic writer of the present age'. Cassandra hurried into spinsterly middle age, and the attachment to her sister became more important than ever: Jane was at once her child to be protected, her friend to be encouraged, and her sister to be given unconditional love.

While 1797 brought tragedy to Cassandra, it resolved the comic emotional tangles of two of her brothers and their cousin Eliza. None of them took Cass's view that you could love only once; Eliza liked to affirm that she was altogether immune to love. Some time in the summer of 1796 she had reappeared at Steventon, and James plucked up his courage to court her. It was a most suitable arrangement, after all, the young widower with a small daughter and his widowed cousin with her poor boy; all the family must approve, and they could live very comfortably together on his income and her fortune. So he danced attendance, riding over from Deane, offering up verse tributes, and whatever took her fancy. Eliza enjoyed being wooed, and toyed with the idea of accepting; then she went back to London to think about it and decided that James had not enough to tempt her, and that she preferred 'dear Liberty, & yet dearer flirtation'.[7] Being confined all the year round in a country parsonage would not do: sermon writing, hunting, tithe gathering and dinners with the same local squires for him; children, and tea with the squires' wives for her. She was used to something livelier. She liked to go to Brighton and other resorts: sea bathing for Hastings, with a little flirting with the officers for his mother, made a very acceptable programme. None of the tragedies life threw at Eliza stopped her from treating it as a game to be played for as much rational enjoyment as could be extracted from it, and at thirty-five she still dressed and behaved as a conquering beauty, carrying a pug dog and, when in London, taking her airings in the Park alongside the Princess of Wales. It was hard to see how James could be fitted into this picture.

James did not allow himself to brood over his cousin's refusal. The Austens were realists, he knew he must find a wife to run the domestic side of his life, and if one woman said no he must simply find another. He settled on a candidate so obvious that you suspect Mrs Austen of arranging matters with 26-year-old Mary Lloyd, who was indeed invited over from Ibthorpe to stay at Steventon. Not only were the Lloyds family friends, Mary had already lived in Deane parsonage with her widowed mother; marriage to James for her meant a return to an entirely familiar house. Mrs Austen expressed her delight at the engagement in a letter welcoming Mary as exactly the daughter-in-law she would have chosen. 'Had the Election been mine, you, my dear Mary, are the person I should have chosen for *James's Wife*, *Anna's Mother*, and *my Daughter*, being as certain, as I can be of anything in this uncertain world, that you will greatly increase & promote the happiness of each of the three.'[8]

Although Mary, whose face was scarred by smallpox, was jealous of James's old passion for Eliza, and Jane came to think she ruled his life too unrelentingly, the marriage was a happy one. James accepted that Eliza was never to be invited to the house; nor did any account of his visit to France and the de Feuillide estates survive, either in prose or verse; which is surprising, given his habit of recording the major events of his life, and the careful preservation of letters such as Mrs Austen's. Family tradition has it that Mary Austen continued to speak ill of Eliza, whom she long outlived, to the end of her days, so the bad feeling must have run deep. Eliza, all innocent of this – or at least pretending innocence – spoke kindly, if condescendingly, of James's choice, as 'not either rich or handsome, but very sensible & good humoured'.[9]

They were married at Hurstbourne Tarrant, near Ibthorpe, where Mrs Lloyd lived with Martha and Mary, on a snowy day in January. As James put it,

> Cold was the morn, & all around
> Whitened with new fallen snow the ground,
> Yet still the sun with cheering beam,
> Played on the hill, & vale, & stream,
> And almost gave to winter's face
> Spring's pleasing cheerfulness & grace.

Little Anna went home from Steventon to Deane; Mrs Chute called on the bride and found her 'perfectly unaffected, and very pleasant', and she fitted in well with all the local gentry, including Anna's grandfather General Mathew, who continued to look favourably on the household. Anna herself was not so pleased, and there were problems between her and her stepmother; and Jane, who was devoted to Anna, failed to warm to Mary as the years went by.

James and Mary were married at the start of 1797, and the news of Tom's death came in May. In June, Eliza de Feuillide took advice from a lawyer and asked to have the money put in trust for her by Warren Hastings removed from the trustees – one of them her Uncle Austen – and made directly available to her. This was promptly done, and six months afterwards, on the last day of the year, she married Henry in Marylebone Church. If the Austens were taken by surprise, Mr Austen at least was delighted enough with the marriage between his favourite son and his niece to send the considerable sum of £40 to the regiment for celebrations.[10] Champagne was not the drink in England in 1797, when the war was at its most dangerous point, but the money was enough for some considerable feasting.

Henry was twenty-six, Eliza ten years older; he had his officer's pay, recently augmented to about £300 a year by becoming regimental Paymaster and Captain, and she had what was left of her fortune, plus the possibility of a very large inheritance in France should the old system be restored there. Both were worldly enough to understand a bargain, sexual and financial, but it looks as though there was a genuine flame burning; one that had flickered, burnt up, been extinguished and revived itself several times over many years. Perhaps Eliza had been piqued by his engagement to Mary Pearson; she was also increasingly worried about the management of her own affairs, with rising rents in London, servants expecting to be paid more, and new taxes. She saw him in London in May 1797, heard he had given up all idea of the Church, and decided he had prospects; and they contrived to meet during the autumn in East Anglia, where his regiment was stationed and she took Hastings for sea bathing. In theory she was planning a visit to friends in the north in December, postponed only on account of Hastings's ill health; so the wedding was an almost impromptu affair. She wrote to Warren Hastings three days before the day from her house in Manchester Square, explaining that Henry had been

> for some time in Possession of a comfortable Income, and the excellence of his Heart, Temper, and Understanding, together with steady attachment to me, his Affection for my little Boy, and disinterested concurrence in the disposal of my Property in favor of this latter, have at length induced me to an acquiescence which I have withheld for more than two years.[11]

There was some truth and some fantasy here, for Henry had been engaged to Mary Pearson in 1796, as all the Austens knew – Jane indeed met her – and Eliza too, who had sympathized with him when he told her he had been jilted. He also owed Eliza money, and his actual income was sufficient for a single man but scarcely comfortable by the standards of Warren Hastings or Eliza herself.[12] The words about little Hastings were closer to reality; he was very ill in December, with convulsions and fever. He could now walk, it seems, but remained backward and delicate; fortunately Eliza had acquired a new 'confidential maid', the charming Françoise Bigeon from Calais, who had fled the Terror with her eighteen-year-old daughter Marie Marguerite and who now took over much of the care of Hastings. Eliza continued to lavish love on him too, and Henry was able to show enough affection to please her. Soon they were all off to Ipswich, she expressing skittish doubts about Henry's coachmanship, Hastings with Madame Bigeon 'on whose care you know I can thoroughly depend'.[13] They took a house with a garden, and the boy was able to be out in the fresh air most of the day which, even in February, Eliza thought better for him than medicine.

In the regiment, Eliza was warmly welcomed by the colonel, Lord Charles Spencer, 'so mild, so well bred, so good . . . if I was married to my third husband instead of my second I should still be in love with him', and Henry's particular friend Captain Tilson ('remarkably handsome').[14] She was delighted to be granted the precedence due to a *comtesse*, and there were calls, parties and dances with the officers and their wives, one so fashionably dressed that even Eliza was shocked by her failure to wear stays, her naked bosom and her ultra-fashionable little black wig: 'Such a mode of dress or undress would be remarked even in London so that you may judge what an uproar it makes in a Country Town.'[15] These excitements aside, Henry was demonstrating that he possessed an 'excellent heart, understanding & temper'; better still, he understood that he should let her have her own way in every-thing, knowing 'that I have not been much accustomed to controul & should probably behave rather awkwardly under it'; and did not mind her aversion to the word 'husband'.[16]

In the same cheerful letter she plans a visit to Hampshire and writes of the threatened French invasion, expected to take place on rafts with wheels. She expresses her belief that the French will make the attempt, and seize her fortune; and tells Phila that the regiment is increasing its numbers and holding itself in readiness to march at the shortest notice; she would not be Eliza if she did not add, 'I am going to be *drilled* & bespeak my regimentals without further delay.'

James, Edward, Henry and Cousin Eliza were now all married and settled; Cassandra had turned her face against the idea, but Jane had not. As though to make amends for her Irish nephew, Mrs Lefroy invited a young Fellow of Emmanuel College, Cambridge, to stay at Ashe in 1797; this was when Jane was working on *First Impressions*. The Revd Samuel Blackall was thought to be in want of a wife for the very good reason that he was due to give up his fellowship, with the prospect of his college appointing him to a good parish; it was the point at which most young clergymen set out on their wooing, and Mrs Lefroy seems to have persuaded herself that he and Jane might suit one another. Jane's laconic account of the meetings that followed suggests that Mr Blackall made his needs and hopes heavily obvious, but failed to charm. Their opportunities for conversation must have been carefully engineered at both parsonages. She warmed neither to him nor to the situation; even her much loved Mrs Lefroy could be tactless. The Lefroys invited him again at Christmas 1798, but although he wrote expressing a hope of 'creating to myself a nearer interest' with the Austen family, something held him back and he failed to return to press his suit in person. Jane was at her sourest explaining to Cassandra that it was 'most probable that our indifference will soon be mutual, unless his regard, which appeared to spring from knowing nothing of me at first, is best supported by never seeing me. Mrs Lefroy made no remarks on the letter, nor did she indeed say anything about him as relative to me. Perhaps she thinks she has said too much already.' You can only sympathize with Jane, wincing away from such clumsy matchmaking efforts and so leaden a pursuit. The best that can be got out of the episode is the hope that Mr Collins's manner of proposing to Elizabeth Bennet may owe something to Mr Blackall's efforts to interest Jane. In life, she bore him no malice. Years later, in 1813, hearing he was to be married, she recalled him as 'a peice of Perfection, noisy Perfection himself which I always recollect with regard'; and expressed the hope that his wife would be 'of a silent turn & rather ignorant' – adding politely, 'but naturally intelligent & wishing to learn'.

She was proud, and quick to suspect she was not wanted. Describing a ball she attended in January 1799, soon after her report on Blackall, she told Cassandra, 'I do not think I was very much in request –. People were rather apt not to ask me till they could not help it . . . There was one Gentleman, an officer of the Cheshire, a very good looking young Man, who I was told wanted very much to be introduced to me; – but as he did not want it quite enough to take much trouble in effecting it, we never could bring it about.' The acuteness that allowed her to formulate this uncomfortable account must have made her an alarming partner to any gentleman not quite sure of himself; however cheerfully she smiled, however lightly she trod the floor, her cleverness disquieted. In *Sense and Sensibility*, Lady Middleton reflects of Elinor and Marianne that 'because they were fond of reading, she fancied them satirical: perhaps without exactly knowing what it was to be satirical'. Similar thoughts no doubt went through the heads of ladies and gentlemen in Hampshire and in Kent.

13

Friends in East Kent

The ladies and gentlemen in Kent whom she risked disquieting with her cleverness were the Edward Austens and their circle; that some of them looked her over with sharp eyes of their own became clear many years later when her niece Fanny took up her pen to describe the impression made by Aunt Jane as a poor relation lacking in refinement. Perhaps she had in mind the sort of jokes Jane and Cassandra exchanged in their letters. When the widowed Mrs Knight, Edward's benefactress, was indisposed, Cass suggested she was really giving birth, and Jane went one further: 'I do not think she would be betrayed beyond an *Accident* at the utmost' – which looks as though she means an abortion.[1]

But Jane's accounts of her visits to Kent are sunny on the surface at least. They normally took place in the warmer months, and the Edward Austens lived very much more spaciously and comfortably than the Steventon Austens. Jane joked about their affluence, writing from Hampshire in winter: 'People get so horridly poor & economical in this part of the World, that I have no patience with them. – Kent is the only place for happiness, Everybody is rich there.'[2] She was in Kent in the summers of 1794 and 1796, and again in 1798, when she went with Cassandra and both parents to Godmersham for the first time. By then Edward and Elizabeth had four children – Fanny was followed by three sons – and were expecting a fifth; they had moved from their first home, Rowling, at the insistence of Mrs Knight, who thought they could do with the space she no longer needed, and took herself off to a house in Canterbury.

The Austen sisters soon became polite and respectful about Mrs Knight. They found she was unusually thoughtful and generous, and extended her generosity to Jane, to whom she gave what appears to have been a discreet annual allowance. Jane herself is our informant; she refers to it as her 'usual Fee', and it makes Mrs Knight her only known patron.[3] Jane's gratitude became real friendship; Mrs Knight at least was exempt from what she referred to as 'the happy indifference of East Kent wealth'.

Rowling was a good-sized family house, Godmersham of another order altogether. It occupies a wide, serene and beautiful grassy site in the valley of the River Stour, between Ashford and Canterbury, standing close to the old pilgrims' route. In 1798 there were deer in the park, and the gently rising hills were planted with picturesque circular copses, meant both to please the eye and provide shelter for game. The house was large and up to date, and set, like most English Palladian houses, in splendid isolation. Modern land-owners did not want their tenants' cottages cluttering the view, and the park was surrounded by walls which kept out everyone but family, guests and servants; a key was needed to get in and out of the private grounds.[4] The central block of the house, with its marble-paved and plaster-worked hall and large main rooms, dated from the 1730s; wings had been added in the 1770s, one for the kitchens, the other for the great library, in which Jane Austen found herself sitting on one occasion with 'five tables, eight and twenty chairs and two fires all to myself'. A Greek garden temple or summerhouse was set high up across the river, to catch the eye and provide an object for a stroll. There was another 'Hermitage' in the grounds, and a bathing house on the river; swimming and boating both became very popular with the children. There was a 'serpentine walk', walled gardens and an orchard; and an ice house, to keep the house supplied with that luxury. The church was within easy walking distance, through the park and out of one of the locked doors in the park wall; a few estate houses were clustered around it. Edward kept horses, carriages and chaises enough to make frequent and agreeable trips into Canterbury and visits to neighbours; he could spend sixty guineas on a pair of carriage horses without stopping to consider. The contrast with Steventon, where the Austens acquired a carriage in 1797 only to be obliged to give it up a year later, was marked.

At Godmersham the rituals of the year were kept with ceremony. Every January and every July there was a rent day, when the estate workers came to the house and Edward dined with his tenants, with a drum and pipes playing at the door of the servants' hall; the ladies did not attend. Christmas was celebrated with carols, card games, blind-man's buff, battledore, bullet pudding[5] and dancing; at Twelfth Night there was another feast, and the choosing of a King and Queen from among the children. Edward's and Elizabeth's wedding anniversary was also fêted by the whole family, and on their birthdays all the children got half-holidays from their lessons with their governesses. There were pets, birds and kittens, and Fanny even had her own cow; and she played at gardening and haymaking. Edward was a jolly father; he took Fanny riding, and one day at breakfast offered her sixpence if she would hold her tongue for five minutes. He enjoyed shooting and fishing, but did not hunt. In the summer there were cricket matches, and he organized trips to the seaside, especially Ramsgate with its pier. His duties as a land-owner included attending the Quarter Sessions in Canterbury; and when a French invasion was feared he was in charge of the volunteers, exercising them, parading them through the park and to church, and marching off to Ashford with them for two weeks' serious training.

The house, airy and spacious, was made for guests. It was maintained by dozens of servants. Fires were lit in all the bedrooms; breakfast was at ten, and dinner might be as late as six thirty; trays of food and drink would be brought to suit everyone's appetite in the hours between. Elizabeth's sisters were the most frequent guests, but Austens were regularly welcomed too. Henry Austen in particular gravitated towards Godmersham whenever he could; even after his marriage, he came several times a year, almost always on his own, like a favourite bachelor friend of the family.[6] He knew how to make himself part of the household, and was popular with the children, handing out sixpences and joining in their games. He would come in winter for the festivities, attend the Canterbury and Ashford balls and make up parties for the theatre, with dinner at the Fountain Inn; and he read Shakespeare aloud to anyone who would listen in the evenings. In summer he went to the races, or for rambles with Elizabeth; once as they walked in Chilham Park he gallantly saved her from an angry buck, getting a finger broken in the process. He would ride over to Ramsgate and Deal. He shot rabbits and went ferreting with Edward, and fished for pike and eels in the Stour; later in the year there would be partridges, pheasant, guinea fowl and landrails to shoot. He enjoyed his brother's good French wine, and drove his various vehicles, the chaise, the chair and the sociable. No wonder he called Godmersham 'The Temple of Delight' and wrote a poem in its praise, casting himself as a modern Canterbury pilgrim:

> Gentle Pilgrim, rest thy feet,
> Open is the gate to thee;
> Do not doubt that thou shalt meet
> Mirth and Hospitality.
> Elegance and grace shall charm thee,
> Reason shall with wit unite –
> Stirling sense shall here inform thee
> How domestic love can find
> All the blessings, which combined
> Make the Temple of Delight.[7]

Henry was Elizabeth's favourite brother-in-law, but Frank was often a visitor too, and when he became engaged to a Ramsgate girl, she was invited to stay. Charles was occasionally there, James brought his family for a few weeks one summer, and Anna was invited on her own when she was old enough. The Austen parents came in 1798. Cassandra was frequently invited to help Elizabeth at her confinements; Jane was there less often. According to her Hampshire niece Anna, who knew them all, Aunt Jane was not much liked by her sister-in-law; Elizabeth was, she wrote, 'a very lovely woman, highly educated, though not I imagine of much natural talent. Her tastes were domestic, her affections strong, though exclusive.' Anna went on to say that, as between Cassandra and Jane, Elizabeth 'very much preferred the elder Sister'. The reason? 'A little talent went a long way with the Goodnestone Bridgeses of that period, & much must have gone a long way too far.'[8] Although Anna's view must be taken cautiously, her comments ring true in the light of everything else we know.

They get confirmation from Fanny, whose memories of Aunt Jane and her deficiencies were jotted down privately in 1869, when she was in her seventies. Fanny remembered that she

was not so *refined* as she ought to have been from her *talent* . . . They [the Austens] were not rich & the people around with whom they chiefly mixed, were not at all high bred, or in short anything more than *mediocre* & *they* of course tho' superior in *mental powers* & *cultivation* were on the same level as far as *refinement* goes . . . Aunt Jane was too clever not to put aside all possible signs of 'common-ness' (if such an expression is allowable) & teach herself to be more refined . . . Both the Aunts [Cassandra & Jane] were brought up in the most complete ignorance of the World & its ways (I mean as to fashion &c) & if it had not been for Papa's marriage which brought them into Kent . . . they would have been, tho' not less clever & agreeable in themselves, very much below par as to good Society & its ways.[9]

This passage has upset and angered Jane Austen's admirers, and been taken as an example of disloyalty and the wrongheadedness of mid-Victorian ideas of refinement; but it should be remembered that Fanny was very fond of her aunt, and that she ended the passage, which was written in a private letter to her sister Marianne, 'If you hate all this I beg yr. pardon, but I felt it at my pen's end, & it chose to come along & speak the truth.' As such it is important, not least because it suggests how Jane was received at Godmersham: kindly, without a doubt, but with enough condescension for her to feel it. For instance, a visiting hairdresser who came regularly to cut and dress the ladies' hair made a point of lowering his rates for her, so obviously did she appear as a poor relative.

For an author who took social discomfort as one of her main themes, it meant that Godmersham was precious as a place in which to observe and record, but not always an entirely congenial place to be. There is nothing unusual about such a situation: in fact it is a classic one for a writer. No one observes the manners of a higher social class with more fascination than the person who feels they do not quite belong within the magic circle. Evelyn Waugh is the obvious example in this century, and there are others; Henry James gave authoritative accounts of life in the grandest English country houses without being more than an outside observer himself. Both learnt, like Austen, to 'put aside all possible signs of "common-ness"'; and, again like her, found themselves hailed as impeccable guides to the behaviour of true gentlemen and ladies.

Jane Austen's comments about the Kentish gentry were not always enthusiastic and sometimes less than polite: 'they called, they came and they sat and they went', was her description of the visit by one group of well-born ladies. Of the daughters of another she wrote, 'Caroline is not grown at all coarser than she was, nor Harriet at all more delicate.' Again: 'Ly Elizth for a woman of her age & situation, has astonishingly little to say for herself, & . . . Miss Hatton has not much more.' A Miss Fletcher, one of the many young women with whom she was supposed to make friends, had in her favour that she had enjoyed *Camilla*, but not much more; she seemed ready to believe the only interesting people in Canterbury were the young army officers. And family evenings at Godmersham could be soporific: 'I guess that Elizth. works, that you read to her, & that Edward goes to sleep,' suggested Jane to Cassandra when she was at Godmersham in December 1798.

None of Edward's many in-laws and their neighbours seem to have become her regular correspondents; instead, the closest friend she made in Kent was a Godmersham employee, the governess Anne Sharp. In Miss Sharp she found a truly compatible spirit. She was delicate in health, clever, keen on acting and quick enough with her pen to write a play for the children to perform; it was called *Pride Punished or Innocence Rewarded*, and was put on, although only to amuse the servants. And she was obliged to earn her bread by the only possible means, the hard labour of teaching. Jane took to her at once, and formed a lasting friendship with her; and although Anne Sharp left Godmersham in 1806, and worked mostly in the north of England afterwards, the two women kept up a regular correspondence.

Miss Sharp became 'my dearest Anne'. In 1809, feeling rather 'languid and solitary' at Godmersham, Jane could not help recalling a much more animated time when Miss Sharp had been present. Jane worried about her circumstances, and invited her to stay more than once; and she did manage to get her to Hampshire at least once, in the summer of 1815. She sent her copies of her books and cared for her opinion of them, some of which we know: *Pride and Prejudice* the favourite, *Mansfield Park* excellent, *Emma* somewhere between. Jane worried about her as she might about a sister. On one occasion she was concerned enough for her to express the desperate romantic wish that one of her employers, the widower Sir Wm. P. of Yorkshire, would fall in love with his children's governess: 'I do so want him to marry her! . . . Oh! Sir Wm – Sir Wm – how I will love you, if you will love Miss Sharp!'[10] Sir William, needless to say, did not oblige; neither he nor Miss Sharp were figures of romance, and it would take a later novelist to marry a working governess to her employer.

It was Jane, not anyone at Godmersham, who wrote to Miss Sharp to inform her when her erstwhile employer, Elizabeth Austen, died. Jane wrote one of her last letters to her dearest Anne; and after Jane's death, Cassandra felt it right to send Miss Sharp – as she still called her – a lock of her sister's hair and a few mementoes. The modest nature of the gifts underlines the poverty and thrift all three women took for granted: one was a bodkin that had been in Jane's sewing kit for twenty years. It was no doubt treasured for another thirty. Miss Sharp lived on into the 1850s. She was found 'horridly affected but rather amusing' by James Austen's son, a judgement that recalls Phila Walter's description of Jane Austen herself as 'whimsical and affected'. It seems that in Kent, Jane found a *semblable* and made her into one of her very few close friends; someone who was neither rich nor particularly happy, but who was entirely congenial. What's more, she was not shared with the family; she was entirely her own friend. That she was also a working woman who was later to set up and run her own boarding school in Everton suggests a good deal about what interested and attracted Jane Austen.

To appear whimsical and affected is a common form of self-defence. Silence is another. Jane Austen's silences are especially problematical because it is hard to know how much they are real silences, how much the effect of Cassandra's scissors. Her silence about politics is famous, and generally taken to represent agreement with the Tory views of her family. As a child, she scribbled 'Nobly said! Spoken like a Tory!' in the margin of Goldsmith's *History of England*, but it is her only known rallying cry. After her death, a niece, trying to recall what opinions she had expressed on public events, was unable to think of 'any word or expression' relating to them; and if she did keep her Tory loyalties, they did not extend to liking the local Tory MP.[11]

Politics were of the masculine world, apart. So were field sports. Henry declared confidently that Cowper was her favourite moral writer in verse, and especially his long poem *The Task*, which she could indeed quote from memory; but she kept quiet about Cowper's detestation of field sports and their cruelty: 'the savage din of the swift pack . . . detested sport,/That owes its pleasures to another's pain,/That feeds upon the sobs and dying shrieks/Of harmless nature'.[12] Living as she did among brothers and friends for whom hunting, coursing and shooting were favourite pursuits, it would have been awkward to invoke her favourite poet's views to them. Henry hardly had a gun out of his hand when he was at Godmersham, all Edward's sons were brought up to field sports, and James and his son were passionate about hunting; so if, privately, she shared Cowper's feelings, she chose not to say so. The only mentions of field sports in her letters are uncritical. In *Mansfield Park* she sends Edward Bertram and Henry Crawford hunting together, and she is sympathetic to ten-year-old Charles Blake's excitement about his first hunt, in *The Watsons*. There is no evidence that Jane Austen herself was ever at a meet; but loyalty to her brothers appears either to have overborne or at least silenced Cowper's moral teaching.

Women's rights were another matter on which she kept quiet. Nobody could live through the 1790s without being aware of Mary Wollstonecraft's *Vindication of the Rights of Woman*, which was published in 1792 and caused a furore; but its opening chapter was not best calculated to appeal to a parson's daughter with two brothers in the navy and, from 1793, one in a militia regiment. *A Vindication* begins with an attack on the monarchy and goes straight on to the army: 'a standing army is incompatible with freedom' – 'every corps is a chain of despots' – 'the needy *gentleman*, who is to rise, as the phrase turns, by his merit, becomes a servile parasite or vile pander'. So much for Henry. Next the navy: 'the naval gentlemen, come under the same description, only their vices assume a different and a grosser cast . . . mind is equally out of the question': that was for Francis and Charles. Then the Church: 'the blind submission imposed at college to forms of belief serves as a novitiate to the curate, who must obsequiously respect the opinion of his rector or patron, if he mean to rise in his profession. Perhaps there cannot be a more forcible contrast between the servile dependent gait of a poor curate and the courtly mien of a bishop. And the respect and contempt they inspire render the discharge of their separate functions equally useless.'[13] This was for her father, her brother James, and half their cousins and friends.

It was out of the question that she would endorse any of these sentiments. This at any rate is the first response. Thinking again, Austen's own presentation of certain army officers, and her portraits of some clergymen as uncharitable, snobbish and sycophantic, suggests she might not entirely dissent from them. And Wollstonecraft's central arguments for the better education and status of women must at the very least have caught her attention. Add to this her ownership of Robert Bage's *Hermsprong*, and we can be certain she was aware of them. Bage was a radical and 'scarcely a Christian' (in his own words), outspoken in his support for Wollstonecraft's claims for women, which are invoked and approved by his hero.[14] Hermsprong indeed challenges every aspect of Tory thinking, as a philosophical American who believes in equality, simplicity and plain speaking as well as women's rights, and confronts the English class system in the shape of an unregenerate old West Country peer and his corrupt entourage of priest, lawyer and mistress. The great charm of the book is in the dialogue, which glints and sparkles with cleverness, much of it in the mouth of Hermsprong's chief ally Maria Fluart, a young woman of independent mind, quick tongue and a great capacity for upsetting the plans of the peer. When he demands a kiss and complains of her resistance, she exclaims, 'A kiss! Lord bless me, I thought, from . . . the mode of your attack, you had wanted to undress me.' Hermsprong and Fluart use frank speaking as a weapon against opponents accustomed to polite lies and social forms, and his frank speakers carry the day. That particular opposition was taken up by Austen in *Sense and Sensibility*, with different results. Her formal silence on the position of women is qualified by the way in which her books insist on the moral and intellectual parity of the sexes; and her delighted remark about the young Oxford man who 'has heard that *Evelina* was written by Dr Johnson' signals her awareness of the situation addressed by Wollstonecraft and Bage.[15]

If she is not silent about religion, she is quiet. Religion is there, as you would expect for the daughter of the parsonage, an essential part of the fabric of her life. It was not something to be questioned or investigated, and never a source of wonder or terror, as it was for Johnson and Boswell. Family prayers, sermons and the sacrament are occasionally mentioned in the letters, but religion is chiefly, and silently, associated with the duty of charity to the poor; more of a social than a spiritual factor. No one prays in her novels, no one is shown in church, or seeking spiritual guidance either from God or a clergyman. Marianne Dashwood, in the depths of misery and contrition, speaks of making atonement to God and regulating and checking her love for Willoughby 'by religion, by reason, by constant employment', but we are not shown her religion in action. More is made of Fanny Price's faith, which gives her courage to resist what she thinks wrong; it also makes her intolerant of sinners, whom she is ready to cast aside, just as Mr Collins recommends that the Bennets should cast aside the sinful Lydia and Wickham. Austen the novelist was interested in the way religion could be invoked in different causes and practised in different styles; about inner spiritual struggles she has nothing to say.

14

Travels with My Mother

Mrs Austen gave a very frank personal reason for welcoming Mary Lloyd as James's wife in 1797. 'I look forward to you as a real comfort to me in my old age, when Cassandra is gone into Shropshire, & Jane – the Lord knows where.' There is something more than uncertainty in the dash and the 'Lord knows': a throwing up of hands, an implied doubt, perhaps, as to whether Jane was likely to make either a comfortable wife or a comfort for her mother's old age. Jane was unpredictable; elusive; and at least as formidable as Mrs Austen herself in her mental and satirical powers. Mrs Austen liked laughing at other people, but no one likes to be laughed at.

As a mother, she wanted her daughters to marry. What else was there? Let them be as lucky as her niece Jane Cooper, who had married her splendid naval officer, already knighted for his successes against the French. Cousin Jane was now established as Lady Williams, however Jane Austen might mock 'his Royal Highness Sir Thomas Williams'; and he was in a position to be good to Charles, who was happy to serve under his command. His wife was always made very welcome at Steventon. Family structures were strengthened, family advancement helped along, by such good marriages.

Only nothing was secure. Within a few months of Mrs Austen writing her letter to Mary, Tom Fowle was dead, and Cassandra no longer had a future in Shropshire. The following year Jane Williams was thrown from her gig by a runaway dray horse colliding with her as she drove along the lanes of the Isle of Wight. She was killed, leaving Sir Thomas a widower only six years after their wedding at Steventon.

Jane Austen showed no sign of finding a husband, either among the local young men – Digweeds, Terrys, Portals, Harwoods, Tom

Chute – or from further afield. She and Cassandra got on with all their old friends and their brothers' friends, but it was sisterly stuff and led to nothing. Cass's bereavement seemed to be pushing them both into – aunthood? spinsterhood? self-sufficiency? – it was hard to say. Their father took to referring to them, affectionately but collectively, as 'the girls'. Their niece Anna, returned to Deane to live with her father and stepmother, remembered them from these years as an almost inseparable pair:

> I recollect the frequent visits of my two Aunts, & how they walked in wintry weather through the sloppy lane between Steventon & Dean in pattens, usually worn at that time even by Gentlewomen. I remember too their bonnets: because though precisely alike in colour, shape & material, I made it a pleasure to guess, & I believe always guessed right, which bonnet & which Aunt belonged to each other.[1]

There is something depressing about the choice of identical bonnets for women in their mid-twenties, almost as though they were signalling that they were indivisible and indifferent to establishing any individual style.

When they were not together, they wrote to one another constantly. 'My Uncle is quite surprised at my hearing from you so often,' wrote Jane to Cass from Bath in 1799, a smooth remark with a rude implication, that their uncle was nosy and impertinent. Yes, they did write to each other very often; they needed to because they could speak to one another freely, their letters acting as safety valves for exasperation, dissipating anger and disappointment, helping them to brave the world as well as carrying gossip, jokes, travel notes and chat about their sad-sounding clothes. Cassandra sometimes tried her hand at a piece of formal prose, sending one such from Godmersham to Steventon in the winter of 1798; 'your essay on happy fortnights is highly ingenious', Jane told her, but she made no attempt at any essays or fine writing herself in her letters. They were only sharpening stones against which she polished the small knives of her prose.

She will suddenly slip in a joke about a neighbouring clergyman's wife, Mrs Hall, giving birth to a dead child, 'some weeks before she expected, oweing to a fright. – I suppose she happened unawares to look at her husband.' E. M. Forster called this 'the whinnying of harpies', but surely it is much closer to the deliberate boyish bad taste of the juvenile stories, an impromptu piece of outrageousness that flew from the end of her pen, because Dr Hall was so repellent. Further on in the same letter she talks comfortably of a new baby in the village, for whom there are baby clothes to be given from the parsonage.

There are other surprises dropped in. 'I do not wonder at your wanting to read *first impressions* again, so seldom as you have gone through it, & that so long ago.' She acknowledges the existence of her work, even though she never discusses it. The denial of initial capital letters in the title is like a lowering of the voice; she is almost unwilling to mention *First Impressions*. But there is no false modesty. It is worth rereading, in spite of the publishers' rejection; later it would be worth rewriting.

Both sisters and parents were at Godmersham in the summer of 1798, and Cassandra stayed on to help Elizabeth with a new baby while Jane travelled home with their parents. The next group of letters offers a detailed picture of her day-to-day relations with her parents; they also offer some more knife sharpening, as Jane turns her mother's fussing about her own health into a running joke. Mrs Austen began to feel unwell during the first lap of their complicated journey. She had to be ministered to, twice with medicinal bitters and several times with pieces of bread; once they reached the Dartford Inn she managed to recover enough to eat a dinner of beefsteaks and boiled chicken. She decided to share the double-bedded room they were offered with Jane, leaving Mr Austen the peace of a single room. Jane makes no comment on this decision, although her next remark, 'My day's journey has been pleasanter in every respect than I expected. I have been very little crowded and by no means unhappy', must rate as a qualified expression of pleasure.

At the inn her father settled down to read a novel while her mother sat by the fire. Jane meanwhile discovered that her boxes had disappeared, with all her money, letters and papers. The landlord thought they must have been put on a coach bound for Gravesend, on their way to the West Indies; and so they had, but were quickly pursued and rescued. As the family party journeyed on towards Staines the next morning, her mother grew dramatically worse, with 'heat in her throat' and 'that particular kind of evacuation which has generally preceded her Illnesses'. Reaching Basingstoke at last, they went straight to Lyford, the family doctor, who prescribed laudanum, twelve drops to be taken at bedtime. Mrs Austen then settled down for a cosy chat about the rival virtues of dandelion tea. They had, incidentally, just missed the excitement of another invalid passing through Basingstoke on his way to Windsor from Weymouth; the town had been full of local people gathered to cheer the King.[2]

Mrs Austen was extracted from Lyford's and taken the last few miles home to Steventon. Jane was now in charge of the laudanum, rather pleased with the responsibility of dropping out the dose for her mother. When James appeared from Deane to greet the returning travellers, Mrs Austen had another revival of spirits and another good talk before retiring to bed; once there, Mr Lyford's good laudanum knocked her out and kept her in bed all the next day. Jane and her father took their three thirty dinner alone. 'How strange!' she wrote to Cass; strange to be giving the orders in the kitchen, strange to be the only Austen child left at home, sitting at the big table. Mr Austen was considering how to help Frank, now in the Mediterranean, stuck at the rank of lieutenant; some paternal intervention in the shape of letters to the great and powerful was needed. Charles, at eighteen also a lieutenant, was eager to be transferred from home waters to a ship more likely to see active service. Mr Austen wrote to Admiral Gambier, a connection of James's first wife; Admiral Gambier consulted with Lord Spencer, First Lord of the Admiralty and cousin of Henry's retiring colonel and friend. His letters were effective, and by Christmas Frank was promoted to Commander and Charles moved to a frigate. Henry was also gazetted Captain and officially appointed Paymaster of the Regiment; it was a triple triumph for the fighting Austens.

At Steventon the days went quietly by, with Jane ordering the household and giving what time she could to writing. From a passing pedlar she bought herself six shifts and four pairs of stockings. Mrs Austen supplied sixteen shillings for a subscription to a new Basingstoke library, which Jane put in Cassandra's name. Her father worried about his sheep and his falling tithes, bought a copy of Boswell's *Life of Johnson*, and prepared to take a special service of Thanksgiving for Lord Nelson's victory on the Nile; in the evening he read Cowper aloud, to which Jane listened 'when I can'. Mrs Austen lay in bed, working up tremendous symptoms which did not always tally with Dr Lyford's diagnoses. Digweeds and Harwoods called, there were problems with servants – a new washerwoman 'does not look as if anything she touched would ever be clean, but who knows?' and Mary, heavily pregnant, took on a young girl at Deane 'to be her Scrub', whom James feared might not be strong enough. A new maid arrived at Steventon too, who cooked well, sewed well and would learn the work in the dairy. Jane unpacked some books returned from Winchester, where they had been bound. Two local women died in child-birth, a piece of news kept carefully from Mary. Mrs Austen did not propose to repeat her feat of walking through the night to attend the birth; this time she asked to be told nothing until it was over; and soon it was. James and Mary had a son, and all was well.

The baby, James-Edward, had large, dark eyes and became a favourite nephew. Jane judged his mother 'not tidy enough in her appearance; she has no dressing-gown to sit up in; her curtains are all too thin', comparing Mary unfavourably with Elizabeth at Godmersham, 'really a pretty object with her nice clean cap put on so tidily and her dress so uniformly white and orderly'. It was obviously unfair to hold up the rich land-owner's lady as a model for the country parson's wife; but Jane was imagining herself with a baby, as she made clear. Mary did not 'manage matters in such a way as to make me want to lay in myself'. Surrounded by pregnant sisters-in-law and neighbours, she allowed herself moments when she dreamt of being in their place, with a husband, a home of her own, and a baby. Why not? She was only twenty-two.

In December, Mrs Austen recovered enough to appear downstairs. 'My mother made her *entrée* into the dressing-room through crowds of admiring spectators yesterday afternoon.' She still, however, com-plained sometimes of 'an Asthma, a Dropsy, Water in her Chest & Liver Disorder', as well as unsettled bowels. Hypochondria on such a heroic scale could be greeted only with delight. 'Gouty swelling & sensation about the ancles' were the next symptoms; they did not interfere with her mother's good spirits, or with Jane's. Nor did they prevent Jane from spending a few days at Manydown with Catherine Bigg, and attending a ball at which she danced every one of the twenty dances. 'In cold weather & with few couples I fancy I could just as well dance for a week together as for half an hour.' She also discovered the pleasure of walking alone. 'I enjoyed the hard black Frosts of last week very much, & one day while they lasted walked to Deane by myself. – I do not know that I ever did such a thing in my life before,' she told Cass, a most surprising remark when you think of the way she makes Elizabeth Bennet scramble unescorted about the countryside. Now that Jane had begun, she must have often walked alone along the lanes made passable by the frost, her feet clinking in their pattens, her imagination working.

In Kent, Cassandra was also going to balls, including one graced by Prince William, the King's nephew. Jane spent a quiet Christmas Day at Deane with the Harwoods, entertained the Digweeds and James at home two days later – 'We shall be a nice silent party I suppose' – and saw the registration of her new nephew's christening at Deane on New Year's Day, 1799. The news of Frank's promotion brought many congratulations, and there were more parties, and a grand ball given by the Dorchesters at Kempshott Park. Eliza Chute noted it as a good one, with soup and sandwiches, and stayed till three; Jane left much earlier, going back to her brother James's house, where she and Martha Lloyd lay talking companionably until two in the morning in the new nursery bed, nurse and baby evicted on to the floor.

In January she was able to revive the regular comic feature of the letters: 'It began to occur to me . . . that I had been somewhat silent as to my mother's health for some time, but I thought you could have no difficulty in divining its exact state – you, who have guessed so much stranger things. She is tolerably well . . . She would tell you herself that she has a very dreadful cold in her head at present . . . &c.' As it happened, Edward was also suffering ill health at Godmersham. He had his mother's gift for interesting symptoms, including 'glow in his hands and feet' and 'Bowel complaints, Faint-nesses & Sicknesses'; and he was making a plan to go to Bath in the spring with Elizabeth and their two eldest, and to invite his mother and Jane to join them.

Jane had been to Bath once before, staying with Uncle and Aunt Leigh-Perrot during a wet and gloomy November, and she had a good reason to want to go back, since much of the action of the book on which she was working (*Northanger Abbey*) took place there. Cass returned from Kent in March to take charge of the household, and Jane and her mother prepared to set off westwards in May.

Bath was still the most famous resort town in England, a modern city that had been expanding around its Roman remains and fifteenth-century Abbey church for the past sixty years, blessed with planners and architects who seemed incapable of getting things wrong as they raised its new streets and terraces in steep, spectacular patterns above the loop of the River Avon. It had the best communications – the London–Bath road was the most perfectly maintained in the country – and it was the place to which everyone who wanted to see and be seen came. Cheltenham and Brighton would both seek to eclipse it, but never quite succeed. People came to take the waters and receive the ministrations of the many doctors who settled there, as Uncle Leigh-Perrot did for his gout, and Edward intended to do for whatever he was suffering from; he would drink and bathe in the waters, and even try the new electrical treatment, administered either as a spark or through an alarming-sounding flesh-brush.

You could also rely on the best available entertainment in Bath. London actors and actresses loved to appear in the theatre. There were concerts, indoor and outdoor, often accompanied by fireworks. There were public breakfasts and carefully organized dances in the two separate Assembly Rooms. There were libraries in which you could gossip as you read the newspapers; above all there were the other people, their fashionable clothes, their outrageous hats, their curricles, their horses, their conversation, their shopping and their symptoms. Bath represented an acme of civilized urban life in which men and women of sufficient means could enjoy themselves and entertain one another in an agreeable setting, very little distracted by the presence of the poor for whom they were responsible at home on their estates; a few beggars and a few pickpockets were less troubling.

Mrs Austen knew the city well from before her marriage, and her brother Leigh-Perrot now came regularly with his wife, and had taken No. 1, the Paragon, an imposing terraced house with views over the countryside. Like many Bath terraces, the Paragon had no private gardens but faced on to a public one; but then the attraction of the city lay chiefly in public activity, public gardens and parties, rather than in domestic pleasures. There was something theatrical about the lay-out of the whole town; everyone was on show, and aware of it. Literature paid its tribute to Bath as much as life. Jane knew it from many sources: in Charlotte Smith's *Emmeline*, it was a city in which you could be anonymous, hiding in lodgings during an indiscreet pregnancy. Charlotte Lennox's heroine Arabella, in *The Female Quixote*, caused a stir by appearing veiled in the Pump Room, and another by being rude to the Bath beaux. Sheridan had eloped from Bath with his first wife, and then made it the scene for *The Rivals*; and she had already sent characters of her own on jaunts to Bath. 'The unmeaning Luxuries of Bath' were warned against in *Love and Freindship*; she also made it the home of 'Mr Clifford', characterized as owner of a magnificent collection of vehicles and horses, and not much else – a clear prediction of the man who was about to sell Edward a pair of carriage horses for sixty guineas, and who 'has all his life thought more of Horses than of anything else'.

The Edward Austens and their party found lodgings in a corner house in Queen Square, within easy reach of the Pump Room, the Upper Assembly Rooms and the Paragon. Mrs Austen and her daughter had connecting bedrooms on the second floor, 'two very nice sized rooms, with dirty Quilts and everything comfortable'; a kitten ran about the staircase and the landlady was 'a fat woman in mourning'. Jane acted as a good aunt to Fanny and Edward, helping them to write letters. Elizabeth kindly presented Jane with a hat; perhaps she had noticed the twin bonnets. They planned to attend a gala evening in Sydney Gardens, although Jane's enthusiasm for the music was oddly expressed: 'the Concert will have more than its' usual charm with me, as the Gardens are large enough for me to get pretty well beyond the reach of its sound'. Uncle Leigh-Perrot overwalked himself and had to rest, but Jane enjoyed some rambles into the country with new acquaintances, one of whom at least lived up to her best hopes, for it was here she met Mr Gould, a very young man who had 'just entered of Oxford, wears Spectacles, & has heard that Evelina was written by Dr Johnson'.*

* *Evelina* was published anonymously in 1778. Its success was tremendous and its author quickly revealed as Miss Frances Burney, who had written it in secret, unknown even to her father. Dr Johnson was one of its warmest admirers, preferring it to any of Fielding's novels.

Edward had to be home at the beginning of July for the Godmersham rent day, but Mrs Austen was eager for more travels. She wanted to make a grand progress, visiting her Leigh cousins in Adlestrop, her nephew Edward Cooper now installed at Harpsden in her childhood home, and yet another cousin, Mrs Cooke, at Great Bookham in Surrey. Jane was not enthusiastic, and told Cassandra she would prefer to have Martha Lloyd to spend the summer with them at home instead. She may have found the prospect of her Aunt Cooke particularly difficult, because she had just published a novel; and although it was anonymous, the family was expected to read it. *Battleridge, an Historical Tale Founded on Facts* was set during the interregnum; the plot turns on a missing document which will restore an estate to its rightful, royalist owners, and is revealed through a dream in its hiding place, a false-bottomed chest. There are other dramatic moments: a young woman is abducted from her 'favourite haunt, the Grotto' on a moonlit night by two horsemen who imprison her in a tower, where she has to sleep in an old ebony bed carved with frightful faces. Mrs Cooke was using established Gothic conventions, and particularly admired Mrs Radcliffe ('Queen of the *tremendous*'); but her false-bottomed chest and lost document prompt a suspicion that Jane, who was working on a first draft of *Northanger Abbey* when *Battleridge* appeared, may have seized on these details with some glee. There could be an element of family teasing in her mockery of Gothic fictional clichés.

She did, however, give way to her mother's wishes, and accompanied her on the cousinly visits. While they were travelling, disaster befell the Leigh-Perrots. Rich Aunt Jane was accused of shoplifting and, almost unimaginably, taken to prison. She was accused of stealing a piece of lace by a Bath shopkeeper. The assistant ran after her after she had left the shop with a purchase, and the 'stolen' lace was found either in her parcel or her pocket – it is not clear which – and she said it must have been put there by mistake when she was served in the shop. The shopkeeper asked for the Leigh-Perrots' address, which they gave, and four days later a constable appeared at the Paragon with a warrant. Mrs Leigh-Perrot, in her mid-fifties and childless, was committed to prison on the sworn depositions of the shop people, accused of a crime that could carry a death sentence, since the lace was worth more than a shilling. In practice, were she found guilty, she would be likely to be transported to Australia for fourteen years; in effect, the equivalent of a capital sentence to a woman of her age and habits.

Her husband supported her with unswerving devotion, insisting on remaining with her in the house of the prison keeper, Mr Scadding, at Somerset County Gaol in Ilchester, to which she was now sent; prison cell and prison garb she was spared, given her social standing and income. But the Scaddings' house was not what she was used to: 'Vulgarity, Dirt, Noise from Morning till Night. The People, not conscious that this can be Objectionable to anybody, fancy we are very happy, and to do them justice they mean to make us so.'[3] The Miss Scaddings sometimes entertained them with music, but the little Scaddings put pieces of toast on Mr Leigh-Perrot's venerable knees and trickled beer down his sleeves; their mother cleaned a knife by licking the fried onions off it; two dogs and three cats disputed the food, the smoke went everywhere but up the chimney, and the children's bedroom, next to the Leigh-Perrots', was as noisy as Bedlam. It must be said that, in this extremity, Mrs Leigh-Perrot not only found descriptive powers almost matching the brush of Hogarth, she also behaved with the greatest dignity. When Mrs Austen offered to send one or both of her daughters to share her miseries, she refused to allow 'these Elegant young women' to suffer alongside her.[4] Whatever Jane thought of her mother's offer, she was no doubt grateful to her aunt for the refusal.

There were some who believed that Mrs Leigh-Perrot was guilty, and her own counsel gossiped maliciously about her being a klepto-maniac, mocking James Leigh-Perrot's uxoriousness for good measure. There is another story of her attempting to steal a plant from a gardener's greenhouse to lend credence to the first accusation, but it may be no more than tattle; it also allegedly happened in Bath, a few years later, in 1804.[5] The more general opinion was that her accusers had been trying to entrap and blackmail her, even though they set about it very inefficiently if that was their object. After seven months with the Ilchester prison keepers, she came to trial at Taunton assizes. Mrs Austen again offered her daughters for the trial, and again Mrs Leigh-Perrot expressed the view that a court room was an unsuitable place for young ladies. She herself had no choice, and stood up in front of what must have seemed a quite terrifying packed court room. She spoke for herself, briefly but to great effect; and after this many testimonials to her character were read out in court. The judge summed up and the jurors found her 'not guilty' in ten minutes; there was much weeping and kissing. The Leigh-Perrots were free, although their expenses came to nearly £2,000, and nobody subsequently prosecuted the shopkeeper, who continued to flourish; but 'I stand some chance of being killed by Popularity', wrote Mrs Leigh-Perrot drily.

Dr Johnson, so much admired by Jane, had written magisterially in the *Rambler* against the sentencing laws of England, particularly the imposition of the same punishment of death for petty theft as for murder; and a story like Mrs Leigh-Perrot's underlines their cruelty and absurdity. Even if she were guilty, nobody could think it right for an elderly woman committing such a misdemeanour to be imprisoned, let alone threatened with hanging or transportation to Botany Bay. In this century, women in her situation have committed suicide after being prosecuted for shoplifting. It was just as well that Jane Leigh-Perrot was a tough old bird with a supremely loyal husband. Jane never referred to the case – no doubt it became an unmentionable subject in the family – but it did not make her love her aunt any better. She found her irritating, as a penniless niece is likely to find a rich, sometimes overbearing and ungenerous old aunt.

James Austen, expected heir to the Leigh-Perrot fortune, had promised to be at his aunt's trial with his wife. Instead, he fell and broke his leg in the heavy snow of February 1800, and could not get out at all. Eliza Chute recorded his absence from church, and Charles Powlett took his services for him. She was busy making broth to feed her villagers. Times were very hard for the poor, and getting worse. At Deane, Mrs Lefroy had set up a 'Straw Manufactory' to enable the women and children of the district to earn a few pence by making mats and other small objects. But such charity could do very little. Eliza Chute wrote to a friend expressing her sympathy with the Hampshire labourers:

> the poor are dissatisfied & with reason: I much fear that wheat will not be cheap this year: & every other necessary of life enormously dear: the poor man cannot purchase those comforts he ought to

have: beer, bacon, cheese. Can one wonder that discontents lurk in their bosoms: I cannot think their wages sufficient, & the pride of a poor man (& why shd we [not] allow him some pride) is hurt, when he is obliged to apply to the parish for relief, & too often receives harsh answers from the overseers. I own I think our political horizon still lowers.[6]

This is a remarkably intelligent and sympathetic letter for the wife of a fox-hunting Tory; she did not always see eye to eye with Chute. In the same letter she expresses herself no less cogently on the position of wives.

Mr Chute . . . seems to think it strange that I should absent myself from him for four & twenty hours when he is at home, tho' it appears in the natural order of things that he should quit me for business or pleasure, such is the difference between husbands & wives. The latter are sort of tame animals, whom the men always expect to find at home ready to receive them: the former are lords of the creation free to go where they please.

A woman with an ironic and independent voice like this sounds a neighbour worth knowing. But there was still no meeting of minds between Eliza Chute and Jane Austen. Jane may have made up her mind to see condescension where Eliza was really shy; she may have found Jane alarming. A case of pride and prejudice, even. The Chutes did of course live very much grander lives; for instance, they attended the great music meeting at Winchester in October 1800, when Haydn's *Creation* was given in the cathedral before 500 county families – Sheridan was among them – and followed by a ball. The Austens could not aspire to such entertainments. In 1800 they were not having an easy time. The farm brought in less than £300, and tithes were affected by the general depression. Like Mrs Chute, Jane writes of distress in the neighbourhood, of bailiffs and seizures of houses, and of taking clothes to the village. And although they were trying to improve the Steventon garden, turfing and planting, and even spending something on new tables for the house, Mr and Mrs Austen were both tired. In November a storm brought down two of their elm trees close to the house with a great crash, and broke the maypole that had borne the weathercock ever since the children could remember. It was a gloomy winter for everyone.

There were no cheerful visits from Henry and Eliza. In March 1799 Henry had been sent to Ireland with his regiment, required to guard the coast against the French and keep down the continuing disaffection among the Irish. He remained there for seven months, mostly in Dublin, and made himself agreeable to the Viceroy, Lord Cornwallis, officially Governor-General of India, but sent by the government to Ireland to crush the rebellion. Such rich and powerful figures appealed to Henry, and he was quick to think of how they might be useful to him after he left the army. With his experience as Paymaster, he began to think of becoming a banker and to discuss it with friends in the regiment.

Meanwhile Eliza retreated to what she called her 'hermitage' near Dorking, in Surrey. She said she preferred her piano, harp and books to any other company; in confirmation, a printed volume of 'Feuilles de Terpsichore', pieces to be sung at the harp, and another of hand-copied songs by Purcell, Handel, Haydn and Mozart, bear her name, 'Mrs Henry Austen' and 'Eliza Austen, 19 August 1799'.[7] Her gaiety was in eclipse. She told Phila, who wrote soliciting help for her brother from Warren Hastings, that she had 'the most insuperable aversion to asking favours'. Her health was poor, and her son's worse: he suffered from frequent and violent epileptic fits. 'Their effects on his mental powers, if his life should not be destroyed by them, must be of the most melancholy nature, and are a constant source of grief to me.' She went on sadly, 'mental & bodily sufferings are ever closely connected'.[8]

15

Three Books

When Jane Austen wrote the first draft of *Pride and Prejudice*, she was twenty, the same age as Elizabeth Bennet. By the time it was published in 1813 she was thirty-seven: almost old enough to be Elizabeth's mother. Seventeen years must be one of the longest delays ever between composition and publication. *Sense and Sensibility* went through the same long, drawn-out process, with a sixteen-year gap between first draft and publication. *Northanger Abbey* took twenty years to find a publisher, and did not appear in print until its author was dead. It is sobering to think how easily any of them might have been lost.

She made some copies; but neither the copies nor any of her good care help us to know how the earlier versions differed from the later. There are no manuscripts of either drafts or final versions of any of the published novels.[1] It makes talking about her revisions almost entirely guesswork. You can have fun speculating whether she was nineteen, or twenty-one, or thirty-five when she wrote a particular passage, but proving anything is like trying to carve a solid shape out of jelly. We know that *Pride and Prejudice* was originally longer than the final version, because she says she 'lop't and crop't' it, and we can suppose that the dialogue was more finely characterized with each revision; there must also be some lost passages we should dearly like to see. A puzzling thread from an early version that hangs into the final one is that Jane Bennet is a horsewoman, while Elizabeth only walks, which seems contrary to their characters. How this came about is anyone's guess; something lop't that should not have been. There are some small late insertions such as references to Scott's poetry and Maria Edgeworth's novel *Belinda*, which cannot have been in the early drafts; beyond this, no certainties.[2] My own assumption is that the central characters and plot structures were in place by 1800, when she had three completed novels, one of them already thought good enough for publication by her father, and that although she did more work on them, they were substantially the books we know. And although the titles of two of them changed before they were published, I shall call them by their final names.

The first striking thing about these three early novels is that each approaches its subject in a radically different way. *Sense and Sensibility* is – roughly speaking – a debate, *Pride and Prejudice* a romance, and *Northanger Abbey* a satire, a novel about novels and novel reading. You might expect a young writer to keep working within the same formula several times, learning as she goes. Not so with Jane Austen. She was too inventive and too interested in the techniques of fiction to settle in any one mode, and she tackled the problems of three such diverse forms with astonishing skill.

In *Sense and Sensibility* Elinor and Marianne act out a debate about behaviour in which Austen compares the discretion, polite lies and carefully preserved privacy of one sister with the transparency, truth-telling and freely expressed emotion of the other. Austen is considering how far society can tolerate openness, and what its effect on the individual may be. The question was keenly debated in the 1790s as part of a wider political discussion, with radical writers like William Godwin and Robert Bage favouring the complete openness practised by Marianne, conservatives insisting that the preservation of the social fabric requires an element of secrecy and hypocrisy. These were serious questions, and one of the things that gives the book its intense interest is that Austen starts as though she is favouring one set of answers, and grows less certain as the book progresses. For me, this ambivalence makes *Sense and Sensibility* one of her two most deeply absorbing books – the other being *Mansfield Park*, which has a similar wobble in its approach. Fiction can accommodate ambivalence as polemic cannot.

Early in the story Elinor and Marianne Dashwood are both engaged in love affairs with slippery young men. Austen sets out to present Elinor as the model of good behaviour, and to back her insistence on the social necessity of discretion and even lying. She speaks of the duty of 'telling lies when politeness required it', and refuses to confide her own difficulties and sorrows even to her much loved sister. Marianne, who will not – cannot – lie, is at first set up as merely silly and self-indulgent, dramatizing her emotions, making things more difficult for others whether she is grieving for her dead father or letting everyone see how much she is in love with her new friend, Willoughby; and she follows the dictates and desires of her heart into unconventional and even risky behaviour, justifying it with the words 'we always know when we are acting wrong'. Like Fanny Price in *Mansfield Park*, she follows an inner voice that tells her what is right and what is wrong.

Marianne's honestly expressed feelings are not all silly. This is how she reproaches her neighbour, the bluff forty-year-old Sir John Middleton, for talking about girls 'setting their cap' at men: 'That is an expression, Sir John . . . which I particularly dislike. I abhor every common-place phrase by which wit is intended; and "setting one's cap at a man," or "making a conquest," are the most odious of all. Their tendency is gross and illiberal; and if their construction could ever be deemed clever, time has long ago destroyed all its ingenuity.' This fierce, and fiercely intelligent, Marianne is surely giving Jane Austen's opinion here, even if Austen herself never spoke such words aloud to the Hampshire squires. Marianne's ability to talk well, her refusal to tell lies, and the fact that she is not afraid to express her views and feelings are shown as attractive. Austen did not break accepted codes of behaviour as she makes Marianne do, by corresponding privately with a man to whom she was not engaged, although she did let everyone see her attraction to Tom Lefroy. As narrator, she makes her disapproval of Marianne's imprudences plain; but as the story proceeds, she shows increasing sympathy for her. Marianne's exaggerated responses may be absurd, and her wild behaviour with Willoughby dangerous to her reputation and peace of mind, but once she is in London her key characteristics become her openness and vulnerability.

Elinor knows, just as her rival, the cunning Lucy Steele, knows, that concealment, disguise, pretended indifference, are almost indispensable props on the social stage. One theme of the book is that survival in society means you cannot afford to live with Marianne's openness, at least not if you are an unprotected woman. Marianne's behaviour is wrong in the light of this social fact; Jane Austen learnt it quickly enough herself. Whether it is absolutely wrong is another question. Marianne goes through the fire of betrayal and humiliation by the man she loves and trusts, and expresses remorse for 'a series of imprudence towards myself'; but the reader is likely to feel that she has acted innocently and purely, and with a consistency that justifies what she has done. The justification is endorsed by Willoughby's continued love for her after he has jilted her and made his prudent, mercenary marriage; and by Elinor's acknowledgement to herself that he would have been the right husband for her sister, in spite of his misdemeanours. Marianne's morality, unfortunate as its effects are on her own life, is not so bad after all, and Austen's answer to the questions posed at the beginning becomes uncertain.

It may be that Austen started with a simple opposition between the sister who follows the correct path – polite lies, suppression of feeling – and the one who rejects it; and that it was in reworking her story that Marianne drew ever more of her sympathy. Rather as Tolstoy created Anna Karenina to show the evils of adultery, and then found himself bewitched by his creation, Austen, beginning with a sometimes crude portrait of a self-indulgent sixteen-year-old, found her appreciation of her character growing as she developed the portrait and traced out her history.

The ball at which Marianne is humiliated is one of her great set-pieces. That it is played out entirely as tragedy, and not as a merely embarrassing social occasion, makes it a unique moment in the novels, and is another sign that Austen credits Marianne with being more than a foolish girl, and allows her depth of character and feeling. And although Austen shifts the story back into the comic mode, the tragic shadow remains over Marianne. Other potential tragedies occur to the reader: that she might have suffered the same fate as Colonel Brandon's niece Eliza Williams, seduced by Willoughby and left pregnant. Or that she might die of her illness, which she herself describes as brought on by a suicidal impulse: 'Had I died, – it would have been self-destruction,' she tells Elinor. Again, it is possible to speculate that an early version of the book might have allowed Marianne to die.

Even as the final version stands, she is punished, and the punishment is never lifted, since she is not allowed to marry Willoughby, whom she loves and who loves her. None of Austen's words about her learning to love Colonel Brandon cut much ice with the reader, and Austen does not risk a single exchange of dialogue between them; always a sign of her lack of commitment to a plot point.

What she does give us is the amazing moment when Elinor finds herself wishing that Willoughby's wife would die: she 'for a moment wished Willoughby a widower'. For Elinor to harbour murderous desires is so surprising that most readers fail to notice that Austen gave them to her. The scene in which Willoughby and Elinor talk, he already married, Marianne lying ill near by, has the surprisingness of art that has lifted entirely away from pattern and precept into truthfulness to human nature.[3]

Sense and Sensibility lies between tragedy and comedy. The tidying up of the love affairs at the end hardly changes that, and the prevailing tone of the book is sombre. Mrs Jennings is a blessed creature, as we learn to appreciate, but a trio of black-heartedly villainous women dominates much of the action. Mrs Ferrars, rich, stupid and cruel, bullies her sons and becomes a dupe herself. Lucy Steele gets her claws into one victim and hangs on, lying and cheating, until she achieves the position in society she has set herself to win; and Fanny Dashwood, all avarice and envy, steals her sister-in-laws' inheritances.

Just as the question of truth versus social lies is of the 1790s, so does Marianne's self-destructive impulse fit the ethos of that decade. The linking of love with suicide became an important theme in literature from the publication of Goethe's hugely influential *Sorrows of Young Werther*; it appeared in English in 1779 and produced a crop of imitations. One who was influenced by it was Mary Wollstonecraft. Her story was much in the air in the late 1790s, and the Austens had a particular reason for hearing about her, because the father of one of their ex-pupils was a benefactor of hers. Sir William East not only sent his son Gilbert to school with them, he was also a neighbour and friend of the Leigh-Perrots. Sir William showed particular kindness to Mary Wollstonecraft in the spring of 1796, as she recovered from a suicide attempt, brought about by the ill treatment she had received from an unreliable lover into whose power she had put herself by her rash behaviour. Wollstonecraft died in September the following year, two months before Austen started revising her first draft of *Sense and Sensibility*, and her friendship with Sir William was mentioned in the *Memoirs* of Mary Wollstonecraft that appeared the following year; or rather it was mentioned in the first edition, and cut out of the second. I am not suggesting that Austen modelled Marianne on her, only that the theme of sensibility, outspokenness, refusal to conform to social rules and attempted self-destruction when love fails are paralleled in the two cases.[4]

Marianne is made to recover from her self-induced illness in a thoroughly chastened state, blaming herself for her death wish. She promises, 'I shall now live solely for my family . . . and if I do mix in other society it will be only to shew that my spirit is humbled, my heart amended, and that I can practise the civilities, the lesser duties of life, with gentleness, and forbearance.' When she goes on to say that the memory of her lover 'shall be regulated, it shall be checked by religion, by reason, by constant employment', she sounds almost as though she is speaking from a manual of advice warning young ladies to avoid passion in any form.[5] And when she sinks into marriage with Colonel Brandon, one in which the reader knows there will be no passion for her, we feel she deserves better; as does Elinor. For Elinor has changed too; rewarded for her prudence, self-effacement and stoicism by the marriage she hoped for, she has also had her views enlarged.

Sense and Sensibility is a book that moves to tears; and this in spite of the schematic plot and reliance on standard subplots to move things forward: seduced and abandoned girls, a tyrannical guardian and a wicked mother with her hand on the purse strings; an unsuitable engagement to a scheming minx; a miraculous reversal of the minx's plan; and so on. Yet it repeatedly bursts into brilliance. Chapter 2 alone stands as a masterpiece of dramatic writing, as Austen makes Fanny Dashwood, in thirteen speeches, turn her husband through 180 degrees without his once being aware of what is happening; a perfectly engineered piece of manipulation, and a *tour de force* of dialogue. When Mary Lascelles wrote that 'it was never to count for as much, to the author or her family, as the later novels', you wonder whether it was simply too strong for the Austens in its portrayal of an openly passionate heroine.[6]

Pride and Prejudice has always been the most popular of Jane Austen's books, inside her family and out. It is the simplest to enjoy, with its good-humoured comedy, its sunny heroine, its dream denouement. Yet it had its origins in a bleak time for the Austen sisters: 1797 was the year of Tom Fowle's death and also when Jane was putting up her defences against what she had felt for Tom Lefroy; a year from which no letters at all survive. The book's detachment from her personal circumstances is notable; never do we feel more strongly that she was 'engrossed in making an artifact which pleased her', and creating a world altogether unlike the one in which she was living.[7] Its setting is a country town, and although there is a farm in the background, and some shooting takes place, you cannot imagine Mr Bennet worrying about the price of pigs or a ploughing competition; his family, with its cook, housekeeper, butler, footman, coachman and maids, is much more comfortably established than the Austens could ever have hoped to be. Mr Bennet has never had to follow a profession, and Mrs Bennet prides herself on her daughters being without domestic responsibilities. Occasional themes and touches tie it to her real world – notably the Brighton camps of the mid-1790s and the militia officers – but essentially she is inventing, absorbed by the form and possibilities of the novel. Elizabeth Bennet is a superb creature, and we may think Jane Austen another; but Elizabeth is not a version of herself, as she would be in the work of a romantic novelist.

The plot moves at a cracking pace, bringing four new young men into the Bennet girls' circle in a few chapters, each of them a potential husband; and the pace is kept up with a series of crises and confrontations. It is a warm story, and a lot of the warmth comes from its steady movement towards consummated love. Elizabeth and Jane Bennet – and Lydia too – are all as intent on this as is their mother on their behalf. The physical attractiveness, beauty and energy of the young women is made much of, in Lydia's case the bounciness of a healthy animal, in Lizzy's given extra edge by her intelligence. In fact intelligence and beauty are almost the same thing in her; Darcy notices how her face is 'rendered uncommonly intelligent by the beautiful expression of her dark eyes'.

Austen endowed her heroine with four admirable qualities, energy, wit, self-confidence and the ability to think for herself, and out of these qualities spring the most dramatic and characteristic moments of the book, when Lizzy is shown in action, running, laughing, teasing, arguing, contradicting and refusing to comply with orders. She resembles Marianne Dashwood in her energy and wit, but unlike Marianne she is tough and knows how to protect herself. She uses humour as both defence and attack, but she does not overstep the rules of society. She is the clear moral centre of the book, and her judgements of character are good in almost every case; this makes her two failures of judgement – about Darcy and about Wickham – surprising enough to provide the pivot on which the plot can turn.

The men, like the girls, are physical beings, strong, young and good-looking, Bingley with his easy nature and pleasant expression, Darcy tall and strikingly handsome, Wickham a charmer in his irresistible uniform. Even Colonel Fitzwilliam is possessed of a sexual charge; although he is 'not handsome' he is very good company, and his exchanges with Lizzy are characterized by their 'spirit and flow'. This line-up of desirable men helps to make Mr Collins seem worse than merely ridiculous. He is disgustingly repellent. He inspires laughter in Mr Bennet, but in Lizzy an almost panicky physical revulsion. She knows enough about sex to find the thought of her friend Charlotte's subjection to his embraces as loathsome as she would in her place, and so incredulous is she that Charlotte can be prepared to endure them that the thought sets up a barrier of confidence between them. (Austen's joke about Mrs Hall losing her baby because she happened to catch sight of her husband, a clergyman of the same age as Mr Collins, seems to relate to a similar physical revulsion in real life.) But Austen allows that Charlotte, ten years older than Lizzy, is making what is for her a reasonable decision in buying herself a social position as a married woman, escaping the humiliations of a dependent daughter at home in exchange for sexual and domestic services. The notion of marriage as a form of prostitution, spelt out by Mary Wollstonecraft and dwelt on by Austen when writing about her Aunt Phila, is surely present again in Lizzy's mind here.

Austen is careful to balance her revulsion with a very fair account of Charlotte Collins's management of her situation as a married woman. She takes pleasure in being in charge of her own small domain – drawing room, cow, poultry, a few servants – and being able to receive her guests; and she is shown developing strategies for minimizing her husband's awfulness. While she blushes for some of his remarks, she tries not to hear others; she encourages him to separate activities such as gardening, and carefully chooses to sit in a back room while he works in his study at the front, to reduce the chances of his interrupting her. Perhaps the delicate implication is that she attempts a similar distancing method upstairs. It would require great firmness to maintain separate bedrooms; the only one of the married Austen brothers whose sleeping arrangements we know anything about would not have considered such a plan. When Edward was away from Godmersham, his wife took his daughter Fanny to sleep with her, and she records in her diary how, at the age of twelve, she was pulled out from beside her mother in the night when her father arrived home unexpectedly, so that he could take his rightful place in the matrimonial bed. Elizabeth Austen was, as we know, almost permanently pregnant.[8] On the other hand, James Austen's strong-minded second wife managed to confine their family to two children, with a seven-year gap between them; Jane believed she dominated him, and perhaps she did, not least in order to preserve herself. James is also, incidentally, the closest to Mr Collins in his social situation, summoned regularly to dine at The Vyne by the Chutes after taking the Sunday service.

Social awkwardness, one of Austen's great themes, supplies a good deal of the comedy in *Pride and Prejudice*, and is so fundamental to the plot that it must have been an important element from the first. The central embarrassment for Lizzy is that her mother is every bit as vulgar, stupid and regrettable as Mr Darcy thinks she is, and acts as an appalling obstacle to any hopes she can have of getting on with an intelligent man under the prevailing social constraints. How much better things are when they meet in Kent and Derbyshire; at home, Lizzy, Jane and their father can only cringe away from Mrs Bennet's excesses. And although Lizzy loves her father, she sees that the infatuation of *his* youth is squarely responsible for landing them all in this painful situation; she is his favourite, and the 'least dear' of her mother's children. Yet Lizzy's vitality – and Lydia's too – comes from their mother, who is not, as she is often represented, a frumpish elderly woman but one in her forties who would like to be taken to Brighton to enjoy herself; when Lydia imagines herself there, 'tenderly flirting with at least six officers at once', we are told that only her mother would understand the fantasy, because 'she might have felt nearly the same'.

Austen had read scenes in Fanny Burney's *Evelina* and *Cecilia* in which vulgar older women say things that make their heroines wince; but they are not mothers. Richardson's *Sir Charles Grandison* does bring on a mother whose behaviour causes her daughter distress, but she is made to reform and becomes presentable. Both writers see the drama of such situations, but neither has anything like Austen's bite. Mrs Bennet is the first modern mother. Lizzy is too polite to formulate, even in the privacy of her own mind, the wish that her mother would drop dead, but she undoubtedly feels something like it.

And Mrs Bennet dominates the book from its opening sentence. We read it as a piece of resounding irony – 'It is a truth universally acknowledged, that a single man in possession of a good fortune, must be in want of a wife' – whereas in fact it is something like a choral statement of the view she shares with every mother in the neighbourhood. As the book proceeds, we see Mrs Bennet proved right more than once. The single men do line up, wanting wives. Her silly predictions about Bingley marrying one of her daughters are justified. Her maddening manoeuvres to leave Jane alone with her admirer are indeed necessary to bring him to the point. Her restored faith that Lydia and Wickham will turn out very well is wonderfully brought to pass. Indeed, her belief that it is better to have ten thousand a year than five, better five thousand than one, and better something than nothing, is also well founded; it was after all a tenet shared by the Austens. Money was important if a married woman was not to be ground down by comfortless child-bearing and drudgery. No question of that for Mrs Darcy, of course; impossible to imagine Darcy inflicting a yearly baby on Lizzy as Edward Austen did on his Elizabeth. The good landlord and master, the kind and imaginative brother, the discerning reader and collector of books, concerned for his sister's cultural development, aware of the civilizing effect of women on society, is surely not going to abdicate his responsibility for his wife's physical well-being and turn her into a 'poor animal' once they are married at the end of the book. Outside its pages, Jane Austen credited him with a mixture of 'Love, Pride & Delicacy' in his attitude towards his wife.[9] No doubt his fine, up-to-date library contained novels. Fiction itself – despised by Mr Collins, for whom it is also the case that one woman is virtually indistinguishable from another when it comes to choosing a wife – is one of the higher pleasures that brings a better appreciation of women's contribution to civilization.

A puzzling weakness of the book is the way in which Darcy, a fastidious and educated man, accepts the many crude conversational manoeuvres of Bingley's sisters, intending to flatter him and put down the Bennets. He even hopes to marry his sister to Bingley, although these tough, shallow young women, their malice polished by 'one of the first private seminaries in town', are surely no models for Georgiana Darcy. It is hard to believe he finds their behaviour or their talk acceptable, let alone companionable; their terrible manners seem to have strayed in from the Austen juvenilia. My guess is that they were retained from the earliest draft into the final version for structural reasons, because they provide a series of opportunities for comic dialogue that allows Austen to dramatize Darcy's developing feelings about Lizzy, obviously neater than describing it. The reason is sound, but it makes an awkwardness in the credibility of the plot.

As to Wickham and his fellow officers, they are the one feature of the book that ties it into Austen's known experience. The attractions of officers quartered in Canterbury to Mrs Lefroy's daughter and her friend are touched on sardonically in one of her letters shortly before she started writing.[10] There were militia officers in Basingstoke (Eliza Chute gave dinners for them, and mentioned the 'fracas' they made in the summer of 1794); Tom Chute was in a militia regiment, and Henry doubtless had stories to tell of his fellow officers in the Oxford militia. All this must have contributed to Wickham, Colonel Forster, Denny, Pratt and Chamberlayne, who was dressed up in women's clothes by Lydia, Kitty and Mrs Forster. And Wickham carries a faint suggestion of Henry Austen, as he hesitates between possible brides and possible careers, and shows himself to be more agreeable than reliable. If Henry was not a villain, it is also true that the story of Wickham's wickedness seems artificial and grafted on, strayed in from a different sort of novel altogether; because as we see him in action he seems frivolous rather than evil, casting about to see what prizes he can win for himself in a competitive society, rather than steeped in cold-hearted villainy.

Wickham's prize is a particularly interesting one. Lydia, presented as a bad girl, and spoilt by her mother, who sees her as a surrogate self, is selfish and stupid; but her outrageous energies propel her into getting what Elizabeth also wanted – i.e., Wickham – and Austen shows that Lizzy cannot quite forgive Lydia's success. It is not only her superior morality at work, you feel, but a touch of envy that makes her so prim and bad-tempered with Lydia, whose careless vivacity and amorality have allowed her to bag the desirable Wickham. Lydia is the id to Lizzy's ego. What's more, she is to be allowed to enjoy him. This is one of the great touches of the book; Austen is too honest to pretend that stories like Lydia's must end as the gloating neighbours predict, with every erring girl either reduced to prostitution – 'on the town' – or banished to lonely penitence and poverty. When she came to write *Mansfield Park* she felt obliged to condemn Maria Rushworth to precisely that formal banishment, insisted on by her father; but not here. Lydia remains pleased with herself and her situation, at ease with her charming if forcibly married husband, with enough money and rich brothers-in-law prepared to pay to ensure her continuing comfort in life. It is even possible to feel a sneaking sympathy for that shameless ability to enjoy herself.

The finest stroke of invention in the whole book is the way in which Austen arranges for Lizzy to accept Darcy. Since Lizzy's best scenes are her refusals – first of Collins, then of Darcy – it is pure genius to allow her another refusal, this time made to Lady Catherine, as the means of signifying her willingness to marry Darcy at last. Not only is the scene intensely dramatic in itself, as every adapter for stage and film knows; it also serves to keep the flag of excitement flying right to the end.

Northanger Abbey was also started in the aftermath of a family tragedy, this time the death of their 27-year-old cousin Jane Williams in August 1798. Again, there is very little trace of personal allusion in the book, although it is written more in the style of a family entertainment than any of the others, with its detailed picture of Bath, familiar to most of the Austens, and its references to novels read and doubtless discussed at Steventon. One of the jokes is that the heroine is not a heroine by any of the usual rules of fiction, neither clever nor beautiful, and without accomplishments or admirers – an ordinary girl, one of ten children of a plain country clergyman. When she is taken to Bath by dull, kindly friends, she falls in love with the first young man who dances with her, and although he likes her for her simplicity and straightforwardness, he does not think of her as a possible wife until he realizes she is in love with him, and notices that she listens with sparkling eyes to everything he says: 'in finding him irresistible, becoming so herself'. Later we learn that 'a persuasion of her partiality for him had been the only cause of giving her a serious thought. It is a new circumstance in romance, I acknowledge, and dreadfully derogatory of an heroine's dignity; but if it be as new in common life, the credit of a wild imagination will at least be all my own.'

The narrator's stance is that of a cheerful elder sister who from time to time disrupts the story by commenting on it, very much in the manner of Fielding in *Tom Jones*: 'And now I may dismiss my heroine to the sleepless couch, which is the true heroine's portion; to a pillow strewed with thorns and wet with tears. And lucky may she think herself, if she get another good night's rest in the course of the next three months.' Fielding-like, she offers maxims: 'A woman especially, if she have the misfortune of knowing any thing, should conceal it as well as she can.' And, most famously, on the status of the novel: ' "And what are you reading, Miss—?" "Oh! it is only a novel!" replies the young lady; while she lays down her book with affected indifference, or momentary shame . . . in short, only some work in which the greatest powers of the mind are displayed, in which the most thorough knowledge of human nature, the happiest delineation of its varieties, the liveliest effusions of wit and humour are conveyed to the world in the best chosen language.'[11]

The second source of humour is at the expense of the fashion for Gothic fiction: mysterious old buildings, secret hiding places, lights suddenly extinguished, night terrors, indecipherable messages, rumours of suspicious deaths, powerful and menacing men. The genre has lasted long enough for modern readers to pick up the joke without having read Mrs Radcliffe or her imitators, and is so precisely and delicately handled that it is as funny today as it was when it was written. Jane Austen was using Mrs Radcliffe as Stella Gibbons used Mary Webb and D. H. Lawrence, finding their weakest points and through them undermining the whole basis of their work. It is an unfair and a deeply enjoyable exercise.

16

Twenty-five

Anyone arriving at their twenty-fifth birthday with three outstanding novels to their name looks well embarked on the road to success; fame, riches, happiness all within easy reach, you would think. This was exactly Jane Austen's situation: she had three substantial and original books completed, owing nothing to anyone but their very bright, energetic and inventive author. There had been a set-back with Cadell, but she was sure of her father's support; and she could joke about her manuscripts, accusing Martha Lloyd of planning to memorize *First Impressions* and publish it from memory as her own work, teasing Cassandra for not rereading it often enough. This is the laughter of a confident person. Everything was set for her to put in a little more work perhaps on the three manuscripts – revising is easier than the first draft – find a publisher who understood his trade, and start on a new novel.

This did not happen. Instead, she fell silent. For ten years she produced almost nothing, and not until she was nearly thirty-five, in the summer of 1809, did she return to the working pattern of her early twenties. On the face of it there was no reason why she should not have gone on writing steadily through the first decade of the nineteenth century. Her family offered no explanation. Her biographer nephew remarked only that 'it might rather have been expected that fresh scenes and new acquaintance would have called forth her powers', but that they failed to do so; and he shrugs her silence off.

The truth is that Austen depended very little on fresh scenes and new acquaintance; her work was done in her head, when she began to see the possibility of a certain situation and set of characters, and her books are never transcripts of what she saw going on around her. She used the odd particular point and incident – the amber crosses

Charles gave to her and Cass become a topaz one given by Midshipman William Price to his sister in *Mansfield Park*; the Cobb at Lyme Regis suggests a dramatic scene; Henry's experiences in the militia may have set her mind working on Wickham and his fellow officers – but she did not draw from life, or write down the stories of her friends and family. A series of thrilling novels could have been based on the adventures of her Aunt Philadelphia and her Cousin Eliza; they seem to cry out for fiction. Or she could have put the oddities and crimes of half a dozen neighbouring Hampshire families into novels; but, as we have seen, Hampshire is missing from the novels, and none of the Austens' neighbours, exotic, wicked or merely amusing, makes a recognizable appearance. The world of her imagination was separate and distinct from the world she inhabited.

What she did depend on was particular working conditions which allowed her to abstract herself from the daily life going on around her; and these she lost just after her twenty-fifth birthday. What made her fall silent was another huge event in her 'life of no event': another exile.

The decision by Mr and Mrs Austen to leave their home of over thirty years, taking their daughters with them, came as a complete surprise to her; in effect, a twenty-fifth birthday surprise, in December 1800. Not a word had been said to anyone in advance of the decision. Charles had been at home on leave in November – he and Jane went to a ball together at Lord Portsmouth's – and when he received the news early in the new year it came as a shock to him too. After his visit both daughters were away, Jane at Ibthorpe staying with Martha, Cassandra at Godmersham, where the arrival of a sixth baby made her presence desirable. This had left the Austen parents on their own; and, like a pair of enthusiastic children left to their own devices, they egged one another on with the possibilities and pleasures of a new life, and agreed to cast off the habits and responsibilities of four decades. So they hatched their plan to leave Steventon, without reference to anyone else, and decided to move to Bath.

No one can blame them for wanting some relief from their long years of labour. And although they might have proceeded a little more tactfully than they did, tact would not have altered the essential point. According to several accounts, Jane was told, immediately and baldly, that the move was settled as she walked into the house on her return from Ibthorpe: 'Well, girls, it is all settled, we have decided to leave Steventon in such a week and go to Bath' is the family version of Mrs Austen's announcement. Jane was greatly distressed. This is Mary Austen's account, who was there; and although she misremembered the presence of Cassandra, there is no reason to doubt the truth of it. She had a reason to stress the bright side rather than insist on Jane's unhappiness, since she was to benefit from the change.[1] James and Mary were to move into Steventon rectory and take over the parish. James's daughter Anna was told her Aunt Jane fainted. Whether she did or not, it can hardly be doubted that the whole thing was a shock, and a painful one.

All the Austen children were affected by it. The fact that every one of them who was absent and could possibly return to Steventon – Edward, Henry, Frank and Charles – made a point of doing so before their parents left – 'while Steventon is ours', as Jane put it – suggests how much they felt it as the closing of a door on their childhood and the end of a way of life. Cassandra destroyed several letters Jane wrote to her immediately after hearing her parents' decision, which suggests they made her uncomfortable, too full of raw feeling and even anger. Jane's spirits were not helped by the obvious keenness of both her parents and her brother and sister-in-law to get the move organized as fast as possible. In January she told Cassandra that she was invited by James and Mary to a party for their wedding anniversary – with Tom Chute, Mary's sister Elizabeth Fowle and her husband – but had turned them down. No explanation was offered or needed: 'I was asked, but declined it.'

She made it clear she felt the James Austens showed too much eagerness to take over Steventon, telling Cass that one of the Steventon horses – the brown mare – due to go to James after their departure 'has not had the patience to wait for that, & has settled herself even now at Deane . . . & everything else I suppose will be seized by degrees in the same manner'. Since both her parents were agreeable to all this seizing, Jane herself was powerless. She could only watch. 'As to our Pictures . . . all the old heterogenous, miscellany, manuscript, Scriptoral peices dispersed over the House are to be given to James.' Her sadness about the family pictures, valued not for their beauty but for their familiarity, will be understood by anyone who has lived with such an odd, random collection in which each picture connects with a memory of family life. She resisted her mother's (and Cassandra's) suggestion that she should give away one of her indubitably personal possessions: 'as I do not chuse to have Generosity dictated to me, I shall not resolve on giving my Cabinet to Anna till the first thought of it has been my own'.

She and Martha set to steady work sorting her father's library of 500 volumes, which he intended to sell, along with most of the furniture, the piano on which Jane had learnt, practised and played over the years, and 'a large collection of music'. The old painted theatre-sets were to go too: James had evidently lost his taste for theatricals entirely. Jane hoped to persuade him to buy her father's books for a guinea a volume; he may have taken most of them, for what price we don't know, since only 200 reached the sale. Jane expressed further anxiety to know what 'my books' fetched at the sale, and was indignant that her father's were valued at only £70: 'the whole World is in a conspiracy to enrich one part of our family at the expense of another'.[2] No need to spell out who was being enriched and who impoverished.

She strained to keep up the easy, gossipy note in her letters, but the jokes to Cass often feel forced. 'We have lived long enough in this Neighbourhood, the Basingstoke Balls are certainly on the decline . . . It must not be generally known however that I am not sacrificing a great deal in quitting the Country – or I can expect to inspire no tenderness, no interest in those we leave behind.' She did look forward to 'summers by the Sea or in Wales'; and she relaxed when she discussed some of her mother's hopes and plans for Bath, falling into the established comic tone for Mrs Austen. 'My Mother looks forward with as much certainty as you can do, to our keeping two Maids – my father is the only one not in the secret. – We plan having a steady Cook, & a young giddy Housemaid, with a sedate, middle aged Man, who is to undertake the double office of Husband to the former & sweetheart to the latter. – No Children of course to be allowed on either side.' Mrs Austen's health naturally remained 'quite stout' through all the excitements, for the good reason that 'she wishes not to be obliged by any relapse to alter her arrangements'.

Mrs Austen believed that Bath would be good for her uncertain health, and for her husband's too; he had now reached seventy. The proximity to her brother Leigh-Perrot, rich, friendly and hospitable, was also important to her; apart from the obvious advantages of living near a wealthy relative, it would allow her to keep an eye on his expected bequest to James. Mr Austen was pleased with the idea that they could easily travel on from Bath into Devon and Wales for holidays, which he felt the girls would enjoy; and here he was right. This was the one aspect of the plan that did appeal to Jane; it interested her mother much less, so that when she got to Bath she maintained she would rather stay put than go travelling further, and had to be coerced by the rest of the family.

There is briskness and brightness in Jane's letters at this time, much keeping up of spirits, but no enthusiasm. She is doing what she has to do, making the best of a situation over which she has no control, watching the breaking up of everything familiar and seeing what was left eagerly taken over; fitting in with plans in which she has no say, losing what she loves for the prospect of an urban life in a house not yet found; no centre, no peace, and the loss of an infinite number of things hard to list, impossible to explain. She had enjoyed Bath as a visitor and used it as a writer, but she had no wish at all to live there. In February she fled from her parents, leaving them to get on with the dismantling of the house, while she went to stay with Alethea and Catherine Bigg at Manydown, where nothing was changed. Then Cassandra came home, Edward and Elizabeth made their last visit, and Frank got leave from the Mediterranean for his; after which he and his father set off for London together, going on to Godmersham, and the three women went to Ibthorpe at the beginning of May. Cass was to remain for a few weeks with the Lloyds, while Jane and her mother travelled on together to Bath, where the Leigh-Perrots, fully restored to their dull dignity, were expecting them at the Paragon. From there they were to look for a rented house.

The four letters written during the first weeks in Bath suggest a mind struggling against low spirits. Bath itself was 'vapour, shadow, smoke & confusion'. Her uncle and aunt were kind and welcoming, but when some old acquaintances appeared, 'we were very happy to meet, & all that': the '& all that' has the function of denying the happiness. Taken to the Assembly Rooms, she amused herself watching a drunken wife chase her drunken husband round the rooms, and picking out a notorious adultress. Then: 'Another stupid party last night; perhaps if larger they might be less intolerable.' But 'I cannot anyhow continue to find people agreable.' This is not a light-hearted remark, like Elizabeth Bennet's 'The more I see of the world, the more I am dissatisfied with it', but a desolate, even frightening statement. Her opinion of people was not raised by the 'old *Toughs*' who came to play whist with her uncle, or by Miss Langley, 'like any other short girl with a broad nose & wide mouth, fashionable dress, & exposed bosom'.

She may have had an extra reason for bitterness if she suspected her parents' intentions in choosing Bath, which was not only an old people's pleasure ground but also a place for husband-hunting. Mrs Austen's parents, on reaching retirement age, had moved to Bath in just the same way, taking their two unmarried daughters, both in their mid-twenties, with them; and, in Bath, Cassandra Leigh had married George Austen, and Jane Leigh had found her husband too. The younger Jane was more than capable of drawing the parallel, and feeling a stinging sense of humiliation at any idea of being paraded in the marriage market. Perhaps it was this that provoked her to accept an invitation to be driven up and down Kingsdown Hill in a phaeton and four with a man she could not be suspected of setting her cap at, Mr Evelyn, who was both married and thought more of horses than anything else; he was the man who had sold Edward a pair for his carriage when they were last in Bath. When Cass warned her not to do anything indiscreet with Mr Evelyn, she assured her that 'he is very harmless; people do not seem afraid of him here, and he gets Groundsel for his birds & all that'.

A Mrs Chamberlayne prompted another withering response: 'As to Agreableness, she is much like other people'; this was after Cassandra had suggested she would make a suitable friend. Cass's interventions seem peculiarly unhelpful at this point. Jane persevered and went for walks with Mrs Chamberlayne, and 'The Walk was very beautiful as my companion agreed, whenever I made the observation – And so ends our friendship, for the Chamberlaynes leave Bath in a day or two.' This was the likely end of most Bath friendships, she might have added. 'We are to have a tiny party here tonight; I hate tiny parties – they force one into constant exertion.' Then she warns

Cass, 'My aunt has a very bad cough; do not forget to have heard about *that* when you come.' There are enough varieties of tedium here to drive someone who wanted to be doing something else to despair; the prospect of them continuing for a limitless period must have been intolerable. But Jane was schooled to keep up appearances even if she was screaming inside her head. Then the letters stop, and there are no more at all for the next three and a half years.

The ejection from Steventon made severe practical difficulties for her; it also depressed her deeply enough to disable her as a writer. Depression may be set off when a bad experience is repeated, and it seems likely that this is what happened here. First as an infant, then as a child of seven, Jane had been sent away from home, frightening and unpleasant experiences over which she had no control and which required periods of recovery; they helped to form the 'whimsical' girl Cousin Phila noticed, cautious with strangers, ready to laugh at herself and others, almost always well defended when it came to showing emotion. That she had deep and often painful feelings is not in doubt. She could not have written the novels without them; but feelings were largely excluded from the letters, or conveyed in the form of jokes.

As a child recovering from the school years, she found the power to entertain her family with her writing. At the same time, through her writing, she was developing a world of imagination in which she controlled everything that happened. She went on to create young women somewhat like herself, but whose perceptions and judgements were shown to matter; who were able to influence their own fates significantly, and who could even give their parents good advice. Her delight in this work is obvious. She was pleasing herself at least as much as she was impressing the family circle, and the possibility of reaching a wider audience was a further excitement and spur.

To remove her from Steventon was to destroy the delicate pattern she had worked out, in which she could take her place within the family but also abstract herself from it when she needed to. She had enjoyed a certain amount of travel, visits to Kent, Bath, London and Ibthorpe; but even before 1801 there are signs of her wanting to protect her time at home, as when she said she preferred the idea of Martha visiting Steventon in the summer of 1799 to joining her mother on her summer tour. So there was both a perfectly good rational basis for wanting to be at home, and a residue of the terrors of infancy and childhood about banishment and exile, ready to spring out when they threatened again. That this new exile was brought about by the same people as before, her parents, against whom she could neither rebel nor complain, must have made it worse.

Her brother James shared something of her deep emotional attachment to their native place. In one of his poems he said he believed he would fall ill if he were ever 'exiled' from Hampshire. When he made a trip away from home, he missed the familiar landscape painfully and experienced a strong sense of relief on returning. He expressed the idea, a little stiffly and solemnly, in his verse:

> It is a feeling to the human heart
> Congenial, and most potent in effect,
> To long, when absent, for the welcome sight
> Of the dear precincts of our native home.[3]

There is another, odder poem in which he imagined lying in the Steventon graveyard beside his wife after their deaths; to him, it was a comfortable and consoling vision of the future, so strongly did he feel himself to be an integral part of the place. It sounds more like a Brontë than an Austen, and James's poetry was intensely personal, with no attempt to deny feelings. He allowed himself to be a romantic as Jane did not; she was nevertheless rooted in Steventon and its surrounding countryside very much as he was. He had suffered no exile to school; hers can only have added to an inborn suspicion of change, and helped to give her a mistrust of strange places and people. The same views from the same windows; the same household routines and daily walks in the garden or to the church or the village; the same sounds and silences, all these samenesses made a secure environment in which her imagination could work.

Jane never wrote of being depressed in the way Dr Johnson was when he spoke of his 'black dog', or Boswell with his low spirits and terror of death. Hers did not take that form. She would not allow herself to indulge anything she might label self-pity; and she never became clinically ill, as Cowper, who brooded on his own sinfulness and feared being cast out of God's mercy, did. Cowper died in 1800; Jane loved his poetry, and gave some of his lines to Fanny Price to quote in *Mansfield Park*. Her account of Fanny's permanent low spirits after a childhood trauma, and her very different account (in *Sense and Sensibility*) of Marianne unable to combat her misery and willing herself into serious illness, show how well she understood depression. And however she dealt with and controlled her own, it struck at the core of her being: it interfered directly with her power to write. The great burst of writing of the late nineties simply came to a halt.

17

Manydown

For the next four years the Austens were on the move almost as much as they were in Bath. Mrs Austen may have settled on city life, but Mr Austen turned out to be as interested in travelling further; he was a true pioneer of all those who, on reaching retirement age, make for the sea coast. At seventy he became a wonderfully enthusiastic and resilient tourist, and he was particularly keen on the resort towns of the Devon and Dorset coast. Although there was another invasion scare in 1801, and Nelson bombarded Boulogne to show Napoleon where the real power lay, the West Country was hardly affected. We read of soldiers posted on the coast marrying local girls, rather than of anyone staying away; and in fact its fishing villages and small towns were expanding and competing for visitors, as the fashion for sea bathing and villas with marine views grew and spread.

The climate on that coast is mild, the scenery delightful. For Jane Austen there was the pleasure of coastal walks and sea bathing, although she seems never to have learnt to swim. She had to be content with a bathing machine and a maid to attend her when she took a plunge; even so, bathing, like dancing, was a bodily pleasure she could joyously indulge to excess. The Austens tried Sidmouth in 1801, and Dawlish and Teignmouth in 1802, possibly going on to Tenby and Barmouth in Wales in the same year. They may have been at Charmouth in the summer of 1803, and were certainly at Lyme Regis in November 1803 – Lyme is noted for its sunny Novembers. Add to this a long autumn visit to Godmersham by the two sisters in the autumn of 1802, another a year later, and a stay of several weeks at Lyme again in the summer of 1804, this time with Henry and Eliza, and the house they took in Bath looks rather more like a perch than a home.

No. 4, Sydney Place, was, however, a good, well-proportioned, newly built terraced house. It was well placed outside the crowded centre of Bath, but within easy walking distance over Pulteney Bridge. From its tall drawing-room windows it looked across the road to the newly laid-out and very agreeable Sydney Gardens at the front, and there was a small garden at the back. Here James, Mary and nine-year-old Anna visited them in the spring of 1802. Anna later wrote sweetly of her grandparents that 'this was the short Holyday of their married life', and that Mr Austen's fine white hair and bright eyes were admired wherever he went.[1] They at any rate clearly enjoyed the change, the relaxation, and cheerfulness of town life.

In Sydney Place they also made good use of the excellent doctors of Bath. Mrs Austen fell ill, and this time it was the real thing; for a time there was even fear for her life. She recovered under the care of a good Dr Bowen, and with much careful nursing from her daughters. The verses she produced on getting better are more proof of her resilience and tough sense of humour. Boldly named 'Dialogue between Death & Mrs Austen', they go:

> Says Death, 'I've been trying these three weeks or more
> To seize an old Madam here at Number Four,
> Yet I still try in vain, tho' she's turned of three score;
> To what is my ill-success owing?'

> 'I'll tell you, old Fellow, if you cannot guess,
> To what you're indebted for your ill success –
> To the prayers of my husband, whose love I possess,
> To the care of my daughters, whom heaven will bless,
> To the skill & attention of Bowen.'

There is an impish serenity about the lines. Mrs Austen can take death or leave it, and crack a joke about it. Her attitude suggests where Jane derived her own unblinking attitude towards death, never a subject for sentimentality or backward-looking with her; something to be avoided, to be sure, but, when it had happened, tidied away as quickly as possible so that the living could get on with what mattered. Mrs Austen's lines also show how, despite the tensions and disagreements that sometimes divided the family, they held together solidly when danger threatened any one member.

*

The single letter of Jane's to break a four-year silence between 1801 and 1805 was written at Lyme in September 1804, and shows that little had changed for her, either inwardly or in her relations with others, since the abandonment of Steventon. She is writing to Cassandra, who has gone on to Weymouth, a much smarter resort along the coast, with Henry and Elizabeth, who have also been at Lyme; Cass is on her way to Ibthorpe, leaving Jane with their parents. The letter is one of her frank ones. She is finding her Aunt Leigh-Perrot's letters to her mother irritating because she does not understand the difference between a sloop and a frigate – which she, as the sister of two naval officers, naturally does. 'My Aunt may do what she likes with her frigates,' she writes rudely.

She has been for a walk on the Cobb with yet another of the young ladies who might possibly turn into a friend, a Miss Armstrong. She 'has Sense & some degree of Taste'; her flaw, one not shared by Jane, is that 'she seems to like people rather too easily'. Jane is much more interested in two of the servants her parents have brought with them, Jenny and James. She finds them books and newspapers to read and, as a thoroughly enlightened employer, sends them off for a long tramp together over the clifftops to Charmouth. Jane expresses her pleasure that Jenny has found a new way of putting up her hair; and she has enjoyed a few dances at the Lyme Assembly Rooms – two shillings for a subscriber, four for non-subscribers, with card room, billiard room and chandeliered ballroom, two violins and a cello for dancing every Tuesday. Mrs Austen plays cards with 'Le Chevalier' – possibly Mrs Hancock's old friend, Sir John Lambert, still in touch with Eliza and returned from France with the peace.[2] Jane dances with a Mr Crawford, but not with the 'odd looking Man' who eyed her for some time and asked her if she intended to dance any more; and whom she suspects of being Irish 'by his ease'. 'I imagine him to belong to the Honble Barnwalls, who are the son & son's wife of an Irish Viscount – bold, queerlooking people, just fit to be Quality at Lyme,' she declares snobbishly. She is interested in who is fit to be Quality and who is not, and nervous that Mrs Austen might bring out her stockings to be darned when visitors are present, as Miss Armstrong's mother did – the sort of anxiety parents induce even in their grown-up children.

Now that Henry had gone, there was no one for Jane to go

rambling with, and she spent too long enjoying herself in the sea, and tired herself out. Her father and mother could not possibly have managed the steep climb up from the seafront at Lyme to the cliff walk to Charmouth, and the wildly overgrown undercliff walk to the west of the town would also have been daunting for them. They were unlikely even to venture on to the Cobb, the famous stone jetty curved like a great hooked finger; it had a sloping surface and rough, tricky steps offering neither handholds nor railing. As a group, the Austens would have kept to the public promenade along the front, and the gentle walk inland beside the Lym, rushing and gurgling through the town on its way to the sea. On Sunday they would all process from their lodgings in Broad Street to attend the parish church, a curious amalgam of Norman and Gothic, Jacobean gallery and pulpit: plenty to look at if the sermon palled. So Jane played the dutiful daughter, and kept an eye on the arrangements at their lodgings: 'I detect dirt in the Water-decanter as fast as I can, and give the Cook physic.'

Years afterwards, when Cassandra was an old woman, she told her niece Caroline that she and Jane became friendly with a young man at one of the Devon resorts who showed signs of becoming fond of Jane, and went so far as to ask whether they might meet again the following summer. This is hardly the approach of an ardent lover like Jane Cooper's Thomas Williams, with his almost instant proposal; but Cassandra had the impression that Jane returned his interest. The next thing they heard was that the man had died; there was no second summer meeting, and this is the whole of the story. If it is true, and if Jane had really hoped for more, it makes another sadness in her life. There is, however, nothing in writing by Cassandra, no name, no precise place or date. When Caroline set down her account forty years after she was told it, it had become as mistily romantic as the wilder shores of Devon itself when the weather is uncertain.

Another episode from the same period is better documented and throws a much clearer light on what was going on in Jane's head. In the autumn of 1802, she and Cassandra were wandering about as usual, spending two nights in their old Steventon home with James and Mary before travelling on to Godmersham with Charles, who was currently unemployed because the peace between the English and the French that spring had put so many ships out of commission. At the end of October, after eight weeks in Kent, the sisters returned with Charles to Steventon, intending to see old friends and one or two enemies also. We know from Eliza Chute's diary, for example, that she dined with all the Austens at Oakley Hall, the Bramstons' house, in November. Two weeks later Jane and Cass were invited by the Bigg sisters for a stay of several weeks at Manydown, where they had so often enjoyed themselves. Alethea and Catherine were both still single, and Elizabeth Heathcote had come home to her father's house with her baby son William after the tragic early death of her husband that spring.

The five young women had much to talk about and were planning long, cosy winter evenings together; the Bigg sisters may have had something else in mind as well. Their father was at home, a hale sixty-year-old; so was their younger brother, Harris, who had reached his majority in May. He had been away finishing his education at Worcester College, Oxford, so Jane and Cassandra had not seen him for some time; the shy, stammering boy, although still awkward in manner, had turned into a broad-shouldered, tall and much more confident young man. He was after all the heir to considerable estates.

On the evening of 2 December, Harris asked Jane to become his wife. It seems likely his sisters conspired with Cassandra for the couple to be left alone together, in the library, perhaps, or one of the small drawing rooms. It may also be that they had encouraged Harris to make his proposal; he was their little brother, and they may have felt he needed some help. Because of his stammer he had been privately educated at home until he went to Oxford, and the stammer still remained, which meant that social life could be something of an ordeal, and made him occasionally aggressive.[3] So perhaps his loving and powerful elder sisters persuaded him that a wife he had known and liked all his life would solve his problems and make him a happy man. Whether Harris fancied himself in love with Jane or not, he decided she would make a good wife, and duly proposed.

Jane, no doubt very fond of her friends' brother, whom she would have danced with when he was a child, accepted his proposal. The discrepancy in their ages was only five years, nothing of any moment; Eliza was ten years older than Henry. The entire Manydown household was delighted. The evening was passed in congratulations, and everyone went to bed rejoicing.

Jane would now become the future mistress of a large Hampshire house and estate, only a few miles from her birthplace, and close to her brother James. She would be almost as grand as Elizabeth Austen at Godmersham. She would be able to ensure the comfort of her parents to the end of their days, and give a home to Cassandra. She would probably be in a position to help her brothers in their careers. She would be surrounded by dear sisters-in-law and friends. She would be a kindly mistress to the estate workers. She would have children of her own. All these thoughts must have rushed through her head, each one like a miracle, offerings of happiness she had given up expecting.

And she would have a perfectly decent young husband. There she paused. Seven years before, she had danced here at Manydown with all the *élan* of her love for Tom Lefroy; she had sat out with him, joked with him, done everything that was profligate and shocking, believed he cared for her and known she cared for him. She had let the world see it, not minding if she were talked about. It was even possible that Harris had kept a vision of Jane as she had been then, dancing so recklessly and happily. She had only to compare the emotions of that night with this one to realize what a gulf lay between real happiness and delusive dreams. The night went by, and Jane stayed awake, like a heroine in a novel who cannot sleep because too many emotions are pressing in on her: 'the sleepless couch, which is the true heroine's portion . . . a pillow strewed with thorns and wet with tears', as she had written mockingly herself. She thought and thought; and in the morning she packed her bag, dressed herself grimly, and sought someone – Alethea perhaps – who would find Harris. Again they were closeted alone in the library, or the small drawing room, and this time Jane explained, with all the delicacy in her power, that she had made a mistake and could not after all marry him. She esteemed him, she was honoured by his proposal, but on thinking it over she realized that esteem and respect were not enough, and that she would not be behaving fairly or rightly towards him if she accepted the offer of his hand.

After this appalling explanation, she and Cassandra could not stay on at Manydown as planned. Alethea and Catherine ordered the carriage and drove with them to Steventon, where a very surprised Mary received them and saw the Austens and the Biggs embrace tearfully by way of farewell. Jane then insisted that James must take them back to Bath the very next day; she was for once peremptory, and when asked for an explanation refused to give any. When Mary found out the reason later, she much regretted Jane's change of mind from a worldly point of view, but said she also understood why she had made it.

To continue the story from Harris's point of view, he did not pine for long. Two years later he found a young woman from the Isle of Wight who could and did love him. They were married and she bore him ten children. Their eldest son became a clergyman, a Whig and a poet; on the one hand he translated the whole of the *Iliad* into English verse, and on the other he was active in supporting the Basingstoke Mechanics' Institute and promoting allotment holdings for agricultural labourers. We would naturally rather have *Mansfield Park* and *Emma* than the Bigg-Wither baby Jane Austen might have given the world, and who would almost certainly have prevented her from writing any further books. At least Harris's son grew up to be a thoroughly good and honourable man, one of whom Jane Austen would have approved.

On the face of it, the effects of the whole episode were no worse for Jane than for Harris. The friendship between the Austens and the Bigg sisters was undamaged. Harris moved away into a house of his own, and Jane was able to continue to visit Manydown as before. In fact, it marked another painful epoch in her life, because this was her last serious thought of marriage and the possibility of having children. After this she, like Cassandra, hurried into middle age.[4]

Hurrying into it was one way of dealing with the fact that it was not an easy prospect to face. Looking around, she saw her friend Martha Lloyd, ten years older than her, living with her old, infirm, widowed mother and her mother's friend Mrs Stent. 'Poor Mrs Stent! it has been her lot to be always in the way; but we must be merciful, for perhaps in time we may come to be Mrs Stents ourselves, unequal to anything & unwelcome to everybody,' she wrote, although she was still in her twenties.[5] Thoughts of this kind, and fears of the future, were on her mind; not unreasonably, given the age of her parents and the question mark over how she and Cassandra would manage their lives without them.

The fiasco with Harris seems to have returned her to her manuscripts. She had been carrying these precious bundles around from place to place, year after year, and purely as physical objects they must have caused her some anxiety. They had to be preserved from water, fire, loss, disintegration and all the hazards of life on the move. Packets of paper are easily mislaid on coaches, in lodgings, at inns: you think of the mistake that sent her bags from the inn at Dartford on their way to the West Indies. Even the houses of relatives and friends do not offer perfect security; there are always maids lighting fires, and children looking for something to make paper darts with. The manuscripts had gone with her to Bath, first to the Leigh-Perrots, then to Sydney Place. They then accompanied her around the Devon coast and Wales, and wherever the Austens travelled during the next years, to Godmersham, and back to Hampshire for their frequent visits to different households there; for it seems unlikely she would have left them on a shelf in an empty or rented-out house in Bath. The more you think about it, the more surprising it becomes that nothing was lost. Keeping them under her eye must have been one of the unmentioned but essential disciplines of her life.

Now she copied out and revised *Northanger Abbey* (still called *Susan*). Henry offered to take over from Mr Austen as her agent, and deputed one of his business partners, a lawyer named William Seymour, to offer the manuscript to Richard Crosby, a London publisher. This was at the start of 1803. Crosby paid £10 for the manuscript, promising early publication. He then advertised the book in a brochure called *Flowers of Literature* as being 'in the Press'; but after this nothing more happened. It was worse than Cadell's blind refusal; this time Jane's hopes had been raised by an acceptance.

She none the less started on a new novel, which she called *The Watsons*.[6] The first thing that strikes you about it is that it is the story of a group of youngish women – four sisters – who are all unmarried, have very little money, and are casting about more or less desperately to remedy their situation before their invalid father dies, when they know they will be even worse off. For the present they have a home at least; but because Mr Watson is a clergyman they will lose that when they lose him. The parallel with Jane's and Cassandra's situation is obvious; and the similarity became more striking. She planned to kill off Mr Watson in the story, only to face the real death of her own father in January 1805. At this point she abandoned the book for good.

Her biographer nephew suggested that she gave up because she found she had placed her heroine too low down in the social hierarchy. A more likely reason is that the theme of the story touched too closely on Jane's fears for herself, Cassandra and their companion Martha Lloyd, whose hopes of marriage had fallen through, and who faced the same bleak uncertainty over her future. For someone who took care not to write autobiographically, this degree of parallel between her fiction and her own life may have become impossibly tricky to handle.

The conversations she wrote for the Watson sisters are strikingly grimmer than anything else in her work. Elizabeth Watson, the eldest, defending the crude husband-hunting of her juniors, remarks, 'but you know, we must marry . . . my father cannot provide for us, & it is very bad to grow old and be poor & laughed at'. Emma, the youngest, who has grown up in affluence with a rich aunt, protests, 'to pursue a Man merely for the sake of situation – is a sort of thing that shocks me; I cannot understand it. Poverty is a great Evil, but to a woman of Education & feeling it ought not, it cannot be the greatest. I would rather be Teacher at a school (and I can think of nothing worse) than marry a Man I did not like.' Elizabeth, better informed about the harsh realities of women's lives, replies: 'I would rather do any thing than be Teacher at a school . . . *I* have been at a school, Emma, & know what a Life they lead; *you* never have.'

The two middle sisters are depressed, quarrelsome and unrealistic in their expectations of men who are merely casual acquaintances; the expression on their faces is 'sharp and anxious'. One brother, Robert, has married the daughter of a lawyer with enough money of her own to allow her to condescend mercilessly to her sisters-in-law. Mrs Watson is dead and Mr Watson is largely confined to his room. Emma Watson finds home life the more difficult because she has been brought up with expectations of inheriting her widowed aunt's riches, only to see her aunt succumb to a fortune-hunting Irish officer as a second husband. Emma was 'sent back a weight upon your family', as her brother delicately puts it; 'By Heaven! A woman should never be trusted with money,' he adds, by way of reproach to his late aunt.

If family life among the Watsons is grim, when the upper classes appear they are no better. Lord Osborne, who admires Emma at a ball, is the sort of man who talks loudly about a woman within earshot: 'Why do not you dance with that beautiful Emma Watson . . . and I will come and stand by you . . . & if you find she does not want much Talking to, you may introduce me by & bye.' Then, 'bring me word how she looks by daylight'. Deciding to have a word with Emma, he returns to the ballroom with the excuse that he is looking for his gloves, not bothering to hide the pair he is holding in his hand. His friend, Tom Musgrave, is a self-satisfied puppy who could appear with very little alteration in a feminist novel of the 1990s. When the young ladies arrive at the inn where a ball is to take place, Musgrave is standing, not yet dressed for the evening, in the doorway of his bedchamber, in order to watch them walk by. He tries to bully Emma into accepting a lift she does not want, and enjoys turning up unexpectedly at the Watsons', and boasting about his grander engagements.

These and other impressions of provincial life, set down from memory as she sat in Bath, strike as truthfully as anything in Austen. There is the cold, empty appearance of the town ballroom before the dancing starts; the powdered hair of the footman in the best house in town, the curl papers in the hair of the daughter of the house, and the mother's two satin dresses 'which went thro' the winter'. We learn that conversation is impossible when driving through the town in an open vehicle, from the clatter of the streets. We see a plate of fried beef make up the whole dinner of Elizabeth and Emma when they are on their own, and serving themselves, at home. There is a lordly invitation to look in on the hunt meeting – 'Everybody allows that there is not so fine a sight in the world as a pack of Fox-Hounds in full cry. I am sure you will be delighted to hear the first Burst' – with the recommendation to wear half-boots or come on horseback, made to a young woman who can afford neither.[7]

The picture of society is bleak and pessimistic, and although the narrative moves fast, Mary Lascelles, who trained a keener eye on

Austen's style than any other critic, finds that she 'seems to be struggling with a peculiar oppression, a stiffness and heaviness that threatens her style'.[8] One scene alone lights up the fragment, when Emma takes pity on little Charles, a ten-year-old who is longing to dance at his first ball, and is let down by his promised partner. Emma offers to dance with him instead, and his delight and gratitude at having such a pretty partner, and staying up so late, and being able to tell her about his life – Latin lessons, his first horse and his first hunt, the stuffed Fox and Badger he would like to show her at the Castle – is tenderly realistic. He is proof of how carefully Austen listened to children talking; and he is the most attractive child in her work.

Little Charles apart, *The Watsons* is cheerless. Deaths feature so little in Austen's novels that you can't help wondering how she would have described the last moments of Emma Watson's father, who was to be killed off, according to Cassandra's recollection of Jane's plan. But before she reached that point, she had to face a whole series of real deaths. In October 1801 Eliza's beloved son Hastings, worn out by increasingly frequent fits, died at the age of fifteen. The fat, fair baby who had been the plaything of all the Austen family at Steventon was more cruelly afflicted than their own George. Although he learnt to speak, and Jane was very struck by his formal phrases, remembering him talking of 'my very valuable friend', his condition deteriorated as he grew, and he endured a 'sad variety and long series of pain'. By the time he died, his mother had come to understand he had no expectation of a normal life, and now turned to the hope that her 'dear child' had exchanged 'a most painful existence for a blissful immortality'.[9] She had him buried in Hampstead beside his grandmother, the stone inscribed 'Also in memory of her grandson Hastings only child of Jean Capot Comt. de Feuillide and Elizabeth his wife born 25th June 1786 died 9th October 1801': choosing not to give him the title his father had claimed.

Eliza went to Godmersham for two weeks, alone; she and Henry were often apart. He had given up his commission and set up as part banker, part army agent, with offices in Cleveland Court, St James's; he also opened a branch of his bank at Alton in Hampshire. Some months after the death of his stepson, he wrote to Warren Hastings to solicit financial help, and was politely turned down. 'I regard with sensations little short of horror the possibility of appearing to you capable of meanness or rapacity,' explained Henry in a further letter; but that source of patronage was now firmly closed off.[10] Another avenue of opportunity opened when the Treaty of Amiens made it possible to travel to the Continent again. Austen family tradition has it that he and Eliza travelled to Gabarret together to try to claim her first husband's estates, or at any rate what was owing to her and her mother from them; and that they were nearly trapped in France by the ending of the peace, and got back to England thanks only to her near perfect French. French tradition suggests that the English Monsieur 'Ostin' was not welcome in the Gers. Jean Capot de Feuillide's brother and sister had already made their claim to the Marais and taken possession; but no one had the resources to restart the drainage scheme, the land was unproductive, and the money that had been poured into it was lost.

Another death that struck Jane Austen more nearly came on her twenty-ninth birthday, when her old friend Mrs Lefroy suffered an accident. She had been riding to Overton to do her shopping, accompanied by a servant. In the village she happened to meet James Austen, and remarked to him on the stupidity and laziness of her horse; but on her way home the same horse bolted. The servant failed to catch the beast, and in trying to dismount she fell on the road. The effects were beyond Mr Lyford's skill, and within a few hours she was dead. Jane had hardly time to come to terms with this news when her father was taken ill. He had 'oppression in the head, with fever, violent tremulousness, & the greatest degree of Feebleness'. Everything happened very fast, and 'being quite insensible of his own state, he was spared all the pain of separation, & he went off almost in his Sleep'.

This was Jane's account to her brother Francis in January 1805. She spoke warmly of their father and his 'virtuous and happy life', and with what seems like curious detachment of 'the Serenity of the Corpse' being 'most delightful! – it preserves the sweet, benevolent smile which always distinguished him'. 'The loss of such a Parent must be felt, or we should be Brutes.' Indeed: although this sounds still more detached. If Jane was reliving her childhood memories of her father, thinking over the times she played in the church vestry and he allowed her to write the names of imaginary husbands in the parish register, she kept such thoughts, and her sorrow, firmly to herself. She was, as always, practical and sensible, and she did what she thought best, finding a pocket compass and a pair of scissors that had belonged to their father to send to Frank; and you can be sure she was attentive in every way to her mother, whatever the dryness and coldness about her heart.

Mr Austen died in a house in Green Park Buildings East to which they had moved not many weeks before, after the lease on Sydney Place ran out, and now they had to move again. They found modest lodgings at 25 Gay Street, while the Austen brothers worked out how best to support their 'dear trio' of women, left with a much diminished income. The Church did nothing for widows and orphans of clergymen, as the Watson sisters knew. Mr Austen's livings went to the next incumbent – in this case his son James – and his little annuity ended. Generous Frank wrote at once offering £100 a year, although he had recently become engaged to a Ramsgate girl with no money of her own; but he felt happy, with his pretty nineteen-year-old Mary Gibson promised to him, and rich, because he had just been appointed Flag-Captain of HMS *Canopus*, a fine French ship carrying eighty guns, captured at the battle of the Nile. It was to be used to chase the French across the Atlantic.

Mrs Austen would accept only half his £100. James and Henry each offered a more cautious £50. Henry wrote of his own 'present precarious income', and mentioned Frank's expectations of £500 a year from the *Canopus*. Both he and James travelled to Bath to see their mother, and James came away thinking she would be happy to spend her summers 'in the country amongst her Relations' and her winters in 'comfortable Lodgings in Bath'. He had nothing to say about his sisters; it did not occur to him that they might like, and benefit from, a permanent home.[11] Charles was far away patrolling the Atlantic for American ships seeking to trade with France; he could do nothing. Edward was expected to add another £100 a year. Mrs Austen and Cassandra each possessed a little capital, enough to produce something like £200 more. Jane had nothing.

The precariousness of Henry's financial situation makes you wonder what had happened to his wife's fortune. There was enough of it left, at least, to finance their expensive life in London, where they kept a carriage and a superbly named French chef, Monsieur Halavent, in their house in Upper Berkeley Street, off Portman Square; and Henry needed well-situated offices, choosing them first in St James's, later at the Albany. He was able to make frequent visits to Godmersham. In fact he was there when the news of his father's death came; and he was back again for three weeks in May and June, then briefly in August, and for another month at the end of the year, which suggests that office routines at the bank were not too onerous. No doubt he believed his business depended more on good contacts with rich men prepared to pay high interest rates on what they borrowed than on day-to-day bookkeeping. Up to a point he was right; but banking was a high-risk business.

Hastings's nurse, Madame Bigeon, was too closely attached to the family to leave their service after the death of her charge. Her own daughter, Marie Marguerite, was married in the Catholic church in King Street, Portman Square, on 7 June 1805, close to her employers' house. Henry was at Godmersham, but Eliza must have given her blessing. The bridegroom was a Frenchman, Pierre Frayté or Fraytet, *dit* Perigord, which suggests he was a soldier from the Périgord district in south-west France; it was a common thing for men in the French army to adopt the name of their place of origin in this way, rather than using their parents' name. He was thirty-five, and the bride was thirty; as it happens, the same age as Jane Austen.[12] The bridegroom disappears from the story again after the wedding, and Madame Perigord, as she always called herself, remained with her mother, childless, and attached to Henry's and Eliza's household.

This same June, Jane left Bath for Godmersham with her mother and sister. On the way they stopped at Steventon to collect Anna. Mary had just given birth to her second child, Caroline, and was naturally very much occupied; this generation of babies was not put out to nurse, and Caroline was not weaned for nine months. In Kent, Edward's Fanny and James's Anna enjoyed themselves together; they read romances in the appropriate Gothic seat in the park, fortified with 'gypsy' baskets of bread and cheese. Fanny's diary also noted that her grandmother and aunts played at school with them, and joined in theatrical performances. It was during this visit that Jane made friends with the governess, Anne Sharp, no mean actress herself.

Wed. 26 June. Aunts & Gmama played at school with us. Aunt C was Mrs Teachum the Governess Aunt Jane, Miss Popham the Teacher Aunt Harriet, Sally the Housemaid, Miss Sharpe, the Dancing Master the Apothecary & the Serjeant, Grandmama Betty Jones the pie woman & Mama the Bathing woman. They dressed in Character & we had a most delightful day. – After dessert we acted a Play called 'Virtue rewarded'. Anna was Duchess St Albans I was the Fair Serena & Fanny Cage a Shepherdess Flora. We had a Bowl of Syllabub in the evening.[13]

In August they put on *The Spoiled Child*, one of the biggest hits of the London stage, in which Mrs Jordan triumphed year after year as 'Little Pickle', the naughty boy of the title. Another part for Miss Sharp, perhaps, given her willingness to take on male roles. There was dancing and much merriment. One evening Jane and Elizabeth went to a ball in Canterbury, where Henry had arranged to meet them. Fanny says nothing in her diary about the troop movements in Kent, caused by another invasion scare, but we know they were worrying her father and his land-owning friends, fearful that their game would be disturbed by the soldiers: a case of weighing up the relative disadvantages of invading Frenchmen and a shortage of pheasants. Fortunately they were not put to the test. This was the last invasion scare of the war, and, at the end of August, Napoleon evacuated the Boulogne camp and turned his attention elsewhere. Edward took Fanny to London to stay with Henry and Eliza; there was a theatre party, and she met Lord Charles Spencer at dinner at the Albany. Then back to Kent, and the whole family, with Mrs Austen, Jane and Cassandra, was taken to Worthing. It was altogether a busy, cheerful, luxurious life at Godmersham.

'Seven years I suppose are enough to change every pore of one's skin, & every feeling of one's mind,' wrote Jane to Cassandra this year, thinking back over the drama and upheavals they had gone through. She did not need too say that in seven years she had lost home and father. Nor did she care to spell out that she now had little prospect of marriage; and that she had almost lost hope of getting anything published. It was unnecessary to state that she was penniless, dependent on her brothers, and obliged to accept whatever living arrangements were chosen for her. These were not things you wrote down; if possible you did not allow yourself even to think about them.

18

Brotherly Love

'We must not all expect to be individually lucky. The Luck of one member of a Family is Luck to all.' The words are put into the mouth of Emma Watson, trying to make the best of a bad situation; Jane Austen may have wanted to convince herself of their truth, or at any rate to try out the idea. Families can be support systems when the lucky ones pass on their luck to the others, but at bad times they feel more like traps from which you want only to escape. Emma Watson discovers as much. So did Jane, in the years immediately following the death of her father. Whatever individual luck her brothers enjoyed, it was not easily passed on to her, as a glance at their situations shows.

James first. He had taken over their father's living at Steventon, and remained comfortably at Steventon rectory with Mary and his three children, Anna by his first marriage, clever, sensitive and unhappy in feeling she was slighted by her father as well as her stepmother; good little James-Edward, and baby Caroline. There were to be no more. James's time was given to Church duties, to hunting – he bought his son a pony and introduced him to the sport early – and a quiet social round that centred on his regular dinners with the Chutes at The Vyne. He also devoted a good deal of energy to writing poetry, some to amuse his immediate family – there is a very funny account of the family cat Tyger stealing the steak meant for his dinner – and some long, serious, melancholy works; but he had published nothing since *The Loiterer*. He was gifted, but he could not channel his gifts effectively. His wife ran the house, garden, cow and poultry; she drove her own little chaise and was on good terms with the neighbours. Once or twice a year they might go to see a play put on in Basingstoke, or attend a Basingstoke ball; nothing ambitious. They were always ready to be hospitable to Cassandra and Jane; this did not prevent considerable tensions between brother and younger sister.

George, the luckless member of the family, his condition unchanged for better or worse, remained at Monk Sherborne; he was approaching forty, and continued to share his life with his Uncle Thomas, who would soon be sixty. James, being so close, was no doubt deputed to keep an eye on their care, and Mrs Austen could, if she chose, visit her son and brother when she stayed with James. Did George recognize his mother? If he suffered from cerebral palsy, he could well have done so, and other members of his family also. To them, although they made sure he was cared for, he remained unmentionable; another silence in Jane's life.

To balance George's bad luck, Edward enjoyed the spectacularly good. He owned not only Godmersham and all its lands but large estates in Hampshire as well. Chawton House, near Alton, was let out to tenants, and Steventon Manor was still leased to the Digweeds. His wife's family also possessed fine houses and estates in Kent; and he could expect a further increase in his fortune when his benefactress Mrs Knight died. He was rich in children too; in 1806 he and Elizabeth already had nine, five sons and four daughters. The bigger boys were at boarding school at Eltham, preparing for Winchester; the girls studied with governesses at home; Miss Sharp, Jane's friend, left at the beginning of 1806, giving poor health as her reason, although she took another job at once. Edward could afford to take his family for seaside holidays and trips to London, staying at a hotel in Jermyn Street, dining with Henry and Eliza and their grand friends, and going to the theatre. He lacked imagination and was uninterested in books or ideas, but had a good head for business and a kindly, uncomplicated nature. He was fond of his family and his wife's family, entertained them all freely, and took pleasure in planning expeditions and treats. But his sisters may well have asked themselves how much of Edward's luck was passed on to them when even the idea of providing a permanent home for them and their mother did not occur to him at the time of his father's death, although he must have had houses at his disposal. What did occur to Elizabeth with increasing frequency was that Cassandra should help out with her children. Cassandra's visits to Godmersham may have given her the chance to put the idea of a house into his head; if so, it took some considerable prompting.

Henry needed little prompting at any point in the conduct of his life. Ambitious and optimistic, he must have envied Edward, to whom everything was given, while he had to struggle and make his own luck entirely by his wits. He is the odd one out among the Austen boys, the one in the middle, quite as adventurous in his way as the brave sailor brothers; and he was the only one of them, George aside, to remain childless. He was always said to be Jane's favourite as well as their father's, who lent or gave him more money than any of his brothers; and she remarked more than once in her letters on how agreeable he was, how he never failed to be amusing, how much she enjoyed his company. At the same time there is something indulgent in her tone when she writes of him, as though she favoured him in the way a sweet unreliable boy may be favoured. I have already suggested Wickham has a touch of Henry; I guess she gave some of his wit to Henry Tilney, and to Henry Crawford his play-reading skills and all-purpose flirtatiousness. Crawford's readiness to be moved by innocent goodness while keeping a taste for dangerous games could owe something to him too. Where Jane and Henry resembled one another was in seeing the possibilities in things: for her, the possibilities presented by her imagination; for him, the possibilities presented by life. An engagement, a career move, a friendship in high places, a possible patron, a new bank branch, even a simple pleasure jaunt would catch his fancy and set him going, alight with enthusiasm.

In 1806 he was expanding his banking business optimistically; later he took the brother of a friend from the militia into partnership, James Tilson, whom Jane was to know well. He and Eliza had moved to Brompton, then on the outskirts of town, where they continued to lead a somewhat semi-attached existence. He spent the New Year celebrations for 1807 at Godmersham without her, joining in plays and other festivities, and was in Kent in July, *en garçon* again, for the races; while Eliza stayed in London, with her music and her books. Fanny's diaries make clear how delightful both she and her mother found him: sociable, entertaining, the perfect house guest.

Clever too; and yet a faint question mark hangs over Henry. Jane's letters suggest that the Miss Pearson to whom he was engaged before he married Eliza bore him a grudge for his treatment of her, despite his claim that she jilted him; she may have felt he gave her cause. He strikes you as a shade too eagerly on the make, with his rich friends – not to mention his rich wife – and his sycophantic letters. All that ambition and optimism had to ride on the hectic, ostentatious society for which the Prince of Wales set the standards, and into which Henry had been introduced through his aristocratic fellow officers in the regiment. With his brains, his charm, his taste, his desires, he was a man of his time, and saw no reason why he should not win for himself the rewards and pleasures he could see there for the taking. I do not for a moment believe he gave up a career in the Church because Eliza expressed a preference for a secular husband; it was because he saw better possibilities elsewhere.

Francis, closest to Jane in the nursery, then away for many years, grew close again, and especially in 1806. What she knew of his experiences in the navy moved her to admiration for his courage, endurance and practical skills; and she was sympathetic when, in the unluckiest moment of his career, he missed the Battle of Trafalgar in October 1805.[1] She could have no opinion of what she did not know, of shipboard brutality, of clandestine services to the East India Company, or high-handed dealings with foreign powers; she saw a sober, sensible, well-conducted brother who served his country single-mindedly at sea and deserved a happy life at home. To his impatience to be married in the summer of 1806 she gave her warm support, even without meeting Mary Gibson, the Ramsgate girl he fell in love with while commanding the Sea Fencibles on the North Foreland. He was thirty-two, an age when a man has surely earned the right to a wife. And he could afford to marry; there was prize money, there were formal thanks from the House of Commons, and other rewards coming in after he chased the French across the Atlantic, commanding the *Canopus*, and contributed to their defeat at the Battle of St Domingo.

As for Charles, no one had set eyes on the youngest brother since the end of 1804, when he departed for the North America Station. He had an affectionate heart, and was lonely for his sisters, whom he loved dearly; and he found comfort by becoming engaged to a sixteen-year-old beauty in Bermuda. Fanny Palmer came of a family of English lawyers who had made careers for themselves on the island, but she had no fortune and was still younger than Francis's Mary. She and Charles were married in Bermuda in May 1807, a romantic match on the edge of the world between the young naval officer and the pink-cheeked, golden-haired child bride, with only her married sister to support her. He naturally had no family present at all. Letters went to and fro, but Fanny did not meet any of the Austens for another four years, when Charles was at last posted back to England, by now with two little daughters; the babies and their girlish mother were then warmly taken into his family, especially by Cassandra and Jane, always tender to their little brother.

And Cassandra? In her own words Jane was 'the sun of my life, the gilder of every pleasure'; which made her the moon and shadow to Jane's brightness.[2] Cassandra is never much more than a darkly seen shape; like the silhouettes which are the only representations of her, outline only. Her niece Caroline (James's younger daughter) wrote, 'I did not *dislike* Aunt Cassandra – but if my visit had at any time chanced to fall out during *her* absence, I don't think I should have missed her.'[3] A good woman, there is no doubt of that, but there is something disquieting too about a once cheerful, pretty girl who elects the role of virgin widow in her early twenties, so certain she will never recover from the loss of one lover that she rejects youth and its pleasures in favour of melancholy and self-effacement. The only passion of hers that has survived is in her letters about Jane, written in the days after her death, when she spoke of her being 'part of myself' and even reproached herself for having loved her so much, accepting that God had punished her for such exclusiveness: 'I can acknowledge . . . the justice of the hand which has struck this blow.' Her submission suggests a particularly nasty view of divine justice: because you love someone better than other people, God punishes you by killing the person you love. If this was Cassandra's view of the working of her maker, her company may not have done much to raise Jane's low spirits.

Jane did once suggest Cass could be funny, and she must have laughed at Jane's jokes; but no one remembers Cass making any. She did not complain either, it seems, about being the permanently useful sister-in-law, nurse and aunt; and may well have done everything she could to protect Jane from being absorbed in the same way. As the only person Jane discussed her work with, she was in a unique position to encourage her and question her about her plans. She was also the closest witness of Jane's depression, seeing before her eyes how the lack of a settled home kept her from writing and wasted her God-given gifts. Cassandra must have worried more than anyone else when Jane fell silent after the marvellous books of the 1790s.

But for the moment there was nothing to be done, and all through 1806 the sisters were as unsettled as ever. Most of the first three months were spent in Hampshire, at Steventon with James and Mary, and at Manydown, where it was agreed that the awkwardness of Harris's proposal should be forgotten. Halfway through March, Jane and Cass returned to Bath; their mother had taken Anna to another set of lodgings, and was negotiating to move yet again. This further removal fell through, to the relief of her daughters, who continued to find the gaieties of Bath disagreeable. They remained in Trim Street, boxed in among buildings and with no gardens in sight, into the summer; Martha Lloyd, whose mother had died, took lodgings near by, and it was agreed that she would join them as a fourth member of the household wherever they settled next. The question was where.

Now one of the brothers did make a proposal. Francis was eager to be married and had fixed on the month of July; he knew he must necessarily be away at sea a great deal, and he suggested that he and his Mary should share a house with his mother, his sisters and Martha. Whatever Mary Gibson felt about the prospect of living with four unknown older women, she did not question Frank's idea. Since they had to be near a naval base, he proposed Southampton, in Hampshire, close to Portsmouth and already familiar territory. It was an attractive town then, still surrounded by its medieval walls, with open walks beyond them beside the sea and along the River Itchen; and it was busily promoting itself as a spa and a resort. The Austens agreed to start off in lodgings and do their house-hunting once they were there.

But first Mrs Austen carried her daughters off for the summer on another of her favourite rounds of visits to the *cousinage*. While they were travelling, Frank was married in Ramsgate, and took his bride to Godmersham for their honeymoon. Jane produced a poem to mark the occasion. It was written for Fanny, in her voice, describing the arrival of the bridal pair at Godmersham, and sent to Fanny to amuse her, although it was certainly meant to reach Frank too. Done with a novelist's eye and ear for the scene in front of the great house where the children are waiting to welcome the 'lovely couple', it sparkles with joy for her brother. You hardly expect Austen to write an epithalamium, but it is her best piece of verse:

> Down the hill they're swift proceeding
>   Now they skirt the Park around;
> Lo! The Cattle sweetly feeding
>   Scamper, startled at the sound!
>
> Run, my Brothers, to the Pier gate!
>   Throw it open, very wide!
> Let it not be said that we're late
>   In welcoming my Uncle's Bride!
>
> To the house the chaise advances;
>   Now it stops – They're here, they're here!
> How d'ye do, my Uncle Francis?
>   How does do your Lady dear?

Jane had not met Mary Gibson, but she knew she was already Fanny's friend; Mary had stayed at Godmersham after becoming engaged to Frank, in the autumn of 1804, when he and Charles were both there, and Fanny's diary describes how the two girls went nutting together in the river walk, and grieved when 'the horrible abominable beastly Admiralty' summoned both the young men to return to their ships in the small hours. Now Fanny wrote stolidly in her diary, 'I had a bit of a letter from Aunt Jane, with some verses of hers.'[4]

The Austen ladies had left Bath at the beginning of July, Jane and Cassandra rejoicing at their escape from the place they had come to hate, to which they never went back; when they needed to take the waters some years later, they chose Cheltenham. But now Mrs Austen took them, after a preliminary stay at Clifton, to Adlestrop in Gloucestershire, where Cousin Thomas Leigh presided at the rectory, with his nephew at the big house. The old gentleman was pleased to show the improvements carried out to the estate by the landscape designer he had employed at great expense, Humphry

'Nutting', illustration from *The Seasons* by James Thomson (1794)

Repton, the most fashionable name available. Repton had opened the grounds of the two houses into one large park, constructed a waterfall to run through the flower garden, and enclosed the village green. This last part of the scene can hardly have been considered much of an improvement by the villagers; but they were powerless against the combined power of Repton, fashion and their landlord.

Their stay in Adlestrop was cut short when Cousin Leigh swept them off to Warwickshire to be his guests at Stoneleigh Abbey. The great house was not quite his, but he had just heard he was in line to inherit it. Hence the hurry: as a result of one of the complicated wills that were such a feature of life among Leighs and Austens, there were other claimants, and Mr Leigh was determined to be on the spot. He installed himself firmly at Stoneleigh among the scores of servants whose mistress had just died, buttressed by his lawyer and a large party of friends, including his fascinated Austen cousins. Other claimants, among them Mrs Austen's brother James Leigh-Perrot, gathered more discreetly in London and complained of his behaviour; but an inheritance was an inheritance. It demanded that you put yourself out.

The Stoneleigh estate and mansion were set in lush country on the banks of the Avon where the original Cistercian abbey had once stood. Mrs Austen wrote to Mary at Steventon, bubbling with enthusiasm for the grandeur of the place, relishing every moment of her stay and alert to every detail of the house, the grounds, the servants and the service. She counted the front windows, making them forty-five (and getting it right). She suggested to her Cousin Thomas that he might install signposts along the labyrinthine corridors ('I have proposed his setting up *directing Posts* at the Angles'). She revelled in the scale of everything from the kitchen garden and fish ponds to the billiard room; she even began to worry about the cost of putting the scores of servants into mourning for their late mistress. She described the state bed chamber, with its high dark crimson velvet bed, as 'an *alarming* apartment just fit for a Heroine' – a nod to Jane – and the shady woods around the house 'impenetrable to the sun even in the middle of August'; Humphry Repton had not arrived here yet, although he soon would.[5] She wrote of visits made to Warwick and Kenilworth castles; and of the chocolate, coffee, tea, plum cake, pound cake, hot and cold rolls and bread and butter on the breakfast table. 'Dry toast for me,' she finished, boasting with some justification of her asceticism.

Yet another distant Leigh cousin, the widowed Lady Saye and Sele, joined the house party. She was a tedious and scatty old woman: 'rather tormenting, tho' something amusing, and affords Jane many a good laugh', wrote her mother. It is a relief to hear of Jane laughing, even satirically, under the assembled weight of so many decrepit family members and hangers-on. She came away with one useful impression at least: the chapel at Stoneleigh is like enough to the one described in *Mansfield Park* to suggest it was the model for the chapel at Sotherton, with its plain sash windows, lack of ornament, wooden pews and gallery for the family.

After this they went on to Cousin Edward Cooper in Staffordshire. Hamstall Ridware was a peaceful rural spot in principle, and the rectory a fine house, but the eldest Cooper boy turned out to be a pompous bully of twelve and all eight little Coopers went down with whooping cough one after another. Jane caught it from them, and coughed her way through the autumn.

So back to Steventon in October, where Frank and his Mary were waiting for them, and on to Southampton. Cass had agreed to spend Christmas at Godmersham, where there was a tenth baby. Fanny wrote in her diary: 'Nov. 16, Mama did not go to Church. About ½ after 8 in the evening, my dearest Mama was safely delivered of a daughter. She had a good night & I saw her afterwards & the baby, which is immense. Fri. 21 Baby to be Cassandra Jane.' Cassandra had earned the compliment, and Jane surely did not mind being tucked in perfunctorily after her. 'Mama' did not leave her room until 15 December, when she dined in the schoolroom; she did not go out of the house until mid-January, and went to church for the first time at the end of January. But the children had the usual Christmas dancing and games, Hunt the Slipper, Oranges and Lemons, Wind the Jack, Lighting a Candle in Haste and Spare Old Noll; the gentlemen enjoyed their rabbit and snipe shooting, and the boys rode in the park.

While this was the Godmersham Christmas, Jane's Southampton one was not so enjoyable. Martha went to her sister Eliza Fowle in Berkshire. Frank's Mary was pregnant and feeling ill, with fainting fits that usually came on after eating a hearty dinner, as her sister-in-law put it, a touch uncharitably. Looking back from our easier century, you feel how wretched it must have been when a longed for marriage brought pregnancy and illness almost before the couple could enjoy one another; but this is a strictly anachronistic piece of sympathy. Then James and his Mary invited themselves with their baby Caroline for the New Year. It was at the end of this visit that Jane wrote to Cass, 'When you receive this, our guests will be all gone or going; and I shall be left to the comfortable disposal of my time, to ease of mind from the torments of rice puddings and apple dumplings, and probably to regret that I did not take more pains to please them all.' It is a classic statement, immediately recognizable to anyone who has taken charge of a family Christmas with limited space and money at their disposal. She loved them, but the demands of that love left her time unprotected, and this made her hate them too.

She never pretended to like James's Mary, who was not in the least interested in books and rather too interested in money; and James himself was not above criticism. When he wrote to say he planned to make another visit, she told Cass, 'I am sorry & angry that his Visits should not give one more pleasure; the company of so good & so clever a Man ought to be gratifying in itself; − but his Chat seems all forced, his Opinions on many points too much copied from his Wife's, & his time here is spent I think in walking about the House & banging the Doors, or ringing the Bell for a glass of Water.'

The eye for detail is perfect and would grace a novel. At once James appears before us, a man not quite at ease either with his sister or himself, making nervous, unnecessary demands and asserting opinions not really his own, but ones he has been browbeaten into by the stronger personality at home. In his wife's diary, incidentally, he is always put down simply as 'Austen', just as Mrs Elton refers to 'Knightley' rather than 'Mr Knightley' in *Emma*, to Emma's disgust. Jane herself never failed to give every gentleman his 'Mr' in her letters, as did Mrs Chute in her diaries. Mary Austen's was standard usage, and implied no disrespect to her husband; but there are nuances to such things, as Jane appreciated. James's banging of doors and ringing of bells somehow seems more 'Austen' than 'Mr Austen'; you cannot imagine his father behaving so.

Jane found little good to say about their Southampton neighbours either. 'Our acquaintance increase too fast,' she grumbled. 'There was nothing to like or dislike' in a friendly admiral and his daughter. Another family 'live in a handsome style and are rich, and she seemed to like to be rich, and we gave her to understand that we were far from being so; she will soon feel therefore that we are not worth her acquaintance.' After this spleen, there was something to cheer her up at last. In February she was writing to Cass, still in Kent, about the house they had found. It was old and not in very good repair but with plenty of room, and a large garden that ran to the town walls; and it was the garden that made her happy. She writes as a long-deprived gardener restored to bliss; and you remember her showing chaffinch nests to Edward's children all those years ago, in the garden at Steventon. She ordered a syringa in honour of Cowper's line: 'Laburnum, rich / In streaming gold; syringa, iv'ry pure'. 'We also talk of a Laburnam,' she went on, and there were to be currants, gooseberries and raspberries as well as new shrubs and roses. It is a relief to find her happy in the prospect.

The house stood in Castle Square, and the landlord was the Marquis of Lansdowne, who had just built himself a mock-Gothic castle alongside which formed part of their view.[6] Jane had some dealings with Lord Lansdowne's house painter, or 'domestic Painter I shd call him,' she wrote, 'for he lives in the Castle – Domestic Chaplains have given way to this more necessary office, & I suppose whenever the Walls want no touching up, he is employed about my Lady's face'. An old-fashioned joke, but the Marchioness was generally despised as having been her husband's mistress before she was his wife, and no doubt she did paint her face. Otherwise she was harmless, and added to the gaiety of the place; she drove a little phaeton drawn by eight extremely small ponies, which appealed greatly to visiting children, who watched them, entranced, from the Austens' windows.

Henry brought Cass home from Godmersham, where he had entertained everyone by reading a play aloud on two successive evenings, and they all moved into the Castle Square house. At once Frank was given a command and had to leave to fit out his ship, the *St Albans*, which was to do convoy duty to the Cape of Good Hope, and then to China. This left his mother and sisters to take charge of Mary's confinement in April. It did not go well. Fanny was kept informed and entered in her diary that Mary was 'so ill as to alarm them extremely', and that she relapsed into bad fainting fits after the birth; an anxious time for her sisters-in-law. Frank's Mary, like Edward's Elizabeth, was destined to bear eleven children, and to die after giving birth to the last; this time she recovered, and Frank got home for the christening of his daughter in May, and stayed with them until the end of June, when he sailed for the Cape.

Before he went, Edward came over to see him in Southampton. He had been visiting his estate at Chawton following the departure of his tenant there, and suggested to his mother and sisters that they might like to join him in September at Chawton House for a family holiday while it stood empty. He could escort his eldest son to Winchester for his first half while they were there, and James and Mary could come over from Steventon too; there was plenty of room for them all. So while Mrs Frank took her child to see her family in Ramsgate, the other ladies made their first visit to Chawton House. Its tapestried walls, intricate corridors, huge old fireplaces, great hall, gallery and family portraits impressed them properly, but not to the exclusion of more modern attractions; Fanny's diary records three shopping expeditions to Alton with Aunt Jane in five days.

The family party went on to Southampton, where the three Austen ladies entertained Edward, Elizabeth, Fanny and her brother William at Castle Square for several days, and Henry came to join them. They went to the theatre to see John Bannister in *The Way to Keep Him*, Arthur Murphy's perennially popular satire on women who stop bothering to please their husbands after marriage. There was a boat trip to Hythe, and another to see the picturesque ruins of Netley Abbey: 'we were struck dumb with admiration, and I wish I could write anything that would come near to the sublimity of it,' wrote Fanny in a letter.[7] Other visitors to Netley objected to the stalls for toys and gingerbread, and the presence of picnicking parties.[8] And Fanny's diary records 'we eat there some biscuits we had taken and returned quite delighted. Aunt Jane and I walked in the High Street till late.' The next day Henry hired a sociable and took everyone for a drive in the New Forest; everyone except Aunt Jane, that is, who had perhaps had enough of the family, and stayed at home alone.

19

A Death in the Family

For another year Jane's time was given to her brothers and their families. She was thirty-three in December 1808, and settling into the role of maiden aunt. If she was not with Francis, Mary and their baby in Southampton, she was at Steventon with James and his three children, or at Godmersham, with Edward's troop of ten. She also went to the Fowles at Kintbury, where the rectory had passed, like Steventon, to the eldest son, Fulwar. Old Mr Fowle was dead, and so was his son Charles, another childhood friend, only in his thirties; now there were eight children in the new generation, ready to be entertained by visiting 'aunts'.

The only childless home was Henry and Eliza's, where she spent a month in June and July. Their house at Brompton was small, but they were good hosts. They had time to make conversation, and kept up a round of dinner parties with London friends as well as theatre and concert-going; Henry even owned his own box at the Pantheon Opera House in Oxford Street.[1] Eliza was distinctively different from the other sisters-in-law, at once stranger and sadder through her complicated cosmopolitan history, and closer to Jane, as a first cousin whose memories went back to her earliest years.[2] There was another pleasant feature to the household in her French women servants, Madame Bigeon and her daughter Marie Marguerite, Madame Perigord; Jane found them charming and interesting. Brompton was altogether a different world, where there was time to sit and talk, and an appreciation of a whole range of the pleasures of life: food and wine as well as music, pictures and reading.

At Manydown too there was leisure for conversation; her two weeks with the Biggs were such a success this year that she invited them for a return visit to Southampton in the summer. It was to be a 'snug fortnight' when her mother would be away at James's, and a happily anticipated release. When she found the arrangement was going to fall through, because she was at Godmersham and no one there could conveniently escort her back to Southampton in time to receive her friends, she was so upset that she was driven, uncharacteristically, to plead with Edward. The family had simply assumed that Godmersham was as good for her as anywhere else, and that she might as well stay there for another two months until Henry was due to come down, when he would take her back. It had not crossed anyone's mind that she might have plans of her own to be taken into account. She must have felt like an awkward parcel.

Jane had to give Edward and Elizabeth a 'private reason' for needing to keep her engagement with the Biggs before they gave way and he agreed to take her home. Perhaps she told him she did not want to offend the Manydown sisters after her treatment of their brother; they were after all an important county family. Even then Edward was ungracious about the journey, and Jane wrote resignedly, 'till I have a travelling purse of my own, I must submit to such things'. Not that there was the least prospect of such a purse.

The snug fortnight would be the last with Catherine Bigg, who was to be married, at thirty-three, to a clergyman approaching sixty, the Revd Herbert Hill. Jane's remark as the wedding day in October approached, 'tomorrow we must think of poor Catherine', suggests how she viewed her friend's fate.[3] She was learning to see that spinsterhood, a condition which had for so long looked fearful, could be a form of freedom. In August, Frank was home again, and told them he and Mary wanted to move to a home of their own on the Isle of Wight. Jane quite saw the point: with 'plenty of each other' they 'must be very happy', and she was happy for them; but for herself she had seen enough of babies and pregnancies to know she could live contentedly without them. The events of the next months confirmed that feeling.

Cassandra went to Godmersham for Elizabeth's eleventh confinement. There was already a nurse installed, and the boys had gone off to school, the two eldest now at Winchester. Fifteen-year-old Fanny wrote in her diary on 27 September, 'Mama as usual very low', but on the 28th, 'About three this afternoon to our great joy, our beloved mother was delivered of a fine boy and is going on charmingly.' On 4 October 'Mama got up for dinner', and the next day 'Papa to Quarter Sessions'. On Saturday the baby was named Brook-John, names from Elizabeth's family. Three days later, the mother was dead, leaving a family stunned by the suddenness of her collapse. The doctor could offer no explanation; she had eaten what Fanny called a hearty dinner only half an hour before the end. She was thirty-five: a well-to-do, well-born, well-looked-after woman who had married for love at eighteen, and been pregnant almost permanently ever since.[4]

Henry dashed to Godmersham, and letters flew to and fro between Cassandra and Jane, and from both of them to more distant members of the family who must be informed. 'May the Almighty sustain you all,' wrote Jane, invoking Him as she had not felt necessary at the time of her father's death. She thought of 'dearest Edward, whose loss & whose suffering seem to make those of every other person nothing', but also 'of Henry's anguish', acknowledging his special position at Godmersham; 'but he will exert himself to be of use & comfort'. She excused herself from 'a Panegyric on the Departed' beyond a line on 'her solid principles, her true devotion, her excellence in every relation of Life', her chief thoughts being with the children, Fanny propelled into the position of mistress of the house and virtual mother to the new baby, and the boys away at school. They were fetched by James to Steventon, to her disappointment: 'I should have loved to have them with me at such a time.' Then there was poor little Lizzy, who was, with seven-year-old Marianne, packed off to boarding school in Essex within three months, neither their elder sister nor their Aunt Cassandra raising any objection. Jane kept worrying about 'dear little Lizzy & Marianne in particular', and the 'poor little girls' were much in her thoughts on the day they were sent away. The little girls protested so strongly that they were allowed home and given a governess, but not before they had spent a year at school in Wanstead.[5]

'I suppose you see the Corpse, – how does it appear?' asked Jane of her sister, with somewhat disconcerting curiosity. She may have been thinking of the only dead body she had seen, her father's, whose sweet and serene expression had comforted her, and hoping for the same reassurance. She went on to imagine Edward 'restless in Misery going from one room to the other – & perhaps not seldom upstairs to see all that remains of his Elizabeth'. Ten days later young Edward and George arrived at Castle Square. They had come by coach from Steventon, insisting on sitting outside with the coachman, and although he gave them his coat they were chilled to the bone.

Now Jane rose magnificently to the task of comforting the two boys. She was too sensible to expect them to pine and grieve or listen to psalms and sermons more than could possibly be helped. Instead, she made paper ships with them, to be bombarded with chestnuts, and organized card games and spillikins. She thought up riddles and charades, and best of all went out on the river with them to see a battleship under construction, allowing them to take the oars of the rowing boat for a good part of the way. She knew from her own childhood what boys enjoy, and felt instinctively how much better it was to cheer them up with excursions and games than to insist on mourning. It is one of the rare moments in the Austen family history when she was in command; and she did exactly the right thing.

In the midst of all these arrangements there was another preoccupation. Edward had at last made the offer of a house to his mother and sisters; or rather he now offered them a choice of two, one close to Godmersham in the pretty village of Wye, the other his bailiff's cottage in Chawton village, the bailiff having died, and his widow being willing to leave at midsummer. Chawton cottage could be put in order without much expense, and there was a garden, some outhouses, six bedrooms and garrets for storage. Mrs Austen was pleased with the idea of Wye, but was easily persuaded by the other three – Martha remained one of the group – to take Chawton. They knew the village and had already appreciated its nearness to Alton. Henry had a branch of his bank there, and James was only about twelve miles away, which was bound to weigh with his mother. And it was rural Hampshire, to which their tastes and loyalties strongly inclined them. So it was decided, and the move set in motion, to take place in July.

Cassandra remained at Godmersham throughout the winter, where the period normally given to festivities, including Edward's and Elizabeth's wedding anniversary, passed sadly. But Jane, in Southampton, had an access of high spirits. She insisted on Martha going with her to the play, advancing absurdly the reason that she 'ought to see the inside of the Theatre once while she lives in

Southampton, & I think she will hardly wish to take a second view'. Next the two of them went dancing, taking themselves to the Assembly Ball at the Dolphin. Jane was surprised to be asked to dance ('You will not expect to hear that *I* was') by a black-eyed gentleman whose name she did not know. After that she and Martha may have danced together, rather than joining the 'many dozen young women standing by without partners, & each of them with two ugly naked shoulders!' If she disapproved of bare shoulders, she enjoyed everything else; there were new dances that year, named as usual for public figures and causes like the anti-slavery bill: 'The Fair Slave' and 'Mr Canning's Waltz', as well as 'The Ocean Fiend', 'Brighton Races' and 'Lady Dashwood's Reel'.[6] Jane reminded Cassandra that they had both attended a ball at the Dolphin fifteen years ago, and went on to say she was quite as happy now as she had been then. It was a claim she would scarcely have made at any time during the past ten years. 'In spite of the shame of being so much older', as she put it, she was reviving, growing cheerful and purposeful. She enjoyed teasing Martha by pretending to believe she was carrying on an immoral love affair with a local clergyman, a respectable married man. Martha was 'the friend and sister under every circumstance', she told Cass, not quite tactfully perhaps. And the friends went dancing again in January, to celebrate Queen Charlotte's birthday, or perhaps simply Jane's good spirits.

In April she wrote to Richard Crosby, the publisher who had bought *Susan* (*Northanger Abbey*) for £10 six years before from Henry's lawyer and done nothing with it. The letter is firm and confident, offering to supply a copy of the book if it had been lost and they were prepared to print it now without delay; otherwise she intended to find another publisher. Her confidence failed only at the thought of other eyes seeing what she was about, and she asked him to answer care of the post office, and to a false name she had chosen for herself, 'Mrs Ashton Dennis'. Crosby was not impressed and wrote back three days later denying that there had been any stipulation as to when he would publish, or that he was bound to do so, and offering to sell the manuscript back to Mrs Ashton Dennis for £10.

She was in no position to raise so much money. Jane's entire spending money for 1807, the only year for which we have her accounts, was something like £50, and it was made up from money allowed her by her mother, plus a little extra from Edward and also the generous Mrs Knight. Of this £14 on clothes, more than £8 on laundry, nearly £4 on postage, above £6 on presents and £3.10s 3½d. on charity; the hire of a piano cost her £2.13s.6d., and rather less than £1 went on plays and 'waterparties'.[7] It was a modest budget, and since she was wholly dependent on other people's goodwill for every penny she had to spend, and could not be certain of next year's income, there was no question of repurchasing her manuscript. Crosby remained both uninterested in publishing and unwilling to return it. She had to let it go, and it was only in 1816 that it was bought back.

The house in Castle Square was given up in May. Martha went to stay with friends in London, the others to Godmersham, where Henry and Eliza also made a rare visit together. Instead of plays Henry now read prayers in the library, a new departure, signifying a change of mood in the family following the death of Elizabeth.[8] Fanny went for walks with Aunt Eliza, and attempted some mimicry of her conversational style in her diary: 'Uncle & Aunt Henry Austen went away early ce matin. Quel horreur!' she wrote when they left. They were moving too, to a house in newly fashionable Sloane Street.

Next to leave Godmersham were Jane and her mother. By 7 July they were in the cottage at Chawton, joined soon afterwards by Cassandra and Martha. The effect on Jane of this move to a permanent home in which she was able to re-establish her own rhythm of work was dramatic. It was as though she were restored to herself, to her imagination, to all her powers: a black cloud had lifted. Almost at once she began to work again. *Sense and Sensibility* was taken out, and revision began.

20

At Chawton

Chawton village, a dozy place startled into attention several times a day by the clatter of rapid coach traffic through its centre, stood where three roads met: to the north, Alton and London; to the south, Winchester if you followed one fork, Gosport along the other. The Austens' cottage was on the corner at the divide, so close to the road that the beds in the front rooms upstairs were sometimes shaken by the six-horse coaches that thundered past. Slower carriages allowed curious passengers to see into the rooms. 'I heard of the Chawton Party looking very comfortable at Breakfast, from a gentleman who was travelling by their door in a Post-chaise,' Mrs Knight wrote to Fanny soon after Mrs Austen had moved in.[1] She liked to look out at the village street, and often sat by the sunny dining-room window to enjoy whatever it offered by way of entertainment.[2] Jane also amused herself with the passing traffic: at the start of the Winchester term she observed 'a countless number of Postchaises full of Boys pass yesterday morng – full of future Heroes, Legislators, Fools and Villains'.

The house was L-shaped, of red brick. Built as a farm about 1700, it later served as an inn; there were two main storeys, and attics above under the tiled roof. Opposite it, between the fork in the roads, was a wide shallow pond, and at the back a 'pleasant irregular mixture of hedgerow, and grass, and gravel walk and long grass for mowing, and orchard, which I imagine arose from two or three little enclosures having been thrown together, and arranged as best might be, for ladies' occupation', according to Jane's niece Caroline, who knew the place well.[3] There was a kitchen garden, a yard and generous outbuildings. The church, the rectory and Chawton House were ten minutes' walk away along the Gosport road. Something like sixty families lived in the village, almost all labourers on Edward's farms and woodlands. They naturally held their employer's mother and sisters in great respect, and carried out work for them on his orders, digging the garden, for instance, and chopping firewood. The ladies in return taught some of the village children to read, and made clothes for the needy, of whom there were a great many in those increasingly needy times; the altogether destitute were maintained from the poor rates. The Austen ladies also extended kindness to another sort of villager in the shape of Miss Benn, sister of a poor clergyman with too much family and too little income to help her, and reduced to renting a labourer's cottage. 'Poor Miss Benn' appears very much oftener in Jane's letters than their few better-off neighbours; she was not very interesting, but then nor were they.

Before the ladies arrived, Edward had the plumbing renewed for them. This did not mean indoor sanitation, of course; some town houses had water closets by then – Henry's and Eliza's, perhaps – but you did not expect the luxury of piped water in a country cottage. An improved pump at the back, and a better cess pit for the privy, well away from the house, would be enough. Some structural alterations were also carried out; however much Mrs Austen liked looking out at the passing world, it was thought better to have the front drawing-room window blocked, replaced by a large and pretty Gothic one on the garden side. The ceilings were low and roughly finished, and none of the bedrooms large, but it was furnished comfortably enough, or at least to the standard of an ordinary country parsonage: this is again according to Caroline.

Mrs Austen and Martha each had a bedroom to themselves, and there was a 'Best Bedroom' kept for guests; family tradition says that Jane continued to share with Cassandra, as they had done at Steventon.[4] Their bedroom was one with a fireplace beside which you could sit comfortably in an armchair in your dressing-gown; and two beds, as at Steventon.[5] We find it surprising that Jane did not want to be alone, claiming the privacy that seems appropriate to a writer; especially since she had often enjoyed a room of her own during the many periods when she and Cass were separated. But sisters can become couples, as dependent on the companionable chat of bedtime as husband and wife; Jane described to Anna how she read aloud to Cassandra 'in our room at night, while we undressed'.[6]

No doubt they also found pleasure in playing the game of contrasting personalities. I knew two middle-aged sisters who, in the innocent days of the 1950s, explained to my mother in so many words that they thought of themselves as being like husband and wife; the elder went out to work wearing a suit, the younger preferred flower-printed dresses and took charge of their house and garden. They were certainly sisters, and not lesbian companions, and had evolved their own way of living which both found quite satisfactory. Neither Jane nor Cassandra adopted a masculine role – they had too many brothers to compete with to allow that – but they enjoyed their complementarity. 'I know your starched notions,' Jane teased Cassandra. To the younger generation, Jane was not the prickly person who appears in many letters but the warm and lively aunt, while Cass was 'colder and calmer'. Where Cass was prim, even dull, Jane was always ready to entertain them. Where Cass gave her niece Fanny a lecture on astronomy which left her with a headache, Jane laughed over a silly story with Anna, and Cass 'would exclaim at our folly'.[7] Their different roles were known and understood within the family.

And Cassandra knew how to leave Jane alone. Jane got up first, and went downstairs to her piano before anyone was about. The piano was an early acquisition at Chawton, and must have stood in the drawing room, at the end of the house, out of earshot of the main bedrooms. While she practised, or simply thought, or wrote, a maid laid the fire in the dining room and filled the kettle. Then Jane prepared the nine o'clock breakfast for the rest of the family. That was, by agreement, her only household responsibility beyond keeping the key of the wine cupboard, and, since breakfast was nothing more than tea and toast, both made on the dining-room fire, it was not a demanding one. In this way she was privileged with a general exemption from domestic chores when Cass and Martha were at home – almost as a man was privileged. They took responsibility for all the arrangements for the other meals of the day, the morning snack and the late-afternoon dinner; Martha's recipe book has survived, with its soups, cakes, cheese puddings and vegetable pies.[8] There was a cook – she was paid £8 a year – but the planning and a good deal of the work must have been in the hands of the ladies.[9] Mrs Austen was now also relieved of being housekeeper-in-chief, and gladly gave herself to the garden. Her granddaughter Anna described her at work there: 'She dug up her own potatoes, and I have no doubt she planted them, for the kitchen garden was as much her delight as the flower borders, and I have heard my mother say that when at work, she wore a green round frock like a day-labourer's.'[10] Mrs Austen in her seventies, dressed as a labourer and putting in potatoes, must have been one of the sights of Chawton.

The Austens did not enter into the social life around Chawton as they had at Steventon. There were no dances and few dinners, and they remained largely withdrawn into their private activities, except when enlivened by family visits. 'Our small family party has been but seldom enlarged by friends or neighbours,' reported Cassandra to Cousin Phila after the Christmas season of 1811.[11] Frank had moved his wife and baby to be near them again while he sailed the China seas, and his second child was born at Rose Tree Cottage on the Alton road just after they moved in. Because the baby was a boy, Jane wrote a congratulatory poem to Francis; she was conventional enough to feel he mattered more than his elder sister. The verses began, 'My dearest Frank, I wish you joy / Of Mary's safety with a Boy, / Whose birth has given little pain / Compared with that of Mary Jane'. The reference to pain suggests she may again have been in attendance at the birth; and from now on, with a sense of the ordeal of childbirth made more sensitive also by Elizabeth's death, she is more inclined to write pityingly of married women. But she never criticizes her brothers.

At the end of the verse epistle she wrote of her pleasure in their new home:

> how much we find
> Already in it, to our mind;
> And how convinced, that when complete
> It will all other Houses beat,
> That ever have been made or mended,
> With rooms concise, or rooms distended.

The metaphor is brilliantly surprising with its suggestion of rooms as living tissue to be cut short or swollen; we have all seen concise bathrooms and distended kitchens.

Some old neighbours turned up at Chawton, and there was news

Chawton, July 26. – 1809. —

My dearest Frank, I wish you joy
Of Mary's safety with a Boy,
Whose birth has given little pain
Compared with that of Mary Jane. —
May he a growing Blessing prove,
And well deserve his Parents' Love! —
Endow'd with Art's & Nature's Good,
Thy name possessing with thy Blood,
In him, in all his ways, may we
Another Francis William see! —
Thy infant days may he inherit,
Thy warmth, nay insolence of spirit; —
We would not with one fault dispense
To weaken the resemblance.
May he revive thy Nursery sin,
Peeping as daringly within,
His curley Locks but just descried,
With "Bet, my be not come to bide." —
    Fearless of danger, braving pain,
And threaten'd very oft in vain,
Still may one Terror daunt his Soul,
One needful engine of Controul

The poem by Jane Austen to her brother Frank on the birth
of his son

of others. Harry Digweed from Steventon had married a Dummer girl, Jane Terry, and moved to Alton. Jane was ferociously condescending about them, the more so when her niece Anna, James's daughter, aged only sixteen, declared her determination to marry Mrs Digweed's brother, Michael Terry, a shy clergyman in his mid-thirties. It was a classic case of the girl who feels bored and unwanted at home rushing into the first love affair that comes along, and it fizzled out after her father had given his reluctant permission for the engagement. She was invited to Godmersham, and Mr Terry travelled to Kent to visit her, and won the approval of Fanny and her father; but on returning home Anna announced she had changed her mind. This annoyed her father and stepmother as much as the original engagement, and she was sent to spend three months at Chawton with her grandmother and aunts in the summer of 1810. Officially, she was in disgrace; in truth, she enjoyed herself and was better entertained than at Steventon.

Jane kept up regular contact with the Biggs; Alethea's nephew William Heathcote and her nephew James-Edward were close friends and went to Winchester together. Through James and Mary as well as through Manydown came news of the Chutes, the Portsmouths, Harwoods, Bramstons and Lefroys. Jane was not much better pleased with Anna's second engagement than with her first, this time to Benjamin Lefroy, the youngest son of her old friend. 'There was *that* about her which kept us in constant preparation for something,' as her aunt wrote, sounding as though the whole family were nervous of what Anna, attractive, wayward and unpredictable, might do next, if not with one young man, then with another. Fifteen years had gone by since Jane herself set out to shock the neighbours by her behaviour with Benjamin Lefroy's cousin, and there must have been some consciousness of this at the back of her mind even as she made her aunt-like pronouncements about the ill-matched temperaments of Ben and Anna, he a solitary with a 'queerness of Temper', she gregarious and unsteady. Anna's alleged unsteadiness disappeared entirely when she became a married woman; and Jane herself had, after all, broken off an engagement. You wonder if the aunt's occasional asperities towards her clever, charming niece are tinged, however faintly, by regrets for her lost Lefroy.

When Ben Lefroy turned down a curacy on the grounds that he was not sure about taking orders, the family was enraged; he told his future father-in-law he would have to give up the engagement rather than be pushed into the curacy. James complained about this during one of his frequent visits to Chawton, made on horseback, alone and across country, as he most enjoyed travelling. Occasionally he brought a poem for them to read. In 1812 there was 'Selborne Hanger':

> Who talks of rational delight
> When Selborne's Hill appears in sight
> And does not think of Gilbert White?
> . . . Oh could my rude and artless lay
> Such sweet attractive charms display . . .
> Ne'er would I seek fictitious theme . . .

As far as we know, James never did seek a fictitious theme after his early efforts in *The Loiterer*, and about these he now spoke slightingly.[12] He does not appear to have offered encouragement to his sister in her writing, although he did later respond warmly to *Mansfield Park*.[13] When he composed his memorial lines to her they were full of love and praise for her character, but remote about the quality and content of her writing. He commended her for not giving offence in spite of her eye for the ridiculous, and for keeping up her share of domestic work while she wrote; also for not succumbing to the vanity or pride that afflicts authors.[14] In another late poem he singled out Scott as a novelist, but did not mention her. All this suggests a somewhat ambiguous reaction from the eldest son, who considered himself the writer of the family, towards the little sister, who claimed the territory from him and used it to produce – well, only novels: 'only some work in which the greatest powers of the mind are displayed, in which the most thorough knowledge of human nature, the happiest delineation of its varieties, the liveliest effusions of wit and humour are conveyed to the world in the best chosen language'. The passage in defence of the novel in *Northanger Abbey* has the ring of personal argument; it also loyally singles out two other women novelists, Burney and Edgeworth, for praise. Whether James and Jane ever discussed the subject of women's fiction openly or not, there are the elements of a debate in their respective writings.

Henry's visits were as likely to be impromptu as announced; he would arrive in his curricle or gig to see his bank partner in the High Street in Alton, and then take one of his sisters for an outing to Selborne or Petersfield. Edward came from Kent in the autumns of 1809 and 1810 and the spring of 1812, with Fanny, now his indispensable companion, so devotedly did she take on her mother's role; they divided their time between Chawton and Steventon, went to Alton Fair, took the boys to Winchester and were invited to dinner at The Vyne.[15] Fanny was always glad to return to Kent, but he found these Hampshire visits so congenial that he decided not to re-let Chawton House when the present tenants' lease expired, but to keep it for family use.

Charles, still in the Atlantic – he did not return to England until 1811 – sent news of his two Bermuda-born daughters and asked his sisters to stand as godmothers. Frank arrived home in July 1810 to see his son for the first time. In the public sphere he received formal thanks from the Admiralty for his effective command at sea; and from the East India Company a thousand guineas and some silver-plate for bringing back 'Treasure' from China to England. Like Warren Hastings, Frank was a pragmatist who worked with high efficiency within the conventions he found and did not think of trying to change them. He had joined the navy to make money as well as to serve the country, and could well take the view that carrying bullion for the East India Company was one way of serving his country. These were in fact his last dealings with the Company; he went on to serve in the North Sea, fighting the Americans in the war that broke out in 1812, and later escorting convoys in the Baltic. Mary bore him a second son in 1811.

All this family business stirs in the letters of aunt, sister, godmother and good village lady. The other life was stirring too, entirely apart from Chawton and her brothers' careers and children: Jane Austen managed the day-to-day routines of a novelist with an efficiency and discipline worthy of her naval brothers. The famous account of her working habits, given by her nephew, credits her with almost miraculous powers in stopping and starting under interruption.

She was careful that her occupation should not be suspected by servants, or visitors, or any persons beyond her own family party. She wrote upon small sheets of paper which could easily be put away, or covered with a piece of blotting paper. There was, between the front door and the offices, a swing door which creaked when it was opened; but she objected to having this little inconvenience remedied, because it gave her notice when anyone was coming.[16]

The picture is admirable, exasperating, painful; and can be only half true. How she juggled with revisions under such circumstances becomes especially mysterious; neat and dextrous as she was, she could not go through a complete manuscript of *Sense and Sensibility*, making changes and rewriting, with only single sheets of paper under her blotter. There must have been times when the other inhabitants of the cottage protected her silence and privacy with something more effective than the creaking door. There was after all no reason why she should not have worked upstairs, or in the early morning during her piano-practising time.[17]

Encouragement and practical help came from Henry. In the last months of 1810 the publisher Thomas Egerton of the Military Library, Whitehall, agreed to publish *Sense and Sensibility*. Henry's army connections may have helped to make the deal, but Egerton was not enthusiastic enough to take any risk when an ex-officer offered him a manuscript by an anonymous lady. He merely agreed to publish on commission, which meant the author paid for the printing, plus something for advertising and distribution, and kept the copyright. 'Printed for the Author' states the first edition of *Sense and Sensibility*: Henry and Eliza's money paid for the printing.[18] And in March he and Eliza welcomed her to Sloane Street again, where she began to correct her proofs.

At this point Jane Austen hoped the book would appear in June. The immediate family, and friends as close as Mrs Knight, were in the know – Jane expected her benefactress to like at least the character of Elinor – but she begged them to preserve strict secrecy as to her authorship. A fellow novelist, Mary Brunton, publishing at the same time, told a friend why she would not consider letting her name be known to the public: 'To be pointed at – to be noticed & commented upon – to be suspected of literary airs – to be shunned, as literary women are, by the more unpretending of my own sex: & abhorred, as literary women are, by the more pretending of the other! – My dear, I would sooner exhibit as a rope dancer.'[19]

A lady naturally avoided any public notice; but the intensity of Jane Austen's feelings about seeing her work in print after so many years was overwhelming. 'No indeed, I am never too busy to think of S&S,' she told Cassandra. 'I can no more forget it, than a mother can forget her sucking child.' It is the rejoicing, vulnerable voice so rarely heard in her letters; much closer to Marianne's voice than Elinor's, and not unlike the one prompted by Tom Lefroy fifteen years earlier. Like every writer, Jane was frightened of the world's response; at the same time her book was the child of her heart; and she must have known in her heart that it was good.

The end of April came and the printer had reached only Chapter 9 and Willoughby's first appearance, not even the end of the first volume. Henry was hurrying him as best he could, but he was about to go away on business. No matter, Eliza would act for him: 'It will not stand still during his absence, it will be sent to Eliza.' The acknowledgement of Eliza's concern with the printing of the book, able to take over Henry's role, and judged reliable to Jane, is important; as the printing went on slowly, the sister-cousins had a common interest and purpose. They had always been friends; now their friendship acquired an extra dimension, and they made plans for Eliza to come to Hampshire for a fortnight's visit in the summer.

Sense and Sensibility was advertised on 31 October 1811 in the *Morning Chronicle* as 'a New Novel by a Lady—'. A week later another advertisement called it an 'Extraordinary Novel!' and at the end of November it had become, in the way of newspaper announcements, 'Interesting Novel by Lady A—'. Who could the mysterious Lady A— be? She was good for publicity purposes at any rate. Publication dates were no more exact then than now, and the number of copies printed is not known but is not likely to have been more than 1,000; the three-volume edition sold for fifteen shillings. It sold out by the summer of 1813, and made Jane a profit of £140. The importance to her of this first money she had earned for herself can be best appreciated by women who have endured a similar dependence. It signified not only success, however modest, but freedom; now she could decide one or two things for herself. She could give presents and plan journeys. A fixed order had been moved.

Well before *Sense and Sensibility* sold out, Egerton saw that it was a success and was ready to buy her next work. There were favourable reviews, well meant if leadenly worded: 'very pleasing and entertaining' and 'well written; the characters are in genteel life, naturally drawn, and judiciously supported. The incidents are probable, and highly pleasing, and interesting; the conclusion such as the reader must wish it should be'.[20] Still more important, it had taken the fancy of the *beau monde*, the people whose taste and opinions were most influential, and was passed round at dinner tables and in letters to friends and lovers. Lady Bessborough, clever and sharp as a pin, friend of Sheridan and the Prince of Wales and sister of the late Duchess of Devonshire, had the perception to complain that it ended 'stupidly', but she was greatly amused by it. Little Princess Charlotte, next in line to the throne, sixteen years old and simultaneously neglected and quarrelled over by her parents, the Prince Regent and his estranged wife Caroline, felt that 'Maryanne & me are very alike in *disposition*, that certainly I am not so good, the same imprudence, &c however remain very like. I must say it interested me much.'[21] The family of Lord Holland was delighted with it too, judging from the remark of his eldest son, who told Charles Austen a few years later that 'nothing had come out for years to be compared with "Pride and Prejudice" and "Sense and Sensibility"'.[22]

Egerton was prepared to pay for the copyright of *Pride and Prejudice*. He offered £110 and, although Jane had hoped for £150, she accepted, no doubt on Henry's advice. This was in November 1812. Copyright at that date was in any case not as it is today; it lasted for only fourteen years, extended for another fourteen if the author were living. 'It's being sold will I hope be a great saving of Trouble to Henry, & therefore must be welcome to me,' Jane wrote to Martha; it meant he did not have to advance money. To Cass she again called the new book 'my own darling Child'. It was advertised as being 'by the Author of *Sense and Sensibility*' and sold for the higher price of eighteen shillings; and was immediately reviewed extremely favourably, with particular attention given to Elizabeth Bennet's character. There was even greater enthusiasm from the public. Sheridan recommended it as one of the cleverest things he had ever read; it must have reminded him of his own mastery of dialogue before he threw away his best talents, and he was generous enough to recognize and hail a greater voice than his own. Henry Austen was told by a literary gentleman that it was much too clever to be the work of a woman. Warren Hastings wrote so admiringly that Jane was 'quite delighted'. The great world read, laughed and bought.

Jane Austen herself was not part of this excitement. She was preserving her anonymity at Chawton, and alone with her mother; Cass and Martha were both away visiting when *Pride and Prejudice* appeared. She had sets sent to her brothers, and celebrated publication by taking turns with her mother to read the first chapters aloud to Miss Benn, as they sat beside their fire on a damp January evening. 'She was amused, poor soul! *that* she cd not help you know, with two such people to lead the way; but she really does seem to admire Elizabeth. I must confess that *I* think her as delightful a creature as ever appeared in print, & how I shall be able to tolerate those who do not like *her* at least, I do not know.' Just for once in her life, whether she knew it or not, Miss Benn was the luckiest person in the kingdom.

When Mrs Austen took over the reading on Miss Benn's second visit, she went too fast, and 'tho' she perfectly understands the Characters herself, she cannot speak as they ought'. Jane could not help being exasperated by her mother, the strong, stubborn old woman used to being in charge, who wanted to make her mark even in appreciating and interpreting her grown-up daughter's work. She found too that anonymity, however ladylike, had considerable drawbacks. Every author hopes to talk about a newly published book, but there was no one at hand to talk to. She wrote to Cass about the typographical mistakes and the sudden realization that she had made the Bennets serve suppers when they would not have done; and how a ' "said he" or a "said she" would sometimes make the Dialogue more immediately clear – '. Since there was no one at Chawton with whom she wanted to discuss any of this, she went out walking, in the mud, to Alton; at least she escaped her mother's visitors, she grumbled.

Then she decided she would let young Anna into her secret. After that, she wrote to Cass at Steventon to inform her that other people in Chawton were reading books by Miss Edgeworth and Mrs Grant; although she does not say so, no author is quite pleased to hear of other books being read when hers is available. Foolish Mrs Digweed had the three volumes of Mrs Grant's *Letters* and 'it can make no difference to *her*, which of the 26 fortnights in the Year, the 3 vols lay in her House'.[23]

When she returned to the subject of *Pride and Prejudice*, she let her pen run on as freely as if she were in love with her 'darling Child'; as indeed she had every right to be.

> The work is rather too light & bright & sparkling; – it wants shade; – it wants to be stretched out here & there with a long Chapter – of sense if it could be had, if not of solemn specious nonsense – about something unconnected with the story; an Essay on Writing, a critique on Walter Scott, or the history of Buonaparte – or anything that would form a contrast & bring the reader with increased delight to the playfulness & Epigrammatism of the general stile. – I doubt your quite agreeing with me here – I know your starched Notions.

She liked to tease Cass when she was happy, and there are few passages in the letters so happy, so witty, so free as this. Here she has no need of defences, and her prose sails as blithely and brightly as any of Elizabeth Bennet's most beguiling speeches.

21

Inside Mansfield Park

In the spring of 1811, when Jane was correcting her proofs while staying with Henry and Eliza in Sloane Street, Eliza gave a musical party. She employed professional pianists, harpists and singers, decorated her drawing room with a hired mirror, special chimney lights and floral arrangements; eighty guests were invited and over sixty came, overflowing from the first-floor drawing room into the passages and front room. The party was a success; it went on until midnight and was mentioned in the *Morning Post*. Jane enjoyed the music, and reported to Cassandra that a drunken naval captain talked to her about their brother Charles. On another evening Eliza took Jane to visit a French friend, the Comte d'Antraigues, with his musical Countess and son Julien. 'It will be amusing to see the ways of a French circle,' wrote Jane.

What neither she nor Eliza knew was that Emmanuel Louis d'Antraigues was a spy, in the pay of both the Russian and the English governments, and now in some trouble; his English protector was Canning, but Canning was no longer Foreign Minister, and d'Antraigues was fearful about his own future. He was also anxious to rid himself of his wife.[1] Naturally none of this was apparent during the Austens' visit. 'Monsieur the old Count, is a very fine looking man, with quiet manners, good enough for an Englishman – & I beleive he is a Man of great Information & Taste. He has some fine Paintings, which delighted Henry as much as the Son's music gratified Eliza.'

'The old Count' was fifty-eight. The Countess was a retired opera singer, Anne de Saint-Huberty, who had been at the height of her fame in the 1780s. The Austens could reflect that such marriages were not unknown in English society, since the Earl of Craven, kinsman to Cassandra's fiancé, had married the popular actress Louisa Brunton in 1807.[2] Eliza's acquaintance with d'Antraigues may have dated from the 1780s, during her first marriage; like Capot de Feuillide, he was a Gascon, and a favourite young officer at Versailles; unlike de Feuillide's, his title was genuine. Beyond this, nothing about him was straightforward. He had veered between free-thinking and religion, between a vehemently expressed republicanism and support for the monarchy, and had to leave France in 1790; his castle was burned down by his peasants, and he never returned, but wandered Europe working for those who would pay. Napoleon imprisoned him in Trieste, and he travelled to Russia, where he was employed by Alexander I, officially as an adviser on education. He arrived in England in 1807, apparently an unfortunate *émigré*, and his wife was invited to set up a singing academy by the Duchess of York.

The quiet manners that impressed Jane Austen were thus a cover for a man who had intrigued all his life, and was now embittered and desperate; and the following year d'Antraigues and his wife were both brutally murdered by their manservant, a deserter from the French army in Spain. The young Comte Julien held Napoleon responsible, but d'Antraigues' biographer believes it was no more than the act of an embittered servant, adding that d'Antraigues' position in England was barely tenable ('il était à peine toléré en Angleterre'). There the story rests, and there is no further mention by Jane Austen. But how did Henry and Eliza come to have such raffish and even dangerous friends? Had they no inkling of their situation, or did d'Antraigues have contacts useful for Henry? There is no knowing. In London society it was difficult to be sure of anyone's credentials; opera singers and actresses became countesses, just as Eliza herself had been a countess, or believed herself one. The long decades of war had stirred the brew so that nothing was dependable. Henry was making his living by finding men whose interests and needs he could serve, and it was a tricky business; he counted on their honesty, they relied on their expectations, and everyone was juggling. In the same year the d'Antraigues were murdered, the Prime Minister, Spencer Perceval, was also shot dead as he entered the House of Commons, by a commercial agent who had been ruined by the economic war with France.

Eighteen-eleven, the year in which Eliza took Jane to meet the dubious d'Antraigues, was the year in which *Mansfield Park* was begun. It was also the year in which the Prince of Wales, after more than two decades of frustrated hopes, was at last appointed Prince Regent. The King was afflicted with madness yet again, and this time he was not expected to recover. In Hampshire his seventy-third birthday was nevertheless celebrated in June, with loyal parades of Volunteers on Selborne Common. In London the Prince Regent celebrated his own elevation, also in June, at Carlton House, rather differently. The party he gave was ostentatious even by his standards. It cost £120,000, money taken from a nation that had been expensively at war for nearly twenty years and was hardly able to feed its poor. To this ill-judged event the Prince failed to invite his own wife, with whom he was engaged in a long-drawn-out war of his own. Jane Austen's view of him is sufficiently indicated by a remark she made about the Princess of Wales some months later: 'Poor Woman, I shall support her as long as I can, because she *is* a Woman, & because I hate her Husband.'

Eighteen-eleven also saw the scandal of the Duke of Clarence's dismissal of his mistress and mother of his ten children, the actress Mrs Jordan. She moved out of their home and into a house in Cadogan Street, just round the corner from the Henry Austens. They may have noticed the arrival of the five younger FitzClarence children in February 1812, brought to the back door by the Duke, and their departure again in June, when their mother returned them sadly to his care, judging it in their best interest. In the House of Lords, Clarence spoke in favour of the slave trade; elsewhere he made himself a laughing stock by pursuing rich young heiresses, urged into matrimony by the Regent, himself quarrelling furiously with his wife over his daughter's custody. The behaviour of Princess Charlotte, who had so much identified with Marianne in *Sense and Sensibility*, was feared to be almost out of control. She spent her time flirting with unsuitable young men, one of them her cousin, the eldest son of Mrs Jordan. On the one hand there was social, moral and political confusion; on the other, patronage ruled. The Regent appointed Clarence Admiral of the Fleet in December 1811, putting him at the head of a system in which advancement depended largely on knowing the right people; as the Austens had always understood.[3]

The princes were able to live with a total disregard for justice, religious principles or the sanctity of marriage; but their behaviour was widely perceived as a liability upon the nation. *Mansfield Park* is, among other things, a novel about the condition of England, and addresses itself to the questions raised by royal behaviour and the kind of society it encouraged. It sets up an opposition between someone with strongly held religious and moral principles, who will not compromise them for any reason, will not consider a marriage that is not based on true feeling rather than opportunism, and is revolted by sexual immorality; and a group of worldly, highly cultivated, entertaining and well-to-do young people who pursue pleasure without regard for religious or moral principles. On the worldly side, Henry and Mary Crawford have been tainted by their uncle the Admiral, who has the power of patronage, keeps a mistress openly and passes on a light-hearted attitude towards unnatural vice in the navy to his niece. Maria and Julia Bertram are led astray by vanity and greed, unable to resist temptation; their corruption is completed by moving from their father's house in the country, where outwardly correct standards are maintained, to London, where anything goes. This is at any rate one way of looking at *Mansfield Park*; and the parallels with the highest Regency society are all there. (Readers who would like to be reminded of the plot of *Mansfield Park* can turn to the endnote.[4])

The championing of morality and criticism of corrupted standards was something many of its earliest readers were particularly pleased with. Jane Austen noted that the publisher himself, Mr Egerton, 'praised it for it's Morality'. Others mentioned the 'pure morality', enthused over its 'moral Tendency', and found its attack on the modern system of education admirable; its 'excellent moral', 'sound treatment of the Clergy' and the 'strong vein of principle' running through the whole book were all lauded.[5] When a second edition was discussed, Austen's nephew James-Edward urged her to produce a further volume 'in which the example of useful, and amiable married life may be exhibited in the characters of Edmund & Fanny'.[6]

But from the beginning there were other readers who reacted differently, among them the two most intelligent women (after Jane herself) in the Austen family. Rather than praising the high moral tone, her mother found the virtuous heroine 'insipid'. Anna also declared she 'could not bear Fanny'. Edward's son George disliked Fanny too, and much preferred Mary Crawford. Lord Holland's family considered the book inferior to the two earlier ones. Alethea Bigg thought *Mansfield Park* lacked the spirit of its predecessor, and Miss Sharp praised its characterization, 'but as you beg me to be perfectly honest, I must confess I prefer P&P.'.[7] As for Cassandra, although she was 'fond of Fanny', she also, according to one of her nieces, tried to persuade Jane to let her marry Henry Crawford; which suggests that the 'moral tendency' so much admired by other readers did not impress her much.[8]

Henry's reaction appears in something like a running commentary in Jane's letters, and very interesting it is. As he read Volume I he expressed his liking for Henry Crawford: 'he admires H. Crawford – I mean properly – as a clever, pleasant Man'. He said he could guess how the story would end; but then found himself growing baffled as he read on. After finishing the book, he appears to have confined himself to more general praise: 'his approbation has not lessened', reported Jane. 'He found the last half of the last volume *extremely interesting*.' This is a remark so noncommittal that you suspect him too of reservations about the way she chose to end the story.

Mansfield Park has remained extremely interesting to readers ever since, and has generated more debate than any of Austen's other books. In 1917 Reginald Farrer, while praising the brilliance of many passages, accused Austen of a 'radical dishonesty', of 'weighting the balance' against the Crawfords, 'who obviously have her artist's affection as well as her moralist's disapproval'. He found Fanny repellent: cold, self-righteous, rigid with prejudice, 'the most terrible incarnation we have of the female prig-pharisee' (and more). He also called the conclusion of the story a 'fraud on the reader' and an artistic failure. Twenty years after Farrer, Queenie Leavis supported his view, saying she found the book, for all its brilliance, 'contradictory and confusing' and undermined by Austen's 'determination to sponsor the conventional moral outlook'.[9] Farrer's line was taken up again vigorously by Kingsley Amis in the 1950s: 'to invite Mr and Mrs Edmund Bertram round for the evening would not be lightly undertaken'. Not only were they not fun, while the Crawfords were; they were also humourless, pompous and morally detestable. Fanny lacked 'self-knowledge, generosity or humility'.

Amis concluded that Jane Austen's own judgement and moral sense had gone seriously astray.[10]

The defence of Fanny and the 'moral tendency' was mounted by Lionel Trilling. He began by praising Mary Crawford, conceding that she 'is conceived – is calculated – to win the charmed admiration of almost any reader . . . She is downright, open, intelligent, impatient. Irony is her natural mode, and we are drawn to think of her voice as being as nearly the author's own as Elizabeth Bennet's is.' This is so well put that you wait eagerly for Trilling's elaboration on why we should admire Fanny rather than Mary; when it comes it is disappointing. He says that Austen asks us to withhold admiration from Mary's lively mind because it 'compounds, by very reason of its liveliness, with the world, the flesh, and the devil'; and that Fanny is a Christian heroine, who supports Edmund's wish to become a clergyman and do his duty in society, because the 'hygiene of the self' demands it. In the light of this hygiene, the theatricals are condemned because they involve adopting false selves; and Trilling claims that, although a first reading of the book gives us the intensely attractive Mary he has described, a second reveals her as insincere, a person for whom style is more important than real character.[11] Tony Tanner followed Trilling in praising Fanny for her 'stillness, quietness, weakness and self-retraction' as opposed to the Crawfords, with their taste for play-acting, 'movement untrammelled by morals, their world-darkened minds and their insincere hearts'.[12]

The trouble with these arguments is that they lose their force as soon as you turn back to the book and come face to face with the characters on the page. As Roger Gard put it, 'The fact is that most readers love the Crawfords, which is why some critics have to work with such nit-picking assiduity to find, or even create, retrospective faults in them.'[13] To claim that acting is bad for the character makes no sense, least of all in the context of Austen delight in it. As to why Jane Austen used it as she did: perhaps Eliza and she had laughed together over memories of *Which is the Man?* and *Bon Ton*, both rather daring plays, and this led Jane to see the possibilities of using theatricals in a novel. There is no need to believe that she condemned them outside the context of *Mansfield Park*, and indeed every reason for thinking otherwise.

Yet Tanner is right in pointing out how Austen gives Fanny, quiet and still as she is, enough moral power to overcome all the bright, lively, divided characters who threaten her peace. Timid and uncomplaining under cruel and thoughtless treatment, she is one for whom 'the advantages of early hardship and discipline, and the consciousness of being born to struggle and endure' bring great rewards. In fact she is both heroic, and a prig.

If Austen used memories of being a shy, unhappy schoolgirl observing a world she could not yet understand in creating 'my Fanny', the displaced child who will in the end triumph over everyone, it made a good starting point for a novel. But if it was the starting point, something happened along the way which changed the nature of the story she set out to tell, rather as it did in *Sense and Sensibility*; and this change of direction, intention or emphasis is exactly what gives the book its strength and power to continue to interest readers after many rereadings. Like *The Merchant of Venice*, it goes on being open to different and opposing interpretations. You can make the case for Mary Crawford and the case against her, as you can for Shylock; and the same for Fanny Price. Shakespeare's play and Austen's book are both so alive and flexible as works of art that they can be interpreted now one way, now another.[14]

Fanny's experience at Mansfield Park is bitter as no other childhood is in Austen's work. Her aunt, Lady Bertram, is virtually an imbecile; she may be a comic character, and not ill-tempered, but the effects of her extreme placidity are not comic. Although her 'tone of calm langour . . . was always heard and attended to' she is wholly ineffectual as the mistress of house and family, and her dignity is largely preserved by the good manners of her husband and her sons. (Her husband's good manners have extended to limiting the number of their children to four.) Her complacent belief that beauty deserves money derives from her own success as a good-looking girl who made a better marriage than was expected, and the only advice she offers Fanny in eight years is 'that it is every young woman's duty to accept such a very unexceptionable offer' as the proposal of marriage made by a man Fanny dislikes. She sends her maid Chapman to help Fanny dress for her ball, too late to be of any use, and is pleased to take credit for Fanny's success. Her generosity extends to giving her nephew William £10 but not to noticing how Fanny is ill-treated under her own roof. Lady Bertram's pug dog and her 'work' –

meaning needlework, much of it done by Fanny – are her chief concerns: interests would be too strong a word. She barely notices her children for much of the time, and hardly misses her husband in his absence. Sleeping on the sofa is one of her great resources, and she sleeps so reliably that people can conduct private conversations in her presence. She hardly goes out. She only 'expects to be agitated' at her daughter's wedding; and when reporting the illness of her elder son, her letter is so feebly written that it reads like 'a sort of playing at being frightened'. She and her sister Mrs Price, both tranquil in their tempers, have lost interest in one another over the years of separation to the point that 'Three or four Prices might have been swept away, any or all, except Fanny and William, and Lady Bertram would have thought little about it; or perhaps might have caught from Mrs Norris's lips the cant of its being a very happy thing, and a great blessing to their poor dear sister Price to have them so well provided for.' The suggestion that poor children might be better off dead, because 'well provided for' in the after-life, provides the sharpest lines in a novel that is deeply observant of the attitudes of the times.

Mrs Norris, Lady Bertram's elder sister, is one of the great villains of literature, almost too horrible to be comic; we laugh because Austen's timing is so good, and we enjoy seeing the horrors coming. She is characterized by meanness, officiousness, sycophancy towards the powerful and bullying of anyone she perceives to be in her power. She is determined to be at the centre of all the activities of Mansfield Park, and is the sort of woman who feels herself strengthened and confirmed in her own position by the sufferings of others. Fanny becomes her particular victim because she is an easy target – the charity child, small, weak, timid – and, as Austen acutely writes, her aunt's spiteful attitude towards her feeds on itself: 'she disliked Fanny *because* she had neglected her' (my italics). Note too her implied reproof to Sir Thomas for keeping on his labourers during the winter months, and the pleasure with which she hears of two maids being turned away at Sotherton 'for wearing white gowns', and prevents one of the estate boys from being given the lunch he expects in the Mansfield kitchen.

Sir Thomas Bertram is not so much better than his wife and sister-in-law. He has the very moderate virtue of dignity, but he chose his own wife badly, and he does not know how to talk to, let alone bring up, his children, or how to control his sister-in-law's bad behaviour in spoiling his daughters and crushing his niece. He lacks any perception of people's characters, allowing one daughter to marry a dolt – she is of course following in his own footsteps – and trying to bully Fanny into a loveless match. Here most clearly he expresses a view Fanny considers wholly wrong, although she won't tell him so; she expects a 'good man' to see that it is unpardonably wicked to marry without affection, but he doesn't, and she is reduced to hoping he will reconsider the matter. Instead he behaves disingenuously towards her, sending her to Portsmouth to bring her round to the advantage of marrying well, although through all the years of her childhood it has not occurred to him that she might wish to visit her parents, brothers and sisters. His self-righteousness and confidence in his own judgement are broken only by the behaviour of his daughters.

Maria and Julia Bertram are a weakness, rather like Bingley's sisters in *Pride and Prejudice*. In both books we are informed that they are charming when they choose to be, without seeing the charm in action. The Bertram sisters are characterized with the broadest strokes, and they are hardly differentiated – both large, blonde and pretty in a full-blown way – almost always presented together, or spoken of together. Even at the end, when their fates diverge, we are told that Julia was saved from behaving as badly as Maria only by virtue of being the younger sister, and so less spoilt, not from any essential difference of character. But since they have never been more than sketches this last piece of perfunctoriness hardly matters.

Their failings raise the question of where Fanny gets her good principles from. Not from them or their governess, not from either of her aunts, and not from Sir Thomas, who only terrifies her as he does his daughters. Yet somehow she does arrive at a morality: it consists of modesty, selflessness and an interest in good works, not unlike the heroine of Hannah More's *Coelebs*, who had hers inculcated by virtuous parents (and was not much admired by Austen).[15] Obedience to parental orders is part of Hannah More's package, but it is in rejecting obedience in favour of the higher dictate of remaining true to her own conscience that Fanny rises to her moment of heroism, as she defies Sir Thomas and Lady Bertram over the question of marriage. This is the mouse-taking-on-the-lion moment when even readers who dislike Fanny find something to admire. She also questions him about the slaves on his West Indian estates. Brian Southam has suggested that her question ('Did not you hear me ask him about the slave trade last night?') is met with dead silence because Sir Thomas could not answer her to his own satisfaction, being necessarily a supporter of the slave trade, and that by raising the question at all, Fanny bravely makes her own abolitionist sympathies clear.[16]

Otherwise Fanny is cautious and censorious. Jokes make her and her cousin Edmund uneasy. She takes joy in the stars, in music and poetry and flowers, and in her brother William; but she is not a joyous person, perhaps because her childhood experiences have dried up something in her spirit. Not only is she the least joyous of all Austen's heroines, she is the most reluctant to open her mouth; when she does she speaks in a stilted and wooden manner. This is credible, but it is one of the things that makes it hard to believe that Henry Crawford could ever fall in love with her. Crawford is supposed to admire her character, her goodness, her strict moral standards, but how does he get to know her? He first takes notice of her at a dinner at which he speaks almost a page of monologue, addressed to Fanny, while she either says nothing or tells herself silently 'Oh! what a corrupted mind!' as he speaks on. Finally she ticks him off on the subject of the theatricals – 'every thing had gone quite far enough' before subsiding into trembling and blushes. The next day he tells his sister that 'I never was so long in company with a girl in my life – trying to entertain her – and succeed so ill!' Not a recipe for attraction.

He then watches her listening to her brother's account of naval life, and 'had moral taste enough to value' what he saw. She becomes aware that he is 'trying to cheat her of her tranquillity'. (Mary's encouragement to her brother is, 'Your wicked project upon her peace turns out a clever thought indeed. You will both find your good in it.' Then 'I know that a wife you *loved* would be the happiest of women, and that even when you ceased to love, she would yet find in you the liberality and good-breeding of a gentleman.') And Henry admires Fanny's 'ineffable sweetness and patience', the neat arrangement of her hair and her 'speaking at intervals to *me*'.

Only since we don't hear her speaking we can't judge for ourselves. Again, when he tells her about her brother William's promotion, and follows this up with his proposal, she is 'exceedingly distressed, and for some moments unable to speak', and then says, 'Don't, Mr Crawford, pray don't. I beg you would not. This is a sort of talking which is very unpleasant to me. I must go away. I cannot bear it.' When he visits her in Portsmouth and reaches his highest point in her favour, he asks her to advise him about the management of his estate; her answer is, 'We all have a better guide in ourselves, if we would attend to it, than any other person can be.' They are almost the last of the few words she addresses to him, and they are her central statement about her moral position. They are also enough, surely, to convince him as well as us that the two of them are unlikely to achieve any satisfactory form of communication.

It is Mary Crawford who can, in Trilling's phrase, bring a conversation to a gallop, and her sprightliness and wit are close to Austen's. Her disrespect for the cloth is not so different from the attitude of the creator of Mr Collins and Mr Elton; and indeed takes some of its justification from within the book, in the shape of her brother-in-law Dr Grant, who schemes his way to a stall at Westminster and dies of gorging on three great institutional dinners in one week. Mary's cynical remarks resemble ones found in the letters, and her improper joke about rears and vices in the navy must have been appreciated by Jane before she gave it to her; which makes it difficult for Jane to be entirely on Edmund's side here (he 'felt grave, and only replied, "It is a noble profession."'). And Mary is not always playing the London sophisticate; there is real sweetness and generosity in her behaviour towards Fanny, as well as thoughtlessness and occasional deviousness. Mary intervenes when Mrs Norris is ranting against Fanny; she also opens her heart to her, letting her into her true feelings for Edmund.

The philosopher Gilbert Ryle decided that William Price, Fanny's sailor brother, was the real hero of the book, because he makes her happy; and that their sibling love is the standard against which all the other loves in the book are measured. By that argument the Crawfords do quite well, their mutual devotion never in question either. Readers who can accept the way the story is tied up will accept too that Fanny is in effect marrying a brother in the cousin she has loved since childhood. Their life will be lived within the orbit of Mansfield, on good terms with Sir Thomas and Lady Bertram for all their faults, unforgiving towards the other sinners. The waif turns into something like Queen Victoria; among its other achievements *Mansfield Park* is prophetic.

Was Jane Austen herself satisfied with her heroine and her denouement? Her own words on the subject of 'Novels and Heroines; – pictures of perfection ... make me sick & wicked' cause you to wonder.[17] The remark was written in the last year of her life, and suggests at the very least that she looked back on Fanny Price with complex and divided feelings.

She was a great enough artist to put more than one truth into a book. That Fanny rises to heroism and also hates Mary Crawford does not prevent Mary Crawford from being delightful and ready to like Fanny. There are different ways of being good, and different degrees of bad behaviour too. The fitting up of Henry Crawford with a piece of standard fictional delinquency – an off-stage seduction, like Willoughby and Wickham before him – suggests rather less commitment to this part of the story on Austen's part than to the fully narrated chapters in which his charm, kindness and irresponsible flirting are on display. We should become suspicious of *Mansfield Park* not where we decide we don't like Fanny's priggishness, or mistrust Mary's high spirits, but only where its art falters. It falters rarely enough for this to be a supremely absorbing and entertaining novel, more complex and more ambitious than any of the three that preceded it. Its great set-pieces – the visit to Sotherton, the whole episode of the theatricals, and the chapters set in Portsmouth – show a mastery in handling the interactions of a large cast and a complex series of events that few novelists have matched.

While Jane was working on *Mansfield Park*, Eliza became ill. Breast cancer tends to run in families, and her illness was almost certainly the same as her mother's. It meant she knew what she had to undergo from the moment she was aware of the first symptoms, and could watch herself as though in a mirror held up to her mother's experience; a terrible prospect lay before her. After her death in the spring of 1813, Jane said that it had been a 'long and dreadful illness' and that Henry 'very long knew that she must die, & it was indeed a release at last'. Henry also referred to the length and severity of her suffering in the epitaph he wrote for her. How long is very long? Eighteen months at least, possibly two years. The chest cold she suffered from in the aftermath of her musical party may have been a sign of something worse, although at the time it only prevented her from walking in Kensington Gardens to see the lilac and chestnut trees in bloom.

During this visit, Jane invited her to Chawton for a summer visit, and in August she arrived as planned to stay for two weeks. Cassandra commented on how well she looked, better than she had ever seen her, and for a week they enjoyed themselves quietly.[18] Then the house was invaded by Charles, newly arrived in England with his unknown wife and tiny daughters – aged three and one – after an absence of seven years. As Cass said, the house was 'running over', but Eliza stayed for another cheerful, noisy week. Then she went on to Godmersham, escorted by Henry; he went shooting with the boys and drove to Canterbury with Edward while she walked with Fanny. 'Mrs HA & I had a tête-à-tête, how agreable!' wrote her niece; evidently not quite agreeable enough, though: 'Mrs HA and I get on a little, but we never shall be intimate.'[19] Something about Eliza jarred with many of the Austens, whether it was simply her style they mistrusted – too clever, foreign and frivolous – or some suggestion of a deeper dereliction.[20] 'A clever woman, and highly accomplished, after the French rather than the English mode' – the description of her in the first *Memoir* of her Cousin Jane – is distinctly cautious. Eliza was as British as they were by blood and had been educated in England, but 'French' was well understood to mean something different and not quite up to the standards prevailing in England, and conveniently expressed what they felt about her.[21] Perhaps she took a light-hearted attitude towards religious observance. Whatever the reason, suspicion of her remained part of the family tradition. The 1913 *Life and Letters* describes Henry as having 'a certain infirmity of purpose in his character that was hardly likely to be remedied by a marriage to his very pleasure-loving cousin'.[22] To fix the label of pleasure-loving on a woman who suffered so much pain, in her own person, through her mother, and over many years with her only child, seems somewhat less than just.

At Godmersham, Henry took Fanny riding, and on another day drove his wife to Saltwood Castle. After this she went on alone to Ramsgate for two weeks of sea air; he returned to London, fetching her home in mid-October. By now she can have been in no doubt that she was ill. Her best supports as the disease progressed were her

French companions – for they had become something more than servants – Madame Bigeon and Madame Perigord. Henry was a true tough Austen, as Jane perceived: 'his Mind is not a Mind for affliction. He is too Busy, too active, too sanguine.' Eliza was over fifty, and he was in his prime, and much occupied with his bank; Francis became a partner in 1812, bringing in prize money and contacts.[23] With only two letters of Jane's for that year we know nothing but that Edward and Fanny 'dined quietly' in Sloane Street in May, when they also saw Mrs Siddons, and made more theatre and opera visits, and Henry visited them in Kent in June. In September he was briefly at Steventon, and in December he was again entertaining Edward and Fanny with theatre visits and shopping in London. At that point Fanny's diary is silent on the subject of 'Mrs H A', whose condition must by now have been very wretched.

Henry was in Oxford in February 1813, but as Eliza visibly approached her end in April, he hurried to Chawton and took Jane back to London to be with her. This was on the 22nd; three days later she died. Jane remained in London for another week, then travelled back to Chawton, taking Mme Perigord with her to stay at the cottage.[24] Gratitude for the nursing of Eliza was a good reason for the invitation, but it was an unusually friendly gesture to a brother's employee; another sign of her particular sympathy for working women in their hard lives.

The funeral took place after the two women had left. Mrs James Austen's diary entries tell their own small story. 'Saturday May 1 Tyger [the Steventon cat] had young ones. Mrs H Austen was buried. Sunday May 2 Put on mourning.' Neither James nor Edward attended their cousin's funeral in Hampstead. Henry had her buried beside her mother and her son: 'Also in memory of Elizabeth wife of H. T. Austen Esq. formerly widow of the Comt. Feuillide a woman of brilliant generous and cultivated mind just disinterested and chari-table she died after long and severe suffering on the 25th April 1813 aged 50 much regretted by the wise and good and deeply lamented by the poor.'[25] It is noticeable that the epitaph makes no mention of Christian faith, only of her charity.

There were other deaths to preoccupy the Austens. Good, generous Mrs Knight had died in October 1812. Edward, as heir, was now obliged to change his name to Knight, along with all his children's, to Fanny's considerable disgust ('How I hate it!!!!'). Early in 1813 two Steventon neighbours also died. Mr Bigg-Wither left his daughters well provided for, but Alethea and Elizabeth Heathcote had to leave Manydown. Mary Austen dined with them there for the last time in July. Another Steventon neighbour, old Mr Harwood at Deane, died at the same time, leaving his family nothing but debts and mortgages. The younger Mr Harwood was a clergyman, and 'If Mrs Heathcote does not marry & comfort him now I shall think she . . . has no heart,' wrote Jane. He had loved Elizabeth Bigg since she was a girl, seen her married to Heathcote and then widowed, reviving his hopes; now he could not offer her anything but poverty. She liked him, but not well enough for that. He sold some land and struggled on at Deane, and she moved to the cathedral close in Winchester, where she and Alethea took a house together.

Edward and what Jane now referred to as his Harem were at Chawton House for the whole of the summer of 1813, while Godmersham was given up to house painters. Henry carried Jane off to Sloane Street again in May, where Mesdames Bigeon and Perigord were organizing his move to Henrietta Street in Covent Garden; he was going to try living above his office. 'Mrs Perigord arrived at a ½ past 3 – & is pretty well, & her Mother, for *her*, seems quite well. [Madame Bigeon was asthmatic.] She sat with me while I breakfasted this morn/g – talking of Henrietta Street, servants & Linen, & is too busy preparing for the future, to be out of spirits.'

The secret of Jane's authorship was beginning to be more generally known. A Miss Burdett, possibly a sister of the reformer Sir Francis Burdett, wanted to be introduced to her. 'I am rather frightened by hearing that she wishes to be introduced to *me*. If I *am* a wild Beast, I cannot help it. It is not my own fault,' Jane complained, meaning that she was not responsible for becoming an exhibit in the parade of London society. What she did enjoy was visiting exhibitions with Henry and looking for portraits of Mrs Bingley and Mrs Darcy; the first she found, 'exactly herself, size, shaped face, features & sweetness; there never was a greater likeness. She is dressed in a white gown, with green ornaments, which convinces me of what I had always supposed, that green was a favourite colour with her. I dare say Mrs D. will be in Yellow.' But Mrs D. was not to be found: 'I can only imagine that Mr D. prizes any Picture of her too much to like it should be exposed to the public eye. – I can imagine he wd have that sort of feeling – that mixture of Love, Pride & Delicacy.' It is as close as she ever came to sentimentality.

Henry talked of a drive to Hampstead, but if they visited the three graves there is no account of it. She was no more given to prolonged grieving for the dead than he was, and her letters are cheerful. She enjoyed being on her own in London, and driving about in her rich brother's open carriage: 'I liked my solitary elegance very much, & was ready to laugh all the time, at my being where I was. – I could not but feel that I had naturally small right to be parading about London in a Barouche.' And she was as sharp as ever. Visiting Charlotte Craven, a cousin of Martha Lloyd's, at her smart girls' school, she found 'her hair is done up with an elegance to do credit to any Education', and the room in which they sat 'full of all the modern Elegancies – & if it had not been for some naked Cupids over the Mantlepeice, which must be a fine study for Girls, one should never have Smelt Instruction'.

Mansfield Park was finished in the summer. Henry was often at Chawton, and the Charles Austens visited with a new baby daughter. Jane read *Pride and Prejudice* aloud to Fanny. 'At:' is Fanny's abbreviation for 'Aunt', and 'At: J.A. as *Mr Darcy*' she wrote in her diary on 21 May: it must have been something to hear. Fanny took to running down to the cottage early in the morning to spend more time with this newly revealed and amazingly clever Aunt Jane. 'At: J & I had a delicious morning together.' On 5 June 'At. Jane spent the morn/g with me & read P & P to me and Papa.' 'Ats C & J. came to read before breakfast, & the latter breakfasted . . . I spent the afternoon at the cottage.' 'Cottage dined here. Aunt J came early.' There is even a unique reference to Aunt Jane on horseback: 'Monday 5 July. Aunt Jane & I rode out with Papa to Chawton Park.' Fanny's diary also shows that Aunt Jane had a troublesome and persistent pain in her face this summer; and that although she made light of it, she often chose to sleep at the big house rather than to walk back to the cottage in the chilly night air at the end of the evening. It did not clear up until the autumn.

In August, Henry paid a visit to Warren Hastings, but 'Mr Hastings never *hinted* at Eliza in the smallest degree.' This is Jane's account, given her by Henry. If it means that he did not mention the death of his god-daughter, it is surprising in a man who was known for his loyalty to old friends. If it meant more, Jane did not see fit to elaborate; but Eliza had been too large a presence in her life to be blotted out. Madame Bigeon and her daughter also had memories of her going back twenty years, and Jane did not forget them either.

For *Mansfield Park* she did something she had not done before, which was to collect and write down the opinions of her readers. It was her early version of a cuttings book, only they were not printed reviews she collected – there were in fact none for *Mansfield Park* – but opinions delivered in private letters or conversation, which she then set down in her own hand. These 'Opinions', which exist only for *Mansfield Park* and *Emma*, are some of the most fascinating personal documents she left, as much for what they tell us about her as for what they say about the books. To begin with, they prove how much it meant to her to have reactions to her work; although she had feared it, the breaking down of anonymity was wholly to the good. Then they demonstrate that she was detached enough to write down rude remarks as well as praise, and without adding any defensive replies of her own. When Mrs Augusta Bramston of Oakley Hall 'owned that she thought S. & S. – and P. & P. downright nonsense, but expected to like MP. better, & having finished the 1st vol. – flattered herself she had got through the worst', it is pretty clear that Austen is rejoicing in Mrs Bramston's extraordinary folly rather than feeling wounded; and something like Olympian laughter arises from the page. On the other hand, you can be sure that when Miss Sharp expressed her preference for P. & P. over MP, she took careful and conscientious note of her view. Her collecting and transcribing, and the mixture of seriousness and silliness that characterizes the result, make the whole enterprise particularly endearing: even authors who know with part of their minds that they are among the great must also doubt themselves. On good days they laugh like gods; on bad days they turn back to the bad reviews and crass comments, and shiver. Jane Austen was surely no different.

22

Dedication

In July 1813, as she came out of mourning for Eliza, her situation was this: *Sense and Sensibility* had sold out, bringing her a profit; *Pride and Prejudice* was a clear hit; she had completed *Mansfield Park*; and ideas for her next book, which was to be *Emma*, were taking shape. She was thirty-seven, and her mind was in an extraordinary state of energy and inventiveness. Her letters over the next two years are lively, rapid, tightly packed as ever, and cheerful. Not only was she full of creative vigour and confidence, she was also rejoicing in being richer than she had ever been; which is not to say she was rich, but that she had money she need not thank anyone else for. 'Do not refuse me. I am very rich,' she urged Cass after sending her a present of dress material.

Henry also thrived, at his own very much grander level. So successful was his bank, and so influential his friends, that he got himself appointed Receiver General of taxes for Oxfordshire; very large sureties were required for this position, and his Uncle Leigh-Perrot happily stood for £10,000, while Edward guaranteed another £20,000. He had become a merry bachelor again, and Jane was amused to see him involved with several women. One was the Miss Burdett who had already asked to meet her, a friend of his partner James Tilson's wife Frances, and an admirer of Jane's novels.[1] Another was 'young, pretty, chattering, & thinking cheifly (I presume) of Dress, Company, & Admiration'. She played chess with Henry; Jane was not a chess player and felt she had 'not two ideas in common' with her. A third was a widow in Berkshire; Henry had a way of spreading his attentions, and he was eager for Jane to know them all. He was also unable to resist blabbing about her authorship; she forgave him, and began to grow used to it, but would not be taken to literary

242

gatherings. An attempt to introduce her to the French writer Madame de Staël, who was in London meeting everyone in the winter of 1813/14, was firmly refused. Later, de Staël expressed her view that Austen's novels were *vulgaire*, too close to the English provincial life she detested for its narrowness and dullness, its emphasis on duty and stifling of wit and brilliance. Brilliant as she herself was, she could not find interest in the small scale; and her English was perhaps simply not good enough to allow her to enjoy brilliance of a different kind.[2]

Jane's life continued on its small scale, although she was often with Henry in London, dealing with publishers, enjoying the company of his circle of colleagues and well-to-do friends, and joining him in many visits to the theatres conveniently clustered around Henrietta Street. In September 1813 she was there with Edward and his three eldest daughters, all on their way from Chawton to Godmersham. Although she had her own money, she was pleased when 'kind, beautiful Edward' gave her another £5 out of his 'East Kent wealth' to spend. Looking across the drawing room at her two brothers in the evening, she used a word of her own to describe them: they were deep in 'a comfortable coze', she wrote.[3] She took the girls to the dentist ('I would not have had him look at mine for a shilling a tooth & double it'), and Lizzy and Marianne were now old enough for theatre-going. They were taken on two successive nights, and particularly enjoyed a version of the Don Juan story, *The Libertine*. 'I must say that I have seen nobody on the stage who has been a more interesting Character than that compound of Cruelty & Lust,' wrote their aunt on her own account.[4]

In Kent she saw Charles with his wife and three daughters, and deplored their failure to look like Austens: 'I never knew a Wife's family-features have such undue influence,' she complained. Edward, as a visiting magistrate, took her round Canterbury Gaol, but if he hoped to give her material for a novel, the visit was a failure. At Godmersham she savoured the luxury of meals especially brought to her on trays, and a fire lit in her bedroom before breakfast. She dined at Chilham Castle, and expressed herself content to leave off being young and sit by the fire, drinking as much wine as she liked. How Madame de Staël would have yawned. There was a ball, with very little dancing, according to Fanny; it was the last Jane attended.

She was about to be thirty-eight, and described herself and Cass collectively as 'we, the formidables'. In November she was back in Henrietta Street. Egerton expressed his willingness to publish *Mansfield Park*, but was not prepared to risk his own money and wanted to revert to the commission arrangement; he was shrewd enough to see that it would not be as popular as *Pride and Prejudice*, which he was putting out in a second edition.

The winter of 1813 was as harsh as the winter of her birth, and became a good midwife to *Emma*, allowing her the whole of January and February uninterrupted at Chawton to think and write. 'Emma begun Jany 21st 1814, finished March 29th 1815,' wrote Cassandra exactly in her memorandum. These precise dates suggest either that she kept a note from the manuscript or – more likely – that Jane kept a diary, as other women in the family did, in which she entered the starting and finishing dates of her last two books; enabling Cassandra to draw on her entries before she destroyed them.[5]

There was still snow about when Henry fetched Jane to Henrietta Street again at the beginning of March. Edward and Fanny joined them, Jane read Byron's *The Corsair* and they all went to Covent Garden to see Mrs Jordan, at fifty-one still 'superlative': the word is Byron's, who saw her three nights after the Austen party. They saw her play Nell in *The Devil to Pay* on 7 March. 'I expect to be very much amused,' wrote Jane before the performance, and she was indeed 'highly amused with the Farce'. The rest of the evening, Thomas Arne's opera *Artaxerxes*, with no Mrs Jordan (it demanded two castrati), was a disappointment to them all.[6]

Back to Hampshire again in April, when the 'glorious news of Buonaparte vanquished and dethroned' arrived. At Alton there were illuminations for the victory, and supper was provided for the poor.[7] *Mansfield Park* was published, without fanfare, on 9 May. Henry came down for his birthday in June, and took Cassandra back to London with him; he celebrated the victory by attending a ball given by White's Club at Burlington House. Jane was impressed, slightly shocked, indulgent: 'Henry at Whites! – Oh! what a Henry.'[8] Like Elinor with Willoughby, she felt his charm too keenly to judge him as she would anyone else, whether for worldliness, unreliability or flirting. He was restless. He decided to move back to his old Chelsea haunts, and took a house in Hans Place, No. 23. Madame Bigeon and her daughter continued to look after him; after so many years of intimacy, they had become more like a part of the family than servants. When Jane went to London again her letters mention an 'appointment' with Madame Bigeon, and discussions about who should provide Henry with raspberry jam; Madame Perigord took clothes to the dyer for her, and found her some plaited willow for making a hat. Otherwise Henry kept only a manservant and one maid at the Hans Place house. Jane was pleased by the attic bedroom she was allotted for her visit, and by a cool downstairs room that opened into the garden. Staying with Henry in August, she describes herself walking in and out between house and garden; it is very much what someone settling down to write does, getting up, pacing, thinking, returning to the page she is working on.

Her nieces were demanding attention as they grew up, following and not following in Cassandra's and her footsteps. Fanny, since the age of fifteen, had been a mother to her brothers and sisters and a companion to her father; now she was having doubts about a love affair, and wanted advice. Anna, clever and headstrong, was filling the time before she could be married by writing a novel. Jane was an exemplary aunt to both, attentive and ready to give good counsel, both emotional and technical. She urged Fanny neither to expect perfection in a suitor nor to marry without affection; and Anna, to get her facts right, avoid phrases like 'a vortex of dissipation', and remember that in fiction 'One does not care for girls till they are grown up.' And she made her famous remark, 'You are now collecting your People delightfully, getting them exactly into such a spot as is the delight of my life; – 3 or 4 Families in a Country Village is the very thing to work on.' It was exactly what she was working on in *Emma*.

She was at Hans Place when news came of the death of Charles's wife Fanny, following the birth of another daughter. Fanny was twenty-four, the fourth and youngest of the melancholy sequence of sisters-in-law to die. Her epitaph in Kentish Town Church ends, 'Sleep on dear Fair one, wait the Almighty's Will / Then rise unchang'd, and be an angel still.' The baby died a few weeks later, the three remaining little girls went to their Palmer grandparents, and Charles took a posting at sea. Small wonder that, as Jane commented when she next saw the children, 'that puss Cassy . . . does not shine in the tender feelings . . . more in the Mrs Siddons line'. Cass was the eldest, and all of six years old.

The security of Chawton cottage was suddenly threatened this year by a law suit brought against Edward and his right to the Chawton estates. Should it succeed, Mrs Austen and her daughters would be once again looking for somewhere to live: a grim prospect. The suit was all the worse for being brought by neighbours, the Hinton family of Chawton Lodge, with whom the Austen ladies at the cottage considered themselves on cordial terms. They were claiming that a deed disentailing the Chawton estate at the beginning of the century had been inaccurately drawn up, making them, and not Edward, the rightful heirs to the great house and all its lands. His wealth would be halved if he lost, leaving him with nothing but Godmersham, as well as depriving his mother and sisters of their home. A writ was served on Edward in October 1814, beginning a legal wrangle that was to last for several years.[9]

This trouble may have cast a shadow over Anna's marriage to Ben Lefroy, which took place from her father's house at Steventon in November. Anna was eager to leave home, and her father and stepmother relieved to see her go. A description of the wedding by Anna's half-sister Caroline, who was nine and acted as bridesmaid, was not written until many years later, but gives an exceptionally vivid impression of the occasion and the setting, which had changed little since Aunt Jane's childhood.

> My brother [James-Edward] had come from Winchester that morning, but was to stay only a few hours. We in the house had a slight early breakfast up stairs; and between 9 and 10 the bride, my mother, Mrs Lefroy, Anne [Ben's niece] and myself, were taken to church in our carriage. All the gentlemen walked. The weather was dull and cloudy, but it did not actually rain. The season of the year, the unfrequented road of half a mile to the lonely old church, the grey light within of a November morning making its way through the narrow windows, no stove to give warmth, no flowers to give colour and brightness, no friends, high or low, to offer their good wishes, and so to claim some interest in the great event of the day – all these circumstances and deficiencies must, I think, have given a gloomy

air to our wedding. Mr Lefroy read the service, my father gave his daughter away. The Clerk of course was there, altho' I do not particularly remember him; but I am quite sure there was no one else in the church, nor was anyone else asked to the breakfast, to which we sat down as soon as we got back. I do not think this idea of sadness struck me at the time; the bustle of the house, and all the preparations had excited me, and it seemed to me as a festivity from beginning to end. The breakfast was such as best breakfasts then were: some variety of bread, hot rolls, buttered toast, tongue or ham and eggs. The addition of chocolate at one end of the table, and wedding cake in the middle, marked the speciality of the day. I and Anne Lefroy, nine and six years old, wore white frocks and had white ribband on our straw bonnets, which, I suppose, were new for the occasion. Soon after breakfast, the bride and bridegroom departed. They had a long day's journey before them, to Hendon; the other Lefroys went home [to Ashe]; and in the afternoon my mother and I went to Chawton to stay at the Great House, then occupied by my uncle Captain Austen and his large family [Frank, Mary and five children at this date]. My father stayed behind for a few days, and then joined us. The servants had cake and punch in the evening, and I think I remember that Mr Digweed walked down to keep him company. Such were the wedding festivities of Steventon in 1814![10]

It was very much the Austen style, such as Mrs Elton sneers at in *Emma*, with her 'Very little white satin, very few lace veils; a most pitiful business!' But you do not have to be Mrs Elton to find it sad that even old Mrs Austen, who loved Anna above all her grandchildren, was not present to see her married; nor a single Austen aunt or uncle. And when Jane, on her next London trip, visited Anna in Hendon, she blamed her for ordering a piano ('they will wish the 24 Gs [guineas] in the shape of Sheets & Towels six months hence') and accused her of secret extravagance on a purple pelisse: 'She is capable of that you know,' she told Fanny, allowing herself to sound for once like a malicious old aunt. What had Anna done to deserve all this? Nobody said. Her Aunt Jane's sour comments were an aberration, and she was soon writing sweetly to Anna again.

On Christmas Day Mrs Austen also wrote to Anna to tell her, 'I have just finished *Waverley*, newly published by Scott, which has afforded me more entertainment than any modern production (Aunt

Jane's excepted).'[11] She was still, at seventy-five, as sharp as a needle. On Boxing Day she said goodbye to both her daughters while they went off to see old friends and neighbours; first to Winchester to stay with Alethea and Elizabeth in their new home in the cathedral close. They went on to James and Mary at Steventon, where there was a Twelfth Night cake with a dance for the young ones, and another party to draw for cake at the Bramstons at Oakley Hall, to which the Chutes also came; a dinner with John Portal and his wife at Laverstoke, an overnight stay with the Lefroys at Ashe; and Tom Chute came twice for dinner at Steventon. He had a parish in Norfolk, presented to him by his family when he left the militia to be ordained; and every winter he brought his horses from East Anglia to Hampshire to hunt from The Vyne alongside his brother and James Austen, and young James-Edward Austen too, when the Winchester term allowed.

More material for Madame de Staël's yawns in this collection of middle-aged Hampshire neighbours who had known one another now for over twenty years: the widow with her boy at Winchester and her clever unmarried sister, the Member of Parliament who never spoke in the House, the hunting squires and clergymen with their families, the land-owning businessmen who made £5 notes for the government, the dull women with their cakes and their conservatories. It was also as far as possible from the world Jane was constructing in *Emma*: a Surrey village that had no basis in any real place, a heroine of twenty, handsome, clever and rich, with a father as foolish as Lady Bertram, a sister married to a London lawyer, a model improving estate-owner for a neighbour, a scheming, oily, unpleasant young clergyman, and a large girls' school in the neighbourhood. Also, of course, a subplot concerning a poor beauty called Jane who breaks the rules of her society and nearly pays the price by becoming a governess, the English equivalent of the slave trade. Jane went back to Chawton and finished writing on 29 March 1815; her last chapters were written as Madame de Staël's enemy, Napoleon, escaped from Elba, marched north collecting his soldiers, and re-established his power in Paris.

Mansfield Park had sold out, but Egerton refused to print a second edition. If he was shown *Emma* on its completion, as seems likely, he delayed, dithered and failed to make a good enough offer; and that was the end of his association with Jane Austen. But it was not until the autumn, after she had already started on another novel, that *Emma* was accepted by a new publisher, John Murray. Murray was the founder of the *Quarterly Review* and the publisher of Byron, and he had Austen's manuscript read by William Gifford, editor of the *Quarterly*, who found 'nothing but good' to say of it, and indeed of her earlier work. Gifford offered to do a little work on the text to tidy it up, and Murray to buy the copyright, with the copyrights of *Mansfield Park* and *Sense and Sensibility* thrown in, for £450. Henry refused this on behalf of his sister. Then he was taken ill; and she settled for publication on commission, Murray to have 10 per cent of the profits. He would also produce a new edition of *Mansfield Park*.

Printing began, while Henry's illness grew worse. The doctors were so alarmed that Jane sent urgently for James and Edward. Both set off at once, James collecting Cassandra on the way. All three arrived at Hans Place to find Henry apparently on the point of death, suffering from what was called a 'low fever'. Madame Bigeon had five Austens to look after and for a week Hans Place was a house of fear. Then, as quickly as the trouble had arrived, it dissipated, and Henry began to mend. James went home, Edward sent his daughter a 'comfortable letter' on 2 November, and went back to Kent the next day. Henry remained weak and in need of care, but he was out of danger.

One of the doctors called in was a court physician; and when the crisis was over, he told Jane that the Prince Regent was an admirer of her novels, and reported to the Prince that she was in London. The result was that the Prince's librarian, James Stanier Clarke, was told to call on her and invite her to visit the library at Carlton House. This she did, on 13 November. She remained entirely silent on the subject of its splendours and equally so on her feelings about the visit; but Mr Clarke was also deputed to convey to her that she might dedicate her next book to the Prince. The result appeared at the front of *Emma*.

TO

HIS ROYAL HIGHNESS

THE PRINCE REGENT,

THIS WORK IS,

BY HIS ROYAL HIGHNESS'S PERMISSION,

MOST RESPECTFULLY

DEDICATED,

BY HIS ROYAL HIGHNESS'S

DUTIFUL

AND OBEDIENT

HUMBLE SERVANT,

THE AUTHOR.

Such a lavish supply of three Royal Highnesses and one Prince Regent was not her idea. She had proposed a simple formula on the title-page, to read 'Emma, Dedicated by Permission to H.R.H. The Prince Regent' until John Murray put her right. He must have supplied the copy as it appeared, on a separate page of its own. Martha Lloyd teased Jane about her mercenary motives in making the dedication; in fact she had resisted the idea until it was pointed out that a royal suggestion was a royal command. Murray was happy, of course, and printed 2,000 copies, her largest edition yet, at twenty-one shillings for the three volumes.[12]

The Prince himself did not trouble to write his thanks for the dedication. Royal etiquette did not demand it; nor did he feel it necessary to give any indication that he had actually read *Emma*. He received his specially bound copy in London in December 1815 and his librarian wrote to Jane three months later, on 27 March 1816, from Brighton. 'I have to return you the Thanks of His Royal Highness the Prince Regent for the handsome Copy you sent him of your last excellent Novel . . . Lord St Helens and many of the Nobility who have been staying here, paid you the just tribute of their Praise.' But what, we should like to know, and Jane Austen must have wondered, did the Prince himself think of Miss Woodhouse and Frank Churchill? A word of thanks, sent many weeks after its delivery, for 'the handsome Copy . . . of your last excellent novel' leaves a good deal to be desired as a response. 'Whatever he may think of *my* share of the work, *Yours* seems to have been quite right,' wrote Jane, dry as ever, to Murray.

The Prince's librarian was not much of an improvement on the Prince, but he was determined to show his own appreciation of Jane Austen's genius, and hit on the wonderful idea of recommending subjects for her next book. First he urged her to write a novel about an English clergyman not entirely unlike himself. He had been a naval chaplain: so why not 'Carry your Clergyman to Sea as the Friend of some distinguished Naval Character about a Court'? (Did he have the Duke of Clarence in mind perhaps?) Or why not 'describe him burying his own mother – as I did, – because the High Priest of the Parish in which she died – did not pay her the respect he ought to do. I have never recovered the Shock'? Austen dealt tactfully with Mr Clarke's suggestions, pleading her own incapacity as an 'unlearned, & uninformed Female' without knowledge of the science, philosophy or classical and foreign languages which would be necessary for such an enterprise. His next recommendation was that she should write a Romance based on the House of Saxe-Coburg, as a tribute to Prince Leopold of that house, about to marry the Prince Regent's daughter Charlotte. Again, Austen made the polite excuse that such a project was beyond her powers.

Mr Clarke did manage to inspire her none the less. The result was the *Plan of a Novel, According to Hints from Various Quarters*, three pages in which she followed his advice, mixing in other suggestions from well-meaning friends. The *Plan* offers a faultless heroine, daughter of a widowed country clergyman, who uses up Volume I telling the story of his life, which includes Mr Clarke's ideas of a chaplaincy to a 'distinguished Naval Character about the Court' as well as the burial of his mother. The heroine contrives to remain beautiful, elegant and 'living in high style' while being driven across Europe, starved and persecuted by unworthy admirers, and cruelly slighted by the hero until the very last moment, when he turns out to have loved her after all. Austen is defending her own taste and methods as she goes along, and enjoying the fun of dragging Mr Clarke at her chariot wheels.

Emma, with its far from faultless heroine, is generally hailed as Austen's most perfect book, flawlessly carried out from conception to finish, without a rough patch or a loose end. It offers a world as carefully and satisfactorily enclosed as any in Racine's plays. It springs a real surprise the first time you read it, so that, as has often been pointed out, the pleasures of a detective story are added to the study of human psychology. Every reading increases understanding and appreciation of its structure and subtlety; like a string quartet or a sonata, it grows in the mind with each new encounter.

Emma shares with Fanny Price the inner voice which tells her exactly what to do. I sometimes think Austen may have had her first flash of an idea for Emma as she wrote Fanny's words to Henry Crawford, 'We have all a better guide in ourselves, if we would attend to it, than any other person can be', and was struck with the comic possibility of an inner voice which turns out to be consistently wrong. Emma's inner guide tells her, for instance, to take up Harriet Smith, an unsuitable friend whose life she proceeds to do her very best to wreck. It tells her to misread Mr Elton's attentions to her, obvious as they are to other people. It tells her to slight Jane Fairfax, to concoct a deeply discreditable story about her, and pass it on to a mere acquaintance, Frank Churchill, who uses it for his own purposes and to hurt Jane. It tells her to flirt with Churchill as heartlessly as he flirts with her, and with no intention of accepting him when he proposes, as she confidently expects him to do.

Emma is not ready for a male suitor because she does not want anyone to encroach on a position which allows her to queen it over the little society in which she lives. She half falls in love with Harriet because her life is becoming dull and she needs something to occupy her, although Harriet is a dim-witted, sycophantic girl with no shred of interest beyond possessing a mildly pretty face, and the fact that she is illegitimate and of unknown parentage. Even about this Harriet shows not a spark of curiosity: something quite hard to believe, however dull she is meant to be. Fortunately her stupidity, and the persistence of her suitor, save her from the humiliation and unhappiness Emma's guidance has contrived for her.

Emma is blind to everything she does not want to see, and is enlightened only when her mistakes are shown up, and the good advice of her brotherlike lover is accepted. Austen's revelation of the unacknowledged sexual tension between her and Mr Knightley is a marvellous touch; her helpless tears on the way back from Box Hill after his reproach are the tears of a woman whose body is telling her what her mind has not yet caught up with. 'Emma felt the tears running down her cheeks almost all the way home, without being at any trouble to check them, extraordinary as they were.' Having started as one whose pleasure is all in thinking, manipulating and imposing her will, she is discovering another pleasure in the passionate surrender of her will. At the end Emma says she will never address her husband as George, even though he invites her to, except on the one day which she blushes to mention; after that he will always be Mr Knightley, preserving the master–pupil relationship which is so satisfying – even delicious – to her. If this makes Emma begin to sound like a D. H. Lawrence heroine, it is an indication of Austen's power to imagine experience outside her own, and to set it down with perfect sureness of touch.

Jane Austen herself was far from confident that *Emma* would be well received. Some of her fears were expressed to Mr Clarke in December 1815: 'My greatest anxiety at present is that this 4th work shd not disgrace what was good in the others . . . I am very strongly haunted by the idea that to those readers who have preferred P&P it will appear inferior in Wit, & to those who have preferred MP. very inferior in good Sense.'[13] The first responses from readers were not reassuring. Out of the forty-three 'Opinions' of *Emma* she noted down, twelve were distinctly hostile, and only six gave unreserved praise. Four said they liked it best of her works so far – two being her brothers Francis and Charles – but, just as she had feared, seventeen said they preferred *Pride and Prejudice*. Within the family, Mrs Austen was one of these. At least she thought it 'more entertaining' than *Mansfield Park*, whereas Cassandra was one of nine who expressed a preference for *Mansfield Park*. Fanny could not bear Emma herself, although Anna, perhaps because she was prone to trouble herself, preferred her to all the other heroines. Alethea Bigg, who read it twice in quick succession, was bored by the match-making theme and by Harriet Smith, and liked it less than the earlier books. Edward 'preferred it to MP. – only'; her nephew Edward also kindly pointed out that she had made Mr Knightley's apple trees blossom in July. Henry was in no state to give an opinion, but one smart London friend of his, Sir James Langham, 'though it much inferior to all the others', and another, a Miss Isabella Herries Jane had dined with and thought clever and accomplished, 'did not like it – objected to my exposing the sex in the character of the heroine'. Austen was close to exasperation in noting Miss Herries's further complaint, that she had 'meant Mrs & Miss Bates for some acquaintance of theirs – people whom I never heard of before'. James and Mary Austen communicated their joint failure to like it 'as well as either of the 3 others. Language different from the others; not so easily read.' They must also have passed on the view of Mary's cousin, Jane Murden, who pronounced it 'certainly inferior to all the others'.

Murray allowed his author twelve complimentary copies, a subject on which she expressed herself sardonically to Cassandra, noting that 'all the twelve Copies . . . were to have been dispersed among my near Connections – beginning with the P.R. & ending with Countess Morley' – who were of course Murray's choices.[14] She felt obliged to send one to the Prince's librarian, but after that all her copies went to the family – all that is but one, which went to Anne Sharp, confirming her unique position as the necessary, intelligent friend. From Anne she wanted frankness, having already begged her to be 'perfectly honest' in giving her opinion of *Mansfield Park*. Now even Anne's verdict was disappointing. She liked *Emma* 'better than MP. – but not so well as P. & P. – pleased with the Heroine for her Originality, delighted with Mr K – & called Mrs Elton beyond praise – dissatisfied with Jane Fairfax'. Sharp Miss Sharp touched here on a weak spot: Jane Fairfax is a thinner character than the girl who behaves so outrageously as to enter into a secret engagement and correspondence should be. Her criticism was to be taken seriously, and pondered.

There was a different sort of interest – and amusement – in writing down merely insulting remarks by dim-witted acquaintances. Among Hampshire neighbours, one woman found *Emma* 'too natural to be interesting', and Jane's 'dear Mrs Digweed' 'did not like it so well as the others, in fact if she had not known the Author, could hardly have got through it'. Dear Mrs Digweed indeed. A Mrs Dickson 'thought it very inferior to P. & P. – Liked it the less, from there being a Mr & Mrs Dixon in it'. Another 'Read only the first & last Chapters, because he had heard it was not interesting.' 'The Authoress wrong, in such times as these, to draw such Clergymen as Mr Collins and Mr Elton.' To make up for the nonsense, there was praise from her brothers, especially Charles, who read *Emma* through three times in quick succession; and the verdict of the great Mr Jeffery of the *Edinburgh Review*, who was 'kept up by it three nights'. Yet the *Edinburgh* ran no review.

Murray had reservations of his own. He sent a copy to Walter Scott, suggesting he should write something about it in the *Quarterly Review*, but introducing it with a remark that consigns him to that circle of the Inferno reserved for disloyal publishers. 'Have you any fancy to dash off an article on Emma? It wants incident and romance does it not?' Scott did dash off something, praising Austen somewhat faintly for 'copying from nature as she really exists in the common walks of life', and more warmly for her 'quiet yet comic dialogue, in which the characters of the speakers evolve themselves with dramatic effect'. He found Mr Woodhouse and Miss Bates tiresome, and he did not mention *Mansfield Park* at all, to Jane's considerable, and justifiable, disappointment. His unsprightly summaries of the plots of *Sense and Sensibility* and *Pride and Prejudice* did them no service. Almost half his review was devoted to a general discussion of the novel, and he ended with a paean to the virtues of romantic love as against the 'calculating prudence' that he discerned in some of Austen's heroines.

Nearly ten years after her death, Scott arrived at a higher opinion of her work. 'That young lady has a talent for describing the involvements and feelings and characters of ordinary life, which is to me the most wonderful I have ever met with. The Big Bow-Wow strain

I can do myself like any now going; but the exquisite touch which renders ordinary common-place things and characters interesting from the truth of the description and the sentiment is denied to me.'[15] The vitality of her voice made him do what everyone has done ever since, assimilate her to the twenty-year-old heroines of the books – Elizabeth, Elinor, Emma – by writing of her as a 'young lady'; although she was dead, and had been forty when he reviewed her much less kindly in the *Quarterly*.

23

The Sorceress

The first year after the peace that followed Waterloo brought a series of disasters for the Austen family. In February 1816 Charles's ship was wrecked in the eastern Mediterranean, where he was pursuing the real pirates Byron glamorized for his *Corsair*. Back in England, Charles found himself poor, struggling to bring up his motherless family; he did not get another command for ten years. His eldest daughter, Cassy, was taken to live at Chawton with her aunts for months at a time, just as Anna had gone to her aunts at Steventon after her mother's death twenty years earlier; and the second little girl, Jane's god-daughter Harriet, fell seriously ill with water on the brain.

Frank remained on half-pay of £200 a year, and had considerable savings invested, so even with a family addition every two years he managed reasonably well. He was also a partner in Henry's bank.[1] At the end of 1815, however, the Alton branch of the bank failed; and on 15 March the other branches, the London bank and the army agency all crashed. They were casualties either of the general economic trouble of the post-war period or of the particular untrustworthiness of some clients; probably a mixture of the two, with Henry's too ready optimism another factor. The result was that Henry was declared bankrupt. Whatever money Eliza had left him went with the rest, and the failure involved his Uncle Leigh-Perrot and brother Edward in paying out the large sums – £10,000 and £20,000 – they had guaranteed for him only a year before; so fast had the whirligig turned and thrown him down. Frank and James both lost smaller amounts, and even Jane saw £13 of her profits from *Mansfield Park* disappear. Neither Henry nor Frank was now able to keep up his annual contribution of £50 to their mother's household;

this, and the threat hanging over Edward, put some strain on the finances at Chawton cottage.[2]

Austen accounts of Henry's crash are reticent. In the first *Memoir* it became 'some family troubles'. At Steventon, Mary Austen's diary for 15 March has 'Henry's bank stopped payments' and the next day 'first heard of Henry being a bankrupt'. At the end of the year Fanny wrote in her diary, 'The principal event of this year has been the failure of Uncle H Austen's Bank & consequent distress to most of the family.' Caroline recalled with amazement later how unaffected Uncle Henry himself seemed when he appeared at Steventon; as cheerful as ever, not at all like a ruined man. His bounciness under every sort of affliction makes you wonder whether the tough Austen infant regime had in his case immunized him against distress.

Jane Austen wrote to Murray on 1 April asking him to communicate with her at Chawton in future, 'in consequence of the late sad Event in Henrietta Street'. There would be no more London trips for her; Henry had to give up Hans Place and Henrietta Street at once. Madame Bigeon and her daughter, with nothing to keep them in London, took themselves to France to see how their country was faring after two decades of revolution and war; they found only poverty and misery, and were back in London in September, their own prospects grim.[3] Without any thought that his popularity might have suffered, Henry turned to his family for support. 'My uncle had been living for some years past at considerable expense, but not more than might become the head of a flourishing bank,' wrote Caroline, 'and no blame of personal extravagance was ever imputed to him.'[4] His Uncle and Aunt Leigh-Perrot were the only ones to hold his failure against him. In Kent and in Hampshire he was welcomed as warmly as ever; and in July he travelled to France with two of Edward's sons, financed by Edward no doubt, and hoping to claim what was still owed to Eliza. It proved a useless quest; in France no one was likely to accept an unenforceable claim made by an Englishman, and least of all in 1816.

Now the Church, that most useful stay in time of trouble, became interesting to Henry once more. He remembered the plan he had abandoned twenty-five years earlier and wrote to Brownlow North, Bishop of Winchester, expressing his wish to be ordained. The Bishop, in his seventies and much more interested in botany than theology, was not severe in his examination of the middle-aged candidate. Putting his hand on a Greek Testament, he said, 'I dare say it is some years since either you or I looked into it'; and by the end of the year, Henry was appointed to the curacy of Chawton. It gave him fifty-two guineas a year, which was a good deal better than nothing, and allowed him to keep his own horse.[5]

Early in this difficult year Jane began to feel unwell in some unspecified way. Neither she nor anyone else took much notice; she may have put it down to turning forty. Her protégée Miss Benn gave them a reminder of mortality by dying in January, at the age of only forty-six; but Jane had smiled at her mother's hypochondria for too many years to allow herself to complain of illness at half her age.[6] She kept busy, working on 'The Elliots' – her working title for *Persuasion*. She also recovered the manuscript of *Susan* (*Northanger Abbey*) from Crosby for the original £10 and went through it, changing the heroine's name to Catherine, and writing a note explaining that it dated back many years, having been finished in 1803. It was now in its final form, although without its final title. But 'Miss Catherine', as she named it to Fanny, stayed on 'the Shelve'.

Looking at the letters for this period, you wonder that she had a moment to do anything but attend to her brothers' children. In April, Charles's little Cass was staying at the cottage, and was taken to Alton Fair with Francis's Mary-Jane, and possibly James's Caroline too. Anna and her husband had moved back to Hampshire, renting half a farmhouse from an Alton shopkeeper (the other half was lived in by the farm manager). It was within easy walking distance of Chawton, and Anna was always eager to see her aunt, and could do with any help on offer; she was already six months pregnant again when her first daughter was christened in April. In May, Edward and Fanny spent three weeks at the cottage; Fanny's diary shows that she walked frequently with 'At: Cass' but only once with 'At: Jane'. Something was amiss with her, and immediately after this visit both aunts set off to try the effect of the waters at Cheltenham, dropping Cassy at Steventon on the way, and promising to collect her again on their return in June.

Cheltenham had great cachet as a fashionable spa town with every amenity, assembly rooms, concerts, a theatre, gaming houses and libraries; but Cassandra was taking Jane for strictly medical reasons. The regime was that you walked to the well from your inn or lodging house early in the morning, and took a pint or two of the salty water before breakfast.[7] Perhaps Jane thought it did her some good; at all events, Cassandra went back to Cheltenham later in the year with Mary Austen, who believed herself unwell. On this later occasion Jane was left in charge of entertaining Frank and all his family to meals, as well as several other visitors. Small wonder that Caroline 'did not often see my Aunt with a book in her hand'.[8] Jane wrote what almost sounds like a complaint to Cassandra during her absence with Mary, saying she needed 'a few days quiet, & exemption from the Thought & contrivances which any sort of company gives. – I often wonder how *you* can find time for what you do, in addition to the care of the House . . . Composition seems to me Impossible, with a head full of Joints of Mutton & doses of rhubarb.'

She began to have a pain in her back. Yet in spite of this, and of the almost uninterrupted family visits, and the cold and rainy summer – 1816 suffered the worst for decades – which made it harder than usual to keep children entertained, she finished writing *Persuasion* on 18 July. Or rather, she wrote 'Finis' and then became dissatisfied with its two concluding chapters. Because of this dissatisfaction, these are the only piece of manuscript from her finished novels to survive (they are now in the British Library). It makes them precious and poignant; it also shows a remarkably tight and economical habit of composition. The dialogue runs continuously, without paragraphing, closely packed in. The abbreviations show how she hurried and kept to essentials: 'P. Office' for Post Office, 'Capt. W.', 'Adml', 'Mr. E'. Many nouns are capitalized in the old-fashioned way, 'Bliss', 'Fatigue', 'Headake', 'Providence'; some underlined as well, as though she paused to think of their significance and stress it: '*Persuasion*', '*Duty*'. The hand, like that of the letters, is clear, tidy, flowing, and the crossing out and corrections very neat.

Before discarding the two chapters, she worked over them once, toning down Anne Elliot's feelings of 'Triumph' at being right where her godmother Lady Russell had been wrong, and deleting altogether a rare interpolation in her own voice. It goes like this:

Bad Morality again. A young Woman proved to have had more discrimination of Character than her elder – to have seen in two Instances more clearly what it was about than her God-mother! But on the point of Morality, I confess myself almost in despair after understanding myself to have already given a Mother offence – having already appeared weak in the point where I thought myself most strong and shall leave the present matter to the mercy of Mothers & Chaperons & Middle-aged Ladies in general.

These were first thoughts, Austen talking to herself, laughing at the people who combed her work for a 'moral tendency' and set out to use her novels as primers for good behaviour. This was never her aim in writing; 'Mothers & Chaperons & Middle-aged Ladies' were Hannah More's province, not hers. When she wrote 'on the point of Morality, I confess myself almost in despair', she was mocking, as artists may mock when they see their work reduced by narrow approaches and definitions. But the passage was too strong; it stuck out of the narrative, a rude disclaimer; and it went.

Then she decided to rewrite the two final chapters entirely. It took her three weeks, and the rewriting was masterly. What now? She put the manuscript aside and did nothing with it for six months. She may have thought of revising further; at some point 'The Elliots' became *Persuasion*, although we don't know when, or even whether the name was her idea. But it was not until the following March (1817) that she told Fanny in a letter that she had 'something ready for Publication, which may perhaps appear about a twelvemonth hence'. Ten days later she wrote, again to Fanny, that Henry had inquired whether she had anything, and 'I could not say No when he asked me, but he knows nothing more of it.' The delay is mysterious; perhaps her energy was simply at too low an ebb for dealing with publishers. *Emma* had made £221.6s.4d. profit, but Murray offset this against the losses on his edition of *Mansfield Park*, so that in February she had received only the depressingly small amount of £38.18s. Money was more important to everyone at the cottage than it had been. 'Single women have a dreadful propensity for being poor,' she reminded Fanny, who was hesitating over suitors.

Persuasion is an extraordinary book on many counts. In one light it can be seen as a present to herself, to Miss Sharp, to Cassandra, to

Martha Lloyd, even to the memory of poor Miss Benn; to all women who had lost their chance in life and would never enjoy a second spring. But it is also a remarkable leap into a new mood and a new way of looking at England. The friendly characterization of the naval officers is more than a compliment to Francis and Charles Austen; it points approvingly towards a society in which merit can rise. There is a remarkable portrait of a distinctly new woman, Mrs Croft, tough, humorous, middle aged and clearer headed than her husband the Admiral; and right in her judgements where the defenders of old-fashioned values of prudence, rank and family turn out to be wrong. Then again there is a strain of romanticism which has hardly appeared since it was rapped over the knuckles in *Sense and Sensibility*, and is now at the centre of Anne Elliot's wholly admirable character.

There are also undeniably rough, cold and undeveloped patches in the book. The Elliot family, Anne apart, are close to caricature, and the plotting around Mrs Clay, Mrs Smith and Mr Elliot is put together without finesse. *Persuasion* is 'at once the warmest and the coldest of Jane Austen's works, the softest and the hardest', wrote Reginald Farrer in 1917, getting it right as usual.[9] (For those who need reminding, the plot is summarized in the endnote.[10]) The warmth and softness of the book is all Anne Elliot's, in her responses to people, landscape and season; she and Marianne alone among Austen heroines cherish the beauty and sadness of autumn. They are quick to think of apposite lines of poetry, and sympathetic to those who share their responses: Marianne to Thomson and Cowper, Anne to Scott and Byron. To Anne the autumn fields, the sea at Lyme and the coast, with its 'green chasms and romantic rocks', the sight of the 'black, dripping, comfortless verandah' on her sister's house in late November, all speak with powerful voices; and, unlike Marianne, she is not mocked for finding that such things as dead leaves speak to the heart.

Anne is also in direct contrast to her predecessor, Emma. Where Emma is intent on imposing her will on society, Anne feels herself in a state of 'perpetual estrangement' from it. Emma looks forward, Anne back. Emma rushes into mistakes, Anne has to live with the mistake of eight years earlier. 'She had been forced into prudence in her youth, she learned romance as she grew older – the natural sequel of an unnatural beginning.' It is a statement you hardly expect from an Austen, but years later Cassandra wrote beside it in the margin of her copy of *Persuasion* the words 'Dear, dear Jane! This deserves to be written in letters of gold.'[11]

Emma lives at the centre of a stable circle, Anne among fragmented and shifting groups. Austen finds an opportunity here, and Anne's isolation, and the way the story is told almost entirely through her eyes and thoughts, gives an extra emotional pull, putting readers into the position of her only confidantes. Her capacity for deep feeling and delight becomes ours; so do her suffering and hope, which she has no sister or friend to share with, only us. We are invited to fill the gap; few resist.

The last two chapters, as she revised them, are so dramatically crafted that they remain, even after many readings, almost unbearably tense and moving, as the lovers, unable to speak directly to one another, communicate by other means. Wentworth drops his pen, and pretends to be writing another letter when really he is writing to Anne. Every word she says to Harville is meant for Wentworth. She speaks from the heart, but Anne Elliot is a formidable woman, and she rises to eloquence and wit in defending her sex: 'Men have had every advantage of us in telling their own story. Education has been theirs in so much higher a degree; the pen has been in their hands. I will not allow books to prove any thing.' Like Marianne reproaching Sir John, she is speaking here for herself, but her creator is at her side; only this time she is not so much endorsing as disproving her words, because she had taken up the pen.

Her illness had not left her. The only letter from the last three months of 1816 is one congratulating her nephew James-Edward on leaving Winchester before going up to Oxford, and on his attempts at novel writing. All three of James's children were now trying their hand at fiction; she had given Anna's work close attention earlier, and kept up a correspondence with Caroline about her little stories too, reading and praising them patiently and kindly. Now she made her disclaimer about the 'little bit (two Inches wide) of Ivory on which I work with so fine a Brush' to her nephew, contrasting her work with his 'strong, manly, spirited Sketches'. It is a generous joke, so finely phrased that no one can forget it; a perfectly acceptable way of comparing herself with – say – Walter Scott, and in that way meant as encouragement to her clever young nephew. The letter is in fact a series of jokes; there is one about Uncle Henry's 'superior Sermons' being just the thing to insert into novels, and another about the vicar of Chawton, Mr Papillon. He is, says Aunt Jane, about to make his long awaited proposal of marriage; the desirability of her marrying Mr Papillon was a family jest which she joined in with remarkable good humour and tolerance, as was expected of a maiden aunt. Tucked in among the fooling, she insists she is 'very well'; in truth she was not strong enough to walk the short distance to Anna's house for dinner.

Other members of the family were also confined to their beds. James had been laid up early in the year with another fracture, probably the result of a fall while hunting; he had already broken his leg once, and an arm. Charles had rheumatism, and his little Harriet, treated with mercury and other horrors for her headaches, was so ill that Jane was driven to wish her dead: 'I hope Heaven in its mercy will take her soon. Her poor Father will be quite worn out by his feelings for her.'[12] And among neighbours too, Mrs Chute's adoptive daughter was reported to be dangerously ill by their common doctor, Lyford; she recovered, but not before Jane expressed her sympathy, imagining Mrs Chute 'would almost feel like a Mother in losing her'. The deaths of children were terrible, but their births were not always welcome. News that Anna seemed to be pregnant again upset her: 'Anna has not a chance of escape; her husband called here the other day, & said she was *pretty well* but not *equal to so long* a walk . . . Poor Animal, she will be worn out before she is thirty. – I am very sorry for her. – Mrs Clement too is in that way again. I am quite tired of so many Children.'

She continued to make resolute statements about her improving health. At the end of January 1817 she declared herself 'stronger than I was half a year ago' – strong enough at any rate to walk into Alton, although not back again. She explained to Alethea that her problem was 'Bile', and that she now knew how to treat herself. To Fanny, she called her illness rheumatism, telling her she was almost entirely cured of it, 'just a little pain in my knee now and then'. She gallantly attempted a donkey ride in the hope that it would do her good. Another letter insists 'I am got tolerably well again', and in any case, 'Sickness is a dangerous Indulgence at my time of Life.' All her willpower was deployed to resist and deny the illness. Her letters to

Fanny seem so high spirited that, while they must have caused delight in Kent, you almost wince to think what they cost the writer. Caroline's recollections from this time underline just how far she was prepared to go in rejecting sickness.

> Aunt Jane used often to lie down after dinner – My Grandmother herself was frequently on the sofa – sometimes in the afternoon, sometimes in the evening, at no fixed period of the day, – She had not bad health for her age, and she worked often for hours in the garden, and naturally wanted rest afterwards – There was only one sofa in the room – and Aunt Jane laid upon 3 chairs which she arranged for herself – I think she had a pillow, but it never looked comfortable – She called it *her* sofa, and even when the *other* was unoccupied, *she* never took it . . . I often asked her how she *could* like the chairs best – and I suppose I worried her into telling me the reason of her choice – which was, that if she ever used the sofa, Grandmama would be leaving it for her, and would not lie down, as she did now, whenever she felt inclined –.

It is a display of good manners carried to perfection; and proof of a fierce refusal to become an acknowledged invalid.

Now her will channelled all her remaining energy into the one essential thing, which was to make a start on a new novel. *Sanditon* is never mentioned in the letters, but between January and March she wrote twelve chapters of this most surprising book. If the appeal of *Persuasion* is linked for some to its being her last book, seen as a gentle dying fall, one glance at what actually came after it throws cold water on any such sentimental thought. What other fatally ill writer has embarked on a savage attack on hypochondria? There is no sign of failing energy; on the contrary, it sets off in an entirely new direction. The theme is unlike anything she had tackled before: a place, the seaside village that is being transformed into a resort, where the newly built Trafalgar House will be followed by the still newer Waterloo Crescent, because 'Waterloo is more the thing now'; and where a young man on the make is speculatively 'running up a little Cottage Ornèe, on a strip of Waste Ground'. The language is as fresh as the subject, and much of it is owed to a Mr Parker, best described as a Regency public relations man.

Mr Parker has given up his comfortable old family house to move to Trafalgar House, flagship of the keenly competitive development of Sanditon. It is 'a second Wife & 4 Children to him – hardly less Dear – & certainly more engrossing. – He could talk of it for ever . . . it was his Mine, his Lottery, his Speculation & his Hobby Horse; his Occupation his Hope & his Futurity.' And it leaves Mrs Parker not a little wistful. The modernity of the theme is startling: selling off the family silver, pouring money into 'growth' while neglecting old values, all the emphasis on competitiveness, restlessness, salesmanship.

Sanditon – known by Cassandra as *The Brothers* and in the rest of the family simply as *The Last Work* until Chapman named and published it in 1925 – offers much broader comedy than she had approached for years, and it extends a technique she had used successfully with Miss Bates and Mrs Elton in *Emma*, that of the monologue. Mr Parker, enthusiastic about the signs of new ideas among the Sanditon shopkeepers, cries, 'Civilization, Civilization indeed! . . . Look my dear Mary – Look at William Heeley's windows. – Blue Shoes, & nankin Boots! – Who wd have expected such a sight at a Shoemeaker's in old Sanditon! – This is new within the Month. There was no blue shoe when we passed this way a month ago. – Glorious indeed! – Well, I think I *have* done something in my Day.' It is as though the spirit of Dickens Future was hovering over Jane Austen.[13]

The descriptive writing promises something entirely new too: a walk in a misty landscape reveals, through a park fence, 'something White & Womanish in the field on the other side; – it was something which immediately brought Miss B. into her head – & stepping to the pales, she saw indeed . . . Miss Brereton seated, apparently very composedly – & Sir E. D. by her side. They were sitting so near together & appeared so closely engaged in gentle conversation, that Ch. instantly felt she had nothing to do but to step back again, & say not a word.' Whether you call this *chiaroscuro* or film technique before its time, it is unlike anything Austen has done before. Sir E. D. is a young baronet who has read enough Richardson to feel 'that he was formed to be a dangerous Man'; this is what he is attempting to be in the mist in the park. Other characters are a stout *malade imaginaire* who prefers cocoa and toast to fresh air and exercise; and Mr Parker's sister Diana, the embodiment of 'Activity run mad', who cannot stop talking and organizing other people's lives. The fragment breaks off before the reader can guess where *Sanditon* is going; only that it will be an original and entertaining journey, conducted by a keen observer with a freely ranging imagination.

The journey was not made, but set aside for a grimmer one. On 18 March she abandoned the manuscript, attacked by 'fever and bilious attack' that made her too unwell 'to write anything that was not strictly necessary'. She and Cass and their mother had just struggled reluctantly into their 'old Black Gowns' again – how they must have hated them – in mourning for a distant cousin when, on 28 March, Uncle James Leigh-Perrot also died. He was eighty-two and his end was peaceful. Mrs Austen grieved particularly for her brother; she also had hopes of what his will would do for her family. At this point Jane insisted that her own condition had improved enough to allow Cassandra to travel to Berkshire to help Aunt Leigh-Perrot. James, Mary and Francis all followed her for this important funeral – more important, one notices, than a family wedding – but when the will was read they found he had left everything to his widow, and that only after her death would legacies of £1,000 be paid to each of the Austen children. At Chawton, Mrs Austen and Jane were stunned by this news. Jane suffered what she called a relapse, which she attributed to the shock, although to us it sounds like a continuation of her existing condition. Whatever it was, she had to ask for her sister's return. This was early in April.

When Caroline and Anna called to see her,

> She was keeping her room but said she would see us, and we went up to her – She was in her dressing gown and was sitting quite like an invalid in an arm chair – but she got up, and kindly greeted us – and then pointing to the seats which had been arranged for us by the fire, she said, 'There's a chair for the married lady, and a little stool for you, Caroline.' . . . I was struck by the alteration in herself – She was very pale – her voice was weak and low and there was about her, a general appearance of debility and suffering; but I have been told that she never *had* much actual pain – She was not equal to the exertion of talking to us, and our visit to the sick room was a very short one – Aunt Cassandra soon taking us away – I do not suppose we stayed a quarter of an hour; and *I* never saw Aunt Jane again.[14]

In mid-April she took to her bed, too weak to struggle on, with night fevers and a discharge, unspecified but alarming enough to make her accept the visit of a surgeon from Winchester, whose 'applications gradually removed the Evil'. After this, and without letting anyone know, she wrote her will, dated 27 April and addressed to 'Miss Austen' but unwitnessed. We can take it that from this point she had not too much faith in her own recovery; and, businesslike, she also wrote out an account of the profits on her novels, 'over & above the £600 in Navy Fives'. They came to £84.13s.

After a visit from James and Mary, she agreed to be taken to Winchester to be under the care of the surgeons there; they were attached to a hospital, and thought likely to be as good as any in London. All this she explained in a letter to Anne Sharp just before setting out from Chawton. She explained that she had been very low but was recovering strength. It is a wonderful letter, written in her best voice, affectionate, vividly phrased, and liable to slip in a sentence you have to read again to catch the full effect: 'If I live to be an old woman I must expect to wish I had died now, blessed in the tenderness of such a Family, & before I had survived either them or their affection.' She has become 'a very genteel, portable sort of Invalid'. James has offered his carriage for the journey: 'Now, that's the sort of thing which Mrs J. Austen does in the kindest manner! But still she is in the main *not* a liberal-minded Woman.' Ill as she is, her language is in perfect health, and used to its full effect. It is funny, it is honest, it is even warm where she is not usually warm: 'my dear Mother . . . suffered much for me when I was at the worst'. Suddenly, surprisingly, she invokes the seventeenth-century French 'sorceress' Eléonore Galigai de Concini who, according to Voltaire, told her judges before she was burned that her magic was simply the force that strong spirits exert over weak ones ('Mon sortilège a été le pouvoir que les âmes fortes doivent avoir sur les esprits faibles'). Was it Eliza who read Voltaire and told her about Eléonore? Whoever it was, 'Galigai de Concini for ever & ever' wrote Jane, her own spirit strong enough for a sorceress. Anne Sharp treasured the letter, which was signed off 'Sick or well, beleive me ever yr attached friend'; and she passed it on before her own death, like a true believer, into safe hands.[15]

Elizabeth Heathcote found lodgings for Cassandra and Jane in

Winchester; Alethea was away in Switzerland, 'frisked off like half England' wrote Jane. They set off on 24 May. Henry rode the sixteen miles from Chawton beside the carriage in which his sisters sat. It rained all the way, a soft veil falling over the green landscape. Edward's fourth son William rode alongside Henry, and Jane worried about the two of them getting wet. Then she settled in to their lodgings at No. 8, College Street, a modest house belonging to a Mrs David. It stood between the school buildings at the back and the old city wall, with a strip of pleasant garden and a few trees at the front; built directly over the water meadows, with no cellars to keep out the damp. But they had the first floor, two sitting rooms, a bow window, and two good bedrooms at the back. She wrote to her nephew James-Edward, 'Mr Lyford says he will cure me, & if he fails I shall draw up a Memorial & lay it before the Dean & Chapter, & have no doubt of redress from that Pious, Learned & disinterested Body.'

Apart from a scrap, this was her last letter.

24

College Street

At College Street, Elizabeth Heathcote called every day. Jane was taken out in a sedan chair and allowed to walk from one room to another, and insisted that she was getting better. It did not seem so to Cassandra. She sent for Mary Austen, who arrived on Friday, 6 June. 'I dined with the Miss Austens and stay'd with Jane whilst Cass went to Church' is her diary entry for Sunday; and on the Monday, 'Jane Austen worse I sat up with her.' Tuesday: 'Jane in great danger.' The diary then falls silent for several days. Meanwhile Henry wrote to Fanny to warn her of her aunt's condition; her diary for 14 June notes, 'A letter to me from Uncle H A – a sad acct of my poor dear Aunt Jane.' He also sent a letter to Charles, suggesting that he should come to Winchester as soon as he could. James wrote to his son at Oxford:

> I grieve to write what you will grieve to read; but I must tell you that we can no longer flatter ourselves with the least hope of having your dear valuable Aunt Jane restored to us. The symptoms which returned after the first four or five days at Winchester have never subsided, and Mr Lyford has candidly told us that her case is desperate. I need not say what a melancholy gloom this has cast over us all. Your Grandmamma has suffered much, but her affliction can be nothing to Cassandra's. She will indeed need to be pitied. It is some consolation to know that our poor invalid has hitherto felt no very severe pain – which is rather an extraordinary circumstance in her complaint. I saw her on Tuesday and found her much altered, but composed and cheerful. She is well aware of her situation. Your mother has been there ever since Friday & returns not till all is over – how soon that may be we cannot say – Lyford said he saw no sign of immediate dissolution, but added that with such a pulse it was

Tom Lefroy is the chief subject of Jane Austen's earliest surviving letter, her 'Irish friend', with whom she enjoyed behaving outrageously at a dance. He was a law student from Ireland, a holiday visitor to his uncle in Hampshire and, at just twenty, the same age as her. He was also financially dependent on the good will of another uncle and, since neither he nor Jane had a penny, an engagement between them was out of the question; when it became obvious that they were falling in love he was sent smartly away. Jane joked about him, but it was a painful experience, and she was still thinking of him three years later. He married an heiress, and became Lord Chief Justice of Ireland. As a very old man he acknowledged, when questioned, that he had loved Jane Austen in 1796.

Below is Manydown House, where Jane and Tom danced together. It was the home of her friends, the three Bigg sisters; and seven years after her romance with Tom Lefroy their brother Harris, heir to Manydown, proposed marriage to Jane while she was staying with them. She accepted his proposal in the evening, but changed her mind during the night.

Mrs Austen's brother James Leigh, who came into a fortune and changed his name to Leigh-Perrot. He and his wife Jane (*right*) divided their time between their Berkshire home and Bath. Their childlessness encouraged Mrs Austen to hope her children would be made their heirs; but they liked to keep the Austens guessing about how they would leave their money.

The Revd George Lefroy, uncle to Tom, and like him of Huguenot descent, lived at Ashe rectory, only a step from Steventon. His wife Anne (*right*) was cultivated and charming, and showed particular friendship to Jane, who credited her with 'genius, taste, and tenderness of soul'. Mrs Lefroy set up a Straw Manufactory to help the poor when the war with France brought hard times to the Hampshire villages. She was killed by a fall from her horse.

Luxurious Godmersham, standing in its idyllic parkland near Canterbury, where Edward Austen became master, brought up his many children and entertained his brothers and sisters. Henry was the most frequent visitor; he wrote a poem in praise of Godmersham, enjoyed the shooting, and read plays aloud in the library in the evening. Cassandra came mostly to help her sister-in-law through her confinements. Jane was conscious of being regarded as a poor relation, and the best friend she made there was the governess, Anne Sharp.

Mrs Knight, Edward's adoptive mother and benefactress, was Jane's only patron, presenting her with an annual 'fee', which, apart from the meagre pocket money the Austen parents were able to allow her, was all she had until she began to earn from her writing in her mid-thirties.

Elizabeth Bridges, daughter of a Kentish baronet, married Edward Austen in 1791 at the age of eighteen. She did not care for Jane, perhaps because she thought her too clever. A devoted wife and mother, she was almost permanently pregnant throughout her married life; she died in 1808, after the birth of her eleventh child.

(*left*) The Revd George Austen as an old man. His granddaughter Anna remembered how his fine white hair and bright eyes attracted admiring glances in Bath, where he moved with his wife and daughters in 1801. He died there in 1805 and is buried in the church of St Swithin at Walcot, the same church in which he was married in 1764.

Jane Austen visited Bath (*below*) in 1797 and 1799, and made precise use of it as a setting for scenes in her early novel *Northanger Abbey* and again in *Persuasion*. She admired the beauty of the surrounding countryside, but came to dislike the city itself, with its 'white glare' and inescapable social round; and although she wrote so well about it, she seems to have done little writing while she lived there.

Lyme Regis (*above*), its houses steeply stacked above the bay where Dorset and Devon meet, laid its spell on Jane Austen during her visits of 1803 and 1804; and she immortalized it in *Persuasion*, not only with a scene of high drama but with her lyrical account of its delights, from the Cobb, the fast-flowing tide, the sands and the bathing machines to the dark cliffs of Charmouth near by and the 'green chasms between romantic rocks' at Pinny.

An early photograph showing Chawton Cottage (*left*). It was offered by Edward to his mother and sisters when it became available after the death of the previous tenant, his farm bailiff, and they settled gratefully in the house in 1809. Here Jane Austen took up her pen again after ten years in which she had produced almost nothing. She was at Chawton when two of her early books were published – *Sense and Sensibility* in 1811, *Pride and Prejudice* in 1813 – and three more were written here, *Mansfield Park*, *Emma* and *Persuasion*, making the very modest house into one of the great sites of literary history. It went unrecognized for more than a century, however, and was divided into tenements for labourers; only in the 1940s were the first efforts made to restore it by the newly formed Jane Austen Society. It is now a museum.

Rowlandson's engraving of the Prince Regent driving a curricle shows just what dashing and precarious vehicles they were. Henry Austen drove one, and his wife wrote of being 'sometimes so gracious or so imprudent as to trust my neck to Henry's coachmanship'. Willoughby, Darcy, Bingley, Henry Tilney and Charles Musgrove were all given curricles to drive by Jane Austen, and Mr Collins, John Thorpe and Sir Edward Denham owned gigs, which were very similar and equally showy. The dreadful Thorpe described his gig as 'Curricle-hung, you see; seat, trunk, sword-case, splashing-board, lamps, silver moulding, all you see complete'.

Willoughby carrying Marianne after she has sprained her ankle: an engraving from the 1828 French edition of *Raison et Sensibilité*.

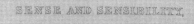

Marianne on her sickbed: the title-page engraving for Bentley's 1833 *Sense and Sensibility*, the first English edition with illustrations. All the illustrations in Bentley's edition are by an otherwise unknown artist called Pickering, engraved by William Greatbatch.

Elizabeth Bennet with Lady Catherine de Bourgh in the garden at Longbourn: the most dramatic scene in the book, in an engraving from Bentley's 1833 edition of *Pride and Prejudice*.

Captain Wentworth removing little Harry Musgrove from his Aunt Anne Elliot's back: an engraving from the 1821 French edition of *La Famille Elliot* (*Persuasion*). This must be the earliest illustration to any of Austen's novels.

Sir Thomas Bertram interrupts Mr Yates while he is rehearsing on the improvised stage at Mansfield Park: another dramatic engraving from Bentley's 1833 edition of *Mansfield Park*.

Emma works at a portrait drawing of Harriet Smith, watched admiringly by Mr Elton: engraving from Bentley's 1833 edition of *Emma*.

A daguerreotype taken in old age of Jane Austen's dear friend Martha Lloyd, who, after sixty-three years as a spinster, became the second wife of Admiral Sir Francis Austen.

The sad survivor: a silhouette of Cassandra Austen, made in later life, showing an imposing-looking woman, but with a cheerless face.

Lastly, Jane's well-loved brother Frank, Admiral Sir Francis Austen, still a handsome man, in a daguerreotype taken in the latter part of his ever active life. He was the longest lived of the family, dying in 1865 at the age of ninety-one. He preserved Jane's letters carefully for fifty years, but immediately after his death they were destroyed by his daughter Fanny, who failed to consult with anyone else: an irreparable loss.

impossible for any person to last long, & indeed no one can wish that – an easy departure from this to a better world is all that we can pray for.[1]

Yet against all expectation she rallied again, and when Charles arrived he found 'Dear Jane rather better'.[2] He rode to Chawton on Henry's horse, where it was Mrs Austen who struck him as 'very poorly'. Then he returned to Winchester on the top of the coach. 19 June: 'Jane a little better. Saw her twice & in the evening for the last time in this world as I greatly fear, the Doctor having no hope of her final recovery.' He could not stay, and travelled sadly back to his difficult life in London; he had lost a wife and child, and now the sister he had loved since he could remember was being taken from him too.

The unexpected improvement in Jane's condition allowed Mary Austen to go home to Steventon. 'You have always been a kind sister to me, Mary,' lied Jane to her, thanking her for her nursing, and perhaps glad to see her go. But Cassandra and Mary were agreed that she would come back when needed; and on 13 June she returned to College Street. Mrs Austen was sent optimistic bulletins, which she passed on to Anna. 'I had a very comfortable acct of yr Aunt Jane this morning, she now sits up a little . . . she hoped to be well enough to see Mrs Portal to day; your Mamma is there, (went yesterday by the Coach) which I am very glad of . . . Tales of My Landlord are at yr Uncle Franks, that is the 3 first are there, I am reading the 4th.' Jane would have liked the idea of her mother cheering herself with Scott's *Tales of My Landlord*; to distract from grief and anxiety is a very proper function of the novel.

It can also be the function of creation. On the morning of 15 July, St Swithin's Day, which was very rainy, and also the day fixed for the annual Winchester races, Jane dictated twenty-four lines of comic verse to Cassandra; she had most likely been writing them in her head for some time, to occupy herself as she lay in bed, but it was still a feat for someone as ill as she was. The verses imagine St Swithin laying a curse on the Winchester races. 'Venta' is an old name for Winchester, already used by James in a poem which may have set her mind to work; Jane makes the saint scold the citizens for setting up races without seeking his permission:

'Oh! subjects rebellious! Oh Venta depraved
When once we are buried you think we are gone
But behold me immortal! By vice you're enslaved
You have sinned and must suffer, then farther he said

These races and revels and dissolute measures
With which you're debasing a neighbouring Plain
Let them stand – You shall meet with your curse in your pleasures
Set off for your course, I'll pursue with *my* rain.'

Cassandra put 'gone' at the end of the second line, where the rhyme clearly calls for 'dead'; but either Jane could not say the word, or her sister could not bring herself to write it down.[3] In the evening of the same day Cassandra noted 'a visible change' in her charge; 'she slept more & much more comfortably, indeed . . . she was more asleep than awake. Her looks altered & she fell away, but I perceived no material diminution of strength & tho' I was then hopeless of a recovery I had no suspicion how rapidly my loss was approaching.'[4]

On 17 July the sun shone all day until the evening, when rain again set in for the night. Mary's diary reads: 'Jane Austen was taken for death about ½ past 5 in the Evening.' What she meant was that Jane had a seizure of some kind and became alarmingly faint; Cassandra, who was out on an errand, arrived back at quarter to six to find her conscious, and the two sisters talked quietly together about the seizure. Mr Lyford was sent for, and pronounced her close to death; he believed, it seems, that a large blood vessel had given way.[5]

Lyford administered something – Cassandra does not say what, but it would have been laudanum – to ease his patient. She knew herself to be dying before it could take effect. 'During that half hour was her struggle, poor soul! she said she could not tell us what she suffered, tho' she complained of little fixed pain. When I asked her if there was anything she wanted, her answer was she wanted nothing but death & some of her words were "God grant me patience, Pray for me oh Pray for me". Her voice was affected but as long as she spoke she was intelligible.' So Cassandra described the last half hour before her sister lost consciousness.

Cassandra settled herself with a pillow on her lap supporting Jane's head, which her last struggle had left half off the bed. Cassandra was

13   *Memorandums.*   Su.

I went to Winton to nurse Jane. W. D. & C. K. dined at Steventon

14   *W: returned from*   M

Kintbury

15   T

16   W

17 *Jane Austen was taken for death about ½ past 5 in the Evening*

18 *Jane breathed her last ½ after four in the morn: only Cass. & I were with her*

19 *Austen & Ed: came, this Latter returned home*

Mary Austen's diary page: 'Jane Austen was taken for death'

unwilling to move her at all, but after six hours sitting like this she allowed Mary to take her place for two hours at one in the morning, returning to her post at three. An hour later, Jane was dead: 'in about one hour more she breathed her last. I was able to close her eyes myself & it was a great gratification to me to render her these last services.'[6] Later Cassandra found the magnificent words partly quoted earlier, in which she was able to express the intensity of her feelings; and which deserve to be read again. 'She was the sun of my life, the gilder of every pleasure, the soother of every sorrow, I had not a thought concealed from her, & it is as if I had lost a part of myself.'

Mary's diary for 18 July read more prosaically. 'Jane breathed her last $\frac{1}{2}$ after four in the Morn. only Cass & I were with her. Henry came.' It was Henry surely who sought permission for their sister to be buried in the cathedral; splendid as it is, she might have preferred the open churchyard at Steventon or Chawton. But Henry knew the Bishop from his recent examination for ordination; Mrs Heathcote was also well known to the Dean, Thomas Rennell, through her late husband; and Rennell was a friend of the Chutes and through them James Austen, so there was no difficulty. The funeral had to take place early in the morning not to interfere with the regular daily services of the cathedral, and was fixed for 24 July. Until then Jane's body lay in its open coffin with a 'sweet serene air over her countenance', in one of the small rooms in College Street. Cassandra cut several locks of her hair to keep and to give away.[7]

Edward and Francis arrived in Winchester on 23 July. Charles could not come, and James felt too unwell to do so, but on the day itself his son James-Edward rode the fourteen miles from Steventon to Winchester very early in brilliant morning sunshine.[8] The coffin was closed and placed on a low bier with a pall over it, to be wheeled along College Street, through Kingsgate and the Close, and so into the cathedral, the three brothers and one nephew walking beside it as the only mourners. A brick-lined vault was ready in the north aisle of the nave, and the Precentor, Thomas Watkins, read the solemn service. A temporary stone was laid while the final one with its epitaph was prepared. She was the third and last person to be buried in the cathedral that year; the arrangements were so relaxed that the entry in the cathedral register gives the wrong date, 16 July, for the funeral.

After this the will was read. Jane made Cassandra her executrix and left her everything but for two legacies of £50. Nothing for nephews and nieces; but £50 for Henry, to mark his special place in her heart, his help in getting her books published, and his present poverty. The other £50 was for Madame Bigeon, Eliza's old retainer. It is a very striking provision, this legacy to an old Frenchwoman with no claim on her but that of friendship, hardship and long service to her cousin and her cousin's child; but then Jane had always been good at noticing those who were overlooked by others.

A few days later the *Salisbury and Winchester Journal* printed an obituary: 'On Friday the 18th inst. died, in this city, Miss Jane Austen, youngest daughter of the late Rev. George Austen, Rector of Steventon, in the county, and authoress of Emma, Mansfield Park, Pride and Prejudice and Sense and Sensibility. Her manners were gentle, her affections ardent, her candour was not to be surpassed, and she lived and died as became a humble Christian.'[9]

The family scattered to their homes. James and James-Edward both turned to poetry and wrote memorial lines. They may also have helped Henry prepare the inscription for the fine black marble grave stone, in three pious, rolling sentences that contrive to omit her greatest claim to fame:

In Memory of
JANE AUSTEN,
youngest daughter of the late
Revd GEORGE AUSTEN,
formerly Rector of Steventon in this County
she departed this life on the 18th July 1817,
aged 41, after a long illness supported with
the patience and the hopes of a Christian.

The benevolence of her heart,
the sweetness of her temper, and
the extraordinary endowments of her mind
obtained the regard of all who knew her and
the warmest love of her intimate connections.

Their grief is in proportion to their affection
they know their loss to be irreparable,
but in their deepest affliction they are consoled
by a firm though humble hope that her charity,
devotion, faith and purity have rendered
her soul acceptable in the sight of her
REDEEMER.

Cassandra sent out letters and mementoes of her sister, to Anne Sharp among others; and life went on. Caroline was sent to school in Winchester. Edward took his daughters Fanny and Lizzy to Paris. Henry stood in for James's clerical duties at Sherborne St John for several weeks in September, as Mrs Chute noted in her diary; she also described how, in December, a performance of *The Rivals* was put on at The Vyne, where James-Edward Austen was a regular visitor. It was thirty-four years since 'some young Ladies and Gentlemen at Steventon' had put on the play in their barn, with Henry speaking the prologue written by James, to the delight of an eight-year-old Jane Austen.

25

Postscript

Cassandra's grief did not prevent her from acting efficiently as her sister's executrix. Five months after Jane's death the two completed manuscript novels, *Catherine* and *The Elliots*, were published together.[1] She and Henry agreed on much improved titles, *Northanger Abbey* and *Persuasion*, and Henry dealt with Murray. He also wrote the biographical note often referred to in the pages of this book. It is dated 'London, Dec. 13, 1817'; a week later, still in London, he added a postscript, giving passages from two of her letters. He described her character as without fault, praised her wit, her modesty where her work was concerned, and her placidity of temper. As befitted a clergyman, he also laid great emphasis on her piety. It is a loving and polished eulogy; his claim that she suffered nothing worse than 'little disappointments' in her life, saw all her wishes gratified, and never uttered a severe expression must be taken as too polite to be the whole truth.

Egerton issued a third edition of *Pride and Prejudice*, squeezed into two volumes; its popularity was assured. *Northanger Abbey* and *Persuasion* were favourably reviewed in the *Edinburgh Magazine*, with the sage prediction that once readers had had enough of the romances of Scott, Byron, Edgeworth and Godwin, 'the delightful writer of the works now before us, will be one of the most popular of English novelists'; but the *British Critic* sourly lamented Austen's 'want of imagination'.[2] For a year Murray's edition sold well, making £500 for Cassandra. After that sales fell off, and in 1820 he remaindered the last 282 copies.[3] Fifteen years went by before another publisher was willing to reprint in England. In France all six of the novels had appeared by the mid-1820s. They were the first illustrated editions, charmingly done; and the title given to *Emma* – *La Nouvelle*

Emma, ou les Caractères Anglais du Siècle – suggests that Austen was taken by the French as a guide to the baffling nature of their English neighbours.

Not long after Jane's death James began to show signs of illness. Like her, he resisted it, determined to continue to ride about the countryside he loved as long as he was strong enough to get on a horse; when he could no longer manage that, he had himself carried out of the house into the open air. He gave up the struggle in November 1819, took to his bed, and died in December. His death meant that his widow Mary and children, James-Edward and Caroline, had to leave Steventon; Henry was to take over the parish and move into the rectory. He planned to take pupils as his father had done, and was also about to marry again. According to Caroline, he 'paid my mother every due attention, but his own spirits he could *not* repress, and it is not pleasant to *witness* the elation of your successor in gaining what *you* have lost'.[4] So history repeated itself, and Caroline and her mother set off sorrowfully for Bath. The following April, Henry married Miss Eleanor Jackson, about whom no one has found much to say except that she was the niece of the Mr Papillon who was always supposed to be about to propose to Jane, and that she made Henry a quiet and loyal wife.

Henry was the last Austen to live in the Steventon family home. He was displaced in the parish by his brother Edward's son William Knight, who took over in 1823. At this point Edward, as landlord, decided that the old house was not worth the repairs it needed. He had always been the brother with a head for business, and proved it now; Mr Austen's rectory, with its strawberry beds and sweep at the front, was knocked down, and a solid, square rectory put up on another site near by. William brought a local bride to his new rectory, Caroline Portal, daughter of the Austens' old friend and neighbour John Portal. They had eight children in twelve years, and the eighth baby killed her; his brother Edward's wife died of her seventh child about the same time, two more casualties of the unquestioned custom of bearing a baby every eighteen months.

James's son James-Edward was also ordained, a year after his cousin William, in 1824, but there was no living for him. He had to become a mere curate; he gave up his early attempts to write novels, and lived the life of a 'hunting, fishing, dancing young man' (his own description), putting in regular attendance at balls, the races and the theatre. He was charming, good-looking and lucky, and like William he found his bride through old connections, marrying Mrs Chute's niece Emma Smith, whom he had first met at The Vyne. Eliza Chute wrote to her niece, 'I must consider your marriage with him as in some degree under my auspices . . . He certainly is a very agreeable companion, cheerful, lively, animated, ready to converse, willing to read out loud, never in the way and just enough of poetry and romance to please me and yet not to overlook sober reason.'[5] She offered the young couple an allowance, and his Great-Aunt Leigh-Perrot also looked favourably on the match; eight years later he inherited her Berkshire house, Scarlets, along with a substantial sum of money. He and his Emma were both blessed with cheerful temperaments, and brought up a large and gifted family of three daughters and seven sons; the boys were kept at home until they were thirteen, before going to various public schools, Eton, Winchester and Harrow. Emma survived the ten births, and James-Edward went on to produce, instead of novels, first a history of the Vine hunt, and then the earliest *Memoir of Jane Austen*. This was in 1869. Before he began to write, he went back to Steventon to look over the old sites; and he had substantial help from both his clever sisters, Anna – widowed, and eking out a penurious existence – and Caroline, who did not marry.

Austen's reputation had advanced only slowly, and her sales remained small. Richard Whateley, later Archbishop of Dublin, published an admiring account in 1821 in the *Quarterly Review* in which he stressed the Christian basis of her morality. Walter Scott's high praise in his journal entry appeared in print in 1837. In 1843 Macaulay hailed her supreme skill in drawing characters who appear both commonplace and unique, which he found akin to Shakespeare's; this was in an article on Fanny Burney for the *Edinburgh Review*. While these were big critical names and ensured her a following, she was not a popular author at the level of Scott, Thackeray or Dickens. During the 1850s visitors began to seek her grave in Winchester Cathedral; the verger did not understand why anyone wanted to see it.[6] And while George Henry Lewes praised her steadily through the 1850s, singling out her dramatic powers especially, he expected her to find appreciation only within a 'small circle of cultivated minds'.[7] One of the cultivated minds was that of George Eliot, whose debt to Austen is clear in the first section of *Middlemarch*. Another woman novelist, Julia Kavanagh, wrote a sharply perceptive account of Austen's work in 1862: 'If we look into the shrewdness and quiet satire of her stories, we shall find a much keener sense of disappointment than joy fulfilled. Sometimes we find more than disappointment.'[8]

This was not at all the view of her memoirist nephew. His beautifully composed portrait of a gentle, cheerful, domestic woman, whose writing was essentially an amateur activity, found immediate favour with the Victorian public and greatly increased critical interest in the novels, and their popularity. New editions began to appear, and by the end of the century there were many, cheap and illustrated, on sale: Dent's in 1892, Macmillan's with Hugh Thomson's illustrations in 1897, Nelson's in 1903, Everyman in 1906, Oxford World's Classics in 1907. In 1923 R. W. Chapman's editions, with the text based on collation of the early editions, began to be issued. As to paperback editions: from 1864 Tauchnitz of Leipzig issued all six of the novels in paperback in his Collection of British Authors, but English paperbacks did not appear until shortly before the Second World War. *Pride and Prejudice* was the first, published as a Penguin Illustrated Classic in May 1938. *Northanger Abbey* appeared in May 1943, and *Persuasion* in September of the same year. *Emma* and *Mansfield Park* were not paperbacked until 1966, *Sense and Sensibility* last in 1969. In America the paperbacks came late too, Houghton Mifflin starting with *Pride and Prejudice* in 1956. In the 1990s you can buy virtually disposable copies, paying £1 for an Austen novel on a station bookstall and throwing it away at the end of the journey if you can bear to. With films and television, sequels, prequels and examination syllabuses, Austen has become very big business.

Henry never made any money again. On giving up Steventon to his nephew William, he moved to Farnham in Surrey, where he taught at the grammar school, and became curate of Bentley. His trail is not easy to follow. Old acquaintances from his palmy days gave him various chaplaincies; he may have gone to Germany in connection with one, and seems to have travelled in France again. In 1825 his attempt to win something from the de Feuillide estate ended, dismissed by the court at Agen. He dabbled in different interests, publishing a well-researched sermon about the persecuted Protestant sect of the Vaudois, intended to raise money to help them; and having Bentley Church partly rebuilt at public expense. It was somehow typical that the rebuilding was faulty, and had to be pulled down again after his death. His one effective action was in negotiating with the publisher Richard Bentley about a new edition of his sister's novels.

This was in the summer of 1832. Henry described himself as 'joint proprietor' of the copyright with Cassandra, which was not strictly the case – she was sole proprietor according to the terms of Jane's will – but she no doubt agreed to the description to make it easier for him to deal with Bentley.[9] She owned five copyrights, for which Henry asked £50 each, a total of £250. Bentley beat him down to £210, because he had also to pay Egerton's heirs for *Pride and Prejudice* to complete the set. He was a shrewd publisher, and asked for more biographical material about 'the Authoress'. Henry offered very little, repeating his phrase 'my dear Sisters life was not a life of events'; and he went on, 'Nothing like a journal of her actions or her conversations was kept by her or others. Indeed the farthest thing from her expectations or wishes was to be exhibited as a public character under any [?] circumstances.' Either Henry had failed to preserve any of the many letters Jane must have sent him and Eliza or, like Cassandra, he was not prepared to let them be seen by other eyes; the former seems more likely. Bentley hoped for a portrait too; Henry explained that the only one he could find was a study in which her face was concealed, which must have been Cassandra's watercolour of 1804 showing only a back view of a seated figure; and, understandably, it was not used. The six novels were put out in one volume each, in Bentley's 'Standard Novels' series, and reprinted several times over the following decades.

We hear of Henry frequently visiting his mother at Chawton cottage in her latter days. She remained safely there after Edward secured his right to the Chawton estates, for which he had to pay out £15,000 to the family who challenged it; and from 1820 she was made more comfortable by an allowance of £100 from her sister-in-law Leigh-Perrot. Like so many hypochondriacs, Mrs Austen turned out to be far tougher than her healthy friends. 'Ah, my dear, you find me just where you left me – on the sofa,' she told her grandson James-Edward when he called to see her. 'I sometimes think that God Almighty must have forgotten me; but I dare say He will come for me in His own good time.'[10] She lived to be eighty-seven; her eyesight deteriorated badly, and during the last year she suffered continual pain and was mostly confined to her bed, nursed by Cassandra and Martha Lloyd; she died in January 1827, alert to the end. She had been a strong force in the family, a tough, self-confident and remarkable woman, not always on easy terms with her most brilliant child, whose genius she nevertheless helped to shape by her example as a writer of verse and her taste as a reader. She was buried in Chawton Churchyard, and a memorial plaque was put up in the church vestry by her children, Cassandra, Charles, Francis, Henry and Edward.

Edward was never ill, but lived out his days calmly and comfortably at Godmersham, reaching the age of eighty-five, looked after by a daughter and a sister-in-law, and died in his sleep. His daughter Fanny, who had received so much good advice on love and marriage from her Aunt Jane, married at the age of twenty-seven a rich land-owning baronet, Sir Edward Knatchbull. The fact that he was a widower with six children meant she continued in the role she had filled since she was fifteen, mothering other people's children, as well as producing nine of her own; and her diaries give the impression that she had to rely rather heavily on her Christian faith to cope with the demands life made on her. Her husband went into Parliament, so strongly conservative that he resigned his seat when he saw the Reform Bill coming, although coaxed back later. He was a fussy man with an obsessive fear of scandal; he twice sacked governesses who attracted the affections of the young men of the family, provoked his eldest daughter into eloping, and did not relent towards her for ten years.[11] Money still multiplied in Kent, and Fanny's eldest son was raised to the peerage as Lord Brabourne. In 1884 he produced the first edition of Jane Austen's letters, but afterwards sold off and scattered many of the originals.

*

Frank's wife Mary was another poor animal, casualty of too much child-bearing; she died, like Edward's Elizabeth, giving birth to her eleventh child at lodgings in Gosport in 1823. He chose his second wife prudently, as a companion and housekeeper, from within the safe circle of the family group: she was Martha Lloyd, lifelong friend and companion of his sisters, aged sixty-three. Martha agreed to marry him and take charge of his house and family; Frank's children were displeased, and so was Mrs Leigh-Perrot, at that stage thinking of leaving him her house, Scarlets. She changed her mind but instead gave him an immediate £10,000; a rather better arrangement for him, since it enabled him to buy his own, Portsdown House outside Portsmouth. Promotion came steadily: Rear-Admiral in 1830 and Knight Commander of the Bath in the last of William IV's investitures; and Vice-Admiral in 1838.

Charles, also pursuing his career in the navy, and as hard working and good hearted as any of the Austens, was dogged by misfortune and poverty. He married his dead wife's sister in 1820, to general disapproval, and had a second family. For years he worked with the coastguard service in Cornwall; and when in 1826 he was given a command at sea again, returning to the West Indies Station, he was injured by a fall from a mast, and was again grounded for eight years. For three decades he remained a captain. Then in 1838 he got to sea once more, serving in the Mediterranean with his two sons, and was at last promoted to Rear-Admiral, only to die of cholera in Burma while commanding the East India Station at the age of seventy-three. His bad luck persisted among some of his descendants; where all the other brothers' families remained fixed in middle- or upper-class life, Charles's son's family sank through the social scale. Almost incredibly, one of his great-grandsons was reduced to driving a bread van, while another was a grocer's assistant; only their sister, showing the spirit of her forebears, became a school teacher. In the fifth generation these Austens shook off England entirely: one emigrated to Argentina, another became a GI bride.[12]

When Martha married Frank, Cassandra was left alone at Chawton cottage; and so she lived for another seventeen years, keeping herself busy with knitting, sewing and the garden.[13] She had her nephew

Edward Knight the younger at Chawton House, and sometimes visited Francis and Martha; and occasionally she would talk to nieces or great-nieces about Jane. In this way the story of the Devonshire admirer was given. A much more surprising remark was remembered by Frank's daughter Catherine; Cassandra told her that 'some of her [Jane's] letters, triumphing over the married women of her acquaintance, and rejoicing in her own freedom, were most amusing'.[14] Jane joking and triumphing is a vision so unlike the official family version – but also so believable – that you want to hear and see more; the letters are naturally not to be found.

Cassandra had many years in which to consider what to do with the papers in her possession. Her niece Caroline gives a clear account of the fate of the letters: she 'looked them over and burnt the greater part (as she told me), 2 or 3 years before her own death – She left, or gave some as legacies to the Nieces – but of those *I* have seen, several had portions cut out.'[15] In this respect, we may regret her decision, but she was confident of doing her duty towards her sister; some of the letters she destroyed were written during periods of stress, some doubtless contained indiscreet, even rude remarks, and some she thought too personal. In her care and disposal of her sister's other writings she was exemplary, given that no museum existed at the time which would have taken them. Of the three early notebooks, she left one to Charles, one to Francis and the third to James-Edward. The manuscript chapters of *Persuasion* and 'the last manuscript' (later called *Sanditon*) went to Anna Lefroy; *Lady Susan* to Fanny Knatchbull; and the *Plan of a Novel* and the 'Opinions' to Charles.

Two years before her death Cassandra sent a gift of £30 to Anne Sharp, something that was surely done with Jane's wishes in mind. She would have been proud of her friend's force of character, because by then Miss Sharp was successfully running her own school for girls in Everton, a suburb of Liverpool, installed in two handsome semi-detached villas with a view over the Mersey. There she retired, and lived until her death in 1853, known as 'a clever, rather dominant woman, much thought of in Everton society of her day'.[16]

One other aspect of Cassandra's devotion to Jane's intentions must be put on record. It is an odd story. Jane's legacy of £50 to Eliza's old servant and friend Madame Bigeon might have marked the end of the association between the French family and the English one, but it did not. In August 1822 Cassandra paid £10 to 'Mr Perigord' (surely a bank clerk's mistake for Mrs Perigord); and in 1824 Henry made three more such payments to Madame Bigeon's daughter, totalling £35.[17] At this point he was awaiting the settlement of his claim in the French courts, and hopeful of being awarded some part of Eliza's fortune; after the failure of his case there were no more payments from him. But now Cassandra took over; by this time Madame Bigeon must have been dead, and ten guineas went to 'Mrs Perigord' from Cass's account at Hoare's Bank in August 1825. Four years later, in 1829, she again gave her £5, and from then on continued with steady payments for the next sixteen years, usually of £5 twice a year, but occasionally more; in 1843, for example, she gave her four payments.[18] In the same year she wrote her will, asking Charles to continue to pay out of his inheritance from her 'twenty pounds a year by quarterly payments . . . to Mrs Mary Perigord now residing in Edward Street Portman Square during the term of her natural life'.[19] Whether this was all done in memory of the two women's service to Eliza and her son, or whether they had actually lost some small savings in Henry's bank failure is not possible to say; or whether Marie Perigord was a relentless petitioner or simply a pitiful figure. It remains that the French connection was kept up by Jane's and Cassandra's goodwill towards two women whose claims upon them were, on the face of it, so slight as to be easily ignored; that they, as the women of the family, perceived a need in those other women, and determined to meet it. Their brothers paid out money at different times to the SPCK and other Bible societies, the 'distressed Irish' and the 'Houseless poor'; Jane and Cassandra saw that Madame Bigeon and Madame Perigord were not forgotten.[20]

Cassandra was remembered by a great-niece as 'a pale, dark-eyed old lady, with a high arched nose and a kind smile, dressed in a long cloak and a large drawn bonnet, both made of black satin'.[21] She died in March 1845, not at home but on a visit to Francis. He had just, at seventy, been appointed Commander-in-Chief of the North American and West Indian Station, and was preparing to sail; older people were not then thought unfit to work. He was a widower again – Martha had died in 1843, like her sister Mary – and was taking two daughters with him, together with one son as his chaplain and another as his flag-lieutenant: a large family party. Cassandra went to say goodbye to them. In all the business of preparation she was left alone at Portsdown House with Henry, and collapsed with a 'seizure' in the head. It sounds like a stroke. Henry sent helplessly for their niece Caroline, who described the situation: 'All the inmates had cleared out and were on board the vessel at Portsmouth when I got there. It was impossible for Uncle [Francis] to delay his departure. He came over to see his sister once – that was all he could do – I found Uncle Henry left in charge. My Uncle Charles joined us ere long.'[22] Cassandra, clear in her mind in spite of the seizure, lingered for a week before she died.

Her body was taken back to Chawton to be buried beside her mother. James-Edward, who had ridden across Hampshire for Jane's funeral in 1817, arrived in his carriage for Cassandra's in 1845. There were very few at the funeral, just two of her brothers, Charles and Henry, and three nephews. It was a fine, blustery March day, and 'it struck me as remarkably emblematic of her age and condition that the wind whisked about us so many withered beech leaves, that the coffin was thickly strewn with them before the service closed', wrote James-Edward to his sister Anna.[23] Henry worked his usual charm: 'he struck me as very agreeable and not very old'; and he departed almost literally in a puff of smoke, taking the night mail train for Leamington.

With Cassandra's death, Edward Knight and his family had no further use for Chawton cottage. The contents were sold off, and it was divided into tenements for labourers. So it remained for a century, until in 1940 Miss Dorothy Darnell founded the Jane Austen Society, its first object being to gain possession of the cottage. It still belonged to the Knight family, and the three tenants were paying two shillings and sixpence a week each; Major Edward Knight was prepared to sell the freehold, but only for a sum quite beyond the means of the newly founded Society: he asked £3,000. The war made everything difficult; fortunately two of the most distinguished authorities on Jane Austen, Elizabeth Jenkins and R. W. Chapman, became involved. Chawton Village Library, which had been using one of the downstairs rooms in the cottage, gave way to the Society; an appeal in *The Times* in December 1946 raised £1,400; and in 1947 Thomas Edward Carpenter bought the freehold from the Knights with the intention of restoring it in memory of his son, killed in action in 1944. The roof was repaired, other accommodation was gradually offered to the families living in the cottage, and in July 1949 it was opened to the public. It seems entirely appropriate that this should have come about through Miss Darnell's initiative, assisted and encouraged by her sister Beatrice, with whom she shared her life, rather than through any rich and powerful institution.

Henry died suddenly in Tunbridge Wells in 1850. Francis lived another fifteen years, reaching the patriarchal age of ninety-one; by then he was Sir Francis Austen, and Admiral of the Fleet. He is the only brother of whom there is a photograph, and you can see what a good-looking man he was, with the alert Austen eyes, mouth firmly downturned and halo of springy white hair. He had kept Jane's many letters most carefully through the fifty years since her death, but surprisingly failed to leave instructions as to what should be done with them; and his daughter Fanny, without consulting anyone else, destroyed the priceless bundles.[24]

Jane Austen's family, with all their remarkable energy, diversity and adventurousness, their power to interest and keep us entertained, would nevertheless have been forgotten without her. It is only because of her writing that we think them worth remembering; and yet she is at almost every point harder to summon up than any of them. She made no claims for herself, for a room of her own, for a place among the English novelists; even her appearance, as we have seen, is hard to visualize at all precisely. The family march towards us, brightly lit in their uniforms or sober in clerical black, surrounded by their children, worrying about wills, installed in fine houses; she is as elusive as a cloud in the night sky.

She has a way of sending biographers away feeling that, as Lord David Cecil put it, she remains 'as no doubt she would have wished – not an intimate but an acquaintance'.[25] Her sharpness and refusal to suffer fools makes you fearful of intruding, misinterpreting, crassly misreading the evidence. Then there are the difficulties that arise from her being one of the few great writers who is popular outside academe as well as in. The critical literature runs to thousands of volumes and tens of thousands of articles, ranging from the brilliantly illuminating to the bizarre; getting through it all is not possible, when you consider that between 1952 and 1972 alone there were 551 books, essays and articles published, not to mention 85 doctoral dissertations.[26] On the other side of the academic fence, many readers feel strongly that she is their personal property, not to be tampered with or subjected to questions and theories.

This is nevertheless an attempt to tell the story of her life, and on the last page I must return to Jane Austen herself. To the child, for whom books were a refuge, offering a world that sometimes made better sense than the one she had to find her way about. To the girl whose imagination took off in startling directions as she began to see the possibilities of telling stories of her own. To the energetic young woman who loved dancing and jokes, and dreamt of a husband even as she apprenticed herself to novel writing with all the force of her intelligence. To the 25-year-old who decided she did not like people and could not write any more; and who was tempted to make a comfortable, loveless marriage, and put the temptation behind her. To the loving sister and aunt who always made time for her family even though she would sometimes have preferred to be left to think and write in peace. To the woman who befriended governesses and servants. To the published author in the glow of achievement and mastery of her art. To the dying woman with courage to resist death by writing in its very teeth. To the person who on occasion preferred to remain silent rather than cut across the views and habits of those she loved; and who kept notes of what people said about her work, to read over to herself. This is my favourite image of Jane Austen, laughing at the opinions of the world. It is lucky she had so much laughter in her; today, the volume of opinions has swelled to something so huge that they could be laughed at for ever.

Appendix I

A Note on Jane Austen's Last Illness

Two hundred years after her death, any diagnosis must be tentative. A carefully argued case was made in 1964 by Sir Zachary Cope that she was suffering from Addison's disease, nowadays responsive to treatment, then incurable. He cited the skin discoloration she mentioned ('black & white & every wrong colour'), her bilious attacks and her deterioration under emotional stress, as when upset by her uncle's will.

Addison's is a tuberculosis of the adrenal glands that produces vomiting and dehydration and skin discoloration, but it has other features which do not seem to fit what we know of Jane Austen's case. The discoloration characteristic of Addison's disease is in fact a tanned, healthy appearance, the effect of increased production of melanin as the pituitary works harder to stimulate the adrenal glands destroyed by tuberculosis, which fail to produce cortisone. This overstimulation, coincidentally, leads to increased skin pigmentation. As a result, observers tend to comment on how well the patient looks; but no one observed such a thing in Jane Austen, and her niece Caroline particularly noted her pallor ('she was very pale').

Addison's does not produce the recurrent fevers from which Jane Austen suffered. It does, on the other hand, lead to what is known as postural hypotension, meaning that the blood pressure drops when the patient stands up, causing sudden faintness and collapse on standing. This was not noted in Jane Austen's case. Again, a steady progress of the disease would be expected with Addison's, whereas her illness fluctuated between periods of improvement and deterioration.

One possibility is that she suffered from a lymphoma such as Hodgkin's disease – a form of cancer – which would produce recurrent fevers and progressive weakening, leading to death.

This could have originated as early as 1813, remaining latent until the winter of 1815/16. In 1813 she suffered from pain in her face for seven weeks between the end of July and the end of September, severe enough to be noted by her niece Fanny in her diary, and referred to by Jane herself in a letter. At Chawton, Fanny wrote of her having a 'cold in her face', 'a very stiff face', and 'suffering sadly with her face'; and of her preferring to sleep at the Great House rather than expose her face to the night air by walking back to the cottage, on six different evenings in August and September. Jane then wrote from Godmersham of 'severe pain' in her face for several days after catching cold on the journey; given her stoicism, severe pain must have been severe indeed.

Anyone suffering from trigeminal neuralgia, or *tic douloureux*, will avoid exposure to cold air for fear of the severe pain in the face it produces. And *tic douloureux* may follow shingles at a time of immuno-suppression such as the beginning of lymphoma. If she had a latent lymphoma in 1813, it could very well have remained without symptoms for another two years or more. The obvious drawback to this hypothesis is that there is no evidence of her having shingles, and it seems unlikely that such a painful affliction would go unmentioned, even by someone as stoical as Jane Austen, or unnoticed by those around her. It is still, however, perfectly possible that her final illness was caused by a lymphoma.

This note was written after consultation with Dr Eric Beck.

Appendix II

'An African Story'
from Fanny Austen's Pocket-book, 1809
with a Note on Attitudes to Slavery

The Revd George Austen became in 1760 a trustee of a plantation in Antigua belonging to an Oxford contemporary, James Nibbs; Nibbs became James Austen's godfather, and sent his own son George to school at Steventon. The Austens thus had a link with slavery, even if a remote one; and indeed few English families of any means in the eighteenth century did not have connections of some kind with slavery.

Jane Austen's reference to the slave trade in *Emma* shows where she stood. When Jane Fairfax speaks of agencies for governesses as akin to the sale of 'human flesh', Mrs Elton answers, 'If you mean a fling at the slave-trade, I assure you Mr Suckling was always rather a friend to abolition.' Jane Fairfax goes on to say that the two activities may be 'widely different certainly as to the guilt of those who carry it on; but as to the greater misery of the victims, I do not know where it lies.' Austen's point here is to do with governessing, not slavery; but there is no doubt that she takes for granted her readers' agreement that the slave trade is a guilty one.

Battleridge, the novel by Mrs Austen's cousin, Mrs Samuel Cooke, and published in 1799, also suggests disapproval of slavery. The story is set in the seventeenth century, when abolitionism would be anachronistic; but when a young man is given a position working for a Barbados planter and sends money home, his small brother lays stress on the fact that 'he did not beat the poor blackamoors to get it'. It is a small point; what matters is that it is made at all.

It is worth remembering too that Cowper, a poet favoured by both Mr Austen and his younger daughter, and read aloud *en famille*, was a fervent abolitionist.

Finally, the following 'African Story', from the printed matter in Fanny Austen's diary for 1809, shows that concern for slaves, and horror at the trade in them, was by then so general that the publishers of ladies' diaries could confidently assume that such a story, wholly sympathetic if also thoroughly naïve, would be entirely welcome.

Owhyhee loved the girl who lived in the next cottage to that in which he resided. She was considered by the young men who inhabited the village, the most beautiful girl round the spot, and she loved, most affectionately loved Owhyhee. They did not know what it was to run counter to the dictates of nature at the instigation of interest, and the day was fixed, on which, according to the rites of the tribe to which they belonged, the marriage was to be celebrated.

'My Ora,' said Owhyhee to her, as they walked together beneath the shade of some spreading palm-trees, 'we will bind together the leaves of the beautiful shade which now keeps the sun from our heads, to make our cot, and you shall fetch water from beneath the mountain, to refresh the fading leaves, and they will look doubly sweet, as though in gratitude at deriving their nourishment from a hand so lovely.'

'And then,' replied the maid, 'thy Ora will smile at thy return, and the dewy heads of the palm tree will let fall a glistening drop, as though in tears to greet thee.'

'And then I shall return so joyful from the chace,' returned Owhyhee, 'and lay the spoils at the feet of my Ora. And when I urge my canoe over the wave, all the fish I collect will be for Ora; the thought of thee will add to my diligence; and whether I hurl the spear at the tiger, or at the monster of the deep, my arm will still be nerved by Ora.'

At length the day arrived which had been fixed as the one on which the union should take place. The elders of the tribe were assembled beneath the protecting shade of a sort of rural tent, which was only inhabited on these occasions, and the marriage ceremony was performed. As was usual, the villagers who were assembled celebrated the union of the young couple with the most lively demonstrations of joy. In the midst of their innocent revelry, an unusual noise was heard, and the innocent villagers rose from their seats. Soon the origin of all this alarm was disclosed. An European vessel had anchored off the coast, which was not far distant, and part of the crew had landed, for the purpose of tearing the unoffending people from their native plains, and all their bosoms held most dear. On their approach, however, finding the whole of the inhabitants of the village together, and not thinking themselves equal to an attack on them, collected as they were, they fired a musquet, in the hope that the alarm would disperse them; finding they had in some measure succeeded, they now fired from three or four different places, and the consternation of the poor victims encreased. The assailants, seizing this opportunity, rushed into the middle of the circle, and the affrighted Africans fled. Owhyhee attempted to take Ora, who had fallen, from the field, but in vain; he was pursued, and together with others, made prisoners by the invaders. He was torn from the arms of his Ora, who, though almost dead with terror, would still have detained him, and with his fellow victims, was conveyed to the ship from which the white men had landed. Soon Owhyhee and his countrymen left the shore which had given them birth, and which now contained all they held dear.

'Oh, my Ora!' exclaimed Owhyhee, as he franticly beat the deck with his chains, 'who will now water the palm leaves by which we were to have been shaded? – Thou wilt, my Ora, but it will be with thy tears.'

His complaints, however, were winds to the rugged hearts which heard them. The ship, after an expeditious passage, arrived at the destined port, and Owhyhee, together with his unfortunate countrymen, were sold for slaves.

In this situation he lived a considerable time. At length, wearied with the cruelty which was every day practised towards himself and his companions, and which their utmost industry and caution could not avoid, Owhyhee and five more made their escape into the woods. Their flight was soon discovered, and the utmost efforts of their tyrants were exerted against them, and were too successful; Owhyhee alone escaped the pursuit. Stealing one evening from his retreat, he bent his way towards the plantation, in order, if possible, to discover the fate of his companions. The first object which presented itself, was a scaffold, on which preparations were making for impaling some unfortunates. – He was soon confirmed in his conjecture that his late friends were about to suffer the horrid punishment. They were dragged to the stake, he saw them bleed – then sought his woods again.

The night was dark, and Owhyhee, wondering why he lived, wandered to the shore. He seated himself beneath an overhanging point of rock, and watched the sea every moment illumined by the lightning. In a moment the blast arose. Owhyhee every instant thought he heard the voice of his Ora calling to him from the winds. He listened – several voices of distress reached him, and the lightning flashing, he saw, at a considerable distance before him, a vessel almost a wreck. As soon as he discovered the unfortunate object, he left the sheltering rock, and stood immediately at the water's edge – the swoln bodies of the drowned floated around him. – At the moment he was anxiously surveying the scene before him, a corpse was thrown at his feet; it was that of a countrywoman, and a moment sufficed him to discover that it was that of his Ora – her wrists still bore marks of chains, and he concluded that she, like himself, must have become the victim of the white marauders. Her ravishers, however, had, in common with the objects of their brutality, met their fate.

'My Ora,' said Owhyhee, taking the hand of his mistress from the ground, and pressing it to his bosom, 'thou hast abandoned thy lover, and yet he must follow thee. When they dragged thee from thy native plains, thou didst not imagine that that violence was a summons to thee from Owhyhee to accompany him to his rest.'

He plunged his knife into his heart, and sunk deep in the wave.

Notes

To avoid overloading the notes, quotations from Jane Austen's own letters are not as a rule given date or page references. They are easily traced either in R. W. Chapman's editions (1932 and 1952) or in Deirdre Le Faye's 1995 edition, now available in paperback.

I 1775

1. George Austen to Mrs Susannah Walter, his half-brother's wife, 17 Dec. 1775, in R. A. Austen-Leigh, *The Austen Papers, 1704–1856* (1942; hereafter cited as *AP*), p. 32.
2. Philadelphia Hancock was expected to help out at Cassandra's birth in Jan. 1773 in spite of the bad time of year for travelling, as Mrs Austen mentions in a letter to her sister-in-law Mrs Walter (8 Nov. 1772, *AP*, p. 28); and she had been before at least once, for George's birth. A woman friend or member of the family was normally asked to be present to assist during childbirth; Mrs Austen went to her sister, Mrs Cooper, in 1770, for example. Philadelphia was in England in 1775, and so easily able to come to Steventon.
3. For the pearls, see Tysoe Saul Hancock to Philadelphia Hancock, 22 May 1775, *AP*, p. 81; for the harpsichord, see Tysoe Saul Hancock to Philadelphia Hancock, 31 Jan. 1772, *AP*, p. 60; for the play, Tysoe Saul Hancock to Elizabeth Hancock, 7 Nov. 1771, British Library Add. MSS 29,236.
4. Eliza Chute's sister, Lady Compton, gave birth on 1 Jan. 1790, went into her mother's bedroom on the 16th, went downstairs on the 27th, went out on the 29th and to the child's christening on 2 Feb. Mrs Austen's daughter-in-law Elizabeth (Austen/Knight) gave birth to her ninth child on 13 Nov. 1804, got up for dinner and walked to her chair on 23 Nov., walked without any support on 2 Dec. and dined downstairs

for the first time on 10 Dec. She did not go out to church until 10 Feb., i.e., three months after the birth. Two years later she gave birth to her tenth child on 16 Nov. 1806, dined in the schoolroom (i.e., upstairs) for the first time on 15 Dec. and went outside for the first time on 10 Jan. 1807. She did not go to church until 25 Jan. All these dates were noted by her daughter Fanny in her diary, held at Kent County Archives, U951 F24/1–69.

5. The godmothers were the wife of Jane's great-uncle Francis Austen, the Kentish lawyer, and Mrs Musgrave, married to her mother's cousin, Rector of Chinnor. Her godfather was the Revd Samuel Cooke of Great Bookham, whose wife was Mrs Austen's first cousin and namesake, Cassandra Leigh, daughter of Theophilus Leigh, Master of Balliol. Mrs Francis Austen died in 1782, Mrs Musgrave was never heard of again. Mr Cooke, described by Fanny Burney as a worthy man, had problems with his own eleven children, of whom only three survived into adult life. Jane did, however, stay with the Cookes in 1814, and he expressed his admiration for *Mansfield Park*.

6. Mrs Cassandra Austen to Susannah Walter, 6 June 1773, *AP*, p. 29. Her sister, Jane Cooper, did stop at two, but she did not marry until she was thirty-two and her husband was forty.

7. George Austen had been presented with the living of Steventon in 1761 by the husband of a second cousin, Thomas Knight, who was overall, and absentee, landlord of Steventon. The living gave Mr Austen only three acres of glebe land to cultivate, but Mr Knight allowed him to run Cheesedown Farm in addition, which meant he was farming a considerable amount of land. He was given special permission by the Archbishop of Canterbury to hold the second living of Deane in March 1773. Mr Austen's selling off of his South Sea annuities is recorded in his account with Hoare's Bank.

8. Mrs Cassandra Austen to Susannah Walter, 6 June 1773, *AP*, p. 29: 'I suckled my little girl thro' the first quarter; she has been weaned and settled at a good woman's at Deane just eight weeks; she is very healthy and lively, and puts on her short petticoats today.' It is possible, of course, that Mrs Austen did not follow the same regime with all her children; she may, for instance, have kept her first-born at home and at the breast for longer. Mrs Thrale breast-fed only her first child, Queenie. James Austen and his mother were noticeably strongly attached to one another.

9. From *Advice to Young Men* (1829), cited in Lawrence Stone, *The Family, Sex and Marriage in England 1500–1800* (1982), p. 100.

10. Susan Ferrier described in Chapter 19 of her novel *Marriage* (published in 1818 but written in 1810 and set earlier) the treatment of twin girls whose mother was unwilling to feed them: one was found a wet nurse, the other handed over to the old aunts of the family to be reared on chopped rusks, gruel, colic powders and other patent medicines administered on a spoon and through a 'sucking pot'. The hand-reared one is narrowly saved from death by being adopted by a young aunt and found a second wet nurse. Sucking pots came into use during the eighteenth century; they were usually of ceramic with a pierced spout over which went a piece of cloth.

    Deirdre Le Faye suggests in 'The Austens and the Littleworths', *Jane Austen Society Report* (1987), pp. 15–20, that a couple called John and Elizabeth Littleworth, with children of their own, all mentioned in Austen letters, may have been regular foster parents to the Austen children. John was sixty-one at the time of Jane Austen's birth, his wife presumably close enough in age to be an unlikely wet nurse. Mrs Austen simply refers to 'a good woman at Deane' in her letter of 6 June 1773 about Cassandra, *AP*, p. 29. Edward is said to have referred to a nurse he remembered as 'Movie'.

    The whole subject of wet nursing is discussed in Valerie Fildes's *Wet Nursing* (1988). See especially Chapter 8, 'Wet Nursing in the Eighteenth Century'. At three months a baby might be fed on pap, semi-liquid food made of milk and flour or breadcrumbs. In the 1760s the philanthropist Jonas Hanway claimed that artificial feeding on animal milk was better than reliance on wet nurses, for foundlings at any rate. 'Bubby-pots' (feeding bottles) were in use in London at the Foundling Hospital, according to Valerie Fildes's *Breasts, Bottles and Babies* (1986), but it seems unlikely they would have been used in Hampshire.

11. This is a statistic for 1764, the year of the marriage of Jane Austen's parents, given in Lawrence Stone's *The Family, Sex and Marriage*, p. 68.

12. Mrs Grant in her *Letters from the Mountains* (3 vols., 1807; written between 1773 and 1803), Vol. I, letter 3, p. 35.

13. James-Edward Austen-Leigh, *A Memoir of Jane Austen* (1870), p. 45. Henry Brooke's *The Fool of Quality*, published in five volumes between 1766 and 1770, was a very popular and influential book.

14. See Mrs Cassandra Austen to Susannah Walter, 8 Nov. 1772, *AP*, p. 28,

in which Mrs Austen writes of having 'all four at home', which must at that date have included George.

15. George Austen to Susannah Walter, 8 July 1770, *AP*, p. 23.

16. In 1827 Edward assigned the whole of his inheritance from his mother (£437.2s.9½d.) to the use of his brother George, *AP*, p. 334. George lived to be seventy-two, dying of dropsy. See W. Jarvis, 'Some Information about Jane Austen's Connections', *Jane Austen Society Report* (1976), p. 15.

17. John Woodman to Warren Hastings, 20 June 1776, British Library Add. MSS 29,137, f. 243.

18. Philadelphia Hancock's account for 1777 at Hoare's Bank, ledger 95, p. 93. The exact sums are £3,438.13s.6d. (on 9 May 1777) and £4,800. There are also a few dividends. Phila bought Consols to the value of £2,669.5s., and paid her uncle Francis Austen £384.12s.7d. She also settled an account with Madame Nettine & Co. in Dec., probably a dressmaker; she figures again.

19. James Woodforde of Long Weston, Norfolk, notes this special service and Fast, which he announced the previous Sunday, and for which he had 'as full a congregation as I have in an afternoon on a Sunday, very few that did not come'. *Diary of a Country Parson* (5 vols., 1924–31), Vol. I, p. 194.

20. The remark comes from p. 61 of *Chawton Manor and Its Owners*, published in 1911, and is attributed to a cousin of Mrs Austen, written down and kept in the Leigh family.

2 MERITOCRATS

1. The Leighs were descended from Sir Thomas Leigh, Lord Mayor of London at the time of the crowning of Queen Elizabeth. The younger branch was ennobled and owned Stoneleigh Abbey in Warwickshire. In the elder branch Mrs Austen's grandfather married Mary Brydges, a sister of the first Duke of Chandos, who was the patron of Handel and the butt of Pope.

2. The document was in the possession of Mrs John Francis Austen of Capel Manor, near Horsmonden, when R. A. Austen-Leigh transcribed it in 1909. He printed it in 1942, in Chapter 1 of *AP*, a book invaluable to all who write about Jane Austen.

3. Information from *AP*, Chapter 1, and from Maggie Lane, *Jane Austen through Five Generations* (1984).

4. William Walter was on good terms with his half-brother and sister, George and Philadelphia Austen. Mrs Austen corresponded with Mrs Walter, and Philadelphia's daughter corresponded with the Walters' daughter, another Philadelphia. The Walter family preserved many of these letters, published in *AP*.

5. I am indebted to Robin Vick for the information about Philadelphia's apprenticeship, which he discovered in the apprenticeship records at the Public Record Office, and also for pointing out the coincidence of Cleland's *Fanny Hill* having a character called Mrs Cole with a millinery shop in Covent Garden that is a cover for a bawdy house. The records show Philadelphia's name spelt 'Philadelphia Austin', a common variant spelling, and a blank for the name of a parent, which fits with her having none living. Other girl apprentices appear in the records, Sarah Harris in 1742 and Rose Keene in 1746.

6. Compare, for instance, Katherine Mansfield's grandmother, a Lancashire orphan sent off by her aunt alone to New Zealand in the mid-nineteenth century.

7. It has been widely believed that Hancock was born in 1711, but this derives from false information on, or a mistranscription of, his tombstone in India, which apparently gave his age at death in 1775 as sixty-four. Robin Vick has found that he was in fact born on Christmas Day, 1723, and baptized at Sittingbourne, Kent, on 10 Jan. 1724, the son of Revd Thomas Saul Hancock and his wife Elizabeth. Thomas Saul Hancock was rector of the nearby parishes of Wormshill and Hollingbourne. The identification is confirmed by the baptisms of four other children at Hollingbourne, including Olivia (1731) and Colbron (1733), both mentioned in Hancock's letters (see *AP*).

For the information about Leonora Austen, I am indebted to researches made by Deirdre Le Faye.

8. Keith Feiling, *Warren Hastings* (1954), pp. 40–41.

9. The suggestion was made by Sidney Grier in an article in *Temple Bar* for May 1905, 'A God-Daughter of Warren Hastings'. It has not been substantiated, although both R. A. Austen-Leigh and Deirdre Le Faye tend to accept it.

10. Keith Feiling, *Warren Hastings*, p. 40.

11. Clive's letter to his wife is cited in Mark Bence-Jones, *Clive of India* (1974), p. 220.

12. Keith Feiling, *Warren Hastings*, p. 51.

13. Cassandra Leigh's leaseholds were in Oxford, George Austen's in Tonbridge, Kent. Some of hers were sold two years after the marriage, the money invested in annuities. Both came into their full inheritances in 1768, when her mother and his stepmother died, after which he too sold off his properties and the whole amount of their inheritances was invested in South Sea annuities. Despite George Austen's financial difficulties, her South Sea investments were never touched, and when she died they were divided among her surviving children.

14. Keith Feiling, *Warren Hastings*, p. 54.

15. Eliza de Feuillide to Philadelphia Walter, 29 Oct. 1799, unpublished portion of letter in Hampshire Record Office (hereafter cited as HRO; 23M93/M1).

16. Deirdre Le Faye conjectures in *Jane Austen: A Family Record* (1989), p. 15, that Warren Hastings first put his son in the care of members of the Leigh family who were neighbours of his impoverished grandfather at Adlestrop in Gloucestershire; and when, by pure coincidence, a Leigh cousin, Cassandra, married George Austen, she was thought suitable to take over the boy's care and education. It is convincingly argued, but not proved.

17. Warren Hastings to Philadelphia Hancock, 31 Jan. 1772, *AP*, pp. 59–60.

18. Tysoe Saul Hancock to Philadelphia Hancock, 23 Sept. 1772, *AP*, pp. 64–5.

19. Tysoe Saul Hancock to Philadelphia Hancock, 23 Sept. 1772, *AP*, pp. 65–6.

20. Tysoe Saul Hancock to Philadelphia Hancock, 17 Jan. 1770, *AP*, pp. 43–4.

21. Whether Jane Austen knew anything of the existence of her Aunt Leonora is not known. In fact she lost two aunts in a short space of time. Jane was at home, having been rescued from the boarding school where she caught a near-fatal fever the previous summer; and the same fever killed her maternal aunt, Jane Cooper, in October 1783, four months before Leonora died.

3 BOYS

1. We know this because Mr Austen's niece Eliza wrote 'my uncle informs us that Midsummer & Christmas are the only seasons when his mansion

is sufficiently at liberty to admit of his receiving his friends'. Eliza de Feuillide to Philadelphia Walter, 23 May 1786, *AP*, p. 118.

2. The packing was James Woodforde's as he set off for New College in Oct. 1762. You can't help hoping his college supplied him with a second towel.

3. Mrs Sherwood, born Mary Butt in the same year as JA, whose father was also a country clergyman who took pupils, gives this game as a popular entertainment of her youth; see her autobiography, edited by S. Kelly (1854).

4. Mrs Austen writes about dancing in the poem she sent to an absent pupil, Gilbert East, in 1779. She upbraids him for staying away in order to dance all the time, but her praise of his dancing – 'That you dance very well / All beholders can tell / For lightly and nimbly you tread' – suggests she saw him dance at Steventon. My version of the poem is taken from a red calf notebook into which Mrs Austen's eldest grandchild, Anna Lefroy, copied various texts. She notes that it was sent to her by the Revd J. B. Harrison, Rector of Evenley Brackley, Northants, which suggests it was valued and circulated, as well it might be. It is now in the possession of Alwyn Austen.

5. James Austen recalled chasing marten cats out of trees to his son James-Edward, who records this in *Recollections of the Early Days of the Vine Hunt* (1865), p. 15: 'My father, when a boy, had sometimes climbed the tree for the purpose of shaking or beating it [i.e., a marten cat] down.'

6. Henry and Ned were the third and fourth Austen sons, and the other three were pupils.

7. See David Gilson, 'The Austens and Oxford: "Founder's Kin"', *Jane Austen Society Report* (1977), pp. 43–5.

8. James-Edward Austen-Leigh, *A Memoir of Jane Austen*, pp. 6–7.

9. John Rowe Townsend has brought to my attention an earlier reference from the *Little Pretty Pocket-Book* of 1744. Under a picture of three boys playing with a ball on a village green, each standing at a large 'stump', is a verse with the heading 'BASE-BALL': 'The *Ball* once struck off, / Away flies the *Boy* / To the next destin'd Post, / And then Home with Joy.'

10. The furniture from Mr Austen's study was sold when he left Steventon in 1801, and the sale list includes 'table and chest of drawers in study, globe, microscope, 8ft by 8ft bookcase, also smaller one; mahogany

library table with drawers'. See Robin Vick, 'The Sale at Steventon Parsonage', *Jane Austen Society Report* (1993), p. 14.

11. The standard work for microscope owners was Henry Baker's *Employment of the Microscope*, first published in 1753 and reissued many times. It gives instructions on preparing slides, and stresses the religious lesson to be learnt from observing 'the amazing Power and Goodness of the Creator', who took as much trouble with the Louse, the Gnat and the Flea as with the Whale, the Elephant and the Lion – providing a lesson for a future novelist too.

12. George Holbert Tucker, *A Goodly Heritage: A History of Jane Austen's Family* (1983), p. 30, citing Emma Austen-Leigh's *Jane Austen and Steventon* (1937), in which the annotated manuscript of the sermon is said to be in the possession of descendants.

13. George Austen to Francis Austen, Dec. 1788, unpublished portion of letter in possession of Alwyn Austen. 'Personal cleanliness, in the hot Country you are going to, will be so necessary to your Comfort & Health that I need not recommend it – I shall only therefore beg of you to be particularly careful of your Teeth.'

14. In her *History of England*, in the section on Edward IV, she so dismisses 'Jane Shore, who has had a play written about her, but it is a tragedy'.

15. The author of *Matilda* was Thomas Francklin, and it was produced at Drury Lane in 1775.

16. First line of the epilogue quoted in G. Sawtell's 'Four Manly Boys', *Jane Austen Society Report* (1982), p. 224.

4 SCHOOL

1. Anna Lefroy to James-Edward Austen-Leigh, Dec. 1864, copy of letter printed by Deirdre Le Faye in 'Anna Lefroy's Original Memories of Jane Austen', *Review of English Studies*, NS xxxix, 155, Aug. 1988, p. 418.

2. Bed sharing was common practice, even at the most expensive and famous boys' public schools. Sir Philip Francis, contemplating his son going to Harrow, specified that he must have a bed to himself. Sir Philip Francis, *The Francis Letters*, (2 vols., 1901), Vol. I, p. 321. Philip Francis to D. Godfrey, 16 Sept. 1776, 'I insist upon his lying alone. His learning may take its fate . . . but his health and morals require all our care.'

3. Arthur Young, *Autobiography* (1898), p. 264.

NOTES

4. See Eric Walkely Gillett (ed.), *Elizabeth Ham by Herself 1783–1820* (1945).
5. See Marilyn Butler, *Maria Edgeworth* (1972), pp. 51–5.
6. JA to CEA, 8 Apr. 1805; *The Watsons* in R. W. Chapman's *Minor Works* of 1954, p. 318; JA to CEA, 1 Sept. 1796.
7. *Emma*, I, 3.
8. See illustration on p. 39, courtesy of the great-grandsons of Admiral Sir Francis Austen. Photographs of the pages appear in *Jane Austen Society Report* (1975), p. 257 in bound collection.
9. Information derived from Mrs Sherwood's *Autobiography*.

5 THE FRENCH CONNECTION

1. George Holbert Tucker, *A Goodly Heritage*, p. 166, citing Christopher Lloyd, 'The Royal Naval Colleges at Portsmouth and Greenwich', *The Mariner's Mirror* (1966).
2. Mrs Cassandra Austen to Philadelphia Walter, 31 Dec. 1786, cited in Deirdre Le Faye, 'Three Austen Family Letters', *Notes and Queries*, Sept. 1985, pp. 333–4.
3. All these London experiences are mentioned by Eliza de Feuillide to Philadelphia Walter in a letter, 9 Apr. 1787, *AP*, pp. 122–3.
4. The phrase 'his two Mammas' comes in a letter, ibid., p. 123.
5. All further quotes in the paragraph from Mrs Austen's letter to Philadelphia Walter, 31 Dec. 1786, cited in Deirdre Le Faye, 'Three Austen Family Letters', *Notes and Queries*, Sept. 1985, pp. 333–4.
6. JA is known to have owned several of the twelve volumes of Berquin in their original French, the first inscribed 'J. Austen december 18th 1786', Vols. II–IX similarly inscribed. In Vol. V another hand has written what seems to read 'Pour dear Jane Austen'. Information from David Gilson, *A Bibliography of Jane Austen* (1982).
7. *The Critic*, III, i, where the stage direction reads 'They faint alternately in each other's arms.'
8. Eliza de Feuillide to Philadelphia Walter, 26 Oct. 1792, *AP*, p. 148.
9. Many are printed in *AP*; a few more have appeared since its publication in 1942, and some are now held in the HRO on microfilm.
10. Tysoe Saul Hancock to Philadelphia Hancock, 11 Dec. 1772, *AP*, p. 68.
11. Her account with Hoare's Bank shows many transfers of money to Sir John Lambert during 1778, and Hoare's Letter-Book refers to a letter

303

of credit on Sir John Lambert at Paris for £200 (letter dated 2 June 1778).

12. Eliza de Feuillide to Philadelphia Walter, 27 Mar. 1782, *AP*, pp. 99–100.

13. Mrs Hancock's account with Hoare's Bank shows payments totalling £370 to Sir John Lambert between Oct. and Dec. 1778, and more in 1780 (ledger 100, p. 406). Eliza asks Phylly to write to her 'au soin de Chevalier Lambert à Paris' in June 1780, *AP*, p. 92.

14. Sir John's father lived on the Isle de Ré, off La Rochelle, at one time, according to *Debrett's Baronetage of England*.

15. e.g., credit entry in Henry Austen's account with Hoare's Bank for 1824.

16. John Woodman to Warren Hastings, 26 Dec. 1781, *AP*, p. 98; original British Library Add. MSS 29,152, f. 150.

17. A Jacques Capot was registered Protestant in 1713, his name in the list of those who went to Geneva. *Bulletins de la Société de l'Histoire du Protestantisme français*, Vol. lxxvi (1926), p. 240.

A Demoiselle Jeanne Capot married in 1683 P. Meulh, the Meulhs being a Protestant family at Nérac. Chaix-d'Est-Ange, G., *Dictionnaire des Familles Françaises anciennes ou notables à la fin du XIXème siècle*, Vol. X (1903–29), p. 441.

18. Eliza de Feuillide to Philadelphia Walter, 27 Mar. 1782, *AP*, p. 100, and 17 Jan. 1786, *AP*, p. 115: 'should a son be in store for M. de Feuillide, he greatly wishes him to be a native of England'.

19. Eliza de Feuillide to Philadelphia Walter, 27 Mar. 1782, *AP*, pp. 104, 100.

20. Eliza de Feuillide to Philadelphia Walter, 23 May 1786, *AP*, p. 119.

21. Eliza de Feuillide to Philadelphia Walter, letter owned by Jane Austen Memorial Trust, cited by Deirdre Le Faye, 'Three Austen Family Letters', *Notes and Queries*, Sept. 1985.

22. Eliza de Feuillide to Philadelphia Walter, 17 Jan. 1786, *AP*, pp. 114–15. Information on Lord Chesterfield from the *DNB*.

23. Eliza de Feuillide to Philadelphia Walter, 17 Jan. 1786, *AP*, pp. 114, 115.

24. Philadelphia Walter to James Walter, 23 July 1788, *AP*, p. 130.

25. James's mixed feelings about France appear in some of his articles in the magazine he started later, *The Loiterer*. One story is of an aristocratic Frenchwoman who tries to involve a young Englishman in a flirtation, from which he flees.

26. *The Chances* was adapted by Garrick from Beaumont and Fletcher.

27. There is a prologue to *Bon Ton* among James's poems, dated this year, HRO 23 M93/60/3/2.
28. This is from James-Edward Austen-Leigh's *Memoir of Jane Austen*, p. 26. He goes on to suggest that his Aunt Jane was 'an early observer, and it may be reasonably supposed that some of the incidents and feelings which are so vividly painted in the *Mansfield Park* theatricals are due to her recollection of these entertainments'.
29. William Cowper, much admired by JA, had been at Westminster School with Hastings, and wrote the following lines at this time:

> Hastings! I knew thee young, and of a mind
> While young humane, conversable, and kind;
> Nor can I well believe thee, gentle then,
> Now grown a villain, and the worst of men.
> But rather some suspect, who have oppressed
> And worried thee, as not themselves the best.

30. Elizabeth de Feuillide to Philadelphia Walter, 22 Aug. 1788, *AP*, p. 133.
31. Philadelphia Walter to James Walter, 23 July 1788, *AP*, p. 130, and Elizabeth de Feuillide to Philadelphia Walter, 11 Feb. 1789, pp. 137–8.
32. Philadelphia Hancock to John Woodman, 5 Feb. 1789, *AP*, pp. 135–6.

6 BAD BEHAVIOUR

1. Philadelphia Walter to Eliza de Feuillide, 23 July 1788, *AP*, p. 131.
2. ibid.
3. Eliza de Feuillide to Philadelphia Walter, 22 Aug. 1788, *AP*, p. 132.
4. George Austen to Francis Austen, Dec. 1788. Letter in possession of Alwyn Austen.
5. These early stories are commonly described as burlesques on whatever Jane was reading at the time, but it is hard to know what this might have been in relation to *Jack and Alice*: nothing in *Sir Charles Grandison* (in which there is a drunken woman, but her intoxication takes place offstage). *Tom Thumb* comes closer, and Charlotte Smith's *Emmeline* may have inspired the two interpolated 'life stories', though nothing else. The tone is entirely Austen's, and the grinning at death points forward to the joke in the letters about the dead baby, and the mockery of a fat mother grieving for her dead son in *Persuasion* – two passages many people find upsetting.

6. James, Edward and Henry each possessed a game duty certificate in 1785 (when Henry was fourteen), acquired from the Clerk of the Peace for three guineas. Mr Austen did not have one; he presumably had never learnt to shoot. See Robin Vick, 'The Sale at Steventon Parsonage', *Jane Austen Society Report* (1993).

7. *The Sultan* by Isaac Bickerstaffe was an enormously popular vehicle for stars like Mrs Jordan, and *High Life Below Stairs* by James Townley equally so: Kitty Clive and Mrs Abington both excelled in playing Kitty, the ladies' maid who aspires to high culture: ' "Shikspur. Did you never read Shikspur?" (Kitty) "Shikspur! Shikspur! Who wrote it? No, I never read Shikspur." "Then you have an immense pleasure to come." (Kitty) "Well then, I'll read it over one afternoon or another." ' Less attractive is the crude stereotyping of two black servants. It is no good suggesting the Austens were ahead of their time in this respect; Henry was also perfectly happy to play a 'Jew' in later charades at Godmersham.

8. Eliza de Feuillide to Philadelphia Walter, 11 Feb. 1789, *AP*, p. 138.

9. Mrs Austen always had a high opinion of him as a writer, praising his 'Literary Taste and the Power of Elegant Composition' after his death. Mrs Cassandra Austen to James Leigh-Perrot, 4 Jan. 1820, *AP*, p. 265.

10. Zachary Cope first suggested that JA was Sophia Sentiment, in the *Book Collector* in 1966; his arguments were summarized in the *Jane Austen Society Report* for the same year. He claimed that 'Sophia's' letter could not have been written by James or Henry, on the grounds of style; and that the suggestions for improving *The Loiterer* 'read like a burlesque of the morbid sentiment prevalent in novels of that period, a type of writing at that very time being satirized in JA's *Love and Freindship*'. He did, however, conclude that it may have been written in collusion with Henry, which seems to me much more likely than that it was her unaided work. The fact that she used the name Sophia for the heroine of *Love and Freindship* more than a year later could indicate that there was a running family joke; on the other hand, Sophia was a very common name. One of the royal princesses, born in 1777, was a Sophia; and the Austens knew their Fielding. Elizabeth Jenkins points out that the phrase 'bitter philippic' occurs in a *Loiterer* essay (no. 58) and in *Sense and Sensibility*, convincing evidence that Jane read her brother's periodical. It would have been strange if she did not, but she did not always use phrases in the same sense as James, for *cara sposa* appears twice quite unsatirically in *The Loiterer*, whereas she gave it to Mrs Elton

as a piece of ridiculous affectation. Admittedly, fifteen years had passed. JA's satirical use of *caro sposo* in *Emma* has made everyone alert to earlier uses of the phrase; Garrick also used *caro sposo* in his epilogue to Mrs Cowley's *The Belle's Stratagem* in 1780.

11. These early stories are sometimes taken as little more than parodies of current fiction, and were so described first by James-Edward Austen-Leigh, in his *Memoir* of 1870, which speaks of nonsense stories and satires on 'sundry silly romances'. There were many sentimental, violent and absurd novels circulating in the 1770s and 1780s, and JA must have read some, but it seems unlikely there would have been many available at Steventon.

12. Henry's biographical note, written after her death in Dec. 1817, appeared in the first edition (1818) of *Northanger Abbey* and *Persuasion*.

13. Her letter of 10 Jan. 1796 makes this clear. See Chapter 11.

14. JA wrote a piece of dialogue about the merits of *Emmeline* and *Ethelinde* in *Catharine, or the Bower*, an unfinished story written in 1792 when she was sixteen.

15. These are Catharine's words; she also speaks of Smith's novels as 'Books universally read and Admired, [and that have given rise perhaps to more frequent Arguments than any other of the same sort].' The square brackets mark Austen's own deletion, but the phrase suggests they were much discussed in the family and among friends. Charlotte Smith, 1749–1806, was the daughter of a Sussex gentleman. She had an early love of reading and started writing at her boarding school, to which she was sent at seven (her mother died when she was three). When her father remarried she was persuaded to marry too, at the age of fifteen, a young man who proved entirely uncongenial. She had seven children before she was twenty-five; at this point she and her husband moved to Hampshire, where they lived at Ly's Farm, Brookwood Park, near Selborne, from 1774 until 1783 or 1784, and were thus neighbours of the Austens. Mr Smith became Sheriff of Hampshire in 1781, but his reckless spending reduced them to poverty and he was imprisoned for debt in the King's Bench in 1783. Mrs Smith saved the situation financially by publishing her poems, and then turned to translating and writing novels; and she parted from her husband. She sympathized with the French Revolution at first and scandalized some readers by allowing that women who committed adultery might not always be irretrievably wicked. She was a friend of Cowper and also of Romney. She went on

writing until the end of her life, producing educational books for children as well as novels. Walter Scott admired her work, especially *The Old Manor House*, published in 1793.

16. James-Edward Austen-Leigh, *A Memoir of Jane Austen*, p. 89.
17. Charlotte Grandison seems to me to stand in the line that runs from Shakespeare's comic heroines to Jane Austen's.

7 WEDDINGS AND FUNERALS

1. Eliza refers to this in a letter of 1792, Eliza de Feuillide to Philadelphia Walter, 26 Oct. 1792, *AP*, p. 148.
2. Eliza de Feuillide to Philadelphia Walter, 7 Jan. 1791, *AP*, pp. 139–40.
3. Goodnestone is pronounced 'Gunstone'.
4. Edward Shorter, *A History of Women's Bodies* (1983), pp. 18–19, gives the end of the eighteenth century as the time of the latest onset of the menarche. In France it was fifteen years and nine months between 1750 and 1799, getting younger steadily thereafter.
5. See JA to CEA, 8 Jan. 1799.
6. Deirdre Le Faye notes that James Austen's name appears in the diary of Kempshott Hunt, made by William Poyntz between 1791 and 1793, and held at the Royal Library, Windsor; and that the Prince of Wales sometimes hunted with the Kempshott during this period.
7. Breast cancer was sometimes eradicated by surgery. Fanny Burney, for example, had an entirely successful operation to remove one breast in France in 1811; but this was a very rare case, requiring an exceptional surgeon and an equally exceptional patient. There was of course no anaesthetic available. She displayed extraordinary courage, and wrote her own account of the operation. She lived for many years afterwards in good health, and died in 1840, aged eighty-eight.
8. Eliza de Feuillide to Philadelphia Walter, 23 June 1791, *AP*, p. 141.
9. Eliza de Feuillide to Philadelphia Walter, 1 Aug. 1791, HRO 23M93/M1.
10. Eliza de Feuillide to Philadelphia Walter, 23 June 1791, HRO 23M93/M1.
11. Philadelphia Walter to James Walter, 9 Oct. 1791, *AP*, p. 143.
12. The sum is given in her will in the Public Record Office.
13. The grave slab is still in place in the churchyard of St John-

at-Hampstead, but the inscription has gone and is replaced by a brief name and date. See Deirdre Le Faye, 'Hancock Family Grave', *Jane Austen Society Report* (1981), p. 182.

14. *Victoria County History of Hampshire* (1900).

15. Eliza de Feuillide to Philadelphia Walter, 26 Oct. 1792, *AP*, pp. 147–50.

16. JA to CEA, 5 Jan. 1801.

17. *Catharine, or the Bower* is printed in R. W. Chapman's *Minor Works* and in the Oxford paperback *Catharine and Other Writings*, eds. Margaret Anne Doody and Douglas Murray.

18. Deirdre Le Faye, *A Family Record*, p. 77, citing the Hubback MS. Anna Austen was actually called Jane Anna Elizabeth, but always known as Anna.

19. The only existing manuscript of *Lady Susan* is a copy made on paper watermarked 1805, and while some commentators have suggested it was written then, most now agree that its composition dates from at least ten years earlier. In particular Brian Southam argues persuasively in *Jane Austen's Literary Manuscripts: A Study of the Novelist's Development* (1964) that she would hardly have reverted to writing an epistolary novel after rejecting the form earlier, as she did when she rewrote *Elinor and Marianne* in 1797. Certain dating is not possible; recent guesses place its writing between 1793 and 1795, before Austen was twenty.

20. Congreve's *Double-Dealer*, Farquhar's *The Beaux' Stratagem*, Vanbrugh's *The Relapse* (reworked by Sheridan as *A Trip to Scarborough*), with the scheming Berinthia and her 'Ah, Amanda, it's a delicious thing to be a young widow', all come to mind. These could well have been in Mr Austen's library, and we know that Garrick's *Bon Ton*, in which the two heroines scheme and betray up to the last scene, was played at Steventon.

21. 'A wholly sinister figure' is the phrase used in *Jane Austen, Her Life and Letters* (1913) by William and R. A. Austen-Leigh. Brian Southam's excellent account of the book in *Jane Austen's Literary Manuscripts* (1964) is odd only in insisting that she is unfeminine because she is aggressive and predatory.

8 NEIGHBOURS

1. Carleton was Governor of Quebec in the 1760s, defended it successfully against the Americans from Dec. 1775 to May 1776, and lived there as

governor again in the 1780s and 1790s. Nothing is left of Kempshott House today but the stables.

2. Hackwood is still standing, a late seventeenth-century house remodelled and enlarged for the Boltons in the early 1800s by Lewis Wyatt.

3. *Northanger Abbey*, II, 9.

4. Mrs Cassandra Austen to Susannah Walter, 6 June 1773, *AP*, p. 29.

5. Mrs Cassandra Austen to Susannah Walter, 12 Dec. 1773, *AP*, p. 30.

6. The house JA visited was built by James Wyatt in the 1770s for the second Earl. It was burned down in 1870.

7. Byron to Hargreaves Hanson, 19 Aug. 1805 and 28 Aug. 1805, Leslie A. Marchand (ed.), *Byron's Letters and Journals* (12 vols., 1973–82), Vol. I, pp. 76, 77. Byron and young Hanson joked in their letters about a 'Mr Terry' who is surely the sporting squire of Dummer, or one of his sons.

8. Leslie A. Marchand (ed.), *Byron's Letters and Journals*, Vol. III, p. 248. Other information from Doris Langley Moore, *Lord Byron: Accounts Rendered* (1974), Appendix 3.

9. *Northanger Abbey* was first written between 1798 and 1799, according to CEA. JA herself wrote in the advertisement she prepared in 1816 that it was 'finished in 1803'. At this stage it was called *Susan*. In 1803, with Henry Austen's assistance, she sold the MS for £10 to publishers called Crosby & Co., who advertised but failed to publish it. Ten years later she paid £10 to have it back, but then did nothing with it until 1816, when she changed its name to *Catherine* and wrote the advertisement. She then did nothing further, and it was Henry who changed the title to the one we know, and published it in 1818, after her death, so that she did not have the chance to revise or read proofs.

10. The manor house can still be seen at Dummer, next to the equally delightful church.

11. Laverstoke House, built by Joseph Bonomi, is still standing, but no longer owned by the Portals, and closed to the public.

12. JA to CEA, 25 Jan. 1801.

13. Mackreth is not mentioned in Austen letters, but appears on p. 45 of James-Edward Austen-Leigh's *Recollections of the Early Days of the Vine Hunt*, where he is described as an Indian nabob who started life as a servant. Only the second part seems to be correct, at any rate according to the *DNB*.

14. The painting, reproduced in the first inset, is by Daniel Gardner (1750?–1805), and is entitled *Sir William Heathcote, the Revd William Heathcote*

and Major Gilbert out Hunting. It belongs to the National Trust and can be seen at Montacute, where it hangs in the main drawing room.

15. The Vyne is now owned by the National Trust, and both house and grounds well repay a visit.

16. Tom Chute's adopted niece, Caroline Wiggett, described him as full of wit and fun in a paper of reminiscences written in 1869, HRO 31M57/1070. There are many references to Tom visiting James Austen in later years in Mrs Chute's diaries, and also in those of Mary Austen.

17. Eliza Chute's diaries, or ladies' pocket-books, are held in HRO. I have examined the volumes for 1790, 1792, 1793, 1794, 1797, 1798, 1799, 1800, 1802, 1804, 1807, 1813, 1814, 1815, 1816 and 1817. The others for the period between 1790 and 1817 are missing. The diaries are beautiful objects, calf bound – mostly red, a few tan, one pale green – with gilt edges and closing flaps, a pocket for extra notes inside, and some with marbled endpapers. They have printed matter at the front, information about hackney-cab prices, names of banks and other miscellaneous practical stuff, and engravings of fashions, theatrical scenes and places. They also print contemporary verse, much of it by women, at the back. Some have obituary and birth notices; for instance, there is a notice of the death of Mary Wollstonecraft in the 1798 diary, and in another the birth of a daughter to 'Mrs Jordan of Drury Lane Theatre'. The fashion for these diaries established itself strongly during this period, and further mention will be made of those belonging to Mrs James Austen and Fanny Austen, the eldest daughter of Jane's brother Edward.

18. A frank was the signature of an MP on a letter, which allowed it to be sent through the mail without payment. The system was so widely abused by MPS giving their franks to friends and neighbours that even the most respectable people asked for them unhesitatingly. Letters without a frank were paid for by the recipient.

19. Mrs Sarah Smith to Eliza Chute, 'Xmas 1793', HRO 23M93/70/3/1.

20. She wrote an account of Box Hill to a friend (HRO 23M93/74/1/3) and mentioned it in her diary a few days before James Austen dined with her on 3 Oct. On 28 Oct. Jane and Cassandra were staying with James.

21. JA to CEA, 15 Jan. 1796, and JA to CEA, 25 Oct. 1800.

22. *Morning* by James Austen, MS poem, no date, HRO 23M93/60/3/1.

23. Mrs Sarah Smith to Eliza Chute, MS letter 1797, HRO 23M93/70/3/16.

24. See Deirdre Le Faye, 'The Austens and the Littleworths', *Jane Austen Society Report* (1987), p. 16, quoting from the Bellas MS.
25. JA to CEA, 27 Oct. 1798, and JA to CEA, 23 June 1814.
26. See Deirdre Le Faye, 'James Austen's Poetical Biography of John Bond', *Jane Austen Society Report* (1992), pp. 9–13. John Bond and his wife buried their first child Hannah four months after their wedding.
27. Mrs Cassandra Austen to Mrs Mary Austen, 19 Nov. 1820, HRO 23M93/62/2/5.
28. James Austen tells the story in a blank verse poem now in the Austen-Leigh Archive in the HRO, 'The Oeconomy of Rural Life'; the relevant part is printed by Deirdre Le Faye in 'James Austen's Poetical Biography of John Bond', *Jane Austen Society Report* (1992), pp. 10–12.

9 DANCING

1. Henry Austen, in his biographical note to *Northanger Abbey* and *Persuasion*.
2. Mrs Bramston was the sister of William and Tom Chute; it was she who later saw a resemblance between herself and Lady Bertram in *Mansfield Park*. The maiden sister is Augusta Bramston. Squire Hicks is Michael Hicks, who married a Bramston cousin in 1779; his son William Hicks-Beach inherited Oakley Hall in 1832.
3. Eliza Chute's diary, Sat., 9 Aug. 1794, HRO 23M93/70/1/4.
4. Henry's movements established by Clive Caplan in 'The Military Career of Captain Henry Thomas Austen of the Oxfordshire Regiment of Militia, 1793–1801', unpublished at time of writing but intended for *Persuasions* (magazine of the Jane Austen Society of North America), 1996 issue.
5. 'Les meubles de feu M. Feuillide furent vendus le 12 thermidor l'an II pour 2858 francs', Abbé Michel Devert, 'Le Marais de Gabarret et de Barbotan', *Bulletin de la Société de Borda* (1970), p. 13. See also 'Cazaubon pendant la période révolutionnaire', *Revue de Gascogne* (1885), p. 328: 'le 8 mai 1794 Lafontan, commissaire del. pour la vente des meubles de Capot-Feuillide, propriétaire du Marais, en Barbotan: J'ai reçu hier soir le certificat qui atteste la résidence du citoyen à Paris (on voulait le faire passer pour un émigré et vendre ses biens). Le domestique de son frère est parti cette nuit pour le faire enregistrer au district.'
6. George Austen to Warren Hastings, 8 Nov. 1794, British Library Add. MSS 29,173, f. 281.

7. See Charles's account of his career in British Library Add. MSS 38,039, f. 181.

8. All this information about Henry's regiment from Clive Caplan's unpublished article 'The Military Career of Captain Henry Thomas Austen of the Oxfordshire Regiment of Militia, 1793–1801'.

9. British Library Add. MSS 29,174, f. 25 (*AP*, p. 153).

10. Anna Lefroy's description of her aunt's rooms comes from family papers, and is quoted in Constance Hill's *Jane Austen, Her Homes and Her Friends* (1902). Deirdre Le Faye's account of the colour of the curtains and wallpaper, taken from George Austen's account with his Basingstoke suppliers, is from p. 69 of her *A Family Record*.

11. Deirdre Le Faye speculates that a 'Small Mahogany writing Desk with 1 long Drawer and Glass Ink Stand' bought for twelve shillings at Basingstoke by Mr Austen on 5 Dec. 1794 was a nineteenth birthday present for Jane.

12. Parson Woodforde witnessed and recorded this incident on 29 Oct. 1795 when he was in London.

10 THE DOLL AND THE POKER

1. These four descriptions – all posthumous, but all from people who saw her many times and three from close relatives – come from Sir Egerton Brydges, brother of Mrs Lefroy, who was the Austens' neighbour from 1786 to 1788, and saw Jane again in 1803, in his *Autobiography* (2 vols., 1834), Vol. II, pp. 39–42; from her niece Caroline Austen, James's younger daughter, born in 1805, writing in 1867 (*My Aunt Jane Austen, a Memoir*, 1952); from her niece Anna, James's elder daughter, born in 1793, who grew up very close to Jane, cited by Deirdre Le Faye, 'Anna Lefroy's Original Memories of Jane Austen', *Review of English Studies*, NS xxxix, 155, Aug. 1988, pp. 417–21; and from her niece Louisa, Edward's daughter, born in 1804, who became Lady George Hill, her remarks reported in a letter of 1856 from Pamela Fitzgerald to Lord Carlyle, and cited by Elizabeth Jenkins, 'Some Notes on Background', *Jane Austen Society Report* (1980), p. 166.

2. A view that persists, though surely without any basis.

3. The four quotations here are from the following sources: Fulwar-Craven Fowle's remarks were recorded by a Mrs Mozley in 1838, and reproduced

by Kathleen Tillotson, *TLS*, 17 Sept. 1954, p. 591. Miss Middleton's description is cited by Deirdre Le Faye, 'Recollections of Chawton', *TLS*, May 1985, p. 495. Sir Egerton Brydges is again from his *Autobiography*, Vol. II, p. 39, and Anna Lefroy as above. Note also Caroline's letter of 4 May 1819 to her brother, about her cousin Marianne Knight: 'I cannot admire Marianne so much as you do. She is certainly I think pretty, but I never saw her look anything like beautiful. Her greatest personal recommendation to me, is being very like poor Aunt Jane' (cited by Deirdre Le Faye, *A Family Record*, p. 236).

4. Anna Lefroy to James-Edward Austen-Leigh, 20 July 1869, cited by Deirdre Le Faye, *A Family Record*, p. 253.

5. Eliza de Feuillide to Philadelphia Walter, 14 Nov. 1791, *AP*, p. 144; Henry's biographical note to the first edition of *Northanger Abbey* and *Persuasion*.

6. James-Edward Austen-Leigh, *A Memoir of Jane Austen*, p. 87.

7. JA to CEA, 20 Nov. 1800. Elizabeth Bennet's untidy hair is criticized by Bingley's sisters after her walk from Longbourn to Netherfield, an indication of their false values.

8. JA to CEA, 8 Jan. 1799.

9. Egerton Brydges, Anna Lefroy, Miss Middleton (neighbour at Chawton), Mary Russell Mitford.

10. James-Edward Austen-Leigh, *A Memoir of Jane Austen*, p. 87.

11. Henry's description from his biographical note, as above. Her step is described by Anna Lefroy, as above.

12. Elizabeth Jenkins reported on the bronze colour of the piece of JA's hair in the possession of the Jane Austen Society. Dark hair fades with time.

13. Mary Russell Mitford (1787–1855), best known as the author of *Our Village*, wrote in Dec. 1814 a letter to Sir William Elford in which she describes Jane Austen first as having been 'the prettiest, silliest, most affected husband-hunting butterfly' who turned later into a 'perpendicular, precise, taciturn piece of "single blessedness"' . . . no more regarded in society than a poker or a fire screen or any other thin, upright piece of wood or iron that fills its corner in peace and quiet' until she became known as the author of *Pride and Prejudice*, when she became 'a poker of whom every one is afraid'. The tone is patently malicious, but this does not mean she is wholly wrong in what she says.

II A LETTER

1. CEA's note, reproduced in R. W. Chapman's edition of the *Minor Works* in 1954 (facing p. 242), reads 'Sense & Sensibility begun Nov. 1797 / I am sure that something of the same story & characters had been written earlier & called Elinor & Marianne'. Family tradition, relayed in William and R. A. Austen-Leigh's *Jane Austen, Her Life and Letters, a Family Record*, suggests that she was writing this early version in 1795 and reading it aloud *en famille*.

2. Such dramas are vividly described in a letter written in Oct. 1795 to one of the Austens' neighbours, Mrs William Chute, from her mother Mrs Sarah Smith, describing a dance in Wiltshire at which

> two blazing Comets made their appearance a Buzz soon went round who are they? – one a foreign Baron, the other a very handsome young Yorkshire Baronet Sir John Coghile . . . no lady was left unengaged with difficulty one Lady was resigned by her Partner to the Baron, & Mrs Dickenson was almost prevailed to dance but when Sir John found she was a Married lady; he preferred a flirtation with Emma, & poor Salmon was obliged to be a Silent witness to the Tryumph of the Baronet who could charm the ear with the account of the gayeties of London, a Theme unknown to the other, our handsome hero flourished . . . , Lounged on the Benches & appeared what he really was, a different Being to those around so that all the Beaus sank in their own estimation, & the Devizes Belles may many a day recount the dangers of that night . . .

HRO 23M93/70/3/15.

3. *Tom Jones*, published in 1749, shocked Dr Johnson among others because it shows both men and women as sexual beings, and regards their sins in these matters as of relatively little importance when weighed against cruelty, snobbery, avarice, meanness and hypocrisy. This is also the view of Squire Western, the hard hunting, drinking and swearing father of the heroine, who was by tradition drawn from a grandfather of the Austens' neighbour, John Harwood of Oakley Hall, where Fielding was a visitor. See JA's nephew James-Edward Austen-Leigh's *Recollections of the Early Days of the Vine Hunt*, p. 65.

4. Henry's plan, like most of his activities, was a complicated one, and involved seeking help from various people. The Chawton living had been in the gift of Thomas Knight, his brother Edward's adoptive father, who died in 1794. Knight had presented the Steventon living to the Revd

George Austen and then to his son James, and the Chawton living to another distant relative, J. R. Papillon, but with the proviso that, if any of them should refuse, they should be offered to Henry Austen next. Henry knew that Papillon already had one parish in Kent, and hoped to persuade him that he would be better off staying there. He started negotiations through Mrs Lefroy, who was acquainted with all those involved.

5. 24 Feb. 1796 Henry repays £35.16s. to his father, but on 25 Feb. he borrows £156 from Eliza. Hoare's Bank archive, ledger 51.

6. JA to CEA, 23 June 1814, the subject then being Henry's attendance at White's Club.

7. Cited in J. H. and Edith C. Hubback, *Jane Austen's Sailor Brothers* (1906), p. 29. Note also 8 Dec. 1795, 'Punished P. C. Smith forty-nine lashes for theft.'

12 DEFENCE SYSTEMS

1. Quoted by R. W. Chapman, *Facts and Problems* (1948), as part of a letter written by Thomas Edward Preston Lefroy to James-Edward Austen-Leigh, 16 Aug. 1870. The nephew wrote, 'As this occurred in a friendly and private conversation, I feel some doubt whether I ought to make it public.'

2. Lefroy MS, in possession of Admiral Sir Francis Austen's great-grandsons.

3. The MS is now at St John's College, Oxford, MS 279.

4. Eliza de Feuillide to Philadelphia Walter, 3 May 1797, *AP*, p. 159.

5. HRO 23M93/60/3/1.

6. Eliza de Feuillide to Philadelphia Walter, 3 May 1797, *AP*, p. 159.

7. Eliza de Feuillide to Philadelphia Walter, 13 Dec. 1796, *AP*, p. 156.

8. Mrs Cassandra Austen to Mary Lloyd, 30 Nov. 1796, *AP*, p. 228.

9. Eliza de Feuillide to Philadelphia Walter, 30 Dec. 1796, *AP*, p. 157.

10. Information from Clive Caplan, 'The Military Career of Captain Henry Thomas Austen of the Oxfordshire Regiment of Militia, 1793–1801'.

11. Eliza de Feuillide to Warren Hastings, 28 Dec. 1797, *AP*, p. 168.

12. Clive Caplan gives his monthly pay as Adjutant, Capt. Lieut. and Paymaster, totalling £281.4s.0d. a year.

13. Eliza de Feuillide to Philadelphia Walter, 11 Dec. 1797, *AP*, p. 167.

14. Eliza Austen to Philadelphia Walter, 16 Feb. 1798, *AP*, p. 169.

15. Eliza Austen to Philadelphia Walter, unpublished letter, 16 Feb. 1798, HRO microfilm.
16. Eliza Austen to Philadelphia Walter, 16 Feb. 1798, *AP*, p. 169.

13 FRIENDS IN EAST KENT

Some of the information for this chapter comes from the unpublished diaries of Lady Knatchbull (Fanny Austen, later Knight) held at the Kent County Archives in Maidstone.

1. JA to CEA, 22 Jan. 1801. Mrs Knight was forty-eight at the time.
2. JA to CEA, 18 Dec. 1798.
3. In a letter to CEA, 20 June 1808. We do not know when Mrs Knight's allowance to JA began, but it was probably not before the death of Mr Austen in 1805.
4. The key to the park is mentioned in Fanny's diaries.
5. The game known as Bullet pudding, as described by Fanny, was played like this:

   You must have a large pewter dish filled with flour which you must pile up into a sort of pudding with a peak at top, you must then lay a Bullet at top & everybody cuts a slice of it & the person that is cutting it when the Bullet falls must poke about with their noses & chins till they find it & then take it with their mouths which makes them strange figures all covered with flour but the worst is that you must not laugh for fear of the flour getting up your nose & mouth & choking you.

6. Why he went without Eliza is not known. She was on friendly enough terms with the Edward Austens to entertain them in London. She did visit Godmersham in Oct. 1801, but then not again until 1809, after the death of Elizabeth, which may suggest that the sisters-in-law did not get on.
7. Copied from papers in possession of Alwyn Austen, which attribute the poem to Henry Austen.
8. Quoted by Deirdre Le Faye in *A Family Record*, pp. 161–2, from the Lefroy MS; and 'Anna Lefroy's Original Memories of Jane Austen', *Review of English Studies*, NS xxxix, 155, Aug. 1988, p. 419.
9. This letter from Fanny, then Lady Knatchbull, to her younger sister

Marianne was first printed in the *Cornhill* magazine, 973, Winter 1947/8, pp. 72–3, 'courtesy of Lord Brabourne and Mr Edward Rice', according to the editor, Peter Quennell (but they were both long dead).

10. JA to CEA, 23 June 1814.

11. Information about the marginal comment in the Goldsmith from Park Honan's *Jane Austen: Her Life* (1987), p. 58 of 1989 edition; her copy of the Goldsmith is in private possession.

Her silence on politics and public events is described by her niece Caroline, who was admittedly only ten when JA died, in *My Aunt Jane Austen*, p. 9. The full passage reads:

> The general politics of the family were Tory – rather taken for granted I suppose, than discussed, as even my Uncles seldom talked about it – and in vain do I try to recall any word or expression of my Aunt Jane's that had reference to public events – *Some* bias of course she *must* have had – but I can only *guess* to which quarter she inclined.

For her dislike of William Chute, MP, see p. 96.

12. The lines are from Book III of Cowper's *The Task*, 'The Garden'.

13. All quotes from Chapter 1 of *A Vindication of the Rights of Woman* by Mary Wollstonecraft.

14. Robert Bage (1728–1801) was a Derbyshire businessman, a papermaker like the Portals and an iron manufacturer. He took up writing in his fifties after a business failure, published several novels before *Hermsprong* (his most successful book) and, like Charlotte Smith, brought down disapproval for allowing female characters to 'recover' from rape and adultery, rather than pine and die in the accepted manner.

15. See below, p. 326, for her references to Anne Grant's *Letters from the Mountains*. JA mentions this popular work which attacked Wollstonecraft several times, but avoids giving any opinion on it. It was, I believe, the first to suggest that women were unfitted to sit in Parliament on the grounds that 'a third of the female members will be lying-in, recovering, or nursing'.

14 TRAVELS WITH MY MOTHER

1. Quoted by Deirdre Le Faye in *A Family Record*, p. 101, from Fanny Caroline Lefroy's notes on family history written between 1880 and 1885.

2. Eliza Chute's diary for 1798 records her riding with 'Lady F' on 22 Oct., HRO 23M93/70/1/6.
3. Jane Leigh-Perrot to Montague Cholmeley, 10 Oct. 1799, *AP*, p. 188.
4. Montague Cholmeley to Jane Leigh-Perrot, 11 Jan. 1800, *AP*, p. 198.
5. Park Honan (*Jane Austen, Her Life*, 1987) quotes R. A. Austen-Leigh's private notes about Jekyll's belief that Mrs Leigh-Perrot was a klepto-maniac and did steal the lace, pp. 150–51.

Sarah Markham gives the account of Mrs Leigh-Perrot stealing a plant in *Jane Austen Society Report* for 1991, drawn from her own book *A Testimony of Her Times: Based on Penelope Hind's Diaries and Correspondence 1787–1838* (1990). She quotes from a letter describing Mrs Leigh-Perrot as being 'of lace-stealing notoriety', and gives some verses written by a Bath magistrate on the alleged plant stealing:

> To love of plants who has the greatest claim,
> Darwin the Bard or Perrot's wily Dame?
> Decide the cause, Judge Botany, we pray,
> Let him the Laurel take and her the Bay.

6. We know about Mrs Lefroy's straw manufactory because Eliza Chute's mother wrote asking for advice from her, hoping to set up something similar herself. Unpublished letter, n.d., HRO 23M93/70/3/16. Eliza Chute to Eliza Gosling, 29 Sept. 1800, unpublished letter, HRO 23M93/74/1/3.
7. Information from Patrick Piggott's *The Innocent Diversion: A Study of Music in the Life and Writings of Jane Austen* (1979), p. 156.
8. All but the last sentence quoted from Eliza's letter, Eliza Austen to Philadelphia Walter, 29 Oct. 1799, *AP*, pp. 172–4. The last sentence, cut in *AP*, I have taken from microfilm of letter in HRO.

15 THREE BOOKS

1. The two cancelled chapters of *Persuasion* are the only manuscripts relating to the six published novels to have survived (see pp. 257–8).
2. R. W. Chapman argues that *Pride and Prejudice* must have been substan-tially rewritten in 1812, on the grounds that he believes JA used an almanac for 1811 in constructing its chronology, as suggested by Sir

Frank MacKinnon; but it is no more than a possibility. Also see n. 5, Chapter 22.

3. For that reason, perhaps, it was omitted from the film version of *Sense and Sensibility*.

4. Sir William East (1738–1819) of Hall Place, Hurley, Berks., was a neighbour in Berkshire both of the Leigh-Perrots and of the Mrs Cotton with whom Mary Wollstonecraft stayed after her second suicide attempt in 1796. See William Godwin, first edition of his memoir of Mary Wollstonecraft (1798), Chapter 8, '1795, 1796', pp. 143–4: 'Her present residence among the scenes of nature, was favourable to this purpose [i.e., casting off her attachment to Imlay]. She was at the house of an old and intimate friend, a lady of the name of Cotton, whose partiality to her was strong and sincere. Mrs Cotton's nearest neighbour was Sir William East, baronet; and, from the joint effect of the kindness of her friend, and the hospitable and distinguishing attentions of this respectable family, she derived considerable benefit.' This passage was cut from the second edition of the memoir, after the first edition had been greeted with violent disapproval and mockery of Godwin's frankness. No doubt Sir William East preferred not to be publicly associated with Wollstonecraft after this.

There are several known links between Easts and Austens. Sir William's son Gilbert was the Steventon pupil to whom Mrs Austen sent the poem quoted above. According to Jane Leigh-Perrot's letter of Jan. 1800 (*AP*, pp. 198–201), Sir William expressed support for her in her shop-lifting ordeal (see pp. 149–51) and 'wished it lay in his power to be of any service as well through the Regard he felt for us as to show his detestation of so much Villainy, for almost a similar Case had nearly involved Lady East in the distress that I was thrown into.' And a portrait of 'Sir Wm East' is mentioned by JA as hanging at Steventon in 1801.

5. JA owned one such manual in French by the Marquise de Lambert – probably another gift from her cousin Eliza – which is insistent on the point that young ladies should never experience love, which might interfere with their parents' marital plans for them. It advises avoiding plays, music, poetry and the reading of romances, i.e., novels, and describes falling in love as 'the most cruel situation a rational person can be in'. Madame de Genlis' stories also condemn passionate feeling, which is presented as wholly destructive and inappropriate in a woman.

Anne Radcliffe also took up the question of excessive sensibility in her *Mysteries of Udolpho*, well known to JA, and published in 1794. Emily, the heroine, is specifically warned by her dying father against its dangers. He tells her, 'Those who really possess sensibility ought to be early taught that it is a dangerous quality, which is continually extracting the excess of misery or delight from every surrounding circumstance . . . beware of priding yourself on the gracefulness of sensibility. If you yield to this vanity, your happiness is lost for ever.' There is a good deal more along these lines, and a central theme of the book is Emily's attempt to follow her dead father's advice through her subsequent trials, which include cruel treatment by her guardians, and the apparent faithlessness of her lover. *Udolpho* is set in a different century and country, and told in a different style, but there was more to it than Gothic effects and romantic evocations of scenery, and it offered more than one theme taken up by JA.

6. Mary Lascelles, *Jane Austen and Her Art* (1939), p. 30.
7. Mary Lascelles, 'Jane Austen and the Novel' in John Halperin (ed.), *Bicentenary Essays* (1975), p. 241.
8. See diaries of Fanny Austen for 5 Aug. 1805, 'I slept half with Mama & half with Sackree [the family nurse]; for Papa came home late in the evening & I was obliged to be pulled out of bed.' She was twelve. Kent County Archives U951 F24/2.
9. JA to CEA, 3 July 1813.
10. JA to CEA, 15 Sept. 1796.
11. Marilyn Butler, in her introduction to *Northanger Abbey* (Penguin Classics, 1995), points out that Johnson's defence of the novel, in the *Rambler* (no. 4), was certainly known to JA; and she suggests that his paragraph in the same essay, mocking ignorant young women readers of novels who are 'open to every false suggestion and partial account', is a likely starting point for *Northanger Abbey*.

16 TWENTY-FIVE

1. Caroline Austen, daughter of James and Mary, gave her mother's account to her brother James-Edward in a letter, 1 Apr. 1869, quoted by Chapman in his *Facts and Problems*. Chapman did not doubt its veracity.
2. See Robin Vick's 'The Sale at Steventon Parsonage', *Jane Austen Society*

Report (1993), pp. 13–16. JA's remarks about the price of the books in letters to CEA, 12 May 1801 and 21 May 1801.

3. Lines from one of a group of MS poems by James Austen copied in unidentified hand, and thought to be written in 1814. HRO 23M93/60/3/1.

17 MANYDOWN

1. Cited by Deirdre Le Faye in *A Family Record*, p. 121, taken from the Lefroy MS.

2. Sir John Lambert was known to Eliza as the Chevalier Lambert when she and her mother stayed with him in Paris. It is quite plausible that she and Henry met him in 1802 or 1803 when they went to France to try to claim her rights in the Capot de Feuillide estates, and that he took advantage of the peace to return to England. Henry was in touch with the Lambert family again later, as is clear from his account at Hoare's Bank.

3. A story from a few years later demonstrates this. In dispute with Winchester Cathedral Chapter about the right to cut timber in his park, Harris invited all the Canons, all of whom were friends, to dinner. He told his butler to mix up several of his very good wines into a punch and served it to them. The mixture was disgusting. When the Canons had tried to drink it, he addressed them, 'Gentlemen, my punch is like you. In your individual capacity you are all very good fellows, but in your corporate capacity you are very disagreeable.' JA might well have appreciated the joke.

4. There may just possibly have been a proposal in 1805 from the Revd Edward Bridges, a brother of Edward Austen's wife Elizabeth, and a few years younger than Jane, whom she had known since the mid-1790s. She at any rate mentioned his particular attentiveness to her, mostly in ordering toasted cheese for her supper at Goodnestone one evening, it must be said. Three years later, in 1808, she recalled (to Cassandra) an 'invitation' from him which she had been unable to accept. It is clear from the letters that she liked him, and he got on well with her brothers, but he held no romantic interest for her. If there was a proposal, no one in either family was informed and there were no regrets. She sent warm congratulations when he became engaged to someone else, and

pitied him when his bride turned out to be a hypochondriac. 'She is a poor Honey – the sort of woman who gives me the idea of being determined never to be well – & who liked her spasms & nervousness & the consequence they give her, better than anything else,' she wrote to Francis, 25 Sept. 1813.

5. JA to CEA, 21 Apr. 1805, just after the death of Mr Austen.

6. Jane Austen's great-niece Fanny Lefroy (granddaughter of James Austen through his daughter Anna) wrote in 1883 in *Temple Bar* magazine (lxvii, p. 277) that she began writing *The Watsons* 'somewhere in 1804'.

7. The passage about the fox-hounds has been deleted in the manuscript. It could be a recollection of Mr Chute, who occasionally persuaded his wife to come and take a look at the hunt, and may well have pressed its charms on other women in the neighbourhood.

8. *Jane Austen and Her Art*, pp. 99–100.

9. Eliza Austen to Philadelphia Walter, 29 Oct. 1801, *AP*, pp. 174–5.

10. Henry Austen to Warren Hastings, 5 June 1802, *AP*, p. 177.

11. JA to Francis Austen, 30 Jan. 1805, *AP*, pp. 235–6.

12. Archives du Ministère des Affaires Etrangères, Quai d'Orsay, I, 20.

13. As already noted, the unpublished diaries of Lady Knatchbull (as Fanny ultimately became) are in the Kent County Archives, U951 F24/1. They start in 1804.

18 BROTHERLY LOVE

1. Francis wrote to Mary Gibson from the *Canopus* when he already suspected he was going to miss the Battle of Trafalgar. He put his feelings very well: 'I do not profess to like fighting for its own sake, but if there has been an action with the combined fleets I shall ever consider the day on which I sailed from the squadron as the most inauspicious one of my life.'

2. CEA to Fanny Knight, 20 July 1817 (the letter is printed in all the complete editions of JA's letters).

3. From *My Aunt Jane Austen, a Memoir* by Caroline Austen, writing in 1867. Her remark is particularly notable since she knew Cassandra for nearly forty years.

4. Entries in Fanny's diary for 16 Sept. 1804, 11 Oct. 1804 and 29 July 1806, Kent County Archives U951 F24/1.

5. Mary Berry visited Stoneleigh four years later, and described it as a 'clumsy house'. She met several of the Leighs, and 'Mr Repton, planning future improvements; very probably . . . for the worse. They gave us the key to the park . . . If this park shows some signs of neglect, it is, at least, unspoiled by improvement.' *Miss Berry's Journal* for 6 Oct. 1810 (3 vols., 1865), Vol. II, pp. 433–4.

6. Just about every old building in this part of Southampton has long since been demolished, and even the ground plan has disappeared, so it is not possible to know exactly where the Austens' house stood, only that the garden ended at the town wall.

7. Nigel Nicolson, *The World of Jane Austen* (1991), p. 110.

8. The novelist Mary Brunton, who visited Netley in 1815, made this objection in a letter.

19 A DEATH IN THE FAMILY

1. Henry's ownership of the box at the Pantheon Opera Theatre, or House, is the discovery of Clive Caplan, to whom I am indebted for the information. The Pantheon opened in 1772, was used by Covent Garden for four years after it burnt down in 1788, and was burnt down itself in 1792; it was rebuilt allegedly on the scale of La Scala, but was never successful, and was reduced to putting on 'Italian burlettas and ballets', according to Erroll Sherson in *London's Lost Theatres of the Nineteenth Century* (1925).

2. Eliza appears so little in the Steventon Austens' records as to suggest a deliberate exclusion, either because of disapproval of her character and marriage to Henry, possibly also going back to the question mark over her parentage. Fanny Austen's unpublished diaries, however, describe dinners, theatre-going and shopping trips in London with Henry and Eliza.

3. Mr Hill's claim to fame was that he was the uncle of Robert Southey, who by now had abandoned the radical opinions of his youth and become a respectable writer with a government pension. JA read some of his works, but without much enthusiasm. She joked about Southey's very popular *Life of Nelson* to Cass, saying she was tired of such lives and never read any, but would read this one if it mentioned her brother Frank (11 Oct. 1813). Later she approved his *Poet's Pilgrimage to Waterloo*,

although moderately, and to Alethea Bigg who was staying with the Herbert Hills: 'parts of it suit me better than much that he has written before' (24 Jan. 1817).

For Catherine's wedding present, Jane stitched some pocket handkerchiefs and sent them with a rather limp four-line verse expressing the hope her friend would have no tears to shed but tears of joy; a better version, not sent, wished 'Slight be her colds, and few her tears.' Both reproduced in Chapman's *Minor Works*, pp. 446–7.

4. Elizabeth's mother, who survived her, had borne thirteen children, the last when she was thirty-seven; so Elizabeth must have been hoping she was nearing the end of her own child-bearing years.

5. Fanny's diary mentions a visit to them at Wanstead with her father the following Oct., so it is likely they were there until Christmas 1809.

6. These are taken from the printed pages in Fanny Austen's diary for the year. Mrs Chute's diaries have similar lists, renewed every year, sometimes with instructions for the steps. In 1810 we find contemporary references again: 'Lord Wellington's Waltz', 'Talavera Reel' and 'The Fair African', as well as theatrical names, 'Elliston's Caper' and 'Catalini's Wriggle'.

7. These accounts are all that survive of a pocket-diary for 1807 owned by JA. The two pages are in the Pierpont Morgan Library.

8. Fanny's diary for Sunday, 9 July 1809, records the prayer reading in the library.

20 AT CHAWTON

1. Mrs Knight to Fanny Austen, 26 Oct. 1809, cited by Deirdre Le Faye, *A Family Record*, p. 161, from Lord Brabourne, *The Letters of Jane Austen* (2 vols., 1884), Vol. II, p. 364.

2. According to Charles Vancouver's 1815 *General View of Agriculture of Hampshire* there were 64 houses in Chawton, 65 families, 171 males and 201 females. Of the men, 61 were agricultural workers, 10 in trade and 301 'other'.

3. Caroline Austen, *My Aunt Jane Austen, a Memoir*, pp. 3–4.

4. The tradition derives from the *Memoir*, in which James-Edward Austen-Leigh writes on p. 16 that the sisters shared a bedroom 'all their lives'. Caroline, however, writes of her 'keeping to her room' when she was

ill, which could indicate it was not shared at that point (*My Aunt Jane Austen*, p. 14).

5. There is no doubt of this. Jane wrote in her letter to Cass of 3 Jan. 1801, *à propos* the departure from Steventon, 'All the beds indeed that we shall want are to be removed, viz: – besides theirs, our own two.' Like just about everyone at that period, she shared a bed on occasion, with her mother, with Martha Lloyd, with her niece Fanny and no doubt with her sister too. Women shared beds with women servants, with children, with friends; just as men might share with total strangers at an inn.

6. JA to Anna Austen, 28 Sept. 1814.

7. James-Edward Austen-Leigh, *A Memoir of Jane Austen*, p. 16. Fanny's diary for the astronomy lecture, 12 June 1811. Margaret Wilson (on p. 29 in *Almost Another Sister*) suggests the 'astronomy' lecture in fact referred to Fanny's emotional entanglements, since she nicknamed one of her young men Jupiter.

Constance Hill, *Jane Austen, Her Homes and Her Friends*, p. 195, for the laughing with Anna and Cass's response.

8. Martha also collected medical information including alleged cures for everything from consumption, worms, sore lips and 'pain in the side' to 'Mad Dog Bite'; and some veterinary treatments. She made cosmetics too, including 'Coral Tooth Powder' and two kinds of cold cream. Information from *The Jane Austen Cookbook* (1995) by Maggie Black and Deirdre Le Faye, p. 36.

9. Mrs Austen wrote to her newly married granddaughter Anna in 1814 about engaging a cook as follows: 'As to a cook, I have to say Mrs Frank Austen gives 10 guineas, I give only 8 – hers is the hardest place, as they have a great wash every fortnight, we have very little washing.' Undated letter cited by Geoffrey Grigson in the *TLS* for 19 Aug. 1955.

10. Anna's daughter, Miss Lefroy, gave this account to Constance Hill, who prints it on p. 176 of her *Jane Austen, Her Homes and Her Friends*.

11. CEA to Philadelphia Walter, now Mrs Whitaker, 20 Mar. 1812, *AP*, p. 250.

12. According to his own son, James-Edward Austen-Leigh, *A Memoir of Jane Austen*, p. 12.

13. See 'Opinions of *Mansfield Park*' in Chapman's *Minor Works*, p. 432. For *Emma*, Mr and Mrs James Austen gave a joint, and unfavourable, opinion: they 'did not like it so well as either of the 3 others. Language different from the others; not so easily read.'

14. The original manuscript of James's poem to his sister is in the Fellows'
Library at Winchester College. I have used George Holbert Tucker's
transcription in his *A Goodly Heritage*, p. 113.

> . . . Though quick & keen her mental eye
> Poor Nature's foibles to descry
> And seemed for ever on the watch,
> Some traits of ridicule to catch,
> Yet not a word she ever pen'd
> Which hurt the feelings of a friend,
> And not one line she ever wrote
> Which dying she would wish to blot;
> But to her family alone
> Her real, genuine worth was known.
> Yes, they whose lot it was to prove
> Her Sisterly, her filial love,
> They saw her ready still to share
> The labours of domestic care
> As if *their* prejudice to shame
> Who, jealous of fair female fame,
> Maintain that literary taste
> In womans mind is much misplaced,
> Inflames their vanity & pride,
> And draws from useful works aside.

15. Fanny's diary notes this, 4 May 1812. 'Beautiful place,' she writes.
16. James-Edward Austen-Leigh, *A Memoir of Jane Austen*, p. 102.
17. Jane Aiken Hodge makes this point in *The Double Life of Jane Austen*
(1972).
18. Jane Aiken Hodge points out that when the second edition was prepared
in Nov. 1813, JA wrote, 'I suppose in the meantime I shall owe dear
Henry a great deal of money for printing &c.' *The Double Life of Jane
Austen*, p. 120.
19. Mary Brunton was three years younger than Jane, a Scotswoman and
the author of *Self-Control*, published in 1810. Jane was trying to get hold
of a copy in the spring of 1811, and said she was afraid of reading it for
fear it would be too clever, and forestall her story and characters. When
she did read it in Oct. 1813 her fears were relieved. Laura is one of the
tribe of perfect heroines who resists first seduction and then the offer
of marriage from the dashing Colonel Hargrave, and goes through
many vicissitudes which culminate in America, where she makes a
dramatic escape in an Indian canoe. It was successful, and is still worth

reading for many incidental touches, like Laura's appalled response to the noise and traffic of London and her humiliating efforts to sell her paintings to earn money.

Mrs Brunton died giving birth to her first child at the age of forty; she had been married at nineteen, and did not expect to survive the confinement, selecting her grave clothes in advance. The letter quoted was to her friend Mrs Izett, given on p. xxxvi of her husband's memoir, prefaced to her posthumous novel *Emmeline* (1819), a fervent tract against divorce.

20. *British Critic*, May 1812, and *Critical Review*, Feb. 1812.

21. Arthur Aspinall, *The Letters of Princess Charlotte* (1949), p. 26.

22. Charles Austen gave this account of his conversation with 'a nephew of Charles James Fox' in a letter to JA dated 6 May 1815. He was in Palermo; Charles Fox was in the navy at this point, aged eighteen. Because he was born before his parents were able to marry (his mother was still married to her first husband) he could not succeed to the Holland barony or ever be legitimized. He gave up the navy, joined the army, and fell in love successively with two of the daughters of the Duke of Clarence and Mrs Jordan; Eliza turned him down in favour of the Earl of Erroll, but Mary FitzClarence agreed to marry him in 1824. The whole of Charles Austen's account, which is printed in J. H. Hubback, *Jane Austen's Sailor Brothers*, p. 270, goes like this: 'Books became the subject of conversation, and I praised "Waverley" highly, when a young man present observed that nothing had come out for years to be compared with "Pride and Prejudice", "Sense and Sensibility" &c. As I am sure you must be anxious to know the name of a person of so much taste, I shall tell you it is Fox, a nephew of the late Charles James Fox. That you may not be too much elated at this morsel of praise, I shall add that he did not appear to like "Mansfield Park" so well as the first two, in which, however, I believe he is singular.' So Charles Fox was a precursor of Kingsley Amis.

23. Mrs Anne Grant's *Letters from the Mountains*, published in 1806 in three volumes, had a great success. They were written between 1773 and 1803, and published when she was left a widow by her clergyman husband, a garrison chaplain at Fort Augustus, with eight living children to support; the letters give an affecting picture of the births and deaths of many more in their remote cottage, halfway between Perth and Inverness. They farmed their patch of land, and spun and wove their own cloth. Her view of family life in these circumstances is well expressed (Vol. III, p. 165):

A large family is a little community within itself. The variety of dispositions, the necessity of making occasional sacrifices of humour and inclination, and, at other times, resisting aggression or incroachment, when properly directed by an over-ruling mind, teach both firmness and flexibility, as the occasion may call forth the exercise of those qualities. – Respect and submission to the elder branches of a family, tenderness and forbearance to the younger, all tend more to moral improvement, if properly managed, than volumes of maxims and rules of conduct. With regard to modesty and deference too, people in our situation must needs enforce those in self-defence. – In a cottage, where children are continually under the eye of their parents, and confined within narrow bounds, petulance would be purgatory.

Mrs Grant had spent her childhood in America, where her father was posted before the War of Independence (she returned to Scotland in 1768). She was an ardent Tory and wrote, 'we detest the Rights of Man, and abominate those of Woman' (Apr. 1795, Vol. III, p. 231).

21 INSIDE MANSFIELD PARK

1. This he wrote in his diaries. All information about d'Antraigues from the second edition of Léonce Pingaud, *Un agent secret sous la Révolution et l'Empire: Le Comte d'Antraigues* (Paris, 1894). Pingaud writes (p. 84), 'Il ne faut malheureusement jamais ni nulle part chercher dans cette vie quelque chose qui soit absolument droit ou absolument pur.' ('There is unfortunately no point in looking for anything entirely straightforward or entirely disinterested in this particular life story.')

2. As Countess of Craven she read and enjoyed JA's novels; JA noted her opinion of *Emma*: 'Countess Craven – admired it very much, but did not think it equal to P & P. – which she ranked as the very first of it's sort.'

3. Francis Austen complained in 1844: 'That I have not served at Sea since 1814 is not from want of inclination or application, but have had no influence of a political or family description to back my pretensions.' British Library Add. MSS 38,039, f. 184. He did, however, receive honours, CB in 1815, Rear-Admiral in 1830, and in 1837 he was invested as Knight Commander of the Bath by King William IV (as the Duke of Clarence became in 1830).

4. For readers who do not remember the details of the book, Mansfield

Park is the Northamptonshire country house of Sir Thomas Bertram, into which he invites Lady Bertram's niece Fanny Price, the eldest daughter of a sister who married a mere lieutenant in the marines. Fanny is younger than the Bertram children, two sons and two daughters, Maria and Julia, both beauties, and she is taken very little notice of by any of them except the younger son, Edmund, who is kind to her and wins her love. She grows up shy and neglected, and tormented by her other aunt, Mrs Norris, who lives near by. The central action begins when Sir Thomas has to travel to his estates in the West Indies, and Henry and Mary Crawford come to stay near Mansfield; they are brother and sister, delightful, witty and well-to-do. Soon both Julia and Maria, who is already engaged to a rich and foolish neighbour, Rushworth, are in love with Henry, who is happy to flirt with both; and Edmund is in love with Mary. She expects to marry an elder son, and turns up her nose at the idea of a clergyman, which is what Edmund plans to be. Two long sequences show the young people spending a day at Mr Rushworth's great house, and then hatching a plan to put on a play at Mansfield Park. Fanny alone opposes the play scheme; even Edmund is drawn in, and the cross-currents of feeling generated by these activities – jealousy, vanity, excitement and pain – are orchestrated with a masterly hand.

Sir Thomas returns, the play is given up and Maria's wedding to Rushworth goes ahead. Mary Crawford finds herself more drawn to Edmund than she meant to be, and Henry to Fanny. When Henry, baffled by Fanny's indifference and impressed by her devotion to her sailor brother William, helps him to promotion and proposes to her, Sir Thomas and Lady Bertram urge her to accept. She refuses, and Sir Thomas sends her to visit her parents in Portsmouth, whom she has not seen since she left them as a child, as a way of bringing her round. The Portsmouth scenes are the other high point of the book, and Austen's fullest representation of poverty; the Prices live in a small house with thin walls and too many noisy children. Mrs Price lacks any capacity to bring order, and Mr Price drinks too much; neither is interested in Fanny. She pines, and Henry Crawford arrives and makes himself extremely agreeable to her by his tactful and charming behaviour. The reader is led to think Fanny will soften, he will mend his light-hearted ways and become a model estate-owner, and Edmund and Mary will marry. Instead, Austen introduces a flurry of activity, mostly reported, in which Henry elopes with Maria Rushworth, Julia also runs off with an admirer, and the eldest Bertram boy falls ill. The Bertrams send for Fanny, whom they now recognize as their only good 'daughter'; and Mary Crawford loses Edmund by failing to condemn her brother's behaviour. The way is open for Edmund to turn to Fanny at last, and on the last page of the book they are settled at the parsonage near his parents at Mansfield Park, while Mrs Norris lives in remote banishment with the disgraced Maria, and the Crawfords disappear into the glittering and corrupt social round of London.

5. Egerton's remark and some of the others are taken from JA's own list of 'Opinions of *Mansfield Park*', printed in Chapman's *Minor Works*, pp. 431–5; others are from contemporary letters cited in Deirdre Le Faye, *A Family Record*, pp. 189–90. There were no reviews, but the first edition, again in three volumes (David Gilson's estimate in *The Jane Austen Handbook*, p. 135, is 1,250 copies) at eighteen shillings, published in May 1814, sold out in six months. Profits for the author were £350.

6. James-Edward sent this request in an anonymous note in Nov. 1814, when a second edition was being considered. It is cited by Deirdre Le Faye, *A Family Record*, p. 197.

7. All from JA's 'Opinions of *Mansfield Park*', Chapman's *Minor Works*, pp. 431–5.

8. This account of Cassandra's reaction is taken from Elizabeth Jenkins's address to the Jane Austen Society, 'Some Notes on Background'. It is attributed to Louisa, née Austen (Edward's daughter), who became Lady George Hill, and told it to Pamela Fitzgerald, who reported it in turn in a letter to Lord Carlyle: 'Lady George says Miss Austen's sister Cassandra tried to persuade her to alter the end of Mansfield Park and let Mr Crawford marry Fanny Price. She remembers their arguing the matter but Miss Austen stood firmly and would not allow the change.' *Jane Austen Society Report* (1980).

9. Reginald Farrer, 'Jane Austen', *Quarterly Review*, July 1917, quoted in Brian Southam (ed.), *Jane Austen: The Critical Heritage*, Vol. II (1987).

Q. D. Leavis's essay on *Mansfield Park* appeared in *Scrutiny* for Jan. 1942, pp. 272–94. She also put forward an unconvincing theory that JA used *Lady Susan* as the basis for *Mansfield Park*.

10. Kingsley Amis, 'What Became of Jane Austen?' (1957).

11. Lionel Trilling, 'Mansfield Park', written for the *Pelican Guide to English*

Literature, first published in the *Partisan Review*, Sept.–Oct. 1954 and reprinted in *The Opposing Self* (1955).

12. Tony Tanner, *Jane Austen* (1986), p. 156. He also blames London (p. 141): 'It is London that has made and formed the attractive Crawfords, who very nearly bring total ruin to the world of Mansfield Park. For if Mansfield, at its best, perfects people, London, at its worst, perverts them.'

13. Roger Gard, *Jane Austen's Novels: The Art of Clarity* (1992), p. 144. An excellent book.

14. The Shakespearean comparison comes readily to mind, because, of all Austen's books, *Mansfield Park* shows most traces of Shakespeare. Eliza and Henry, to whom Jane was close during the period in which she planned the book, were keen theatre-goers and knew their Shakespeare and, as we have seen, he enjoyed reading aloud, exactly as Henry Crawford does. Lady Bertram tells Crawford his reading is as good as a play, and he says how much he would like to play Shylock or Richard III. The Bertram brothers have also from boyhood read Shakespeare with their father, and Fanny often reads to Lady Bertram out of the volumes of Shakespeare in the drawing room. When the young people wander in the wilderness at Sotherton, avoiding and pursuing one another at cross purposes, the resemblance to the lovers in the wood in *A Midsummer Night's Dream* is obvious; what is more, it leads on to theatricals, in which lovers are again divided and humiliated, and even those who would expect to remain aloof find themselves drawn in, as Titania was. When Edmund urges Fanny to accept Crawford, her cry of 'Oh! never, never, never; he never will succeed with me' is a reminder of King Lear's five times repeated 'Never' as he holds his youngest daughter dead in his arms; and Fanny is in effect Sir Thomas Bertram's Cordelia, the misprized third daughter who alone remains staunch.

15. JA accused Hannah More of 'pedantry and affectation' in her *Coelebs in Search of a Wife*, published in 1809 to considerable success. One of its themes is the contrast between corrupt town ladies and innocent country girls. Coelebs chooses as his bride one who is constantly examining her own conscience for possible failings, and devotes herself to gardening and good work with the poor in the village.

16. Support for the view that ladies were generally in favour of abolition is found in Fanny Austen's diary, or pocket-book, for 1809, which contains an anti-slavery story in the printed matter at the front (see Appendix

II). The publishers who printed and sold the pocket-books must have had good reason to assume this would be popular. Brian Southam's arguments are made in 'The Silence of the Bertrams', *TLS*, 17 Feb. 1995, pp. 13–14. Southam argues convincingly that JA places the book in the years 1810–13, i.e., after the dates which made the shipping of slaves illegal. From May 1807 no ship could legally sail from any port in the British Empire with slaves, and from Mar. 1808 no slaves could be landed. This did not mean the trade stopped – it continued illegally – and it remained a divisive issue; slavery itself was not abolished in the Empire until 1834.

17. JA to Fanny Knight, 23 Mar. 1817.
18. CEA to Philadelphia Whitaker, 18 Aug. 1811, *AP*, p. 248.
19. Fanny's diaries for 15 July 1809 and 9 Sept. 1811.
20. JA wrote to CEA after Eliza's death, 16 Sept. 1813, saying she and their niece Fanny were sharing accommodation at Henrietta Street and were 'very well off indeed, & as we have poor Eliza's bed our space is ample in every way'.
21. James-Edward Austen-Leigh, *A Memoir of Jane Austen*, p. 26.
22. William and R. A. Austen-Leigh, *Jane Austen, Her Life and Letters, a Family Record*, pp. 106–7.
23. 'Austen, Maund, Austen & Co. 10 Henrietta St' appears in the printed list of banks in Eliza Chute's diary for 1813; the second Austen can only be Francis.
24. Fanny Austen, then at Chawton House with her father, wrote in her diary that her Aunt Jane arrived on 30 Apr. 'with Mrs Perigord'.
25. The epitaph can no longer be seen, but the text is given by Deirdre Le Faye, 'Hancock Family Grave', *Jane Austen Society Report* (1981), p. 183. It was copied in 1881 when St John-at-Hampstead recorded all the tombstone inscriptions.

22 DEDICATION

1. Chapman conjectures that she was Frances Burdett, who died in 1846, and was the aunt of Baroness Burdett-Coutts. She told JA that she liked *Mansfield Park* less than *Pride and Prejudice*, noted in the 'Opinions', *Minor Works*, p. 432.
2. Madame de Staël had a hard time with English literary ladies. Fanny

Burney also broke off friendship with her because of de Staël's irregular private life. But Miss Berry went to her dinners during her stay in London in the winter of 1813/14, meeting there among others John Murray the publisher, Mrs Siddons, Kemble and the Duke of Gloucester; and she went to the theatre with Byron.

3. The *OED* suggests that 'coze' is an amalgam of 'cozy' and the French *causer*. It gives no earlier usage than Austen's in *Mansfield Park*, which suggests it is her coinage.

4. This *Don Juan* was nothing to do with Mozart, although it was done with music; it was a 'pantomime', based on the Restoration playwright Thomas Shadwell's comedy of 1675, *The Libertine*.

5. James's wife Mary Austen kept one from 1810, Fanny Austen from 1804. Since the fragment of a JA diary exists for 1807, it is possible JA destroyed such earlier ones herself, leaving only the later ones for CEA to refer to, since only *Emma* and *Persuasion* are given exact dates in her memorandum.

JA could also have used them in relation to the internal chronology of some of her novels, since they laid out the weeks and holidays clearly. Sir Frank MacKinnon (1871–1946), a high court judge with an interest in the eighteenth century, first suggested that JA used almanacs in fixing dates. Chapman agreed with him, but between them they assembled only partially convincing evidence that she did so for the final version of *Pride and Prejudice* and for *Mansfield Park*.

6. Arne's opera of 1762, with a text from Pietro Metastasio, was popular and continued to be performed well into the nineteenth century; it was written with two parts for castrati, but presumably adapted. Mrs Jordan played Nell on 7 Mar., Miss Hoyden in *A Trip to Scarborough* on 10 Mar., when Byron saw her. JA does not name her, but Genest gives the dates of all her performances of this, her last London season. She fell ill in April, and was then summoned to Essex to care for one of her married daughters during a difficult confinement (a reason JA would have sympathized with). After this she returned to Covent Garden and continued to act until the end of the season in June. Henry Austen's house at 10 Henrietta Street was two doors away from her first London lodgings at No. 8.

7. The phrase is from Fanny's diary for 8 Apr. 1814; so is the account of the Alton illuminations and supper for the poor, which she walked into Alton to watch, being at Chawton with her father in May.

8. Fanny's diary for 20 June, when she was staying at Henrietta Street, reads: 'Uncle HA went to Whites Fête at Burlington House.'

9. The case was not settled until after JA's death, and Edward was obliged to pay £15,000 to get the Hintons to agree to a settlement. Information from Caroline Austen, *Reminiscences* (1986), pp. 38–9, and Deirdre Le Faye, *A Family Record*, pp. 194–5.

10. Caroline Austen, *Reminiscences*, p. 40.

11. Text given by Geoffrey Grigson in the *TLS* for 19 Aug. 1955, p. 484. Although Scott published *Waverley* anonymously, the Austens were among the many in the secret, doubtless through John Murray.

12. See Caroline Austen's *My Aunt Jane Austen*, pp. 11–12, for JA's initial reluctance about the dedication. Within a year 1,250 copies of *Emma* were sold, but sales fell sharply after this. As Jane Aiken Hodge points out on p. 125 of *The Double Life of Jane Austen*, Murray remaindered both *Emma* and the second edition of *Mansfield Park* he published in 1816 five years later, in 1821. Neither was reprinted until Richard Bentley's edition in 1833.

13. JA to JS Clarke, 11 Dec. 1815.

14. JA to CEA, 26 Nov. 1815.

15. From Scott's diary for 14 Mar. 1826, first published by J. G. Lockhart in his *Life* (1837–8).

23 THE SORCERESS

1. Francis Austen's account at Hoare's Bank gives his half-pay and investment income.

    Clive Caplan has found from directories and bank notes that Francis was a partner from 1806 to 1809.

    Eliza Chute's diary for 1816 has a printed list of London banks at the front which gives 'Austen, Maunde, Austen & Co.'. I think it reasonable to assume the second Austen is Frank.

2. See Mrs Austen's account of this in a letter to Jane Leigh-Perrot, 4 Jan. 1820: 'from the unfortunate spring of 1816 poor Henry has had hardly anything for himself. – Frank also was so much a loser that he was unable to make me any remittance.' *AP*, p. 264, corrected text from Deirdre Le Faye's private transcript. James continued to give £50 a year, and there was no rent to pay, and free firewood supplied by Edward. In 1820, after the death of James and the settling of Edward's

case, he was allowing his mother £200 a year.

I have not been able to trace any will made for Eliza; if she died intestate, her estate would have gone to her husband.

3. JA reports this to CEA in her letter of 8 Sept. 1816.

4. Caroline Austen, *Reminiscences*, p. 48.

5. Deirdre Le Faye gives Henry's stipend and the date of his appointment, *A Family Record*, p. 212.

6. She does not mention being unwell, but Henry's biographical note reads: 'the symptoms of a decay, deep and incurable, began to shew themselves in the commencement of 1816'.

7. The novelist Mary Brunton described the regime during her visit to Cheltenham in 1815.

8. Caroline Austen, *My Aunt Jane Austen*, p. 8.

9. Reginald Farrer, 'Jane Austen', *Quarterly Review*, July 1917, quoted at length by Brian Southam in Vol. II of *Jane Austen: The Critical Heritage*; this quote from p. 270.

10. Anne Elliot is the second daughter of Sir Walter Elliot, a vain and foolish baronet, a widower with no son; the Somerset estate will go to a cousin, William Elliot. Eight years before the story opens, Anne had been engaged to a young naval officer, Wentworth; her mother's friend Lady Russell had advised her to break off the engagement on the grounds that he had no fortune, and she had unhappily done so. Eight years later, her younger sister Mary has married a neighbouring land-owner, Charles Musgrove; Anne is slighted by all the family, her looks are fading, and she deeply regrets breaking her engagement.

Sir Walter is obliged to curtail his expenses and decides to let his house to Admiral Croft and move to Bath for a season. Anne goes to stay with Mary and becomes part of the large Musgrove family party. Mrs Croft turns out to be Captain Wentworth's sister, and he is introduced to the Musgroves; he has made a fortune in prize money, and is now a most desirable husband. He and Anne meet, with shrinking unhappiness on her side and an apparent indifference on his; his attentions are all for the two pretty Musgrove sisters, and there is a general assumption he will marry one of them.

A party is made up to visit Lyme Regis, where Wentworth's friend Captain Harville is staying; he is mourning for his sister, who has died young, and consoling her fiancé, Captain Benwick. In Lyme, Louisa Musgrove falls from the Cobb and seems to be seriously injured;

Wentworth blames himself – they had been fooling about on the steps – and realizes everyone expects him to marry her should she recover. Anne joins her father and sister in Bath; they are both somewhat in the power of a flattering widow, Mrs Clay, daughter of the family lawyer, who accompanies them. Young Mr Elliot turns up; he has noticed Anne at Lyme and been struck by her appearance. Lady Russell encourages his attentions to Anne, but Anne remains doubtful about him. News comes that Louisa is better, and that she and Benwick are now engaged. Wentworth appears in Bath; he becomes jealous of Mr Elliot's attentions to Anne. She learns from an old friend that he is a person of bad character; and soon he and Mrs Clay both prove themselves such. When Wentworth proposes to Anne again, she joyfully agrees to marry him at last.

11. See R. W. Chapman, 'Jane Austen's Text', *TLS*, 13 Feb. 1937, p. 116.

12. JA to Fanny Knight, 13 Mar. 1817. It is a relief to know that Harriet survived the medical treatment and the illness, and lived another fifty years.

13. Dickens was five in 1817. The Dickens family home in Portsmouth must, incidentally, have been rather like the Price household in *Mansfield Park*; they left for London in 1816. As it happens, monologues were in the air; Dickens was later greatly influenced by the actor Charles Mathews (1776–1835), who devised and performed 'monopolylogues' on stage, impersonating a series of characters with great brilliance. He began these in 1808, but they did not become famous until around 1817. And although JA saw Mathews perform in London in 1811 and 1814, the first time at least was in a Molière adaptation, and it is unlikely that she ever heard him do his solo performances. Her credit is all her own.

14. Caroline sets this visit in Mar. rather than Apr., but it does not seem to fit with other events and is more likely, I think, to have taken place after CEA's return from her uncle's funeral in Berkshire.

15. She gave it to a friend, James Carter, and it was still in the possession of his granddaughter in 1926, when she had it published in *The Times*. Now in the Pierpont Morgan Library. All this from R. W. Chapman's notes to his edition of Jane Austen's letters, supplemented by Deirdre Le Faye's notes in her edition, and research by Robin Vick, who has established Anne Sharp's place and year of birth from the 1851 census: London, 1776.

24 COLLEGE STREET

1. James Austen to James-Edward Austen, 12 June 1817, cited in George Holbert Tucker, *A Goodly Heritage*, p. 111–12. The words 'an extraordinary circumstance in her complaint' suggest that Lyford did diagnose a specific illness. Cancer would be expected to produce pain, and would be likely to go unnamed.
2. Charles's diaries are in the National Maritime Museum, Greenwich (AUS/109).
3. This is Margaret Anne Doody's persuasive conjecture in her 1993 edition of *Catharine and Other Writings*.
4. The comic verses 'Venta', dated 15 July 1817, were said by Henry in his biographical note to have been written by Jane on 'the day preceding her death'. I agree with Chapman that it seems unlikely she would have produced the six stanzas even three days before her death. He suggests they might be James's lines, although it seems equally unlikely he would be writing comic verse while his sister lay dying. Chapman points out that neither the *Memoir* of 1870 nor the *Life* of 1813 makes any mention of them. He did, however, print them among the *Minor Works*, p. 451–2.
5. So he told Mrs Austen, who passed it on to Anna in a letter cited by Deirdre Le Faye in *A Family Record*, p. 230.
6. CEA to Fanny Knight, 20 July 1817.
7. CEA's letter of 20 July speaks of her appearance as she lies in the coffin. When Cassandra died in 1845, her nephew James-Edward Austen told his sister Anna that her coffin in the dining room prevented the assembled family from eating there, obliging them to take their meals in the drawing room. Of the two front rooms at College Street (now made into one, but then separate), both low ceilinged, one is about 10 ft by 15 ft, with a sashed bow window; the other is slightly larger, with windows front and back.
8. Eliza Chute's diary for 24 July records 'fine pleasant' weather.
9. 'Candour' did not mean what it means today, as R. W. Chapman explained in his note 'Miss Austen's English' in Vol. I of his 1923 edition of the novels. It was defined by Dr Johnson as 'free from malice; not desirous to find faults' and used by JA herself in *Pride and Prejudice* to mean 'to take the good of every body's character and make it still better, and say nothing of the bad'.

That Jane Austen lived by the highest Christian values of self-abnegation and charity needs no spelling out; equally, the three prayers she wrote for herself, carefully composed as they are, are also entirely conventional, and indicate that her faith was calm rather than questing. As Henry wrote at the end of his biographical note, 'her opinions accorded strictly with those of our Established Church'.

25 POSTSCRIPT

1. Although the title-page bears the date 1818, they were ready for sale at the end of Dec. 1817. It was a four-volume edition costing twenty-four shillings.
2. Both cited by Deirdre Le Faye, *A Family Record*, pp. 234–5.
3. He had printed 1,750 copies.
4. Caroline Austen, *Reminiscences*, p. 57.
5. Eliza Chute to Emma Smith, letter of 1828, quoted by Maggie Lane, *Jane Austen's Family through Five Generations*, p. 210.
6. James-Edward Austen-Leigh, *A Memoir of Jane Austen*, p. 117.
7. Lewes writing in 1859, cited by Brian Southam in his introduction to Vol. II of *Jane Austen: The Critical Heritage*, p. 21.
8. Cited by Southam in Vol. II of *Jane Austen: The Critical Heritage*, p. 18.
9. Henry Austen to Richard Bentley, 24 July 1832, British Library Add. MSS 46611, ff. 305.
10. James-Edward Austen-Leigh, *A Memoir of Jane Austen*, pp. 11–12.
11. Mary Dorothea Knatchbull married at nineteen Edward Knight the younger – they were not related by blood, but connected through the marriage of Fanny (his sister) to Sir Edward Knatchbull (her father), which was one of the reasons for his opposition to the marriage. The couple settled at Chawton Manor and were very happy but for the rift with her father. He finally agreed to see her again after ten years, and the next year she died in childbirth. Edward Knight then married Adela Portal and fathered a second large family.
12. Information from Joan Corder's unpublished thesis of 1953, 'Jane Austen's Kindred' at the College of Arms, London. Of the four children of Charles's grandson Charles John, the eldest (another Charles John), born in 1881, started work as a bricklayer and moved on to driving the bread van because he liked horses; he died in 1905, leaving a son

Geoffrey, who became a salesman for Morris Motors and had no children. Francis, the grocer's assistant, was born in 1887 and died unmarried in 1916. Edith, born in 1884, made a good career for herself teaching in schools, mostly in the West Country, and aware of her connection with Jane Austen; she died in 1949. The youngest boy, Herbert, born in 1889, was apprenticed to the printing trade, served in both world wars, married in 1915 and was proprietor of the Eastgate Press in Bridgwater in 1952. He told Joan Corder that he had in his possession 'the Davenport which belonged to Jane Austen and a family tree going back to 1500 and some (crested) silver'. It was his son who emigrated to Argentina, and his daughter Margaret, born in 1918, who married Melvin Greengrass of New York in 1945.

13. 'my garden is also a constant object of interest': CEA to Philadelphia Whitaker, 6 Feb. 1833, *AP*, p. 289.
14. R. W. Chapman, *Facts and Problems*, p. 67.
15. Caroline Austen, *My Aunt Jane Austen*, p. 10.
16. The words are taken from a letter to *The Times* of 12 Feb. 1926, written by Mrs Creaghe-Howard of Ottery St Mary about Miss Sharp. 'My aunt Miss Middleton [1817–94] knew her well and often spoke of her,' she explained. 'From what she said I gather that Miss Sharp was a clever, rather dominant woman, much thought of in Everton society of her day. She was very reticent about her early life before coming to Liverpool, and also made a mystery of her age.' Miss Middleton is mentioned in Anne Sharp's will.
17. Henry's account at Hoare's Bank actually shows payments to 'Mr Perigord' on 26 Mar. (£5) and 12 July (£20); the payment on 7 Dec. (£10) is to Mrs Perigord. Later payments are sometimes to 'M Perigord', or to 'Mrs M Perigeux'. I suspect the variations are clerks' errors, and all the payments are really to Madame Perigord.
18. All these payments can be seen in CEA's account with Hoare's Bank.
19. Cassandra's will appears in *Jane Austen Society Report* (1969), p. 106.
20. I have been unable to trace the date or place of death of either Madame Bigeon or Madame Perigord.
21. Mary Augusta Austen-Leigh, *James-Edward Austen-Leigh, a Memoir by His Daughter* (1911), p. 164.
22. Caroline Austen, *Reminiscences*, p. 65.
23. James-Edward Austen-Leigh to Anna Lefroy, 29 Mar. 1845, *AP*, p. 294.
24. According to Maggie Lane, *Jane Austen's Family through Five Generations*,

NOTES

p. 231, the destruction of the letters angered Sir Francis's daughter Catherine, who had some of her aunt's intelligence and spirit. Married to John Hubback, who became insane, she supported herself and her children by writing novels, first 'finishing' *The Watsons* and going on to write nine more original ones. In her fifties she went out to California to help one of her sons, and died in America.

25. Lord David Cecil, *A Portrait of Jane Austen* (1978), p. 10.
26. Barry Roth and Joel Weinsheimer, *An Annotated Bibliography of Jane Austen Studies 1952–1972* (1973).

'An African Story' from Fanny Austen's Pocket-book, 1809: Centre for Kentish Studies U951 F24/6.

Short Bibliography

To list all the studies of Jane Austen's work, the books, the articles, the prefaces read over the years, would be ridiculous. Similarly, the works of her contemporaries – novels, plays, letters and essays – which I began to read systematically in the early 1970s, when researching a book on Mary Wollstonecraft, are not listed here; the notes should sufficiently indicate references to them. This bibliography is therefore a short and basic one.

Unpublished material

In the Hampshire Record Office: the Austen-Leigh Archive; poems of James Austen; diaries of Mrs James Austen; letters of Eliza de Feuillide on microfilm; diaries and letters of Mrs William Chute and her mother; Heathcote papers

In the British Library: the letter-book of Tysoe Saul Hancock; the Hastings papers; letters from Henry Austen to Richard Bentley; letters of Sir Francis Austen and Charles Austen

At Hoare's Bank: ledgers relating to accounts held by members of the Austen family and by Philadelphia Hancock

In the Kent County Archives: diaries and letters of Lady Knatchbull (Fanny Austen, later Knight)

Archives du Ministère des Affaires Etrangères, Quai d'Orsay, L 20

At the College of Arms, London: thesis by Joan Corder, 'Jane Austen's Kindred' (1953)

Papers in possession of Mr Alwyn Austen

Hampstead Burial Register

Caplan, Clive, 'The Military Career of Captain Henry Thomas Austen of the Oxfordshire Regiment of Militia, 1793–1801', forthcoming issue of *Persuasions* (magazine of the Jane Austen Society of North America)

Published material

Austen, Henry, 'Biographical Note', prefaced to first edition of *Northanger Abbey* and *Persuasion* (1818). He revised it and added a little extra information for Richard Bentley's edition in 1833

Brydges, Sir S. E., *Autobiography* (1834)

[Austen-Leigh, James-Edward, but published anonymously as] 'by a Sexagenarian', *Recollections of the Early Days of the Vine Hunt* (1865)

Caroline Austen, *My Aunt Jane Austen, a Memoir*, written in 1867 and published by the Jane Austen Society in 1952
—*Reminiscences*, written in the 1870s and published by the Jane Austen Society in 1986

Austen-Leigh, James-Edward, *A Memoir of Jane Austen* (1870), the first biography, with material from his sisters Anna Lefroy and Caroline Austen

Pingaud, Léonce, *Un agent secret sous la Révolution et l'Empire: Le Comte d'Antraigues* (Paris, 1894)

Hill, Constance, *Jane Austen, Her Homes and Her Friends* (1904)

Hubback, J. H., and Edith C., *Jane Austen's Sailor Brothers* (1906)

Bigg-Wither, R. F., *Materials for a History of the Wither Family* (1907)

Austen-Leigh, William, and Knight, George Montague, *Chawton Manor and Its Owners* (1911)

Austen-Leigh, William, and Austen-Leigh, R. A., *Jane Austen, Her Life and Letters, a Family Record* (1913). An edition with further hand-written notes by R. A. Austen-Leigh is held in the HRO; and see Le Faye, below

Austen-Leigh, Mary Augusta, *Personal Aspects of Jane Austen* (1920)

Chapman, R. W. (ed.), *The Manuscript Chapters of* Persuasion (1926)
—*The Watsons, a Fragment* (1927)
—*Works of Jane Austen*, 6 vols. (1923–54)
—*Jane Austen's Letters to Her Sister Cassandra and Others*, 2 vols. (1932)
—*Jane Austen: Facts and Problems* (1948)

Tompkins, J. M. S., *The Popular Novel in England* (1932)

Jenkins, Elizabeth, *Jane Austen: A Biography* (1938)

Lascelles, Mary, *Jane Austen and Her Art* (1939)

Harding, D. W., *Regulated Hatred: An Aspect of the Work of Jane Austen* (1940; printed in *Scrutiny*, viii, 4)

Leavis, Q. D., *A Critical Theory of Jane Austen's Writings* (1941–2; printed in *Scrutiny*, x, 1, 2 and 3)

Austen-Leigh, R. A. (ed.), *Austen Papers, 1704–1856* (1942)

Jane Austen Society Reports from 1949 to 1996

Mudrick, Marvin, *Jane Austen: Irony as Defense and Discovery* (1952)

Trilling, Lionel, *The Opposing Self* (1955)

Southam, Brian, *Jane Austen's Literary Manuscripts* (1964)
—*Critical Essays on Jane Austen* (1969)
—*Jane Austen, The Critical Heritage* (Vol. I, 1968; Vol. II, 1987)

Laski, Marghanita, *Jane Austen and Her World* (1969)

Abbé Michel Devert, 'Le Marais de Gabarret et de Barbotan', *Bulletin de la Société de Borda* (1970)

Hodge, Jane Aiken, *The Double Life of Jane Austen* (1972)

Butler, Marilyn, *Jane Austen and the War of Ideas* (1975)

Hardy, Barbara, *A Reading of Jane Austen* (1975)

Cecil, Lord David, *A Portrait of Jane Austen* (1978)

Piggott, Patrick, *The Innocent Diversion* (1979)

Gilson, David, *A Bibliography of Jane Austen* (1982)

Tucker, G. H., *A Goodly Heritage – a History of Jane Austen's Family* (1983)

Lane, Maggie, *Jane Austen's Family* (1984)
—*Jane Austen and Food* (1995)

Tanner, Tony, *Jane Austen* (1986)

Grey, J. David, *The Jane Austen Handbook* (1986)

Honan, Park, *Jane Austen: Her Life* (1987)

Abbé Michel Devert, 'La Dame du Marais', *Bulletin de la Société de Borda* (1988)

Le Faye, Deirdre, *Jane Austen: A Family Record* (1989)
—(ed.), *Jane Austen's Letters* (1995)

Wilson, Margaret, *Almost Another Sister* (1990)

Nicolson, Nigel, *The World of Jane Austen* (1991)

Collins, Irene, *Jane Austen and the Clergy* (1994)

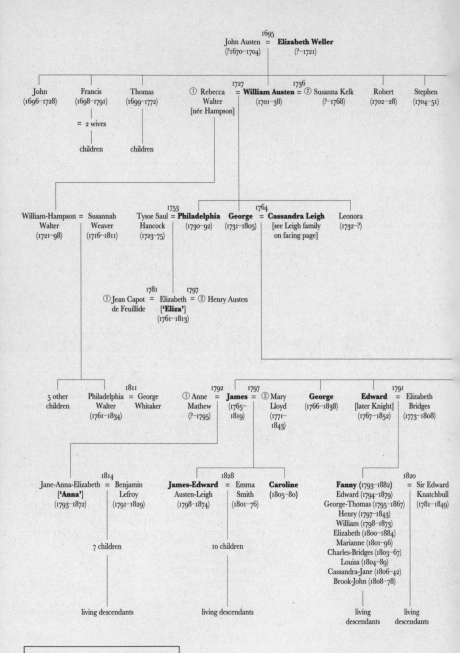

John Austen = **Elizabeth Weller**
(?1670–1704) (?–1721)
1695

John (1696–1728) | Francis (1698–1791) | Thomas (1699–1772) | ① Rebecca Walter [née Hampson] = **William Austen** (1701–38) = ② Susanna Kelk (?–1768) | Robert (1702–28) | Stephen (1704–51)
1727   1736

= 2 wives

children   children

William-Hampson Walter (1721–98) = Susannah Weaver (1716–1811) | Tysoe Saul Hancock (1723–75) = **Philadelphia** (1730–92) | George (1731–1805) = **Cassandra Leigh** [see Leigh family on facing page] | Leonora (1732–?)
1753   1764

① Jean Capot de Feuillide = Elizabeth ['**Eliza**'] (1761–1813) = ② Henry Austen
1781   1797

5 other children | Philadelphia Walter (1761–1834) = George Whitaker | ① Anne Mathew (?–1795) = **James** (1765–1819) = ② Mary Lloyd (1771–1843) | **George** (1766–1838) | **Edward** [later Knight] (1767–1852) = Elizabeth Bridges (1773–1808)
1811   1792   1797   1791

Jane-Anna-Elizabeth ['**Anna**'] (1793–1872) = Benjamin Lefroy (1791–1829) | **James-Edward** Austen-Leigh (1798–1874) = Emma Smith (1801–76) | **Caroline** (1805–80) | **Fanny** (1793–1882) = Sir Edward Knatchbull (1781–1849)
1814   1828   1820

Edward (1794–1879)
George-Thomas (1795–1867)
Henry (1797–1843)
William (1798–1873)
Elizabeth (1800–1884)
Marianne (1801–96)
Charles-Bridges (1803–67)
Louisa (1804–89)
Cassandra-Jane (1806–42)
Brook-John (1808–78)

7 children   10 children

living descendants   living descendants   living descendants | living descendants

**A concise family tree showing the
members of Jane Austen's family
mentioned in this book**

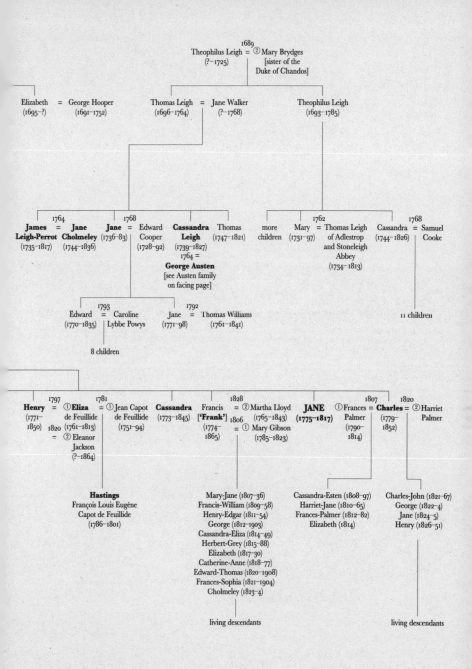

1689
Theophilus Leigh = ② Mary Brydges
(?–1725) [sister of the
Duke of Chandos]

Elizabeth = George Hooper   Thomas Leigh = Jane Walker   Theophilus Leigh
(1695–?)   (1691–1752)   (1696–1764)   (?–1768)   (1693–1785)

1764   1768   1762   1768
James = **Jane**   **Jane** = Edward   **Cassandra**   Thomas   more   Mary = Thomas Leigh   Cassandra = Samuel
Leigh-Perrot **Cholmeley** (1736–83) Cooper   **Leigh**   (1747–1821)   children   (1731–97) of Adlestrop   (1744–1826)   Cooke
(1735–1817) (1744–1836)   (1728–92)   (1739–1827)   and Stoneleigh
                                 1764 =   Abbey
                         George Austen   (1734–1813)
                         [see Austen family
                         on facing page]

      1793   1792
Edward = Caroline   Jane = Thomas Williams   11 children
(1770–1835) Lybbe Powys   (1771–98) (1761–1841)

    8 children

Henry = ① **Eliza** = ① Jean Capot   **Cassandra**   Francis = ② Martha Lloyd   **JANE** ① Frances = **Charles** = ② Harriet
(1771– 1797 de Feuillide 1781 de Feuillide   (1773–1845)   ['**Frank**'] 1828 (1765–1843)   (**1775–1817**) Palmer 1807 (1779– 1820 Palmer
1850) (1761–1813) (1751–94)   (1774– 1806 = ① Mary Gibson   (1790– 1852)
= ② Eleanor 1820   1865)   (1785–1823)   1814)
Jackson
(?–1864)

Hastings   Mary-Jane (1807–36)   Cassandra-Esten (1808–97)   Charles-John (1821–67)
François Louis Eugène   Francis-William (1809–58)   Harriet-Jane (1810–65)   George (1822–4)
Capot de Feuillide   Henry-Edgar (1811–54)   Frances-Palmer (1812–82)   Jane (1824–5)
(1786–1801)   George (1812–1903)   Elizabeth (1814)   Henry (1826–51)
                       Cassandra-Eliza (1814–49)
                       Herbert-Grey (1815–88)
                       Elizabeth (1817–30)
                       Catherine-Anne (1818–77)
                       Edward-Thomas (1820–1908)
                       Frances-Sophia (1821–1904)
                       Cholmeley (1823–4)

                       living descendants   living descendants

Index

Page numbers in italics indicate illustrations on pages cited; *ill. 1* and *ill. 2* indicate illustrations included in the groups of illustrations between pp. 76 and 77, and pp. 236 and 237, respectively.
Titles of works of literature are listed under the names of their authors.

Addison's disease 289
Adlestrop, Gloucestershire 44, 199
'African Story' 291−4, 332
Alton, Hampshire 205, 217, 264, 334; bank 188, 209, 257; Fair 219, 259; victory celebrations 244
Amis, Kingsley 229−30
Angier, Mr: attempts to cure Lord Lymington's stammer 89
Antigua 291
Armstrong, Miss 180
Arne, Thomas: *Artaxerxes* 244, 334
Ashe, Hampshire 96, 97, 116, 131, 248
Austen, Alwyn xiii−xiv
Austen, Anna (*1793−1872*; later Lefroy; niece of JA; daughter of James): birth 83; childhood 107−8, 129, 136, 179, 191, 193, 198; youth 214−15; character 193; first engagement 215−17, 223, 245; view of *Mansfield Park* 228−9; JA's advice to on writing 245; marriage

246−7; after 259, 264, 267, 279; writes of Austens 35, 111, 136, 144, 171, 214−15, 334; describes Steventon rectory 108
Austen, Anne (née Mathew; first wife of James): meets James 78; married life 80, 81, 97; death 107
Austen, Caroline (niece of JA; daughter of James) 181, 191, 197, 258, 259, 260, 263, 276, 278, 279, 284, 286, 313, 318, 321, 323, 325; describes Chawton Cottage 212−13; describes Anna's wedding 246−7; describes JA during her last illness 265, 267
Austen, Cassandra (*1739−1827*; née Leigh; mother of JA) *ill. 1*; family and early life 11−12, 174; character 11, 12, 143, 179, 223; marriage 12, 20−21, 22−23; in JA's childhood 1−2, 3−4, 5−8, 24−31, 34−5, 38, 39, 46, 296, 297; running school 21, 24−5, 62; verses by 26, 105, 179;

Austen, Cassandra – *cont.*
mother of adults 83, 128, 143; hypochondria 145–8; visits Bath (1799, 149–50, 151, 152; 1800, 154); leaves Steventon 170–73; in Bath 173, 174–5, 178–9; travels 178, 180–81; widowed 190; finances 190, 335; subsequent life 191–2, 198, 200–201, 209; at Chawton 211, 212–15, 222–23, 247–8, 267, 282; attitude to JA's writing 228, 254; in JA's last illness 270, 271; death 282

Austen, Cassandra (niece of JA; daughter of Charles) 246, 259

Austen, Cassandra Elizabeth (*1773–1845*; sister of JA) *ill. 1, 2*; childhood 1, 2, 5, 6, 8, 24–5, 33, 34–5, 39, 42; boarding schools 34–5, 38, 43–4; youth 61, 62, 104, 108, 112, 114; character 214; engagement 81; death of Tom Fowle 126–7; adult life 136, 143–5, 148–9, 173, 181–84, 190, 191, 192, 194–5, 197–8, 202, 207, 209, 211, 259; relationship with JA 197–8, 213–14, 223; at Chawton 213–15, 237, 259, 283; attitude to JA's writings 229, 263, 331; in JA's last illness 267, 268–9, 270, 271–2; at JA's death 274, 275; acts following 139, 276, 277, 281; later life 283–85; death 285–6, 338; funeral 285–6; will 284–5; JA's letters to 101–102, 114–15, 116–19, 120, 124–7, 132, 137–8, 144–5, 148, 171, 172, 173–4, 180, 192, 202–203, 204, 209–10, 220, 222, 223–4; destroys JA's letters 4, 124, 171, 284

Austen, Cassandra Jane (niece of JA; daughter of Edward) 202

Austen, Catherine (niece of JA; daughter of Frank) 284, 340–41

Austen, Charles John (*1779–1852*; brother of JA) *ill. 1*, 136, 170, 181–2, 190, 196, 219, 222, 264; birth 26; childhood 34, 45, 63, 83; youth 109, 200; character 196; naval career 83, 106, 118, 146 (shipwreck and following years 257; later years 283); first marriage and family 196–7, 237, 243; widowed 245; in JA's last illness 270, 271; second marriage and later career 283; death 283; descendants 283, 339–40

Austen, Edward (*1767–1852*; from 1812 Knight; brother of JA) *ill. 1*; childhood 3, 24–5, 30, 297; adopted by Knights *ill. 1*, 27, 39; youth 44, 45, 63; character 39, 194; estates and family 39, 194–5; marriage 76, 78, 80; married life 109, 125–6, 133, 134–6, 138, 148, 149, 151, 164, 165, 204–5, 207, 209, 298; widowed 208–9; life as widower 213, 218–19, 238, 239, 243; inherits from Knights 238–9; law suit over inheritance 246, 281, 335; demolishes Steventon rectory 278; death 282

Austen, Edward (from 1812 Knight; nephew of JA; son of Edward) 209, 278, 283, 286, 339

Austen, Eleanor (née Jackson; second wife of Henry) 278

Austen, Elizabeth (née Weller; great-grandmother of JA) 12–14

Austen, Elizabeth (of Tonbridge; later Butler-Harris) 104

Austen, Elizabeth (née Hancock; later Austen) *see* Elizabeth Hancock

Austen, Elizabeth (*1773–1808*; née Bridges; wife of Edward) *ill. 2*; early life 76; character 136; engagement 76; marriage 80; married life 81,

109, 133, 135, 138, 145, 147, 150, 164, 165, 194, 202, 207–8, 295–6; opinion of JA 136; death 139, 208–9

Austen, Elizabeth (from 1812 Knight; niece of JA; daughter of Edward) 208, 243

Austen, Fanny (née Palmer; first wife of Charles): marriage 196–7; in England 237, 243; death 245

Austen, Fanny (1793–1882; later Knight, then Lady Knatchbull; niece of JA; daughter of Edward) birth 83; childhood 135, 150, 164, 191–2, 195, 202, 205, 207–8, 321; and Mary Gibson 198–200; and cousin Eliza 211, 237, 238; mother's death 208, 211; subsequent life 211, 217, 219, 237–8, 247; on change of name to Knight 238–9; at Chawton with JA 240, 259; marriage 282; JA's letters to 261, 264–5; diaries 191, 195, 199, 202, 205, 207–8, 238 (describing JA 133, 136–7, 290; on Henry's bank failure 258)

Austen, Fanny (1821–1904; niece of JA; daughter of Frank) destroys JA's letters 4, 287

Austen, Francis (1698–1791; great-uncle of JA) 296; career 14, 15, 16, 20; entertains JA and family 61; death 83

Austen, Francis (1774–1865; brother of JA) ill. 1, 2; childhood 8, 28–9, 40; naval school 3–4, 62; appearance 109, 286; youth 126; character 196; naval career 30, 62–63, 83, 97, 104, 106, 118, 146, 148, 173, 190, 196, 219, 283, 284, 287, 323, 329; engagement 136, 190; relations with JA 196; proposes sharing house in

Southampton with mother and sisters 198; first marriage 190, 196, 198–200, 207; absent at birth of first child 204; first son 215, 216; finances 257; second marriage 283; death 287

Austen, Revd George (1731–1805; father of JA) ill. 1, 2; early life 14, 18, 27; character 30, 62; ordination and career 19–20; marriage and children 12, 20–21, 22–23, 26; in JA's childhood 1, 2–3, 5, 7, 8–10, 24–30; advice to son on departure 30, 62; finances 5, 8–9, 10, 20, 61–3, 296, 299; runs school 21, 24–6, 30; library 30, 68–9, 172; and niece Eliza 61–2, 80; father of adults 62, 67, 121, 129, 146–7, 154; and JA's writings 67–9, 123–4, 169; closes school 122; leaves Steventon 170–73; in Bath 174–5, 179; travels 178, 180–81; death 188–90; trustee of Antigua plantation 291

Austen, George (1766–1838; brother of JA) 7–8, 194, 297–8; birth 21, 23; childhood 27–8

Austen, George (1795–1867; from 1812 Knight; nephew of JA; son of Edward) 209, 229

Austen, Harriet (née Palmer; second wife of Charles) marriage 283

Austen, Harriet (niece of JA; daughter of Charles) illness 257, 264, 337

Austen, Henry Thomas (1771–1850; brother of JA) ill. 1; childhood 3, 24–5, 30, 33; youth 39, 41, 45, 46, 47, 56, 57, 58, 63, 64, 66, 75, 80–81, 97, 104, 117–18, 306; college 55–6, 58–60, 83, 106, 118; poem by 136; character 166, 195–6, 244; military career 83, 105, 106, 118,

Austen, Henry Thomas – *cont.*
129, 146, 155, 166, 188, 312–13; in
Ireland 155; finances 118, 129, 190,
315–16; as banker 188, 191, 195,
219, 257, 316; bankrupt 257–8, 335;
and Warren Hastings 106–7,
188–9, 240; proposes to cousin
Eliza 106–7; engagement to Mary
Pearson 130, 195; marries Eliza
129–30; at Godmersham 135–6,
195; married life 135–6, 178, 180,
190–91, 192, 195–6, 204, 205, 206,
208, 211, 219, 225–6, 237–8, 322;
clerical career 83, 118, 258–9, 264,
278, 280, 315–16; and JA's writings
185, 220, 221, 223, 249, 261, 277,
280–81; view of *Mansfield Park* 229;
widowed 236, 238; as widower
239–40, 242–3, 244–5, 249; in
JA's last illness 269, 270; after JA's
death 4, 274, 275, 276, 310; second
marriage 278; subsequent life
280–81, 286; death 287; writes of
JA 68–9, 111, 113, 277, 281, 307
Austen, James (*1765–1819*; brother of
JA) *ill. 1*, 101, 140, 153, 312;
childhood 1, 3, 24–5, 296, 301;
college 26–7, 40; youth 30, 31, 33,
39, 41–2, 45, 54, 55, 57–8, 63–4,
77, 94; character 176 (JA's view of
203); clerical career 77–8, 80, 97,
102; first marriage 78, 80; widowed
107, 115; refused by cousin Eliza
127–8; second marriage 128–9,
147, 148, 164; takes over Steventon
parish 170–72, 176; Rector of
Steventon 184, 193–4, 208, 217,
218, 264, 268, 274, 275; on father's
death 190; view of JA's writing 218,
327; letter in JA's last illness
270–71, 338; death 278
   WRITINGS: *The Loiterer* 64–6,
305, 306–7; verses 193 (theatrical

prologues and epilogues 33, 41–42
57; on Tom Fowle's death 126–7;
on marriage to Mary 129; on home
176; on Selborne Hanger 218; on
JA 327)
Austen, Jane (*1775–1817*) *ill. 1*; family
11–23, 287; birth 1–3; christening
3–4; childhood 4–8, 24–33,
34–44, 45–9, 57–9, 61–3; reading
68–74; boarding schools 34–6,
38–9, 43–4; youth 76–7, 87–9, 95,
98–102, 103–5, 107–9, 110–13,
114–23; appearance 110–13;
character 175–7, 287–8
   ADULT LIFE: living at Steventon
124–6, 131–2, 133–4, 136–42,
143–8, 154; finances 133–4, 210–11,
221, 242, 260, 267; visits Bath,
148–52; reaction to leaving
Steventon 170–73, 175–6;
depression and period without
writing 169–70, 175–7; after move
to Bath 173–6, 178–92, 193; Harris
Bigg-Wither proposes 182–4; death
of father 192; after father's death
193, 198–205; in Southampton 202,
203–5, 206–11; on death of
Elizabeth Austen 208–9; after
move to Chawton 211, 212–21,
225–7, 237–41, 242–9, 257–9; last
illness 263–5, 267–9, 270–71,
289–90; death 272–4; funeral
274–5; will 268, 275; obituary 275,
338–9; grave 275–6
   RELATIONSHIPS: with father
67–8, 121; mother 143, 145–8, 223;
niece Anna 107, 245, 259; Mmes
Bigeon and Perigord 206, 238, 275,
285; sister Cassandra 197–8,
213–14, 223; brother Edward 80,
207; brother Charles 197; cousin
Eliza 9, 46–9; niece Fanny 240,
245, 259; brother Francis 196;

brother Henry 47, 118, 195, 220, 229, 238, 244; brother James 203, 218; Anne Lefroy 40, 41; Tom Lefroy 114–22; Martha Lloyd 77, 210; Anne Sharp 138–9

WRITINGS: early 31–33, 47–8, 63, 306–7; *Catharine* 82–3, 307, 309; *Evelyn* 80; *History of England* 67–8, 70; *Jack and Alice* 63, 305; *Lady Susan* 70, 84–6, 284, 309; *Lesley Castle* 66–7; *Love and Friendship* 48, 75, 150; *The Mystery* 58–9; for new nieces 83; *Plan of a Novel* 251–3, 284; *The Three Sisters* 80

LETTERS: to Fanny Austen 261, 264–5; to James-Edward Austen-Leigh 269; to Anne Sharp 268, 337; *see also under* Cassandra Austen (sister); published 282; and other papers, posthumous disposal 4, 282, 283–84, 286–7, 340

NOVELS: *Emma ill. 2*, 39, 42n, 102, 244, 248, 252–55, 262–3, 306–7 (dedication 249–50, *250*; in France 277–8; 'Opinions' on 253–4; publication 248, 249, 250, 261, 335; slave trade in 291); *Mansfield Park ill. 2*, 69, 86, 99, 102, 140, 142, 157, 158, 167, 170, 176–7, 195, 201–203, 228–36, 244, 329–31 (and Shakespeare 332; 'Opinions' on 228–40, 241; publication 244, 248, 249, 261, 335); *Northanger Abbey* (*Susan; Catherine*) 70, 92, 112–13, 123, 150, 156, 157, 167–8, 218, 321 (publishing negotiations 185, 210, 259, 310; published 277); *Persuasion ill. 2*, 102, 259–61, 261–3, 336–7 (MS 284; published 277); *Pride and Prejudice* (*First Impressions*) 70, 102, 103, 104, 107, 122, 123–4, 145, 156–7, 160–67, 169, 239–40, 319–20 (publication 222–24, 277,

281); *Sanditon* 265–7, 284; *Sense and Sensibility* (*Elinor and Marianne*) ill. 2, 39, 69, 109, 118–119, 122–24, 132, 141, 142, 156, 157–61, 211, 262, 315 (publication 220–22; reviews 221–22); *The Watsons* 140, 185–8, 193, 341; posthumous publication 277–8, 280–81; critical literature 288

VERSES: on death of Mrs Lefroy 41; on Frank's marriage 199–200; on birth of Frank's first son 215, *216*; on Winchester races 271–2, 338

Austen, John (great-grandfather of JA) 12

Austen, Leonora (aunt of JA) 14, 18, 21, 23

Austen, Louisa (niece of JA; daughter of Edward) 313, 331

Austen, Marianne (niece of JA; daughter of Edward) 208, 243

Austen, Martha (née Lloyd; second wife of Frank) *see* Martha Lloyd

Austen, Mary (née Gibson; first wife of Frank): engagement 190, 199; marriage 196; honeymoon 198–200; married life 202, 204–5, 207, 216, 219, 260; birth of first son 215, *216*; death 283

Austen, Mary (née Lloyd; second wife of James): character 31, 128–9, 164, 203; first comes to Steventon 77; moves to Ibthorpe 80; marriage 128–9, 143; first baby 147; moves to Steventon rectory 171; as James's wife 184, 191, 193–4, 202–203, 258; in JA's last illness 268, 270–74; widowed 278; death 285; diary entries (on husband 203; on death of Eliza 238; on death of JA *273*, 274); view of JA's writing 326

Austen, Mary-Jane (niece of JA; daughter of Frank) 259

Austen, Philadelphia (later Hancock; aunt of JA) *ill. 1*; early life 14–18, 81, 299; in India 16–19, 81; finances 5, 8–9, 52, 298; marriage 17–19, 21–22, 81–2; intimacy with Warren Hastings 18–22; returns to England 19, 21, 49–50; widowed 8, 50; on Continent with daughter 50–54, 60; in England (1765–6, 21–22; 1775–6, 2–3, 8–10, 49–50; 1786–7, 45, 46–7); illness and death 78–9

Austen, William (*1701–38*; grandfather of JA) 14

Austen, William (*1798–1873*; from 1812 Knight; nephew of JA; son of Edward) 269; Rector of Steventon, and marriage 278, 280

Austen-Leigh, Emma (née Smith) 279

Austen-Leigh, James-Edward (nephew of JA; son of James) birth 147; childhood and youth 148, 193, 217, 248, 263, 275; character 278–9; career 278–9; marriage 279; on JA's death 274, 275; later life 279, 280, 286; view of *Mansfield Park* 228, 330; comments on Miss Sharp, 139; letters to 338 (JA's, about writing 263–64; JA's last 269; father's, in JA's last illness 270–71, 338); *Memoir of JA* 4, 71, 111, 113, 219, 279, 280, 305, 308, 314

Bage, Robert 157, 318; *Hermsprong* 125, 141

Basingstoke, Hampshire 2, 77, 81, 95, 172, 184; Assembly Rooms 97, 104–5; Club 95; library 146; Mechanics' Institute 184; militia in 105, 166

Bath *ill. 2*, 80, 278; Assembly Rooms 173–4; JA's mother in, before marriage 12, 20, 174; Coopers'

home 34; visit (1799) 148–52; Austens move to (1801) 170–72; Austens living in 173–5, 178–9, 187, 190, 198, 200

Beaumont, Francis: *The Chances* (with John Fletcher) 57

beds, sharing 325–6

Benn, Miss (clergyman's sister) 213, 223, 259, 262

Bentley, Richard (publisher) 281

Bentley Church 280

Bermuda 196–7

Berquin, Arnaud: *L'Ami des Enfants* 47–8, 303

Berry, Mary 324, 334

Bessborough, Lady 222

Bickerstaffe, Isaac: *The Spoiled Child* 192; *The Sultan* 64, 306

Bigeon, Françoise: serving de Feuillides 130, 191, 206; death of Eliza 238; serves Henry Austen 239, 244–5, 249; visits France 258; in JA's will 275, 284–5; death untraced 340

Bigeon, Marie Marguerite (later Perigord) *see* Marie Perigord

Bigg, Alethea 77, 93–4, 96–7, 104, 116, 173, 182–84, 206–7, 229, 239, 253, 264, 269, 325

Bigg, Catherine (later Hill) 77, 93–5, 96–7, 147, 173, 182–4, 206–7; wedding 207, 325

Bigg, Elizabeth (later Heathcote) *see* Elizabeth Heathcote

Bigg-Wither, Harris: early life 94; proposes to JA 182–84; later life 184, 322

Bigg-Wither, Lovelace 93, 96, 182, 239

Blackall, Samuel 131–3

boarding schools 34–9, 43–4

Bolton, Thomas Orde, Lord 88

Bond, John 101, 312

Boswell, James 176; *Life of Johnson* 69, 146
Box Hill 98, 102, 253, 311
Brabourne, Lord 282
Bramston, Augusta 105, 241, 312
Bramston, Mary (née Chute) 94, 95, 97, 105, 182; and *Mansfield Park* 312
Bramston, Wither 95, 97, 182
breast cancer 78–9, 308
Bridges, Edward 322–3
Bridges, Elizabeth (later Austen) *see* Elizabeth Austen
British Critic 277
Brompton 195, 206
Brooke, Henry: *The Fool of Quality* 7
Brunton, Louisa, Countess of Craven 224, 329
Brunton, Mary 220, 324, 336; *Self-Control* 327–8
Brydges, Anne *see* Anne Lefroy
Brydges, Sir Egerton 313
Brydges, Mary 298
Burdett, Frances 239, 242, 333
Burdett, Sir Francis 239
Burney, Fanny 333–4; breast cancer 308; novels 97, 218 (*Cecilia* 74, 163; *Evelina* 150, 165)
Butt, Mary (Mrs Sherwood) 37, 301
Byron, George Gordon, sixth Baron 90, 92, 334; and Lord Portsmouth 90–91; poetry 262; *The Corsair* 244

Cadell, Thomas (publisher) 123–4, 169
Canterbury 133, 134, 135, 138, 166, 192; Gaol 243
Carlton House 227, 249
Carpenter, Thomas Edward 287
Cawley, Mrs (schoolmistress) 34–5, 37, 38, 39
Cecil, Lord David 287
Centlivre, Susannah: *The Wonder!* 57

Chamberlayne, Mrs (Bath acquaintance) 174
Chapman, R. W. 110, 266, 280, 286, 295
Chard, George 62
Charlotte, Princess 222, 227, 251
Château de Jourdan *ill. 1*, 53
Chawton, Hampshire 212–15, 325; benefice 118, 258, 315; Churchyard 282, 286; Cottage *ill. 2*, 209, 211, 212–15, 219–20, 222–23, 237, 238, 240, 244, 256, 281, 283, 286–7; House 194, 204–5, 239, 247; Library 286; Lodge 246; Manor 339; Park 240; law suit over ownership 246, 281, 335; after Henry's bankruptcy 257, 258, 335
Cheesedown Farm, Hampshire 29, 296
Chelmsford, Essex 106
Cheltenham 199, 259–60
Chesterfield, Philip Stanhope, fourth Earl of 54
Christmas celebrations 2, 135, 202–203, 317–18
Chute, Elizabeth (née Smith) *ill. 1*, 102; character 96, 97–8; marriage 96–7; adopts Caroline Wiggett 98; at The Vyne 98, 99, 101, 104, 148, 153–4, 164, 166, 264, 276, 279; diaries *98*, 182, 311; letters 153–4
Chute, Mary (later Bramston) *see* Mary Bramston
Chute, Thomas Vere *ill. 1*, 94–5, 96, 98, 99, 166, 248; character 311
Chute, William John, MP (formerly Lobb) *ill. 1*, 94–6, 98, 102, 104, 154, 164, 323
Clarence, William, Duke of 227–8
Clarke, James Stanier 249, 250–51
Cleland, John: *Fanny Hill* 15, 299
Clive, Robert 19

Cobbett, William 6
Coghile, Sir John 315
Cole, Hester (milliner) 14–15, 299
Compton, Lady (née Smith) 295
Cooke, Cassandra (née Leigh) 151, 296; *Battleridge* 151, 291
Cooke, Revd Samuel (godfather to JA) 296
Cooper, Edward (uncle of JA) 27
Cooper, Edward (cousin of JA) 24, 44, 118, 151, 202
Cooper, Jane (née Leigh; aunt of JA) 5, 34, 38, 296
Cooper, Jane (later Lady Williams; cousin of JA) childhood 33, 34, 38, 42, 43; youth 64, 77; marriage 81, 118, 143, 181; death 143, 167
Cope, Sir Zachary 289, 306
Cowley, Hannah 69; *Which is the Man?* 56, 57
Cowper, William 291; illness 176; poetry 69, 139–40, 146–7, 176, 204, 262; lines to Warren Hastings 305; *The Task* 139, 140
Craven, Charlotte 240
Craven, Countess of (Louisa Brunton) 226, 329
Crosby, Richard (publisher) 185, 210–11, 259

d'Antraigues, Comte Emmanuel Louis 225–6, 329
dancing 56–7, 103–5, 115–16
Darnell, Dorothy 286–7
Dawlish 178
Deane, Hampshire: benefice 5, 296; Deane Gate Inn 29; Deane House 94, 96, 116, 148, 239; parsonage 21, 77, 80, 128, 129, 147
de Feuillide, Elizabeth Capot (née Hancock; later Austen) *see* Elizabeth Hancock
de Feuillide, Hastings François Louis

Eugène Capot 45, 46, 52, 55, 60, 76, 79, 80, 130–31, 155; birth 54–5; death 188
de Feuillide, Jean François Capot 45, 46, 188; early career 51; marriage 51–2, 60; land drainage project 52–4, 55, 75; and French Revolution 75–6, 79, 80, 83–4; estates 75–6, 105, 189, 258, 312, 322; arrest and execution 84
de Saint-Huberty, Anne 224–6
de Staël, Anne Louise Germaine 243, 333–4
Dickens, Charles 4, 337
Digweed, Harry 92–93, 217
Digweed, Hugh 3, 101
Digweed, Jane (née Terry) 92, 215, 224, 254
Dorchester, Guy Carleton, Lord 87–8, 309–10
Dummer, Hampshire 92, 310

East, Gilbert 26, 160, 301, 320
East, Sir William 160, 320
East India Company 8–9, 16–17, 196, 219
Edgeworth, Maria: schools 37, 38; novels 69, 218, 223, 277 (*Belinda* 156)
Edinburgh Magazine 277
Edinburgh Review 255, 279
Egerton, Thomas (publisher) 220, 221, 222, 228, 244, 248–9, 277, 281
Eliot, George 280
Evelyn, Mr (Bath acquaintance) 174

Fables choisies 40, 41
Farnham, Surrey 280
Farrer, Reginald 229, 262
Fenton, Lavinia, Duchess of Bolton 88–9
Ferrier, Susan: *Marriage* 297
Fielding, Henry 69; *Tom Jones* 69, 117, 168, 315; *Tom Thumb* 58, 69

Fletcher John: *The Chances* (with Francis Beaumont) 57

Fowle, Charles 25, 114, 206

Fowle, Elizabeth (née Lloyd) 77, 202

Fowle, Fulwar-Craven 25, 33, 77, 206, 313–14

Fowle, Tom: youth 25, 33; engagement to Cassandra Austen 81; army chaplain 108, 114; death 126–7

Fowle, William 25, 33, 77

Fox, Charles 328

France: Le Marais (near Nérac) 52–4, 75, 79, 105, 175, 189; wars 105, 106, 108, 131, 178, 181–2, 189, 192, 196, 248, 322; victory celebrations 244; Eliza Hancock in (1778–84, 50–5; 1788, 60; 1790–91, 75–6; 1802, 189, 322); Bigeons visit in 1816 258; JA's novels in *ill. 2*, 277–8

Francklin, Thomas: *Matilda* 32–33, 302

Francis, Philip 302

French Revolution 50, 75–6, 79, 80, 83–4, 105, 130

Galigai de Concini, Eléonore 268

Gambier, Admiral James 146

Gard, Roger 230

Garrick, David 304, 307; *Bon Ton* 56, 58, 230, 309

George III, King 146; in 1795 riots 108–9; 73rd birthday celebrated in Hampshire 227

George IV, King (as Prince Regent) 196, 308; hated by JA 227; behaviour 227–8; dedication of *Emma* to *ill. 2*, 249–51

Gibson, Mary *see* Mary Austen

Gifford, William 249

Godmersham Park, Kent *ill. 2*, 133, 134–8, 139, 140, 145, 151, 170, 178, 188, 191–2, 194–5, 198–200, 202, 204, 206; described 134; ceremonies 134–5; theatricals 191–2; after death of Elizabeth Austen 207–9, 211, 237, 239, 243

Godwin, William 157, 320

Goethe, J. W. von: *Sorrows of Young Werther* 160

Goldsmith, Oliver: *History of England* 139, 318

Goodnestone Park, Kent 76, 126

Grant, Anne: *Letters from the Mountains* 224, 318, 328

Hackitt, Sarah (Mrs La Tournelle) 43, 44

Hackwood Park 88–9, 310

Hall, Mrs (clergyman's wife) 144–5

Ham, Elizabeth 36–7

Hamstall Ridware, Staffordshire 202

Hancock, Elizabeth (*1761–1813*; later de Feuillide, then Austen; Betsy, Eliza; cousin of JA, first wife of Henry) *ill. 1*; birth 19; childhood 20, 21, 22, 49–50; youth in England 3, 8–10, 45, 46–7; character 9, 46; relations with JA 9, 46–9; finances 8–9, 50; first marriage 45, 46–7, 51–3; as mother 9, 55, 188; in France (1778–84, 50–55; 1788, 60; 1790–91, 75–6; 1802, 189, 322); in England (1786) 55–60, 61–2; at Steventon (1790, 75; 1792, 80–84); mother's illness and death 78–80, 221, 324; widowed 84, 105; refuses Henry Austen 106–7; refuses James Austen 127–8; marries Henry 129–31; as Henry's wife 155, 178, 180, 188–9, 195, 206, 220, 225, 237–8; illness and death 236–7, 238, 240; Austens' view of 237, 317, 324; letters 127

Hancock, Philadelphia (née Austen; aunt of JA) *see* Philadelphia Austen

Hancock, Tysoe Saul 5, 8, 17–20, 21–23, 49–50
Hanson, Charles 91
Hanson, John (lawyer) 90–91, 102
Hanson, Laura 91
Hanson, Mary-Ann (later Lady Portsmouth) 91–2, 102
Hanway, Jonas 297
Harpsden 11, 151
Harvey, Richard 126
Harwood family 92–3, 148, 239, 315
Harwood, John 92–3; and Elizabeth Bigg 94, 96, 116, 239
Hastings, Elizabeth 18, 19
Hastings, George 18, 299–300; death 21, 23
Hastings, Warren *ill. 1*, 9, 18–20, 48, 49–50, 51, 52, 106, 219, 223, 240, 299–300; sent to India 17; intimacy with Mrs Hancock and putative father of Eliza 18–21; settles money on Eliza 22, 49–50; second marriage 22; trial 59, 106; Henry Austen approaches 106–7, 188–9, 240; on Eliza's second marriage 130; Cowper's poem to 305
Heathcote, Elizabeth (née Bigg) 96–7; moves to Manydown 77, 93; marriage 94, 116; widowed 182, 239; in Winchester 239, 248, 268, 270, 274
Heathcote, Revd William *ill. 1*, 94, 116
Heathcote, William (Jr) 217
Hicks, Michael 105, 312
Hill, Catherine *see* Catherine Bigg
Hill, Herbert 207, 324–5
Hoare's Bank 9, 285, 296, 316, 335, 340
Holder, James 93
Horsmonden 12, 13
Hubback, John 341

Huguenots 93, 120–21
Hurstbourne Park 89, 90–92

Ibthorpe, Hampshire 128, 129, 170, 173, 180
Ilchester Gaol 152
Imhoff, Mrs (later Hastings) 22
India 16–18, 21–2, 81–2
Ipswich 130–31
Ireland 115, 121–2; Henry in 155

Jackson, Eleanor (later Austen) *see* Eleanor Austen
James, Henry 137
Jane Austen Society 286
Jenkins, Elizabeth 286
Johnson, Samuel 40, 69–70, 150, 176, 315, 338; in JA's poem 41; *Rambler* 40, 64, 69, 70, 97, 153, 321
Jordan, Dora 192, 227, 244, 334
Jourdan, Château de *ill. 1*, 53

Kavanagh, Julia 280
Kempshott Hunt 308
Kempshott Park 87–8, 148, 310
Kentish Town Church 245
Kew, Elizabeth 99
Kintbury, Berkshire 206
Knatchbull, Catherine *see* Catherine Knight
Knatchbull, Sir Edward 282
Knatchbull, Lady *see* Fanny Austen
Knatchbull, Mary Dorothea 339
Knight, Caroline (née Portal) 278
Knight, Catherine (née Knatchbull) *ill. 1, 2*, 194, 212, 220, 317; honeymoon 27; adopts Edward Austen 39; JA's and Cassandra's rude jokes about 133; allowance to JA 133–4; death 238
Knight, Edward (formerly Austen) *see* Edward Austen
Knight, Major Edward 286

Knight, Thomas 27, 39, 296, 315

Laclos, Pierre-Choderlos de: *Les Liaisons Dangereuses* 84, 85
Lambert, Sir John 50, 51, 180, 303–4, 322
Lansdowne, third Marquis of 204
Lascelles, Mary 161, 187–8
Laverstoke House 93, 310
Le Faye, Deirdre xiii, 295, 297
Leavis, Q. D. 229
Lefroy, Anna (née Austen) *see* Anna Austen
Lefroy, Anne (née Brydges; wife of George) *ill. 2*, 46, 96–7; character 40; JA's poem to 41; and Tom's flirtatious affair with JA 121; match-making for JA 131–2; Straw Manufactory 153; death 189
Lefroy, Anne (niece of Benjamin): at Anna's wedding 246–7
Lefroy, Benjamin (son of George): engagement 217–18; marriage 246–7
Lefroy (Isaac Peter) George *ill. 2*, 40, 96–7, 117, 121
Lefroy, Thomas Langlois *ill. 2*, 183; JA meets 115, 116–18, 119; leaves Steventon 120–21; marriage and career 122; confesses to early love for JA 119
Leigh, Cassandra (later Austen; mother of JA) *see* Cassandra Austen
Leigh, Cassandra (later Cooke; daughter of Theophilus) *see* Cassandra Cooke
Leigh, James (uncle of JA) *see* James Leigh-Perrot
Leigh, Jane (later Cooper; aunt of JA) 12, 20, 27, 174
Leigh, Theophilus (Master of Balliol; great-uncle of JA) 11, 12, 27, 296

Leigh, Sir Thomas (Lord Mayor of London 1559) 11, 298
Leigh, Revd Thomas (*1696–1764*; grandfather of JA) 11, 12, 20, 174
Leigh, Revd Thomas, of Adlestrop (*1734–1813*) visits JA at school 44; estate improvements 199; at Stoneleigh Abbey 200–201
Leigh, Thomas (*1747–1821*; uncle of JA) 7, 8, 27–8, 194
Leigh-Perrot, James (uncle of JA) *ill. 2*, 5, 12, 20, 148, 149, 150, 151–3, 173, 201, 242, 257; death 267
Leigh-Perrot, Jane (née Cholmeley) *ill. 2*; school 35; married life 148, 173, 180, 257, 319, 320, 335; tried for shop-lifting 151–3; widowed 267; later life 279, 281, 282, 283
Lennox, Charlotte: *The Female Quixote* 150
Lewes, George Henry: on JA 279–80
Littleworth, John and Elizabeth 99, 110, 297
Lloyd, Elizabeth (later Fowle) 77, 202
Lloyd, Martha (later Austen; second wife of Frank) *ill. 2*, 129, 148, 151, 169, 170, 172; moves to Steventon 77; leaves for Ibthorpe 80; joins Austen household 198; with JA in Southampton 209–10; at Chawton 211, 213, 214, 250, 262, 282; marriage 283; death 285
Lloyd, Mary (later Austen; second wife of James) *see* Mary Austen
Loiterer, The 64–6, 304, 306
London: Hancocks in (1760s, 21–22; 1770s, 3, 8–9); 1792 riots 80; JA in 92, 125, 240, 243, 244, 245; Henry living in 92, 190–91, 192, 195, 206, 225–6, 227, 239, 244–5, 257, 334; theatres 192, 206, 244, 334, 337

Lyford, John (doctor) 116, 146, 189, 264; and JA's last illness 269, 270, 272, 338
Lyme Regis *ill. 2*, 178, 180–81
Lymington, Lord (later third Earl of Portsmouth) 89–92

Macaulay, Thomas Babington 279
MacKinnon, Sir Frank 334
Mackreth, Sir Robert 93, 310
Manydown House, Hampshire *ill. 2*, 77, 96, 97, 147, 173, 182–84, 198, 206
Mathew, Anne (later Austen; first wife of James) *see* Anne Austen
Mathew, General Edward 78
Mathews, Charles 337
Mitford, Mary Russell 113, 314
Monk Sherborne, Hampshire 8, 27, 194
More, Hannah: *Coelebs in Search of a Wife* 233, 332
Morning Chronicle 221
Murphy, Arthur: *The Way to Keep Him* 205
Murray, John 249, 250, 251, 258, 259; asks Scott for review 254; remainders JA's books 277, 335
Musgrave, Mrs (godmother to JA) 296

Napoleon 178, 192, 226, 244, 248
Nérac, France 53–4
Netley Abbey, Hampshire 205
Newhaven riots 106
Nibbs, George 291
Nibbs, James 291
North, Brownlow, Bishop of Winchester 258–9, 274
Norton, Grace (later Lady Portsmouth) 89–90, 91

Overton, Hampshire 77, 189

Oxford: school in 34–5; University 64–5, 117–18; militia 83, 166. *See also* St John's College

Palmer, Fanny (later Austen; first wife of Charles) *see* Fanny Austen
Palmer, Harriet (later Austen; second wife of Charles) *see* Harriet Austen
Pantheon Opera Theatre 206, 324
Papillon, Revd J. R. 264, 278, 316
Paris 50, 60, 64, 75–6
Pearson, Mary 118, 130, 195–6
Pearson, Sir Richard 118
Perceval, Spencer 226
Perigord, Marie Marguerite (née Bigeon): serving de Feuillides 130, 191, 206; marriage 191; taken to Chawton by JA 238; serves Henry Austen 239, 244–5; visits France 258; in Cassandra's will 285; subsequent Austen payments to 285, 340
Perigord, Pierre Frayté 191, 283
Pitt, William 80, 108–9
Portal, Adela 339
Portal, Benjamin 64
Portal, Caroline (later Knight) 278
Portal, Henry 93
Portal, John *ill. 1*, 116, 248, 278
Portal, Mrs John 271
Portal, Joseph 93
Portsmouth, third Earl 89–92
Portsmouth, Hampshire 105, 286; naval school 46, 106; Portsdown House 283, 286
Powlett, Charles 88–9, 97, 105, 153

Quarterly Review 249, 254, 255, 279

Radcliffe, Anne 151, 168; *Mysteries of Udolpho* 321
Rambler 40, 64, 69, 70, 97, 153, 321
Rennell, Thomas 274

Repton, Humphry 199–200, 201, 324
Richardson, Samuel: *Sir Charles Grandison* 68, 70–74, 72, 165
Rowling, Kent 125, 133, 134
Ryle, Gilbert 235

Salisbury and Winchester Journal 275
Saye and Sele, Lady (née Leigh) 201
Scadding family 152
Scott, Walter 254–5, 263, 279, 308, 335; novels 262, 277 (*Tales of My Landlord* 271; *Waverley* 247, 335); review of *Emma* 255–6
Selborne, Hampshire 1, 219, 227
Sevenoaks, Kent 14–16, 61
Seymour, William 185
Shadwell, Thomas: *The Libertine* 243, 334
Shakespeare, William, plays of 69, 135, 332 (*The Merchant of Venice* 231); French versions 50
Sharp, Anne 191–2, 194, 261–2, 337, 340; friendship with J A 138–9; opinions of J A's works 229, 241, 253–5; J A's last letter to 268, 337; gifts from Cassandra after J A's death 276, 284
Sherborne St John 97, 276
Sheridan, Richard 150, 154; attacks Warren Hastings 59; admires *Pride and Prejudice* 222–23; *The Critic* 303; *The Rivals* 41–3, 150, 276; *A Trip to Scarborough* 309, 334
Sherwood, Mrs (Mary Butt) 37, 301
Sidmouth 178
slave trade 227, 234, 291–4, 332–3
Smallbone, Daniel and Jane 99
Smith, Charlotte 307–8; novels by 68, 69, 70, 97, 307–8, 318 (*Emmeline* 70, 150; *Ethelinde* 70; *The Old Manor House* 70)
Smith, Elizabeth (later Chute) *see* Elizabeth Chute

Smith, Emma (later Mrs James-Edward Austen-Leigh) 279
Smith, Joshua 95–6
Smith, Sarah: letters 120, 315, 319
Somerset County Gaol 152
Southam, Brian 234, 309, 333
Southampton, Hampshire: school at 38; 1793 visit 104; Frank moves to 198; J A living at 198, 202, 203–4, 206–7, 211; with Martha in 1809 209–10
Southey, Robert 324
Spencer, Colonel Charles 106, 131, 146
Spencer, George, second Earl 146, 192
St John's College, Oxford 16, 20, 26–7, 35, 55–6, 59–60
Staples, Elizabeth 99
Stent, Mrs (friend of Mrs Lloyd) 184
Sterne, Laurence: *Tristram Shandy* 69
Steventon rectory *ill. 1*; J A's childhood in 1–4, 21, 23, 24–6, 28–33, 38, 40 (1786–7, 45–7); school 5, 24–6, 28–9, 31–2, 122; theatricals 32–33, 41–3, 57–8, 63–4, 107–8; 1800 damage 154–5; George Austens leave 170–73, 175–6; sale 172, 301, 321–3; James takes over 171–3, 176; James's tenure 181–2, 184, 193–4, 208, 209; Henry takes over 278; demolished 278; William Knight in new rectory 278, 280
Steventon village, Hampshire *ill. 1*, 1–4, 5, 7, 10, 24, 25, 29, 34, 176; benefice 5, 20, 296, 315–16; church of St Nicholas *ill. 1*, 2–3, 4, 10, 30; families near by 99–102; Manor 194
Stoneleigh Abbey, Warwickshire 11, 200–201, 324

Tanner, Tony 230, 332
Teignmouth 178
Terry family 92, 102
Terry, Jane (later Digweed) 92, 217, 223, 253
Terry, Michael: engagement to Anna Austen 92, 217
Terry, Robert 92
Terry, Stephen 92
Thomson, Hugh 280
Thomson, James 96; 'Nutting', *The Seasons* 200
Thrale, Cecilia and Harriet 37
Thrale, Hester 37, 296
Tilson, Frances 242
Tilson, James 131, 195, 242
Times, The 286-7
Tolstoy, Leo: *Anna Karenina* 159
Tonbridge, Kent 14, 16, 20
Tonbridge School 14, 20
Townley, James: *High Life Below Stairs* 64, 306
Trilling, Lionel 230
Tucker's Seminary, Weymouth 36
Tunbridge Wells 56

Vanbrugh, John: *The Relapse* 309
Vyne, The, Sherborne St John 94-5, 96-7, 98, 164, 276

Wallop, Coulson, Hon. *ill. 1*, 89, 104-5
Wallop, Newton, Hon. *ill. 1*, 89, 91
Walter, Philadelphia (cousin of JA) 46, 49, 56-7, 299; opinion of Austens and JA 61

Walter, William 14, 299
Warren, John 117-18
Watkins, Thomas 274
Waugh, Evelyn 137
Weymouth 178; boarding school 36
Whateley, Richard 279
White, Gilbert 1, 2, 218
White's Club 244
Wiggett, Caroline 311; childhood adoption 98-9, 264
Williams, Jane, Lady (née Cooper) *see* Jane Cooper
Williams, Sir Thomas: marriage 81, 181; naval career 118, 143
Willoughby, Cassandra 11
Winchester, Hampshire 95; Biggs at 239, 248; JA's last days in 268-9, 270-76; school 194, 205, 207, 217, 219, 276, 279; JA on schoolboys 212; races 271-2, 338
Winchester Cathedral: Chapter 322; 1800 musical event 154; JA's funeral 274; JA's grave 275-6, 279
Wollstonecraft, Mary 4; suicide attempt 160-61, 320; *Vindication of the Rights of Woman* 125, 140-41, 163, 318, 320
Woodforde, Revd James 298, 301, 313
Woodman, John (lawyer) 8, 9, 50, 52, 60
Worthing 192
Wye, Kent 209

Young, Arthur 36
Young, Bobbin 36

CLAIRE TOMALIN

CHARLES DICKENS: A LIFE

A major new biography of our greatest novelist, published for the 200th anniversary of his birth

Charles Dickens was a phenomenon. A demonically hardworking journalist, the father of ten children, a tireless walker and traveller, a supporter of liberal social causes, but most of all a great novelist – the creator of characters who live immortally in the English imagination: Sam Weller, Mr Pickwick, the Artful Dodger, David Copperfield, Little Nell, Lady Dedlock, Mrs Gamp, Pip, Miss Havisham and many more.

At the age of twelve he was sent by his affectionate but feckless parents to work in a blacking factory. By the time of his death in 1870 he drew adoring crowds to his public appearances, had met princes and presidents on both sides of the Atlantic, and had amassed a fortune. He was truly 'the inimitable', as he jokingly described himself. When he died, the world mourned, and he was buried – against his wishes – in Westminster Abbey.

Charles Dickens: A Life is the examination of Dickens we deserve. It gives full measure to his heroic stature - his huge virtues both as a writer and as a human being - while observing his failings in both respects with an understanding but unblinking eye. Claire Tomalin has written a full-scale biography of the writer, a story worthy of Dickens' own pen: a comedy that turns to tragedy as the very qualities that made him great, his indomitable energy, boldness, imagination, showmanship and enjoyment of fame, finally destroyed him. The man who emerges is one of extraordinary contradictions, whose vices and virtues were intertwined as surely as his life and art.

Published in Viking hardcover 6 October 2011

CLAIRE TOMALIN

THE INVISIBLE WOMAN:
THE STORY OF NELLY TERNAN AND CHARLES DICKENS

Winner of the NCR Book Award, the Hawthornden Prize and the James Tait Black Memorial Prize

'This is the story of someone who — almost — wasn't there; who vanished into thin air. Her names, dates, family and experiences very nearly disappeared from the record for good . . . '

Claire Tomalin's multi-award-winning story of the life of Nelly Ternan and Charles Dickens is a remarkable work of biography and historical revisionism that returns the neglected actress to her rightful place in history as well as providing a compelling and truthful portrait of the great Victorian novelist.

'Will come to be seen as one of the crucial women's biographies because of its vivid dramatization of the process by which women have been written out of history and have been forced to deny their own experiences'
Sean French, *New Statesman*

'The most original biography I read this year. Starting out with scarcely the bare bones of a story, Tomalin convinces by the end that she has got as near to the truth as anyone will' Anthony Howard, *Sunday Times*

'Tomalin tells with great alacrity and with much sympathy and understanding the story that Dickens would never have cared, or indeed dared, to write'
John Mortimer, *Spectator*

'A biography of high scholarship and compelling detective work'
Melvyn Bragg, *Independent*

CLAIRE TOMALIN

THE LIFE AND DEATH OF MARY WOLLSTONECRAFT

'There is no better book on Mary Wollstonecraft nor is there likely to be'
J.H. Plumb

Witty, courageous and unconventional, Mary Wollstonecraft was one of the most controversial figures of her day. She published *A Vindication of the Rights of Women*, lived through the Terror in France, had an illegitimate daughter and married the philosopher William Godwin before dying in childbirth at the age of 38.

Claire Tomalin's first book inaugurated a glittering career, and brought to life one of the great figures in the history of women.

'A most intelligent and sympathetic biographer, aware of her subject's many failings, yet with the perception to present her greatness fairly' *Daily Telegraph*

'A vivid evocation of how women lived in the second half of the eighteenth century' *Evening Standard*

'Gripping. Illuminates Mary's courage and pioneering political foresight'
Sunday Times

read more ⓟ

CLAIRE TOMALIN

MRS JORDAN'S PROFESSION:
THE STORY OF A GREAT ACTRESS AND A FUTURE KING

The story of the love between a prince and a famous actress.

Acclaimed as the greatest comic actress of her generation, Dora Jordan played a quite different role offstage as the mistress of one of the sons of George lll. Dora bore him ten children, and they lived in quiet happiness in Bushy Park on the Thames until the unexpected news arrived of his ascendancy to the throne as William IV at which point he was forced to abandon her.

Claire Tomalin vividly recreates the political, theatrical and royal worlds of the late eighteenth century. The story of how Dora moved between stage and home, of how she battled for career and family, makes for a classic tale of royal perfidy and womanly courage.

'Wonderfully readable. As gripping as the best fiction' Jan Dalley, *Independent*

'The strangest and most sensational story Tomalin has written so far' Hilary Spurling, *Daily Telegraph*

'A compelling story and Tomalin tells it with clarity and warmth' Lucy Hughes-Hallett, *Sunday Times*